RADICAL HISTORY *Review*

Issue 151

Economic Miracles and Their Afterlives

Issue Editors: Ravinder Kaur and Barbara Weinstein

FEATURES

INTERVENTIONS

TEACHING RADICAL HISTORY

Waiting for the Miracle

Future Histories of Economic Enchantments

Ravinder Kaur and Barbara Weinstein

Four snapshots of miraculous futures, some past, even eroded, others still awaited.

1972, Brazil

The military dictatorship accelerated the Trans-Amazonian Highway project, an ambitious infrastructure program that would cut through the rainforest lands to the ports near the Atlantic coast. The opening of the Amazon promised to open up "an area half as big as the United States to settlement and exploitation" and "make raw materials far more available to the outside world." While concerns were raised about the "extremely precarious ecological situation" and the consequences for the Indigenous population, the project billed as economic development of the hinterland had stoked nationalist pride. A newspaper reported: "There are 'Brazil: Love It or Leave It' stickers on car bumpers in Rio de Janeiro, while 2,000 miles north, school children sport T-shirts with the yellow and green Trans-Amazon symbol on them."[1]

2004, India

A decade into the opening up of its economy, India launched a global publicity campaign—India Shining—to celebrate the success of its economic reforms. India, dubbed a leading emerging market, was already at the heart of the BRICS nations, exciting new destinations for global capital. The campaign invited potential investors to come and partake in its growth story: "Opportunity has a new geography.

Radical History Review
Issue 151 (January 2025)   DOI 10.1215/01636545-11506833
© 2025 by MARHO: The Radical Historians' Organization, Inc.

*When global companies look at India, they see more than the vastness of our markets.
They see the power of a nation that can drive a whole new world economy. For the
world's business leaders, investors, marketers, exporters, and tourists, that land of
opportunity is India. India is shining, and you've never had a better time to shine
together."*[2] *Though initially celebrated as a success, the India Shining campaign
came to be seen as a sign of the failure of India's neoliberal growth model. A few
months after its launch, the then ruling party lost elections. India was shining, it
was said, but only for a few. The rest were still waiting for the profits to trickle down.*

2016, Côte d'Ivoire

*Global capital rediscovered Côte d'Ivoire in the early twenty-first century, decades
after it had been abandoned as a "lost cause." The crumbling 1960s–70s concrete
modernism in Abidjan, a reminder of an earlier economic miracle gone bust, was
awash in a fresh coat of optimism. Foreign investors were back, drawn to the second-
fastest-growing economy in Africa. The signs of the new unfolding miracle were visible, the* Economist *wrote:*

> *[Besides] the Burger King, Abidjan now has a Carrefour supermarket, a new
> Heineken brewery, a Paul bakery, and plenty of new infrastructure. Sharp-
> suited, French-educated ministers explain in perfect English what they are
> doing to 'open up,' 'improve the ease of doing business' and 'sustainably grow
> the middle class. . . . ' [Yet] the deepest fear of today's investors in Africa is that
> it (the economic collapse) may be happening again."*[3]

2021, Saudi Arabia

*A new techno-utopia begins taking shape. The glossy video envisions "the startup the
size of a country that will change the way we live and work forever. Healthier, happier with more time for the things that really matter. A truly global culture from
every place and background you can imagine that can show the rest of the planet
how it's done. With energy that flows from the sun and wind. Neighborhoods that
can feed and clean themselves. Technologies that make life everything it can be. This
is where we can prepare together for the next era of human progress."*[4]

Economic Enchantments

To witness the world through the many unfolding "economic miracles" is to behold
dreamworlds and catastrophes all at once. It is to be confronted with many spectacular visions of capitalist modernity, of hope and wonderment, but also ruins left
behind when the promised futures fail to emerge. We began with a few snapshots
of the many economic miracles that have emerged, unraveled, or are still waiting to
happen across the twentieth- and twenty-first-century worlds: Brazil, India, Ivory
Coast, and Saudi Arabia. They capture the manifold frictions at the heart of the phenomenon: the old desire to enter the magical world of prosperity and eternal peace,

this time through the path laid out by unfettered capitalism, along with the persistent fear of not "making it" to the enchanted place, of being left behind, plagued by anxieties that what at first seemed to be a miracle is just a mirage. The story of economic miracles appears as a global serial production, a spellbinding play staged around the world, carrying with it the promise of the spectacular reign of capitalism. However, a closer look reveals that the push to generate previously unattainable, high growth rates has left behind zones of abandonment and despair, inequality, displacement, and political repression.

The four snapshots above disclose how the lure of the economic miracle and the specter of a mirage are never too far apart. Nor, for that matter, is the risk of being deceived and getting stuck in a trail of destruction. Consider the "Brazilian miracle": Brazil was once celebrated as "the new Japan," a new engine of growth previously considered unattainable. Impressed by the economic miracles of Japan and West Germany, the Brazilian planners believed they not only could replicate them but "do much better, and in a shorter time."[5] Their push toward double-digit growth rates coupled with low inflation also coincided with the most repressive era of the twenty-one-year military dictatorship. It allowed the state to create an illusion of its economic triumphs, as Melissa Teixeira shows in her article in this issue. It wasn't just austerity and severe wage repression for workers that the miracle had wrought, but also massive violation of the rights of the Indigenous people, as well as ecological destruction. The colossal infrastructure campaign by companies or government entities in the rainforest had created what has been called "a Brazilian miracle but an Indigenous disaster."[6] In 2024 Brazil formally apologized to the Indigenous people, an acknowledgement that came after more than half a century.

Now move half a world away from Brazil to India to witness another incarnation of the economic miracle. In the early 1990s, faced with a severe financial crisis, India embarked on an economic liberalization program it hoped would not only help avert the immediate "balance of payment" crisis but also realize its old dream of joining the high table of world powers.[7] India's subsequent rise as an "attractive investment destination" came to be celebrated as a spectacular growth story in the twenty-first-century world economy. India Shining wasn't just a publicity campaign name; it signaled a deep transformation of the postcolonial nation's transition to capitalism, a refuge for global capital with the promise of high returns, rejuvenation of its cultural identity, and prosperity for its citizens.[8] Yet, over the past three decades, the promised miracle turned out to be hollow for many Indians; India became more unequal than it had been for a century, and it took a familiar turn toward authoritarianism.[9]

On the African continent, the second coming of the "Ivory Coast miracle" traces a similar journey of the rise, fall, and rise again of the capitalist growth story. Once deemed a growth-oriented, prosperous nation, Côte d'Ivoire became an epicenter of speculative booms and busts, shiny infrastructures and their ruins, all shaped by the flows and ebbs of fickle foreign capital, which led to plummeting commodity prices, a stagnant economy, and violent conflicts.[10] The description of these events as a "lost cause" signaled something far worse than an economic downturn: failed prospects for development in Côte d'Ivoire and, by extension, in Africa. As Abou Bamba shows in his contribution, the Ivorian experience exposes how similar economic events are bestowed with different labels as miracles or failures, and how Black Africa has historically been positioned in the global economy. Similarly, Hannah Borenstein shows the constant turbulence and chaotic shifts between hope and despair that marked the instability of the Ethiopian miracle. Contrast this with the telling of the Chilean miracle, which didn't die even when faced with a series of crises (see Johanna Gautier Morin's article). Franco Barchiesi, in his roundtable commentary, reminds us how the term *economic miracle* was imbued, in Africa, with a racialized meaning, a pessimistic view in which the miracle wasn't growth but Africa's capacity to avoid failures. Thus the return of global capital to the Ivorian economy was indeed celebrated as a miraculous event. What is telling in this fluctuation of fortunes is the absence of disillusionment; the seduction of the miracle remained intact even in its failure.

The latest and perhaps the most ambitious reincarnation of the economic miracle is the newly launched NEOM city project in Saudi Arabia. It expects not only to boost Saudi Arabia's modern image but also to get ahead in the race to attract global capital and technology. Envisioned as "a civilizational leap for humanity," it sets out to create a futuristic smart city "that will be bigger than Dubai and have more robots than humans" by 2030.[11] The promotional presentations suggest an artificial intelligence (AI)–driven, energy-efficient $500 billion business zone in the desert along the Red Sea coast that will be home to nine million residents. This vision of a twenty-first-century utopia has raised the specter of surveillance and human rights violations.[12] For now, the project has been scaled back for financial reasons, but what it reveals is the near immortality of the economic miracle.

The idea of the economic miracle has never truly expired, as these still-unfolding utopias show. It continues to be resurrected, brought to life in even more seductive forms. Dressed up in ever-new garbs, it keeps returning to new and old locations, reaffirming the prosperity gospel and the promise of the laissez-faire formula to bring salvation. We might ask: How and why has it endured so long and been embraced widely even when it left behind a trail of destruction? What dreamworlds does it promise or what new forms does it continue to mutate into? What might account for its resilience, its capacity to conjure new dreamworlds even as it remains intricately tied to crises of poverty and repression? These observations raise an even more crucial question: could it be that the enigma of the economic miracle lives off the crises that unrestrained capitalism creates? Might we say that the economic miracle is not just an answer to crisis but also its genesis, a contemporary historical condition that calls for a more rigorous interrogation? This essay, along with many of the contributions to this issue, addresses the possibility of these interconnections, which continue to shape the many lives and afterlives of the economic miracle.

We explore the enigma of *economic enchantments*: the modern belief in the power of economic growth that keeps the miracle alive even when it fails to deliver, or the neoliberal deification of the market that continues to promise to salve the humiliation of defeat in wars and colonial rule. The hope is that accrued economic worth could be traded to recover the lost mana of national glory and prestige, even rejuvenation of its neotraditional cultural forms (see Rebecca Karl's essay). Our aim in this issue is to generate further debate on the enduring nature of economic miracles and the implications they may hold for political and economic life in the twenty-first century. To this end, we trace three intertwined critical dimensions of the economic miracle: the connections between the crisis and the miracle; new forms of economic enchantments, or what we might call an economic miracle by another name; and the miracle's expansion into new geographies, especially in the Global South. In what follows, we lay out a brief history of how the word *economic* joined with the concept of miracle before we turn to the makings of economic enchantments.

Lineages of the Economic Miracle

When and how did the economic miracle become a dazzling embodiment of capitalism? We begin by returning to the philosophical roots of the concept to trace the bloodlines of the miracle in the field of political economy.

Miracle, derived from the Latin *mirari* (to wonder, marvel), simply means an event that excites wonder or astonishment, denoting something extraordinary, outside the expected routine.[13] In the theological sense, a miracle is the work of God or a divine figure akin to God, a sign of intervention of a superior being. The occurrence of these events cannot be explained through human actions or natural causes. A central philosophical discussion emerges around the proposition of miracles as a "violation of the laws of nature," a proposition that has raised questions about both the nature of violation and what constitutes natural law.[14] The key question is the credibility of claims of a miracle that require an incontrovertible proof, usually the testimony of witnesses, that an improbability has occurred. A violation can only be miraculous if it is nonreplicable, a one-off event that does not occur as a matter of routine. Furthermore, even if such a violation can be established, it can never be proven with certainty that it was the work of a divine being. In short, claims of miracles are never beyond dispute or doubt. But what their existence affirms is the core spirit of religion: the love of wonder and enchantment, the magical state of being spellbound. Note here that the concepts of the miracle and the mirage have always been closely related, deriving from the common etymological roots of *mirus* (wonderful), *mirari* (to wonder), and *mirare* (mirror). If the miracle conjures a world that exceeds the productive power of nature, the mirage signals the optical illusion, the risk of being deceived by shiny images. The miracle is a matter of belief, the mirage an embodiment of doubt. Yet, for all their differences, they work to bolster enchantment as a way of being in the world. After all, an encounter with a mirage does not necessarily lead to disillusionment. It can also induce one to move on, to search harder for the real thing. This aspect is crucial to understanding the enduring lure of miracles.

In the domain of economy, the miracle is popularly associated with the phenomenon of the *Wirtschaftswunder* (economic miracle) that turned postwar Germany into an economic powerhouse, the desirable "dream-state" shaped by capitalist growth (see Aimée Plukker's article). Yet this is not where the story begins. The economic miracle had already made its debut in the late nineteenth century, albeit in a different form. Long before *miracle* became shorthand for capitalist growth, the economic miracle was an ironic telling of tensions between labor and capital, on the one hand, and economic injustice under colonial rule, on the other. Remember, this was the age of imperial capitalism, colonial extraction, mass industrial production, inventions, patents, and international trade wars. The Great Exhibition of 1851 in London showcased marvels of modern industry and raw materials from the colonies in a great spectacle of wealth and enterprise. That age also brought to the surface the underbelly of mass manufacturing: the material conditions of workers. In this turmoil, efforts to organize trade unions and strikes were seen as "formidable weapons of industrial warfare" that would cause injury to the industrial system and yield few returns to the workers. The very goal of social equality was dismissed as an unattainable "economic miracle," a pipe dream that went against the laws of economics. In a similar vein, in an 1892 report on the "sweating system," the exploitation of workers was dismissed as inherently improbable as it would entail their "taking part in the economic miracle of voluntarily selling their labor at less than its market price."[15] The economic miracle, Quinn Slobodian suggests in his roundtable remarks, was derided at this point as an economic absurdity to counter the growing aspirations and demands of contemporary social movements. The theme of economic absurdity resonated in colonial India as well. In 1904, writing on the economic distress that colonialism had brought to India, the economic historian R. C. Dutt noted with despair: "If manufactures are crippled, agriculture overtaxed, and a third of the revenue remitted out of the country, any nation on earth would suffer from permanent poverty and recurring famines. Economic laws are the same in Asia as in Europe. . . . If India were prosperous under these circumstances, it would be an economic miracle. (But) science knows no miracles."[16] The economic miracle was summoned as a metaphor—for the impossibility of achieving prosperity for the colony under imperial rule—a theme that would become central to anticolonial mobilization throughout the twentieth century. It also represented the nature of the extractive colonial economy, which accrued profits to the empire even as it depleted the colony, a miraculous arrangement where almost nothing was traded for something.

Back in the imperial metropole, the economic miracle was transmuting into more than an expression of impossibility. It now conveyed a sense of wonder but was duly tempered with caution. In 1917 the economist J. A. Hobson marveled at how the British war economy during the First World War had managed to produce a surplus and even raise the standard of living of the civilian population: "What this country [England], in particular, has done amounts to an economic miracle," he exclaimed.[17] However, as he analyzed patterns of production, the economic miracle began to appear more like a sign of a transient boom before the bust arrived. The postwar economy, he feared, would be faced with the payment of war expenses and greater taxation, a scenario that might lead to a reduction of real wages and an intensification of class conflict.

In this fluid moment, the idea of the economic miracle underwent a further shift. The economic miracle now came to be associated with economic recovery, especially when enforced with resolute authoritarian action. The Nazi regime had started referring to the rise of industrial output and decline in unemployment as an "economic miracle . . . attribute[d] to the daring spirit of Nazi leaders who did not hesitate to violate the principles of orthodox finance."[18] Germany's minister of economy, Hjalmar Schacht, had even been given the honorific title "economic miracle man," for "he has to feed the Reich's fast rising numbers of babies, born in and out of wedlock," wrote *Life* magazine. "He has further to provide, by miracles of economic juggling, the steel, rubber, oil, and nitrates needed to sustain one of the hugest war machines of history."[19] The wartime economy had turned the economic miracle from a foolish pursuit into a desirable goal, duly incorporated into the to-do list of dictatorships. This alliance between the economic miracle and strong states would later shape Brazil's "technocratic developmental state" (Paula Vedoveli's contribution) and the repressive violence that unfolded in the shadow of the Mexican miracle (Christy Thornton's commentary). Miracles could be manufactured as the handiwork of authoritarian leaders, who meant business in more ways than one.

The Miracle Market

It wasn't until the postwar era that the economic miracle would emerge as a distinct phenomenon, its currency tied to its capacity to work wonders on crisis-ridden economies. The mid-twentieth-century economic miracle was a nearly magical formula: a package of high growth rates and rapid economic reconstruction that could turn depressed economies torn by wars, colonialism, ethnic conflicts, external debts, and financial downturns into economic powerhouses.

The poster child of this reincarnation of the economic miracle was postwar Germany. Reeling from the cumulative effects of high inflation and economic collapse due to the war, Germany made a spectacular economic recovery in the 1950s–60s. Called the "Miracle on the Rhine," this restored Germany's position as a leading European economy. It also became an aspirational formula that would circulate in many incarnations around the world. The Japanese miracle, the miracle on the Han, and Asian tiger economies, or what is broadly called the East Asian miracle, along with Mexico, Brazil, Chile, Côte d'Ivoire, and Ethiopia, among others, would soon be the shining stars in the topography of capitalism, with many more still waiting to witness the miracle.[20]

By the late twentieth century, another shift had begun to rearrange the economic miracle. Here enters a new language of markets that reimagined the Global South as a new frontier of the world economy. The collapse of the Soviet Union and the attendant triumph of liberalism had opened the postcommunist and postcolonial worlds to the seductions of free-market capitalism. With this, the alternate vision of "Soviet futures"—the socialist edition of economic miracles (discussed in this issue by Ellis Garey) that had once animated anticolonial mobilizations—was cast aside. Though international financial institutions had already in the 1950s started promoting private capital as an agent of development in the Third World, these efforts made little headway until the 1980s. The shift began when many parts of the developing world were redubbed as "emerging markets"—territories with untapped market potential. With abundant, unutilized raw materials and vast consumer markets, emerging markets held out the promise of economic growth that markets in the developed world did not.[21] Once raw materials turned into a commodity, their market value soared or fell subject to speculative cycles of boom and bust (see fig. 1). At the turn of the millennium, the largest, most populous territories, including China, India, Brazil, post-Soviet Russia, and post-apartheid South Africa, were rebranded as BRICS, the constellation of successful "growth stories" ready to "take off" and expand the territory of capitalism beyond the West.[22] The phenomenon of emerging markets, an economic miracle by another name, had once again reenchanted the world. The language of markets subsumed the language of miracles; now the true miracle was the endless production of markets.

What ties economic miracles, new and old, is the promise to undo crises—from wars and colonialism to debts and economic collapse—even to turn "failed states" into wonders to behold. Consider the recent push in Pakistan, a nation beset with serial crises, to turn its coastline into a glittering combination of the "Dubai model" of investments and the "Shenzhen model" of infrastructure (see Hasan Karrar's essay). Yet this utopic imagination created its own neoliberal dystopias over the past several decades—from military dictatorships or authoritarian rule to the violent capture of natural resources, austerity, and extreme inequality that created zones of abundance and deprivation (as Andre Pagliarini notes in his essay on Brazil and Chile).[23] However, these ruptures did not always weaken the temptation of the economic miracle. They often led to new calls to have faith in the miracle, for deeper reforms to boost economic growth, and to wait just a bit longer to taste the fruits of capitalist progress. This enduring enchantment of the economic lives off an endless replay of the prosperity gospel, a phenomenon we witness in ever-new

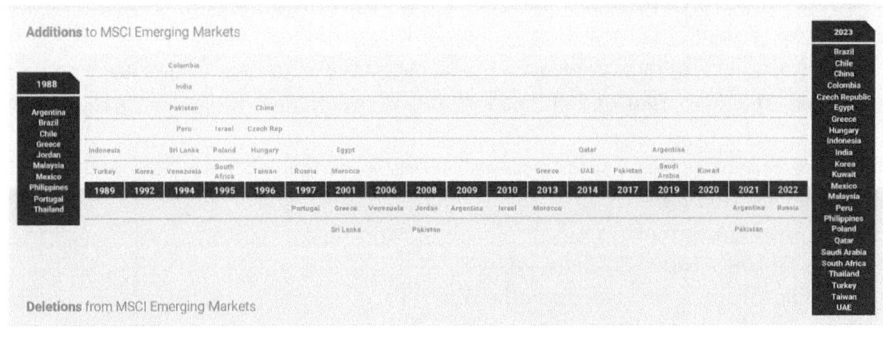

MSCI Emerging Markets Index[2]

24
Countries

10.9%
Weight in MSCI ACWI Index

1,379
Constituents

Figure 1. MSCI Emerging Markets Index (1988–2023).

frontiers of the global economy. Each miracle is a reenchantment, a reconfirmation of the spell of capital. And each failure is a mirage, a deception that tests belief, a call to wait for the true miracle.

Ravinder Kaur is professor of modern South Asian studies at the University of Copenhagen, where she also directs the Asian Dynamics Initiative. Her publications include *Since 1947: Partition Narratives among Punjabi Migrants of Delhi* (2007), and *Brand New Nation: Capitalist Dreams and Nationalist Designs in Twenty-First-Century India* (2020).

Barbara Weinstein is Silver Professor of History at New York University. Her work focuses mainly on modern Brazil, particularly the Amazon during the rubber boom and industrialization and labor in São Paulo. Her most recent book is *The Color of Modernity: São Paulo and the Making of Race and Nation in Brazil* (2015).

Notes

1. Hummerstone, "Cutting a Road through Brazil's 'Green Hell.'"
2. India Shining, "Opportunity Has a New Geography."
3. *Economist*, "1.2 Billion Opportunities," 3.
4. Neom, "Made to Change."
5. *New York Times*, "Brazil, 'the New Japan.'"
6. Phillips and Rogero, "Brazil Apologizes to Indigenous People."
7. The 1990 Gulf War and attendant rising oil prices had created a "balance of payment" crisis, with the risk of external debt default, as inward remittances declined and imports became expensive.
8. Kaur, *Brand New Nation*.
9. Bharti et al., "Income and Wealth Inequality in India"; Roy, "Is India Heading towards an Autocracy?"; *Hindu*, "85 per Cent Indians."

10. Hecht, "Ivory Coast Economic 'Miracle'"; Groff, "Ivory Coast"; Woods, "Tragedy of the Cocoa Pod"; Bamba, *African Miracle, African Mirage.*

11. Carey, Nereim, and Cannon, "Saudi's Crown Prince Wants a Dubai of His Own."

12. Neom, "The Line"; Bostock and Porter, "Saudi Arabia's Neom"; Beaumont, "End of the Line?"

13. Online Etymology Dictionary, s.v. *miracle*, https://www.etymonline.com/word/miracle.

14. Hume, "Of Miracles."

15. Lee, "Sweating System," 128.

16. Dutt, *Economic History of India*, xvi–xvii.

17. Hobson, "Shall We Be Poorer after the War?," 43.

18. Katona, "'Miracle' of German Recovery."

19. *Life Magazine*, "Reich Economic Wizard."

20. Diebold, review of *Asia's Next Giant*; Gulati, "Foundations of Rapid Economic Growth"; Page, "East Asian Miracle"; Ito and Weinstein, "Japan and the Asian Economies"; Stiglitz, "Some Lessons from the East Asian Miracle"; Wang, *China's Age of Abundance.*

21. Agtmael, *Emerging Markets Century*; Mobius, *Little Book of Emerging Markets*; Logue, *Emerging Markets for Dummies.*

22. Rostow, *Stages of Economic Growth*; O'Neill, *Growth Map.*

23. Bharti et al., "Income and Wealth Inequality in India"; Slobodian, *Crack-Up Capitalism*; Gordin, Tilley, and Prakash, *Utopia/Dystopia.*

References

Agtmael, Antoine van. *The Emerging Markets Century: How a New Breed of World-Class Companies Is Overtaking the World.* London: Simon and Schuster, 2008.

Bamba, Abou B. *African Miracle, African Mirage: Transnational Politics and the Paradox of Modernization in Ivory Coast.* Athens: Ohio University Press, 2016.

Beaumont, Peter. "End of the Line? Saudi Arabia 'Forced to Scale Back' Plans for Desert Megacity." *Guardian*, April 10, 2024. https://www.theguardian.com/world/2024/apr/10/the-line-saudi-arabia-scaling-back-plans-105-mile-long-desert-megacity-crown-prince.

Bharti, Nitin Kumar, Lucas Chancel, Thomas Piketty, and Anmol Somanchi. "Income and Wealth Inequality in India, 1922–2023: The Rise of the Billionaire Raj." World Inequality Lab, Working Paper no. 2024/09, March 2024. https://shs.hal.science/halshs-04563836/file/WorldInequalityLab_WP2024_09_Income-and-Wealth-Inequality-in-India-1922-2023_Final.pdf.

Bostock, Bill, and Tom Porter. "Saudi Arabia's Neom Is a $500B Futuristic City Being Built in the Desert—but It Could Morph into a Surveillance Dystopia." *Business Insider*, updated April 26, 2023. https://www.businessinsider.com/neom-what-we-know-saudi-arabia-500bn-mega-city-2019-9.

Carey, Glen, Vivian Nereim, and Christopher Cannon. "Saudi's Crown Prince Wants a Dubai of His Own. So He Plans to Build One." *Bloomberg.com*, April 26, 2024. https://www.bloomberg.com/graphics/2017-neom-saudi-mega-city/.

Diebold, William, Jr. Review of *Asia's Next Giant: South Korea and Late Industrialization*, by Alice H. Amsden. *Foreign Affairs* 69, no. 2 (1990): 171–72. https://doi.org/10.2307/20044328.

Dutt, Romesh Chunder. *Economic History of India in the Victorian Age.* London: K. Paul, Trench, Trübner, 1904.

Economist. "1.2 Billion Opportunities." April 14, 2016. https://www.economist.com/special-report/2016/04/14/12-billion-opportunities.

Gordin, Michael D., Helen Tilley, and Gyan Prakash, eds. *Utopia/Dystopia: Conditions of Historical Possibility*. Princeton, NJ: Princeton University Press, 2010.

Groff, David H. "Ivory Coast: A Tarnished Miracle?" Review of *The Political Economy of the Ivory Coast*, edited by I. William Zartman and Christopher Delgado; *État et bourgeoisie en Côte-d'Ivoire*, edited by Y.-A. Fauré, J.-F. Médard; and *La civilisation quotidienne en Côte-d'Ivoire: Procès d'occidentalisation*, by Abdou Touré. *Africa Today* 35, no. 1 (1988): 61–68.

Gulati, Umesh C. "The Foundations of Rapid Economic Growth: The Case of the Four Tigers." *American Journal of Economics and Sociology* 51, no. 2 (1992): 161–72.

Hecht, Robert M. "The Ivory Coast Economic 'Miracle': What Benefits for Peasant Farmers?" *Journal of Modern African Studies* 21, no. 1 (1983): 25–53. https://doi.org/10.1017/S0022278X0002303X x0002303x.

Hindu. "85 Per Cent Indians Support Rule by a Strong Leader or Military Says Pew Survey Data." March 8, 2024.

Hobson, J. A. "Shall We Be Poorer after the War?" *Contemporary Review* 3 (1917): 43–53.

Hume, David. "Of Miracles." In *Enquiries Concerning Human Understanding and Concerning the Principles of Morals*, edited by L. A. Selby-Bigge. Oxford: Clarendon Press, 1975.

Hummerstone, Robert G. "Cutting a Road through Brazil's 'Green Hell.'" *New York Times*, March 5, 1972.

India Shining. "Opportunity Has a New Geography, India Shining Campaign." Ministry of Finance, Government of India, 2003. https://openthemagazine.com/lounge/books/marketable-idea-india/#google_vignette.

Ito, Takatoshi, and David E. Weinstein. "Japan and the Asian Economies: A 'Miracle' in Transition." *Brookings Papers on Economic Activity* 1996, no. 2 (1996): 205–72. https://doi.org/10.2307/2534622.

Katona, George M. "The 'Miracle' of German Recovery." *Foreign Affairs* 14, no. 2 (January 1936): 348.

Kaur, Ravinder. *Brand New Nation: Capitalist Dreams and Nationalist Designs in Twenty-First-Century India*. Stanford, CA: Stanford University Press, 2020.

Lee, Joseph. "The Sweating System in General." *Journal of Social Science: Containing the Transactions of the American Association* 30 (1892): 105–37.

Life Magazine. "Reich Economic Wizard." May 3, 1937, 67.

Logue, Ann C. *Emerging Markets for Dummies*. Hoboken, NJ: Wiley, 2011.

Mobius, Mark. *The Little Book of Emerging Markets: How to Make Money in the World's Fastest Growing Markets*. London: Wiley, 2012.

NEOM. "The Line: A Revolution in Urban Living." n.d. https://www.neom.com/en-us/regions/theline.

NEOM. "NEOM: Made to Change." 2021. https://www.neom.com/en-us.

New York Times. "Brazil, 'the New Japan.'" January 28, 1973.

O'Neill, Jim. *The Growth Map: Economic Opportunity in the BRICs and Beyond*. London: Penguin, 2013.

Page, John. "The East Asian Miracle: Four Lessons for Development Policy." *NBER Macroeconomics Annual* 9 (1994): 219–69. https://doi.org/10.2307/3585089.

Phillips, Tom, and Tiago Rogero. "Brazil Apologizes to Indigenous People for Persecution during Dictatorship." *Guardian*, April 3, 2024.

Rostow, W. W. *The Stages of Economic Growth: A Non-communist Manifesto*. Cambridge: Cambridge University Press, 1991.

Roy, Vaishna. "Is India Heading towards an Autocracy?" *Frontline*, March 21, 2024.

Slobodian, Quinn. *Crack-Up Capitalism: Market Radicals and the Dream of a World without Democracy*. New York: Metropolitan, 2023.

Stiglitz, Joseph E. "Some Lessons from the East Asian Miracle." *World Bank Research Observer* 11, no. 2 (1996): 151–77.

Wang, Feng. *China's Age of Abundance: Origins, Ascendance, and Aftermath*. Cambridge: Cambridge University Press, 2024.

Woods, Dwayne. "The Tragedy of the Cocoa Pod: Rent-Seeking, Land, and Ethnic Conflict in Ivory Coast." *Journal of Modern African Studies* 41, no. 4 (2003): 641–55.

The Rise and Fall of Economic Miracles

Quinn Slobodian

How and when did miracles become profane? This essay tracks the rise and relative decline of the term *economic miracle* across the twentieth century to explain how wonders became part of mundane policy talk. The term emerged first in the late nineteenth century to scorn the irrationality of socialist and populist claims that distribution could be achieved at the stroke of a legislator's pen. It was a rhetorical means of disciplining political aspirations and emphasizing the limits of government power. The definition held until the First World War, when the unexpected resilience of production under conditions of mass mobilization lent the economic miracle plausibility. After the success of the fascist and then post-fascist states in rapid rearmament and reconstruction, the economic miracle was pitched as an ambitious but reachable goal for developing countries. From the 1970s on, it became a proxy term for debates about the relationship between industrial policy, authoritarian governance, and rapid growth. By the last decade of the twentieth century, achieving an economic miracle was a baseline demand for newly industrializing countries. If you were not having an economic miracle, you were doing something wrong. No longer the province of magic, the miracle became a state imperative.

From Economic Absurdity to Economic Aperture

When the term entered circulation in the late nineteenth century, to speak of an economic miracle was to deride an economic absurdity. "We cannot work economic miracles for the benefit of any man or class of men," said a Connecticut pastor in

Radical History Review

Issue 151 (January 2025) DOI 10.1215/01636545-11506868

© 2025 by MARHO: The Radical Historians' Organization, Inc.

1885. "The State cannot work any social miracle through legislation."[1] An article in 1874 described British iron and coal workers on strike against wage reductions "bivouacking around silent works and deserted mines, in sullen idleness, in the vain hope that some economic miracle will be wrought in their favor."[2] The charge was intended to lower aspirations and counter the demands of contemporary social movements. Against magical thinking, liberals of the time preached self-help and the virtues of "frugality, management, self-control, temperance, purpose, pluck, persistence."[3]

The Populist Party and its presidential candidate William Jennings Bryan were special targets of criticism. The party, it was claimed, "seeks to perform economic miracles, and promises if given power to do things at one sitting that no earthly agency could possible accomplish in seventy-five years."[4] Theodore Roosevelt was also reportedly luring in those with "a silly confidence in his ability to perform political and economic miracles."[5] "Demagogism," another commentator concluded, "has encouraged certain classes to look for the realization of economic miracles, which are beyond the achievement of any legislation or public authority."[6] In such commentaries, "facts" and "the multiplication table" were posed against "hallucination" and "exclusive lunacy." One observer in 1910 captured the dominant tenor when he harumphed, "We are dealing with economics not miracles."[7]

The mood of conversation changed dramatically during the Great War, when miracle talk underwent its most important shift in the twentieth century. The miracle in question was the maintenance of British productivity despite the conscription of half of working-age men into the armed forces. By the old measures of economic thinking, feeding that number of young bodies into the meat grinder of the front should have crippled productivity. The loss of the crucial input of labor should have led mathematically to a collapse of output in production. Yet "the war has brought an economic miracle to England which may well amaze the world," wrote one newspaper in a representative passage. "She finds that despite the work of four million men withdrawn, and of two million men transferred from constructive work to that of making munitions, the remaining laborers" were able to maintain the prewar standard of living for all.[8]

The economic miracle had future implications. If the figures were correct, then "before the war work was so ill-adjusted that not more than one-half the possible production obtained and the standard of living was twice as low as it need have been."[9] Surely this meant that the economy would be organized differently later. "If such methods are going to work economic miracles during the war," asked one journalist, "what is the matter with continuing them after the war is over?"[10] The *New Republic* observed that "before the war no economist would have pronounced what has occurred as possible. The experts were all wrong."[11] The economic miracle had mutated from an economic absurdity to an economic aperture through which one might see a different future.

The Cost of Fascist Miracles

In 1920 the British journalist and Labour Party politician Norman Angell took stock of recent experience.[12] "Suppose before the war you had collected into one room all the great capitalist economists in England" and told them that the country would maintain its prewar standard of living despite the absence of "five or six millions of the best workers." "There would not have been one," he concluded, "who would have admitted the possibility of the thing or regarded the forecast as anything but rubbish."[13] "Yet that economic miracle has been performed," he wrote, "and it has been performed thanks to nationalization and Socialism."[14]

The First World War refuted economic orthodoxy and showed that productivity was a flexible capacity open to radical engineering. Even the editor of the *Economist*, the bastion of liberal orthodoxy, conceded in 1922 that "economic miracles were certainly wrought during the war and as has been shown it may have been possible for still more miraculous miracles to have been performed."[15] The first performers of postwar economic miracles were the United States and France, which rebounded from wartime destruction to reach high levels of employment and output.[16] Aided by new forms of mass production pioneered by Henry Ford (described as a "worker of economic miracles" in the 1923 campaign to draft him for president), the United States became an object of fascination in Weimar Germany, where the economics professor and former state secretary in the Economics Ministry Julius Hirsch published a widely read book on "the American Economic Miracle."[17]

Before long, Weimar Germany itself was being described as an economic miracle along with postimperial Austria, whose "resuscitation" leading US economist Irving Fisher called "the economic miracle of Europe" in 1924.[18] The survival of superior industrial capital stock was largely to be thanked. As an American banker observed in 1924, "Germany is building on a wreck of ten years, but what a wreck it has to build on."[19] The missing ingredient was capital. The German journalist Maximilian Harden saw the relaxation of reparations through the Dawes Plan as "working an economic miracle" by restoring confidence to investors.[20]

Further south, the Italian leader Benito Mussolini's "economic miracle" was regularly acknowledged while its costs were noted. "There are no strikes because Mussolini has forbidden them," a US journalist observed in 1927. "There are no lockouts because factory owners have to keep their places going or incur Mussolini's wrath. Railways run on time . . . because the two Blackshirts on the trains report the cause of any delay and there has to be an accounting."[21] By 1936 similar reports were coming from Germany, where the "economic miracle" of eliminating unemployment had been accomplished by "the immense new armies that have been created and by the large armies of boys and girls in the labour camps."[22] That year a book on the "German economic miracle" appeared in German bookstores.[23] While other voices countered that Hitler's hothouse approach was unsustainable and thus "no economic miracle" had taken place, the material effectiveness of the strategy offered additional evidence of at least the short-term manipulability of basic economic forces.[24] Miracles were within reach of human hands.

In the handful of decades leading up to 1945, a U-turn in miracle talk occurred: economic outcomes once seen to defy the laws of classical political economy were accomplished through concerted state effort and often violent suppression of potentially inflationary internal forces. The postwar decades would see what could be called the universalization of economic miracles not through the "magic of the market," where private forces acted on their own, but precisely through the guiding and often iron-mailed hand of the state.

From Miracles to Tigers

The postwar resurrection of the defeated fascist powers is the most familiar of economic miracles. In many ways, it is also the least miraculous. To use the metaphor from above, West Germany, Italy, and Japan were building on beautiful "wrecks." Combined with their integration into the US bloc, and with export orientation in times of overseas deployment (including the demand-boosting Korean War), these countries enjoyed rapid growth rates until the first recession of the late 1960s.[25] By 1955, the economist Roger Opie wrote that the German economic miracle had "been analyzed in everything from the most learned econometric journal to the *Reader's Digest*."[26]

German protagonists disputed the occult quality of the success while also using it to counter challenges from the socialist Left. A 1952 advertisement titled "the German Miracle" began by saying, "We don't call it that, foreign travelers do," and praised the decisions of the Christian Democratic government and the efforts of the people.[27] Economics Minister Ludwig Erhard said there was "no mystery" to the "miracle," which was actually just commitment to sound currency and open trade policy.[28] Use of the term blossomed to describe postwar Germany after the currency reform of 1948, when Erhard was able to achieve the market turn he had always pushed for when he was advising the National Socialists by replacing the defunct Reichsmark with the new deutsche mark in the Western zone.[29] This helped inaugurate the era of the "one easy trick" version of the economic miracle.[30] Campaigning for Margaret Thatcher in 1979, a British Conservative would say that they would "like to think that what Erhard did for Germany after the war we could do in this country now."[31]

While the apparent gimmick of a new currency appearing overnight drew attention, many observers remarked that the post-fascist economic miracles required "political miracles" too.[32] Stability could be achieved in different ways. In the Federal Republic of Germany, consent was secured through the carrot of rising standard of living and the revival of democratic culture, combined with the stick of the 1956 ban on the German Communist Party and an extensive US military presence.[33] By the late 1960s, a consensus emerged that the biggest threats to economic miracles were social. Most dangerous were developments that threatened the capacity to direct the apparatus of investment and production. Workers were the most volatile variable. Should waged workers begin to organize in an effective way to expand their profit share through collective bargaining or wildcat strikes, the "economic miracle" would be threatened.[34] When a strike wave hit Germany in 1971, the *New York Times* reported that mobilized workers were angry that "the economic miracle has done more for employers than for the workers who made it possible."[35]

The 1970s opened two debates about economic miracles. The first was about the necessity of political repression for economic growth. Visiting Greece, in 1971, where Parliament and much of the constitution had been suspended in the name of an authoritarian "disciplined democracy," the US secretary of commerce Maurice H. Stans praised the rule of the generals. "You have provided an economic miracle up to now," he said, "and I'm sure that miracle will continue to grow."[36] Fascist Spain under Franco was similarly credited with an economic miracle.[37]

With the exception of Chile, where the "miracle" was achieved through the "original sin" of dictatorship, in the words of economist Sebastian Edwards, the symbiosis between authoritarianism and growth was discussed nowhere more than in the case of Brazil.[38] From 1969 to 1974, the "Brazilian miracle" saw world-beating growth rates that provoked persistent questions about the social costs. "Is the practice of political repressions—censorship, arbitrary arrest, police and army persecution—essential for Brazil's 10 per cent growth rate?" asked the *New York Times* in 1974. "Must the rise of Brazil's spectacular economic development continue to be a widening gap between rich and poor—even a net drop in real income for those lowest on the economic scale?"[39] Seymour Hersh reported on mobilizations against the displacement of Indigenous populations for the expansion of agriculture, logging, and mining in the Amazon River basin.[40] Oppositional Catholic bishops claimed that the miracle was only another means "to make the rich richer and the poor poorer" and that it relied on censorship, repression of civil society, and "the most varied forms of imprisonment, tortures, mutilations and assassinations."[41]

The form of political economy taken by Brazil under Antônio Delfim Netto, credited as the "architect of the economic miracle," was "a combination of state capitalism and local and foreign private investment."[42] The intended centerpiece was a Trading Company Law to create large Brazilian-controlled firms with foreign investment and minority ownership stakes.[43] These were inspired by the *zaibatsu*, or Japanese conglomerates, which worked closely with government planners in a partnership that was perceived by contemporary observers as having helped "create the 'economic miracle.'"[44]

For a time, Brazil was discussed as "the new Japan."[45] But when the Brazilian miracle (along with the lesser "Mexican miracle") faded under the skyrocketing interest rates of the Volcker shock, which doomed a model reliant on high levels of foreign debt, new Japans were found to be closer to the old one.[46] "Phrases like 'economic miracle' and 'development success story' have crept into descriptions of South Korea's rapid growth in recent years," wrote a journalist in 1973.[47] As in Brazil, rapid growth relied on both political repression and access to foreign markets and foreign credit. In the late 1970s, Chinese academics began to talk about South Korea along with Singapore, Taiwan, and Hong Kong as the "four little tigers," the "four young tigers," or the "four little dragons." The term migrated into English. The *New York Times* noted in 1979 that the "four young tigers" had the fastest-growing economies in the world.[48] In the 1980s and 1990s the success of the tiger economies sparked a policy debate about the proper role of the state in aiding economic development.

From the Economic Miracle to the Developmental State

By 1983, President Ronald Reagan was giving speeches praising the Korean and Japanese "economic miracles."[49] Three years later, he was claiming the category for his own. "The United States is the economic miracle," he said to Congress, "the model to which the world once again turns."[50] One of the president's leitmotifs was that miracles came to those nations who "believe in the magic of the market place."[51] Yet an unexamined paradox hid here. One could argue—and many did—that South Korea had not achieved its success through surrender to market forces but through the interventionism of the state. Following the discussions into the 1980s and 1990s, we find that even as neoliberal talking points such as Reagan's colonized the political discourse of the parties of the Right and eventually the Left in the North Atlantic, talk of "economic miracles" went in the other direction, remaining more attentive to the centrality of targeted state action in achieving growth. Up to the turn of the century, political economists and development professionals remained aware of the insight that stretched back to the First World War: that there was no magic without an interventionist state.

The locus classicus for the most recent debate about economic miracles is the World Bank report published in 1993 titled *The East Asian Miracle: Economic Growth and Public Policy*.[52] The report had a revealing genesis. It was pushed by the Japanese Ministry of Finance and paid for entirely by the Japanese government. The Japanese felt that the World Bank had not given enough credence to the model being used by it and its neighboring "tiger" economies.[53] The finished product was notable as the first major report to acknowledge the role played by industrial policy in East Asia beyond Japan.[54] It offered a record of a debate among economists about what was most responsible for the East Asian miracle economies. On one side were what the report's lead author, John Page, referred to as the "fundamentalists," who attributed the success of the "high performing Asian economies" to "getting the basics right," by which he meant trade openness, "a stable macroeconomic environment and a reliable legal framework to promote domestic and international competition."[55] On the other side were heterodox economists—labeled "mystics"—like Alice Amsden and Robert Wade, who argued for the importance of East Asian economies moving up the value chain through targeted technology acquisition and new export sectors. This did not always mean simply following the demands of the market. As Amsden argued in her most famous book, "getting relative prices wrong" was sometimes important to direct investment to high-growth industries.[56] Both sides saw the importance of investment in human capital, but the "mystics" saw industrial policy, planning, and activist government as necessary conditions for the East Asian miracle.

Debate about the East Asian miracle's "lessons for development policy" abated in mainstream circles when a financial crisis rocked the region in 1997. What began as a debt crisis became a full-fledged "development crisis."[57] Joseph Stiglitz, who had worked on the World Bank report, wrote that "pundits have been quick to pronounce the end of the region's economic 'miracle.' Some have even declared that there never was a miracle, only a mirage." He contended that this was not the case but that the crisis "underscored the challenges presented by a world of mobile capital—even for countries with strong economic fundamentals."[58] After the Asian crisis, Stiglitz's own work turned toward more frequent critiques of globalization. To Stiglitz, the crisis had prematurely foreclosed open questions, namely, on the fact that East Asian miracles "had been successful not only in spite of the fact that they had not followed most of the dictates of the Washington Consensus, but because they had not."[59] Where once had been awe at a successful growth model now became an occasion to pathologize. The historian Bruce Cumings was among those dubious of the volte face. "How," he asked, "can the 'miracle' economies of Asia turn overnight into cesspools of 'crony capitalism'?"[60] "When the crisis broke out," Stiglitz wrote, "it was almost as if many of the region's critics were glad: their perspective had been vindicated."[61] The time was ripe for those who wanted to redefine economic miracles as the product of state restraint rather than state intervention.

Economic miracle talk never returned at full strength after the Asian financial crisis.[62] Across the twentieth century, discussion of miracles had been about what form and degree of state action was possible or necessary to accelerate economic growth. Paradoxically, it evanesced in policy debates even as the astounding success story of the the People's Republic of China took its own unique combination of policy experimentation and selective state intervention into the 2000s. Isabella Weber and others have described "how China escaped shock therapy" and developed an approach that was neither "fundamentalist" nor "mystic" in the World Bank's sense.[63] Even as it was more important than ever to ask how state action created certain possibilities for accelerating growth and productivity and shut down others, the development establishment opted for a "legal turn" that fetishized rule of law as the defense of private property rights, chased gimmicks like "microfinance," and let the global bond markets do the rest.[64]

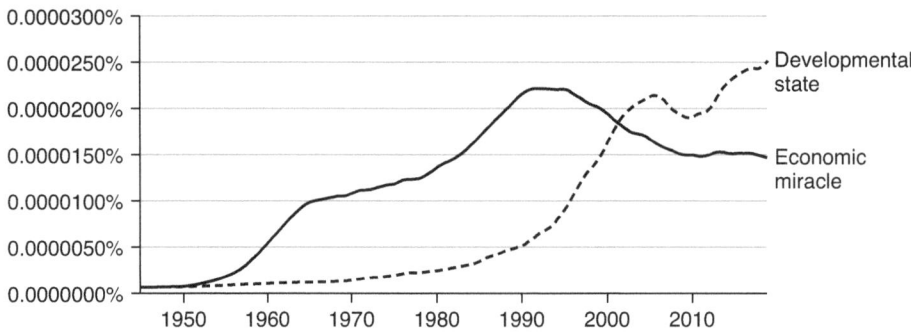

Figure 1. Ngram showing relative frequency of terms in scanned corpus of Google Books. Google Books Ngram Viewer, https://books.google.com/ngrams.

So where had the discussions gone that had once traveled under the category of the economic miracle? It is worth looking again at the so-called mystics, who were not so mystical at all. Amsden, for one, eschewed miracle talk. Rather, she saw the success of countries like South Korea as the rational outcome of rational policy choices.[65] These were not counterintuitive wonders but accomplishments of the "developmental state," a term whose use exploded in the 1990s and 2000s even as "the economic miracle" declined. By 2002, *developmental state* appeared more in the scanned corpus of Google Books than *economic miracle* (see fig. 1).[66]

The rise of the term tracks a shift in public discourse in the last decade in the United States, when reflexive fealty to the market has given way to acknowledgement of the uses of the state for economic ends. The triple shock of the global financial crisis, trade war with China, and the coronavirus pandemic has meant that, at least rhetorically, "big government is back."[67] The absence of a Reaganite language of dreams, miracles, and magic in the present moment is striking. Allusions to the fabulous and Promethean have been replaced by a zero-sum language of geoeconomics, neomercantilism, and rivalry.[68] If the horizon of the imaginable expanded during the First World War, it seems to have shrunk in our current polycrisis of climate catastrophe, trench warfare, and genocide. Concluding its arc across a century dominated by assumptions of endless growth, the age of miracles appears to be over.

Quinn Slobodian is professor of international history at Boston University. His most recent monographs are *Crack-Up Capitalism: Market Radicals and the Dream of a World without Democracy* (2023), and *Globalists: The End of Empire and the Birth of Neoliberalism* (2018). Forthcoming is *Hayek's Bastards: Race, Gold, IQ, and the Capitalism of the Far Right*.

Notes

1.   *Journal and Courier*, "Social Problems."
2.   *Maitland Mercury*, "Suez Mail."

3. *Journal and Courier*, "Social Problems."
4. *Lincoln Nebraska State Journal*, "Daily Drift."
5. *Springfield Leader and Press*, "American Superstition."
6. *Weekly Examiner*, "Huddersfield Chamber of Commerce."
7. *Guardian*, "Cotton Trade and Tariff 'Reform.'"
8. *Times Leader*, "Less Workers, More Production."
9. *Times Leader*, "Less Workers, More Production."
10. Logan, "Behind the Scenes at Nation's Capital."
11. *Lincoln Nebraska State Journal*, "Experts Were Wrong" (reprinted from *The New Republic*).
12. Angell, *Great Illusion*.
13. Angell, "Nationalisation for War."
14. Angell, "Nationalisation for War."
15. Withers, "Political Uncertainties Stifle Recovery."
16. *Box Elder News*, "When Disaster Helps Progress."
17. *New Britain Daily Herald*, "Want Ford to Run"; Hirsch, *Das Amerikanische Wirtschaftswunder*. On Hirsch and the broader German fascination with the United States, see Nolan, *Visions of Modernity*, 19.
18. *Salt Lake Telegram*, "Germany Fast Coming Back"; *Stockton Evening and Sunday Reporter*, "Irving Fisher."
19. *Brattleboro Reformer*, "Economic Miracle."
20. *Oakland Tribune*, "Sunday Tribune Writers Says U.S. Rescued France."
21. *Kansas City Star*, "Mussolini, the Autocrat."
22. *Courier-Mail*, "Germany's Ugly War Talk."
23. Priester, *Das deutsche Wirtschaftswunder*.
24. See, e.g., Chambers, review of *Private Investment in a Controlled Economy*.
25. For classic accounts, see Abelshauser, *Die langen fünfziger Jahre*; Reich, *Fruits of Fascism*; Crafts and Toniolo, *Economic Growth in Europe since 1945*; and Johnson, *MITI and the Japanese Miracle*.
26. Opie, review of *Two Post-War Recoveries*, 281.
27. Spicka, *Selling the Economic Miracle*, 134. On the promotion of the economic miracle, see also Schindelbeck and Ilgen, *Haste was, biste was!*
28. Erhard, "Germany's Economic Goals, 611.
29. *Montreal Star*, "German Money Plan Launched." See Ptak, *Vom Ordoliberalismus zur sozialen Marktwirtschaft*; and Nicholls, *Freedom with Responsibility*.
30. The strengths and limitations of the "Erhard shock" would be discussed for decades, including in reforming China. See Weber, "Ordoliberal Roots of Shock Therapy."
31. Hershey, "Tories Try Desocializing 'Fossilized' UK Economy."
32. See, e.g., Burmeister, review of *Germany and Freedom*, 93.
33. See Angster, *Konsenskapitalismus und Sozialdemokratie*; and Verheyen, *Diskussionslust*.
34. See Chamayou, *Ungovernable Society*.
35. Fellows, "Five Hundred Thousand Germans Idle in Dispute."
36. Modiano, "Stans, in Athens, Hails the Regime."
37. Eder, "Madrid: Three Pablos amidst the Ghosts."
38. Edwards, *Chile Project*, 2.
39. Hovey, "Brazil: Cost of Growth."
40. Hersh, "Ouster of Indians from Amazon Lands Is Charged."

41. *New York Times*, "Bishops in Brazil Denounce Regime."
42. *New York Times*, "'Economic Miracle' in Brazil Is Over."
43. *New York Times*, "Brazil Plans Trading Companies."
44. Griffin, "Revival of Japanese Military Ambitions"; see also Vogel, *Japan as Number One*; and Johnson, *MITI and the Japanese Miracle*.
45. Maidenberg, "Giant's Shadow Lengthens."
46. See Babb, *Behind the Development Banks*; Kiernan, "Modern Capitalism and Its Shepherds," 93.
47. Sterba, "Growth Helps Some Poor."
48. Silk, "Shifting away from the State."
49. Clines, "Reagan Bids Seoul Seek Democracy"; Reagan, "Excerpts from President's Speech in Japan."
50. Reagan, "President Reagan's Speech before Joint Session of Congress."
51. *New York Times*, "Reagan Talk to World Bank and IMF." On Reagan's rhetoric, see Rodgers, *Age of Fracture*, chap. 2.
52. World Bank, *East Asian Miracle*.
53. Wade, "Japan, the World Bank, and the Art of Paradigm Maintenance," 17–18.
54. Chang, *East Asian Development Experience*, 229.
55. Page, "East Asian Miracle," 224. See also Krugman, "Myth of Asia's Miracle." For critiques, see Amsden, "Why Isn't the Whole World Experimenting with the East Asian Model?"; Lall, "East Asian Miracle"; and Chang, *East Asian Development Experience*, chap. 7.
56. Amsden, *Asia's Next Giant*, 139.
57. Veneroso and Wade, "Asian Crisis," 4.
58. Stiglitz, "How to Fix the Asian Economies."
59. Stiglitz, *Globalization and Its Discontents*, 91.
60. Cumings, "Korean Crisis and the End of 'Late' Development," 44.
61. Stiglitz, *Globalization and Its Discontents*, 91.
62. It persists among conservative think tanks that remain keen to identify the "Estonian economic miracle," and trade business books promoting the "start-up nation" that is "Israel's economic miracle," but has little of the power to conjure it once had. Laar, "Estonian Economic Miracle"; Senor and Singer, *Start-Up Nation*.
63. Weber, *How China Escaped Shock Therapy*.
64. See Krever, "Legal Turn in Late Development Theory"; and Geismer, "Agents of Change."
65. See Amsden, *Asia's Next Giant*, 139.
66. Google Books Ngram Viewer, https://books.google.com/ngrams (accessed May 28, 2024).
67. Gerbaudo, "Big Government Is Back."
68. See Slobodian, "Backlash against Neoliberal Globalization from Above," 51–69.

References

Abelshauser, Werner. *Die langen fünfziger Jahre: Wirtschaft und Gesellschaft der Bundesrepublik Deutschland, 1949–1966*. Düsseldorf: Schwann, 1987.

Amsden, Alice H. *Asia's Next Giant: South Korea and Late Industrialization*. New York: Oxford University Press, 1989.

Amsden, Alice H. "Why Isn't the Whole World Experimenting with the East Asian Model to Develop? Review of *The East Asian Miracle*." *World Development* 22, no. 4 (1994): 627–33.

Angell, Norman. *The Great Illusion: A Study of the Relation of Military Power in Nations to Their Economic and Social Advantage.* New York: G. P. Putnam's Sons, 1910.

Angell, Norman. "Nationalisation for War—but Not for Peace." *Daily Herald*, September 16, 1920.

Angster, Julia. *Konsenskapitalismus und Sozialdemokratie: Die Westernisierung von SPD und DGB.* Munich: R. Oldenbourg Verlag, 2003.

Babb, Sarah. *Behind the Development Banks: Washington Politics, World Poverty, and the Wealth of Nations.* Chicago: University of Chicago Press, 2009.

Box Elder News (Box Elder, UT). "When Disaster Helps Progress." December 28, 1923.

Brattleboro Reformer. "An Economic Miracle." October 25, 1924.

Burmeister, Werner. Review of *Germany and Freedom: A Personal Appraisal*, by James Bryant Conant. *International Affairs* 35, no. 1 (1959): 93–94.

Chamayou, Grégoire. *The Ungovernable Society.* Cambridge: Polity, 2021.

Chambers, S. P. Review of *Private Investment in a Controlled Economy: Germany, 1933–1939*, by Samuel Lurie. *International Affairs* 24, no. 3 (1948): 416.

Chang, Ha-Joon. *The East Asian Development Experience: The Miracle, the Crisis, and the Future.* London: Zed, 2006.

Clines, Francis X. "Reagan Bids Seoul Seek Democracy." *New York Times*, November 12, 1983.

Courier-Mail (Brisbane, Australia). "Germany's Ugly War Talk." September 15, 1936.

Crafts, N. F. R., and Gianni Toniolo, eds. *Economic Growth in Europe since 1945.* New York: Cambridge University Press, 1996.

Cumings, Bruce. "The Korean Crisis and the End of 'Late' Development." *New Left Review*, no. 231 (1998): 43–72.

Eder, Richard. "Madrid: 3 Pablos amidst the Ghosts." *New York Times*, November 8, 1971.

Edwards, Sebastian. *The Chile Project: The Story of the Chicago Boys and the Downfall of Neoliberalism.* Princeton, NJ: Princeton University Press, 2023.

Erhard, Ludwig. "Germany's Economic Goals." *Foreign Affairs* 36, no. 4 (1958): 611–17.

Fellows, Lawrence. "500,000 Germans Idle in Dispute." *New York Times*, November 26, 1971.

Geismer, Lily. "Agents of Change: Microenterprise, Welfare Reform, the Clintons, and Liberal Forms of Neoliberalism." *Journal of American History* 107, no. 1 (2020): 107–31. https://doi.org/10.1093/jahist/jaaa010.

Gerbaudo, Paolo. "Big Government Is Back." *Foreign Policy*, February 13, 2021. https://foreignpolicy.com/2021/02/13/big-government-is-back/.

Griffin, Stuart. "Revival of Japanese Military Ambitions." *Guardian*, May 26, 1970.

Guardian. "The Cotton Trade and Tariff 'Reform.'" November 3, 1910.

Hersh, Seymour M. "Ouster of Indians from Amazon Lands Is Charged." *New York Times*, November 9, 1974.

Hershey, Robert D., Jr. "Tories Try Desocializing 'Fossilized' UK Economy." *New York Times*, August 19, 1979.

Hirsch, Julius. *Das amerikanische Wirtschaftswunder.* Berlin: S. Fischer, 1926.

Hovey, Graham. "Brazil: Cost of Growth." *New York Times*, July 9, 1974.

Johnson, Chalmers. *MITI and the Japanese Miracle: The Growth of Industrial Policy, 1925–1975.* Stanford, CA: Stanford University Press, 1982.

Journal and Courier (Lafayette, IN). "Social Problems." February 23, 1885.

Kansas City Star. "Mussolini, the Autocrat." August 25, 1927.

Kiernan, Victor. "Modern Capitalism and Its Shepherds." *New Left Review*, no. 183 (1990): 75–94.

Krever, Tor. "The Legal Turn in Late Development Theory: The Rule of Law and the World Bank's Development Model." *Harvard International Law Journal* 52, no. 1 (2011): 288–319.

Krugman, Paul R. "The Myth of Asia's Miracle." *Foreign Affairs* 73, no. 6 (1994): 62–78.

Laar, Mart. "The Estonian Economic Miracle." *Heritage Foundation Backgrounder*, no. 2060 (2007).

Lall, Sanjaya. "The East Asian Miracle: Does the Bell Toll for Industrial Strategy?" *World Development* 22, no. 4 (1994): 645–54.

Lincoln Nebraska State Journal. "Daily Drift." November 17, 1894.

Lincoln Nebraska State Journal. "The Experts Were Wrong." November 4, 1917.

Logan, Thomas F. "Behind the Scenes at Nation's Capital." *Philadelphia Inquirer*, September 17, 1917.

Maidenberg, H. J. "The Giant's Shadow Lengthens." *New York Times*, January 28, 1973.

Maitland Mercury. "The Suez Mail." August 27, 1874.

Modiano, Mario S. "Stans, in Athens, Hails the Regime." *New York Times*, April 24, 1971.

Montreal Star. "German Money Plan Launched." October 2, 1948.

New Britain Daily Herald. "Want Ford to Run." April 12, 1923.

New York Times. "Bishops in Brazil Denounce Regime." May 19, 1973.

New York Times. "Brazil Plans Trading Companies." July 30, 1972.

New York Times. "Brazil, 'the New Japan.'" January 28, 1973.

New York Times. "The 'Economic Miracle' in Brazil Is Over." February 8, 1976.

New York Times. "Reagan Talk to World Bank and IMF." September 30, 1981.

Nicholls, Anthony. *Freedom with Responsibility: The Social Market Economy in Germany, 1918–1963*. New York: Oxford University Press, 1994.

Nolan, Mary. *Visions of Modernity: American Business and the Modernization of Germany*. New York: Oxford University Press, 1994.

Oakland Tribune. "Sunday Tribune Writers Says U.S. Rescued France." December 27, 1924.

Opie, R. G. Review of *Two Post-War Recoveries of the German Economy*, by Horst Mendershausen. *Economica* 22, no. 87 (1955): 281.

Page, John. "The East Asian Miracle: Four Lessons for Development Policy." *NBER Macroeconomics Annual* 9 (1994): 219–69.

Priester, Hans Erich. *Das deutsche Wirtschaftswunder*. Amsterdam: Querido Verlag, 1936.

Ptak, Ralf. *Vom Ordoliberalismus zur sozialen Marktwirtschaft: Stationen des Neoliberalismus in Deutschland*. Opladen: Leske + Budrich, 2004.

Reagan, Ronald. "Excerpts from President's Speech in Japan." *New York Times*, November 11, 1983.

Reagan, Ronald. "President Reagan's Speech before Joint Session of Congress." *New York Times*, February 5, 1986.

Reich, Simon. *The Fruits of Fascism: Postwar Prosperity in Historical Perspective*. Ithaca, NY: Cornell University Press, 1990.

Rodgers, Daniel T. *Age of Fracture*. Cambridge, MA: Belknap Press of Harvard University Press, 2011.

Salt Lake Telegram. "Germany Fast Coming Back, Visitor Says." June 27, 1924.

Schindelbeck, Dirk, and Volker Ilgen. *Haste was, biste was! Werbung für die soziale Marktwirtschaft*. Darmstadt: Primus, 1999.

Senor, Dan, and Saul Singer. *Start-Up Nation: The Story of Israel's Economic Miracle*. New York: Twelve, 2009.

Silk, Leonard. "Shifting away from the State." *New York Times*, September 5, 1979.

Slobodian, Quinn. "The Backlash against Neoliberal Globalization from Above: Elite Origins of the Crisis of the New Constitutionalism." *Theory, Culture, and Society* 38, no. 6 (2021): 51–69.

Spicka, Mark E. *Selling the Economic Miracle: Economic Reconstruction and Politics in West Germany, 1949–1957.* New York: Berghahn, 2007.

Springfield Leader and Press. "An American Superstition." March 27, 1910.

Sterba, James P. "Growth Helps Some Poor in a Few Asian Countries." *New York Times*, March 22, 1973.

Stiglitz, Joseph. "How to Fix the Asian Economies." *New York Times*, October 31, 1997.

Stiglitz, Joseph E. *Globalization and Its Discontents.* New York: W. W. Norton, 2003.

Stockton Evening and Sunday Reporter. "Irving Fisher Urges Need for U.S. in League of Nations." July 29, 1924.

Times Leader (Wilkes-Barre, PA). "Less Workers, More Production." January 1, 1917.

Veneroso, Frank, and Robert Wade. "The Asian Crisis: The High Debt Model versus the Wall Street-Treasury-IMF Complex." *New Left Review*, no. 288 (1998): 3–36.

Verheyen, Nina. *Diskussionslust: Eine Kulturgeschichte des "besseren Arguments" in Westdeutschland.* Göttingen: Vandenhoeck & Ruprecht, 2010.

Vogel, Ezra F. *Japan as Number One : Lessons for America.* Cambridge, MA: Harvard University Press, 1979.

Wade, Robert. "Japan, the World Bank, and the Art of Paradigm Maintenance: The East Asian Miracle in Political Perspective." *New Left Review*, no. 217 (1996): 3–36.

Weber, Isabella M. *How China Escaped Shock Therapy: The Market Reform Debate.* New York: Routledge, 2021.

Weber, Isabella M. "The Ordoliberal Roots of Shock Therapy: The German 'Economic Miracle' in China's 1980s Reform Debate." In *Market Civilizations: Neoliberals East and South*, edited by Quinn Slobodian and Dieter Plehwe, 139–62. New York: Zone Books, 2022.

Weekly Examiner. "Huddersfield Chamber of Commerce." September 30, 1911.

Withers, Hartley. "Political Uncertainties Stifle Recovery of European Trade, Withers Declares." *New York Tribune*, September 3, 1922.

World Bank. *The East Asian Miracle: Economic Growth and Public Policy.* New York: Oxford University Press, 1993.

African Miracles and Black Damnation

On Economic Thaumaturgy

Franco Barchiesi

The fortune of *miracle* as a term in the arsenal of capitalist rhetoric has much to do with how it articulates the inconspicuous with the spectacular and the quotidian with the extraordinary. The classical image of competitive markets rests on the everyday but also counterintuitive and seemingly inexplicable reproduction of stable social orders through individual self-interested actions. Yet miracles are also meant to be seen and marveled at. In Latin, *miraculum* is etymologically connected to *admiratio*, or "regard with wonder." Economic miracles are such if they are witnessed and ratified by experts in ways that immediately resonate with laypeople's affects. The public's identification with national economic miracles speaks to its own witnessing, which often underscores the sacrifices those generations made in their optimistic faith in the days ahead. Delayed gratification for consumers and the grounding of future hedonism in present savings, hard work, and productivity deals guaranteed by the state have informed stories of Western European and East Asian postwar reconstructions as prodigious achievements. The development of the ancient Greek *mártus* (witness) into the Christian *martyr* also fits precepts of self-abnegation, hardship, and austerity, which capitalism has intimately woven into the economically miraculous, making the idea that markets, as godlike entities, are pleased with one's sacrifices perfectly intelligible and commonsensical in the avowedly secular and rational vocabulary of our times.

Radical History Review

Issue 151 (January 2025)   DOI 10.1215/01636545-11506882

© 2025 by MARHO: The Radical Historians' Organization, Inc.

The extramundane denotations of the miracle as a category of global capitalism have long interested theorists of the theological foundations of economics. For Giorgio Agamben, faith in an ultimately providential order is not only necessary to provide ethical foundations to seemingly arbitrary boom-and-bust cycles and related feelings of injustice resulting from privileged and malevolent actors benefiting from such conjunctures.[1] The management, public or private, of economic uncertainty confers on the economy itself the miraculous attributes of weathering the very storms it generates. In her analysis of religious traces in economic discourse, Sylvia Wynter places a stronger emphasis on discontinuity than does Agamben.[2] For Wynter, modern humanism starts with the assumption that "Man" possesses a divinely ordained yet rational capacity to dominate the natural world. The universalism of those early Christian roots is nonetheless discarded once it proves ultimately inadequate to sustain the racial hierarchies of global European expansion: enslavement and colonization. Under the authority of the racial, economics itself becomes a quasi-theological discourse whose "postulate of significant ill" is no longer ontological sinfulness but backwardness or underdevelopment, while the "plan of salvation" no longer conforms to God's dictates but to rules of capitalist competition.

The following pages confront the imagery of African economic miracles with an eye to the religious groundings of capitalism and a focus on how the anti-Black racialization of the continent signifies a "miracle" by reflecting Africa's abjection in global capital's political as well as libidinal economy. The imbrication of the classical categories of political economy, such as production and consumption, in drives, desires, and emotions invests capitalism with peculiar libidinal forces. The "miraculous" performances of Germany or Italy had something of the unexpected and the messianic in their rupture of postwar poverty and their ushering in of a sense of well-being through relatively original experimentations of a welfarist or "ordoliberalist" type, aligning, through state intervention, workers' demands with private property and the market. Alain Lipietz's classical account of postwar "global Fordism" momentarily departed from its solidly materialist tone by calling "almost a miracle" the fact that, with "no *a priori* reason," productivity and the technical composition of capital rose at the same rate across "developed" economies, inaugurating a surely short-lived "Golden Age."[3]

Modernization theory incorporated the miraculous in the discourse of the Global South's postcolonial economic development, but this time framed in a temporality of sequential stages rather than rupture. Poverty, hunger, and ignorance were assumed to be vanquished by entrenching the pillars of capitalist cosmology—landed property rights, proletarianization, export promotion—in East Asia or Latin America, where self-sustaining growth "would make the miraculous transformation a reality."[4] Rather than unexpected results through innovative solutions, non-Western economic miracles came to be categorized as the ability to replicate

Euro-American policies and results. Across this entire geopolitical spectrum, the baseline characteristic that defined economic miracles remained the fact that they did spectacularly occur and determined the transition from a lower to a higher socioeconomic and civilizational state. When it comes to Africa, however, none of these assumptions was meant to apply, at least in the eyes of the "international community." In the continent's postcolonial economic lexicon, *miracle* carries instead a distinctly racialized flavor, which speaks to a temporality drastically at odds with the progressive narratives of Western-inspired hagiography. For an African country to be globally recognized as a "miracle" it had to *avoid* an expected outcome—as a "failed state," a "basket case," a chaotic repetition of stagnation and failure—rather than *become* anything in particular.

As observers of African colonization, Frantz Fanon and Walter Rodney warned against belief in miracles.[5] They were concerned instead with the long-duration processes and structural conditions—resource extraction, elite consumption, predatory terms of trade and investment, exoticizing tourism—and encrusted dynamics of European rule that, in the absence of a revolutionary path to liberation, would beset the expectations of independence. Aimed at mundane transcendence as it surely was, Fanon's vision of Black liberation as a "leap" into a new world refused to see it as the result of "magical, supernatural powers," be they spiritual or economic.[6] Rupturing Africa's peculiar temporality, in which the event of independence was reabsorbed into the paradigm of racialized and capitalist rule, depended instead on deliberately radical political praxis. Otherwise, Western values and criteria would continue to decree Africa's ultimate inadequacy in freeing itself from the atavistic stagnation and unreason that colonial powers had identified with its Blackness. African leaders would then turn disappointment into violence on their own subjects—constantly accused of immaturity, indiscipline, or poor work ethics—rather than a critique of the global economic system that, in predetermining Africa's "failure," also demanded from the continent the "miracle" of being something other than itself, or "not to be Black," in Fanon's terms.[7]

Earlier expert commentaries even by Western critics of neocolonialism—arguing that "Black Africa" had "started badly" after the Europeans' departure—implied that African countries had to prove worthy of the independence bestowed on them by their former colonizers.[8] Whether they incorporated European legacies too passively or self-servingly, or failed to follow European examples at all, African nation-states became figurations of lack and shortcoming. Their being "left behind" signified not so much delay as an ontological condition of incompleteness.[9] Sociological descriptors of the continent's troubles—from "*un*captured peasantries" to "*in*formal economies" or *de*tribalized yet *semi*proletarianized workers—cast Africa as a byword for absence and void.[10] Despotic conditionalities under the "structural adjustment programs" of the 1980s and 1990s deepened Africa's distress, ratifying, in Western opinion, a disillusionment with independence that had in many ways been preordained and anticipated. In the no-alternative landscape of neoliberalism, the dilemma of whether Africa could make economic miracles was overwritten by the question "Why not Africa?"—why would the continent not churn out the macroeconomic indicators the "Washington consensus" claimed as its payoff for disciplining every other corner of the world into liberal norms and business-friendly approaches?

By the turn of the present century, economists surveyed the continent looking for "success stories" whose departure from what they presented as Africa's depressing sameness—corruption, conflict, and politically lubricated rent-seeking—could miraculously inspire a continental lift-off. Periods of rising commodity prices and the appearance of new investors, now also from Latin America, East Asia, and the Middle East, accompanied hopes for *Africa's turn*. In his contribution to a volume with that title, the influential economist Paul Collier suggested that there is indeed "a boom at the bottom."[11] Its causes, however, are neither the continent's democratization, corrupted by the elites' machinations in the absence of functioning liberal institutions, nor rising commodity earnings, which African leaders would likely pilfer, squander, and waste. Prospects of self-sustaining miracles depended instead, for Collier, on how one benefits from "knowledge . . . gained through failure," the ultimate example of which was, for sure, provided by a European country, Germany.[12] In his earlier book *The Bottom Billion*, widely praised in the corporate press, Collier elaborated on the meaning of the "failure" African leaders should learn to eschew by studying European success. Analyzing insurgency in the Niger Delta, where militant movements seized resources that, under the control of multinational corporations and their local allies, fueled generalized violence and environmental devastation, Collier condemned African rebellion as nothing more than organized crime financing itself through protection rackets and drug trafficking. The result, he concluded, was that the region had come to resemble an "American gangland."[13] Collier's thinly racialized coding lends itself ideally to a symptomatic reading of the underlying libidinal economy: transoceanic Blackness is in this case the abyss, which Black Africa, as the bottom of humanity, could only avoid by a miracle. In a trope subsequently propelled to public consumption by speculative Disneyfication, Wakanda came to represent the African "miracle"—an engine of prosperity and positive cultural diversity in partnership with corporate capital and NGO expertise—in antithesis to the apocalypse of Blackness everywhere else.

Measured as the capacity to "work," or function, in accordance with externally defined prescriptions, the African "success story" verges more on a thaumaturgical definition of *miracle*—healing something through supernatural intervention—than on apotheosis, or the portended rise toward the pinnacle of a global order of things, as in the case of the European or Asian miracles. Despite being incessantly demanded by neoliberalism, African economic miracles would then not occur along the same temporality Agamben alludes to in his critique of economics as an updated redemptive theology. Injunctions for Africa to work miracles instead reflect the secularization of white supremacy, which, for Wynter, is necessitated by the racialized imperative of positioning Blackness as uniquely pathological, or, in Wynter's term, "dysselected." In the wake of the nineteenth-century abolition of racial slavery in the western hemisphere, the core dilemma for political economy applied to plantation-centered nation-states was whether formerly enslaved Blacks would make themselves economically useful (and usable) without coercion.[14] Dereliction—in the form of either African sociocultural inertia or internalization of the passivity and dependence of slave status in the "new" world—was assumed as the condition of Blackness; thus Blackness was removed from progress and civility not only as defining categories of Euro-American societies but also, as postcolonial theorists have argued, as terrains of negotiation and contestation between European rule and colonized subaltern. Black freedom was "burdened," Saidiya Hartman writes, by expectations that its beneficiaries prove deserving of it by embracing subordination through labor contracts and relinquishing radical expectations.[15]

Can Africa become useful to global capitalist profitability without being colonized or otherwise coerced? The question retains its long-standing association with the anti-Blackness that, in the post-abolition era, instigates worries about what Africans might be able to perform besides dereliction. Meanwhile, African economists reputed to be, if not critical, at least lukewarm toward economic dogma are almost entirely excluded from the sites where the question is posed, chiefly the World Bank, which, having lost its once dominant position in development funding, has refocused its activities around knowledge production.[16]

Even when certified by the officiants of economic thaumaturgy, African miracles occur within worldly racial and colonial coordinates. Mozambique, for example, became one of the top destinations for foreign direct investment in sub-Saharan Africa in the first decade of the twenty-first century, following a postindependence history mostly characterized by socioeconomic devastation linked to internal armed conflicts and, initially, aggression by racist Rhodesia and South Africa. Hailed as a "miracle" by the global financial press, Mozambique's performance largely benefited a small fraction of millionaires connected with the governmental actors presiding over the privatization of state assets. As poverty deepened and fostered new social insurgencies,[17] which those very same media now present as the illness the miracle is supposed to cure, capital accumulation has mostly been in the form of financial speculation on the country's extractive prospects, in itself a legacy of colonial ways of "valorizing" African territories through ecological depredation.[18] A recent issue of the *Review of African Political Economy* accurately debunks the mythology surrounding the Mozambican "miracle."[19] The contributors focus on how new and old profit-making modalities in the country pose again a dilemma that scholars have pondered with regard to the continent at large: why did valorization not hatch "real" capitalism? In that scenario, instead of speculating on mineral or agricultural commodities, capital would manufacture stuff and create "good" jobs, allowing social reproduction to be disentangled from hyperexploitative survivalism, emancipating women from intersectional oppression, and creating conditions for the development of a proper working class.[20] The idea that capitalism, through self-interested means, can unwittingly pursue progressive goals and possibly lay the foundations for socialism through the dialectical resolution of its contradictions also resonates with a political-economic imagination verging on the portentous.

Aspirations to socialist miracles have not been better prepared than capitalist ones to confront the key fact that Blacks under white domination have resisted becoming proper working classes, be it in colonial Africa or in the post-abolition Americas, where the identification of freedom with the labor contract perpetuated the condemnation of Blackness as a type of surrogate humanity.[21] Operational in this long-duration transcontinental arc was not so much a calculation of alternative economic means to satisfy objective necessities but rather a critique of wage labor's associations with anti-Black violence. In a classical site of colonial and postcolonial extractivism—the Katanga region of the currently named Democratic Republic of the Congo—Timothy Makori shows how artisanal mining became an attractive, if exhausting and dangerous, path to income and consumption for young people in the aftermath of the World Bank–mandated dismantling of established, state-owned mining conglomerates. While artisanal diggers (*creuseurs*) may or may not be connected to global capital's circuits of extraction and export, their activity—which revives precolonial economic and cultural practices—is generally an object of antagonism from the state and private companies. Far from toiling for mere survival, however, *creuseurs* respond, in Makori's words, to "the evisceration of their pasts."[22] To their parents' generation, a mining job was presented as a colonial economic miracle, complete with European-style visions of stable waged employment and company-based, if racially paternalist, welfarism in the form of accommodation, schooling, and social services. The ruins of that dream, revoked in the neoliberal tide of the 1980s and 1990s, are widespread poverty and environmental collapse. Amid the ensuing precarity, artisanal mining was one of many volatile activities aimed at improving living conditions and household care. Surely problematic and fraught with contradictions, such strategies also reveal growing distrust toward the promises of the state or global investors. In fact, even African countries with a domestic business structure based on ingrained indigenous patterns of landownership and class formation—such as Côte d'Ivoire, one of the quintessential continental miracles of the 1960s and 1970s—had their hopes of self-propelled growth crushed by the very Euro-American development assistance actors that had once boosted African rulers' faith in economic miracles and were now presiding over the dismantling of their economies in the name of debt repayment.[23]

In conclusion, I have here shown how the semantic flexibility of "miracle" has underscored the adaptability of this quintessentially religious category to the allegedly secular realm of political economy. That is also because the economy itself is a flexible category, fusing social, political, and affective dimensions aimed at producing governable subjectivities in contexts (the current global financialized hypercapitalism is a case in point) where seemingly solid orders melt into air—as in Marx's famous metaphor—at an unprecedented speed. The affective or, as I put it here, libidinal investment in economic miracles has placed Africa in a peculiar position that speaks to the structural positionality of global Blackness across time. Applied to non-African contexts, the image of the economic miracle has served to denote breaks and becomings toward desirable self-reproducing states. Such was the meaning conveyed by "takeoff" in modernization theory as well as "sustainable" growth under neoliberalism. When it comes to Africa, however, miracle has meant—in the post-abolition, colonial, and postcolonial episteme—*not* being in some state (a condition of dereliction and dysfunctionality) that had been otherwise preordained and naturalized. Proponents of capitalism and liberal political economy have deemed it a miracle for Blackness—whether embodied by formerly racially enslaved people in the Americas or formerly colonized states in Africa—to overcome its essential incapacity and accede to proper economic activity. The association of Blackness with incapacity and dereliction was thus confirmed along the duration of what Christina Sharpe calls "ship time," which Africa's economic, social, and environmental destruction shares with locales—Haiti, Lampedusa, post-Katrina New Orleans, to name a few— caught in the same, paradigmatically anti-Black temporality.[24] If Blackness stands for a status that humanity has condemned, expectations that African miracles will eventually move out of it have failure built into them, as Fanon intuited. The world's anti-Black violence is then redoubled by the violence of a redemption that is never meant to be achieved and becomes instead the motivation for new rounds of privatization and austerity aimed to conjure miracles that keep receding.

Political economy remains, in the end, reluctant to account for anti-Blackness as structural power and positioning. By nailing Africa to timeless Black dereliction, economic discourse also suppresses specific cultural or spiritual local practices, from the Congolese *creuseurs* to Kenyan women's mobilization to reclaim their land in the name of a common maternal generation of life opposed to a corporate economy of death.[25] The separation or even autonomy of these movements from capital and patriarchy is, for sure, precarious, fleeting, and provisional; to idealize their being "outside" the state would imply a peculiarly miraculous longing. The experimental dimension of those practices instead has a critical potential that relies on their illegibility for established critical repertoires, including those trying to align Africa with a generic decoloniality, and confronts a Black strategic use of "opacity."[26] Social sciences accustomed to canonizing miracles would have much humility to learn from Black experiments with liberation.

Franco Barchiesi is associate professor in the Departments of Comparative Studies and African American and African Studies at the Ohio State University. He is the author of *Precarious Liberation: Workers, the State, and Contested Social Citizenship in Postapartheid South Africa* (2011) and a former fellow at the Hutchins Center for African and African American Research at Harvard University. His current research is on liberalism's groundings in the anti-Blackness of labor regimes across the Atlantic world in the late nineteenth and early twentieth centuries.

Notes

1. Agamben, *Kingdom and the Glory*, 126–29.
2. Wynter, "Unsettling the Coloniality of Being/Power/Truth/Freedom."
3. Lipietz, *Mirages and Miracles*, 36–37.
4. Latham, *Modernization as Ideology*, 81.
5. Fanon, *Wretched of the Earth*; Rodney, *How Europe Underdeveloped Africa.*
6. Fanon, *Wretched of the Earth*, 19.
7. Marriott, "Inventions of Existence."
8. Dumont, *L'Afrique noire est mal partie.*
9. Ferguson, *Global Shadows.*
10. Mbembe, *On the Postcolony.*
11. Miguel, *Africa's Turn?*, 109.
12. Miguel, *Africa's Turn?*, 111.
13. Cited in Watts, "Oil, Development, and the Politics of the Bottom Billion," 112.
14. Hall, *Civilising Subjects.*
15. Hartman, *Scenes of Subjection.*
16. Chelwa, "Does Economics Have an 'Africa Problem'?," 94.
17. Castel-Branco and Greco, "Mozambique: Neither Miracle nor Mirage."
18. Bruna, "Green Extractivism and Financialisation in Mozambique."
19. Ali and Stevano, "Work in Agro-Industry."
20. Ali and Stevano, "Work in Agro-Industry."
21. Cooper, *Decolonization and African Society*; Hartman, *Scenes of Subjection.*
22. Makori, "Mobilizing the Past," 783.
23. Bamba, *African Miracle, African Mirage.*
24. Sharpe, *In the Wake.*
25. Brownhill and Turner, "Feminism in the Mau Mau Resurgence."
26. Glissant, *Caribbean Discourse.*

References

Agamben, Giorgio. *The Kingdom and the Glory: For a Theological Genealogy of Economy and Government*. Translated by Lorenzo Chiesa and Matteo Mandarini. Stanford, CA: Stanford University Press, 2011.

Ali, Rosimina, and Sara Stevano. "Work in Agro-Industry and the Social Reproduction of Labour in Mozambique: Contradictions in the Current Accumulation System." *Review of African Political Economy*, no. 171 (2022): 67–86.

Bamba, Abou B. *African Miracle, African Mirage: Transnational Politics and the Paradox of Modernization in Ivory Coast*. Athens: Ohio University Press, 2006.

Brownhill, Leigh, and Terisa Turner. "Feminism in the Mau Mau Resurgence." *Journal of Asian and African Studies* 39, nos. 1–2 (2004): 95–117.

Bruna, Natacha. "Green Extractivism and Financialisation in Mozambique: The Case of Gilé National Reserve." *Review of African Political Economy*, no. 171 (2022): 138–60.

Castel-Branco, Carlos N. "Mozambique: Neither Miracle nor Mirage." *Review of African Political Economy*, no. 171 (2022): 1–10.

Chelwa, Grieve. "Does Economics Have an 'Africa Problem'?" *Economy and Society* 50, no. 1 (2021): 78–99.

Cooper, Frederick. *Decolonization and African Society: The Labor Question in French and British Africa*. Cambridge: Cambridge University Press, 1996.

Dumont, René. *L'Afrique noire est mal partie*. Paris: Éditions du Seuil, 1962.

Fanon, Frantz. *The Wretched of the Earth*. Translated by Richard Philcox. New York: Grove Press, 1963.

Ferguson, James. *Global Shadows: Africa in the Neoliberal World Order*. Durham, NC: Duke University Press, 2006.

Glissant, Édouard. *Caribbean Discourse: Selected Essays*. Translated by J. Michael Dash. Charlottesville: University of Virginia Press, 1981.

Hall, Catherine. *Civilising Subjects: Metropole and Colony in the English Imagination, 1830–1867*. Chicago: University of Chicago Press, 2002.

Hartman, Saidiya. *Scenes of Subjection: Terror, Slavery, and Self-Making in Nineteenth-Century America.* New York: Oxford University Press, 1997.

Latham, Michael E. *Modernization as Ideology: American Social Science and 'Nation Building' in the Kennedy Era*. Chapel Hill: University of North Carolina Press, 2000.

Lipietz, Alain. *Mirages and Miracles: The Crises of Global Fordism*. Translated by David Macey. London: Verso, 1987.

Makori, Timothy. "Mobilizing the Past: *Creuseurs*, Precarity, and the Colonizing Structure in the Congo Copperbelt." *Africa* 87, no. 4 (2017): 780–805.

Marriott, David. "Inventions of Existence: Sylvia Wynter, Frantz Fanon, Sociogeny, and the 'Damned.'" *CR: The New Centennial Review* 11, no. 3 (2012): 45–90.

Mbembe, Achille. *On the Postcolony*. Berkeley: University of California Press, 2001.

Miguel, Edward. *Africa's Turn?* Cambridge, MA: MIT Press, 2009.

Rodney, Walter. *How Europe Underdeveloped Africa*. Washington, DC: Howard University Press, 1981.

Sharpe, Christina. *In the Wake: On Blackness and Being*. Durham, NC: Duke University Press, 2016.

Watts, Michael. "Oil, Development, and the Politics of the Bottom Billion." *Macalester International* 24 (2009): 79–130. http://digitalcommons.macalester.edu/macintl/vol24/iss1/11.

Wynter, Sylvia. "Unsettling the Coloniality of Being/Power/Truth/Freedom: Towards the Human, after Man, Its Overrepresentation—An Argument." *CR: The New Centennial Review* 3, no. 3 (2003): 257–82.

State Violence and the Bitter Ends
of the *Milagro Mexicano*

Christy Thornton

For decades, scholars tasked with analyzing the demise of the "Mexican miracle" would concentrate largely on the *economic* fallout of the miracle's end—and not without reason. Mexico's transition from the high-growth, rapid-industrialization model of "stabilizing development" during the 1950s and 1960s to the stagnation of the 1970s and the crisis of the 1980s seemed a shocking turn of fortune.[1] In 1974 the Yale development economist Gustav Ranis could still note that "Mexico invariably appears on the list of that select group of cases of postwar development that have achieved success," but he did so in the context of asking if what had seemed a miracle was now "turning bitter."[2] As Ranis and other contemporary observers noted, as Mexico entered the 1970s, rates of industrialization and overall economic growth were slowing, unemployment was rising, and—as population growth continued to soar in Mexico and across Latin America—income distribution was worsening. A conventional view emerged over the following decades, arguing that Mexico's failure to upgrade its manufacturing capacity beyond the easy phase of import substitution and to invest in export-led industrialization had doomed its development strategy.[3]

The economic shift that followed became a well-known story, too. As growth slipped, the Mexican government under presidents Luis Echeverría Álvarez and José López Portillo took advantage of the good credit rating Mexico had established during the preceding decades to borrow unprecedented sums from private banks,

Radical History Review
Issue 151 (January 2025)   DOI 10.1215/01636545-11506861
© 2025 by MARHO: The Radical Historians' Organization, Inc.

with which they massively expanded government spending and funded social programs. Mexico's foreign debt grew from some US$7.5 billion in 1970 to more than
$24 billion in 1976; by 1981, it would reach $80 billion.[4] When interest rates in the
United States spiked with the Volcker shock, rolling over Mexico's ballooning debt
quickly became unsustainable, and Mexico threatened to default in 1982. In the
United States, this threat triggered worries that a Mexican default could imperil a
sizeable part of the global financial system, and so the US Treasury and the Bank for
International Settlements, supported by the International Monetary Fund, put
together a rescue package to ensure that Mexico could continue to pay its creditors
and Wall Street could avert a major crisis.[5] The agreement imposed a new model for
economies in crisis: structural adjustment. As the neoliberal "lost decade" of the
1980s coalesced, the miracle came to seem little more than a mirage.

  The well-known economic story of the miracle's aftermath has long obscured
another bitter narrative, however—one more hidden but no less consequential for
today's Mexico. In fact, the rise and fall of the Mexican miracle was shadowed by a
spiraling campaign of state violence, a campaign whose depth and breadth has only
recently begun to be recognized, investigated, and documented—by scholars and by
the state—as a *guerra sucia*, a dirty war.[6] As the inequities and failures of the Mexican development model became increasingly obvious in the late 1960s and 1970s,
many of those who denounced and fought against Mexico's injustices faced state surveillance, torture, extrajudicial execution, and forced disappearance, as did many of
their associates, family members, and neighbors.[7] Elsewhere in Latin America, the
shift from redistributionist aspirations or state-developmentalist plans to neoliberal
austerity was carried out by military dictators and US-backed regimes whose campaigns of state violence were obvious for those who cared to look: in the dirty wars
of the Southern Cone, for example, or the brutal counterinsurgencies of Central
America. But for many scholars, the notion of the *pax priísta*—a veil of Mexican
exceptionalism wrapped around the managed democratic stability of the hegemonic
Partido Revolucionario Institucional (PRI)—remained strong.[8] Thus, as Benjamin
Smith and Alexander Aviña have recently written, "For three decades, Mexico's dirty
war did not exist."[9] Scholars and activists in Mexico and beyond, however, have been
fighting to bring this other story to light, and to reveal its deep connections to the
economic processes that underpinned the supposed miracle. As a result of these
efforts, our reckonings with the ends of the Mexican miracle can no longer remain
in the antiseptic world of growth rates and debt-to-GDP ratios. Today, looking
back on the afterlives of the *milagro mexicano*, historians are now reckoning with
the bodies left in its wake.

. . . . .

Until the turn of this century, the state violence that accompanied the miracle was
rarely the subject of in-depth inquiry by historians. It was not that the violent

repression of the second half of the twentieth century was unknown or that its relationship to Mexico's state-led modernization plans was obscure. After all, Mexican security forces had quite publicly repressed political opponents and trade union activists, especially teachers and railway workers, in the 1950s; they had turned their guns and truncheons on campesino and student movements in the late 1950s and 1960s; and they had deployed brutal counterinsurgent warfare tactics to root out armed guerrilla movements and their supposed sympathizers in both countryside and cities in the 1960s and 1970s. To justify their actions, Mexican leaders derided those who dared question the results of the state-sponsored *milagro* as communist subversives, dangerous terrorists, or delinquent criminals, and the party-aligned media were often eager to parrot this line—or faced state pressure to force them to do so.[10] All the while, activists and public intellectuals within Mexico tried to bring attention to the repression of students, campesinos, and workers; but what Hector Aguilar Camín and Lorenzo Meyer called the "institutional monologue of the decades of the Mexican miracle" proved a resilient narrative.[11] Their early synthetic study of contemporary Mexican history, written during the 1980s, highlighted how the postrevolutionary state had worked to channel dissent through co-optation, though they noted that "whatever escaped the norms of these intramural negotiations was violently suppressed."[12] Detailed historical study of that violence, however, remained difficult. The history was too recent, much of the relevant archive was still inaccessible, and the political stakes were still uncomfortably high for the ruling party in power.

To be sure, state repression, especially the spectacular violence of the 1968 Tlatelolco massacre, did trigger a historiographic shift. But these new analyses tried to make sense of contemporary state violence largely by unseating the official nationalist narrative of Mexico's past, particularly the revolutionary period. Works like Adolfo Gilly's 1971 *Revolución interrumpida*, famously written inside the *palacio negro* of the Lecumberri prison in Mexico City—where Gilly and scores of other political prisoners were held for years and which today holds Mexico's national archives—and other "revisionist" histories provoked a historiographic debate about the nature of the revolution and the postrevolutionary state that continued for decades.[13] But to study the post-1940 history of Mexico at all remained relatively rare through the close of the twentieth century, as Tanalís Padilla pointed out in her 2008 book about the movement led by Rubén Jaramillo during the miracle period. "This history is still one in desperate need of telling," she wrote, calling for a history that would portray "not the golden age the PRI sought to project at home and abroad but a modernization dependent on the rollback of social reforms, a population fighting to preserve them, and a political machine whose wheels were greased through repression."[14] Nearly a decade into the twenty-first century, Padilla argued, there was still a great deal unknown about the state violence of the twentieth.

. . . . .

One of the key reasons that historians did not begin to grapple with what Fernando Herrera Calderón and Adela Cedillo called "the unknown Mexican dirty war" until the first decades of the twenty-first century was the halting process of opening state files to scrutiny.[15] It was only in the 1990s that it was possible to gain access to government documents about the 1968 massacre at Tlatelolco, for example. Of course, survivors of state violence and victims' families had already been organizing for years, coalescing into a nascent human rights movement in Mexico that won the release of political prisoners and leveraged international connections to force the establishment of a National Human Rights Commission in 1990.[16] In 1993, the twenty-fifth anniversary of the Tlatelolco massacre, a makeshift truth commission composed of prominent activists and public intellectuals—among them Sergio Aguayo, Carlos Monsiváis, and Elena Poniatowska—argued for the release of archival material about 1968, saying it would be "a precedent for the democratic future of the country," as the former student leader Salvador Ruiz Villegas put it.[17] Among nearly 1,300 boxes of archival material from the Dirección General de Investigaciones Políticas y Sociales (IPS), a state intelligence service under Mexico's interior ministry (Secretaría de Gobernación), some forty boxes were identified as containing information about 1968. The commissioners, together with political figures such as Cuauhtémoc Cárdenas, called for the IPS files to be disclosed, along with files from the Secretaría de la Defensa Nacional (SEDENA) and the government of Mexico City, among other agencies. For years they received no response.

Finally, facing national and international pressure (heightened, perhaps, as the question of resistance and repression resurfaced with the 1994 emergence of the Zapatista struggle in the state of Chiapas), archivists at the Archivo General de la Nación (AGN), Mexico's national archive, declared that the Tlatelolco documents would be disclosed thirty years after their production; they were released at last in 1998. At the same time, the National Security Archive in Washington obtained a set of newly declassified US documents that detailed what the Central Intelligence Agency, for example, knew in the lead-up to October 1968.[18] And the 1998 anniversary of the events at Tlatelolco also occasioned the release of a wave of new works by former student leaders and public intellectuals, adding new testimonies to what had been disclosed in the historical record.[19] While today, scholars have come to understand that 1968 was only one small piece of a much larger history of state repression, these initial releases began to form an archival basis for writing new histories of the miracle and its many critics.

The campaign to release files related to the violence at Tlatelolco brought together a coalition that included opposition politicians from both Left and Right to push for more government transparency. Legislators from the right-wing Partido de Acción Nacional (PAN) had played an important role in the effort, and when their candidate, Vicente Fox, won the presidency in 2000 and broke the seven-decade stranglehold of the ruling PRI, the incentives to keep secret the crimes of the single-party state were considerably lessened. A new federal law governing transparency and access to information was passed in 2002, and while appointing a full-fledged truth and reconciliation commission proved too controversial, Fox did appoint a new special prosecutor to investigate state violence from the 1960s to the 1980s, promising to prosecute those responsible for historical crimes.[20] Pushed by advocates and activists, that same year, Fox released more archival material from the IPS and another intelligence agency, the Dirección Federal de Seguridad (DFS). More than four thousand boxes containing sixty thousand files were turned over to the AGN, and transparency became a key promise of Mexico's apparent transition to democracy.

Of course, some worried that the PAN's commitment to transparency was fundamentally political in nature, little more than a strategy by the longtime opposition party to air the dirty laundry of its political rivals. Critics wondered what actions the state would take to hold former officials accountable, and their skepticism came to seem justified as the special prosecutor's work unfolded. In late 2005, the investigative team appointed by the special prosecutor presented to the prosecutor's office a detailed draft of the report it had compiled over the preceding years. It documented not just the brutality of 1968 but a widespread campaign of torture, executions, and hundreds of forced disappearances over nearly two decades.[21] But the prosecutor's office then appeared to stall, and it was only at the end of 2006 that a significantly revised final version was uploaded to the attorney general's website and then quickly taken down, triggering a response from the report's original authors accusing the government of censorship.[22] When the special prosecutor then sought to bring Echeverría to justice for his role at Tlatelolco and other incidents, the charges were overturned by the courts. In fact, none of the more than five hundred criminal complaints investigated was brought to trial, and the special prosecutor's office itself was closed in 2006.[23] What's more, files used by the investigative team for their report became effectively sequestered from outside researchers, leading Kate Doyle of the National Security Archive to wonder if the state had created, in the name of transparency, "a convenient tool for identifying the most damaging and dangerous material in the archives" and removing it from further scrutiny.[24] As researchers began to descend on the archive, it became clear that the IPS and DFS files that had been opened were quite difficult to use; they were barely catalogued and access to them was regulated by an official from the successor state security agency, the Centro de Investigación y Seguridad Nacional (CISEN). If transparency was to be the hallmark of the Mexican transition to democracy, the experience of attempting to consult the intelligence archives demonstrated some very clear limits to that transition.

. . . . .

Despite these limits, however, a new generation of scholars began to use this material to seek answers to historical questions about the *milagro mexicano* and its aftermath that few had previously even been able to ask.[25] Over the next decade or so, researchers began to pore over the newly released files. As they navigated the often arbitrary and inscrutable restrictions of the AGN, historians began compiling their own guides to the files, sharing information with one another, noting keywords that had produced productive searches from among the seven million index cards that accompanied the files, and—in the case of particularly tenacious and resourceful historians such as Adela Cedillo—locating the family members of victims of state violence so that they could request files containing personal information otherwise not available to researchers.[26] At the same time, the AGN began to create some three thousand redacted "public versions" of some of the DFS files, cataloged online, making access to at least some of the material easier. While the research remained far from straightforward, the result was a profusion of new histories that put resistance and repression at the center of the history of the second half of the twentieth century.[27] Scholars used these files to reconstruct the ways the state cataloged, surveilled, and—too often—violently repressed campesino organizations, labor unions, student movements, foreign radicals, Indigenous organizers, and guerrilla groups, both urban and rural.[28]

Much of this work explicitly sought to address not just the collapse of Mexico's development model in the 1970s but, as Alex Aviña wrote, "the so-called 'Mexican Miracle'" itself, which, he argued, had "depended upon the coercive disciplining of industrial workers and the countryside."[29] This new interpretation understood economic modernization and state repression as not merely parallel contemporaneous phenomena but as inextricably linked by a logic of capitalist accumulation that, as Padilla put it, depended "on the rollback of social reforms" of the earlier revolutionary era, as well as the deployment of violence for those who resisted that rollback.[30] Contrary to the idea of a corporatist consensus undergirded by growth, scholars began to show that Mexico's modernizing project had in fact been contested from the beginning by workers, peasants, and opposition parties and politicians, among others, who "witnessed at the local level the socioeconomic inequality produced by the PRI's capital-friendly economic policies," as Aviña put it.[31] Thus "those who resented and questioned the social costs of developmentalism were marginalized or repressed in many ways," as Elisa Servín noted, including by the use of state violence.[32] In a groundbreaking work, for example, Tanalís Padilla showed how the rural movement led by Rubén Jaramillo in Morelos in the 1940s and 1950s did not oppose modernization in the name of tradition but instead "sought the state support necessary to make the campesino economy viable in a rapidly modernizing nation," demanding "credit, technical assistance, better prices for their products, and basic state services."[33] This was contestation not just over political representation and growing authoritarianism (though it was also that, in Morelos and beyond), but over the contours of development itself. The Jaramillistas, Padilla wrote, "rather than resist political and economic modernization, wanted to partake in its fruits" and insisted that the supposed miracle not leave them behind.[34] As was the case in Guerrero, Chihuahua, and elsewhere, leaders' initial efforts to promote this vision electorally and through civic organizations were met with ruthless repression on the part of the state and powerful landholders. In response, Jaramillo and his followers took up arms; for this he would be arrested by the military in 1962 and brutally murdered, along with his wife and three of their children, their bodies dumped, riddled with bullets.

In uncovering these new narratives of the miracle period, historians thus began to show how the geographic, ethnic, and class unevenness of Mexico's apparently successful development model had not only generated opposition beginning as early as the 1940s, but that its appearance of success had depended on co-opting, dismissing, and often repressing that opposition through violence. Once the miracle began to unravel and growth began to slow during the 1960s, the stakes of such opposition became even higher for the state, particularly as both student and guerrilla movements began to grow in number and size. Echeverría attempted to make the bitterness easier to swallow with a concerted counterinsurgency campaign that involved a potent mix of developmental assistance and lethal violence. In the countryside, guerrilla groups such as those in Guerrero led by Génaro Vásquez and Lucio Cabañas "forced the state to implement a rural developmental program in a region largely neglected until the 1970s"; they were met, Aviña argues, by a staggering campaign of torture, disappearance, and extrajudicial execution by the Mexican military, including the use of notorious "death flights" in which alleged guerrillas were thrown into the ocean from small planes.[35] Fernando Herrera Calderón and Adela Cedillo argued that by the end of the administration of José López Portillo in 1982, "more than forty armed revolutionary organizations had been virtually eliminated from the political scene."[36] Not only was this a striking indicator of the scale of state repression, but it also demonstrated the importance of the IPS and DFS files, when read against the grain, to the new scholarship being produced about armed resistance groups.[37] And the countryside wasn't the only locus of such terror, though in the capital, Mexico City, most residents had considered themselves relatively removed from state violence (with the memory of the 1952 massacre of opposition supporters in the Alameda Central all but erased); this veil was lifted with the 1968 Tlatelolco attack and the 1971 massacre called El Halconazo.[38] At that point, even the Mexican middle classes living in the relative comfort of the capital were, as Louise Walker put it, shaking off their "political quiescence" and "waking from the dream" that the so-called miracle had engendered.[39]

As this new scholarship that drew from the DFS and IPS archives flourished, historians began to debate how the release of these files was shaping the historiography of Mexico after 1940, raising methodological, ethical, and even legal questions. Particularly given that archives for so many other state agencies in Mexico were (and are) still missing, uncataloged, or unavailable, how should historians use and interpret what they found in these intelligence files? How should historians understand the relationship between the state's projects of economic modernization, ideological hegemony, and repressive violence? Would an emphasis on the repressive power of the intelligence and security apparatus risk reproducing an image of an all-powerful PRI, able to successfully understand the challenges to its hegemony and ruthlessly root out its enemies? Scholars were careful to acknowledge the limits of files produced by the often paranoiac and poorly informed eyes of the single-party state, creating what Aviña called "archives of counterinsurgency" filled with official narratives that were frequently exaggerated, distorted, or simply wrong.[40] But, as Herrera Calderón and Cedillo argued, the files did appear to reveal a much wider campaign of repression than had been acknowledged by either the state or the earlier scholarship. Still, some worried that the emphasis on repression overstated the strength of the PRI and the state it controlled. Pablo Piccato, for his part, argued in 2013 that "these documents and the intelligence practices underlying them reveal a weak state rather than one able to easily eliminate dissent."[41] And despite using these files themselves, Walker and Padilla worried that that these new archival collections "could begin to loom too large" in the scholarship, creating "a distorting effect on our understanding of this period" in the absence of other archival evidence.[42]

. . . . .

If historians thought they were settling in for a long historiographic debate on the repercussions of this new wave of scholarship, however, the Mexican state foiled those plans. State violence had surged under Vicente Fox's successor, Felipe Calderón, who launched what he called "a war on drugs and organized crime" that sent the military into the streets of major Mexican cities. Calderón's policies resulted in an epidemic of killing and forced disappearance across the country. The resulting insecurity was at least partially responsible for Mexican voters returning the PRI to power in the 2012 elections, when Enrique Peña Nieto, scion of a powerful party family, was elected to the presidency. With the PRI back in power, even the halting efforts at transparency undertaken by the previous administrations were quickly targeted for reversal. A new director took over at the AGN in 2013, and a new archives law took effect that year codifying a thirty-year embargo on confidential records while adding an additional seventy-year restriction on records deemed "sensitive."[43] Then, in 2014, a horrific attack on students from the Ayotzinapa Rural Normal School, the teacher-training college in Guerrero from which Lucio Cabañas had graduated, resulted in multiple deaths and the unexplained forced disappearance of forty-three of the students. As the world watched, horrified, the attorney general quickly moved to produce an obviously false *verdad histórica*, "historical truth," about the Ayotzinapa events that absolved the military and security forces of responsibility, blaming drug traffickers and a few low-level police officers. With the PRI back in power, comparisons to the earlier *guerra sucia* period were frequent, and as Mexicans took to the streets to protest the state's version of events, they rallied behind the cry "It was the state" (*fue el estado*).

It was during this crisis that the AGN suddenly announced new regulations governing the security files in 2015. Deciding that the seventy-year embargo applied to everything in the collection, archivists drastically restricted access to the DFS files, leaving only a selection of the redacted "public versions" available for consultation. In addition, new rules were imposed that limited the number of documents researchers could request on site from any collection, and in 2017, a long-planned move of the AGN's files to a new climate-controlled wing was undertaken by a team of amateur movers with no archival expertise. The result, Andrew Paxman wrote, was organizational chaos, during which "entire collections went missing."[44] Suddenly the advancement of the burgeoning historiography drawing on the previous thirteen years of access was threatened; Padilla and Walker, who had worried a few years earlier about overreliance on the archives, now lamented that "the historiographical loss cannot be understated."[45] As the Peña Nieto administration tried desperately to control the media narrative about the role of the state in the disappearance of the Ayotzinapa students, the archives became ever more closely guarded, imperiling not just the further development of the historiography but the course of justice for the victims of state violence, historical and contemporary.

. . . . .

There was reason to hope that the election of Andrés Manuel López Obrador in 2018 would bring renewed transparency. López Obrador promised to support an independent truth commission about Ayotzinapa and, facing pressure from ongoing mobilizations of families and rights groups, supported the creation of a Comisión Nacional de Búsqueda—a national search commission—to coordinate efforts to locate the more than one hundred thousand Mexicans officially registered as forcibly disappeared. Upon taking office, López Obrador announced not only that the DFS files would be reopened but that he would also declassify files of the successor intelligence agency, CISEN, which had operated from 1985 to 2018. He tasked the newly appointed head of the AGN with overseeing this effort, but the damage wrought to the archives during the Peña Nieto administration was substantial, and the jurisdictional questions were thorny. In 2019, the AGN officially took control of the DFS files from the now-defunct CISEN and promised that access to all files would be restored. Confoundingly, however, in early 2020, the IPS files from after 1950 were also briefly withdrawn from public consultation under the seventy-year restriction, leading survivors of state violence and their families to stage public protests outside Lecumberri. By mid-2020, access was restored to all the files that had been restricted under Peña Nieto, but by then, of course, the COVID-19 pandemic had shuttered in-person access to the archive, so researchers would have to continue to wait to return.

In October 2021, López Obrador issued a decree forming an official Truth Commission which included the creation of the Mecanismo para la Verdad y el Esclarecimiento Histórico, a group tasked with investigating state violence between 1965 and 1990. In 2022, as the Mecanismo members were beginning their work, the separate commission investigating the Ayotzinapa attack and subsequent cover-up issued a report declaring the 2014 events to have been a "crime of the state," finally acknowledging what many had long suspected.[46] Now, seemingly for the first time, the Mexican state itself would acknowledge and investigate state violence, both past and present. Members of the Mecanismo have used the work that historians have produced over the preceding decades, as well as the ongoing labor of archivists at local, state, and federal levels and the testimonies of victims and their families all around the country. And at the AGN, archivists worked diligently not just to restore access to the files that had been restricted but to produce new finding aids that allow for digital consultation of the millions of index cards that organize the security files, which were uploaded into the AGN's new Digital Document Repository in early 2024. After a decade of uncertain access, Mexico's archives of state violence are once again open.

The optimism that comes with restored access to files about Mexico's *guerra sucia* is tempered, however, by an obstacle that both the Ayotzinapa and the historical commissions have faced in recent months and years: lack of cooperation from the military. López Obrador increasingly relied on the military to oversee not just public safety but also to carry out infrastructure development, public health, and other government programs around the country. But even as the armed forces have taken on a rapidly growing share of state functions, SEDENA officials have refused to comply with requests for information, even those coming from their own government.[47] A massive trove of military documents leaked in 2022 revealed a host of military surveillance and training activities they had publicly denied, raising additional concerns about their growing role in Mexican governance.[48] And recent scandals involving secret surveillance of Mecanismo leaders such as the historian Camilo Vicente Ovalle, using Pegasus software licensed in Mexico only to the military, demonstrates the extent to which the historical truth about military violence remains threatening to the country's most powerful institutions.[49]

The intransigence of the Mexican military represents a real impediment not just for those seeking justice for recent crimes but also for those trying to reconstruct how the history of state violence has shaped Mexico today. One of the more recent advances in the historiography, pushed forward even as files have been restricted, are new investigations that detail the ways that political violence gave way seamlessly to the violence of the nascent war on drugs.[50] In fact, as historians like Nathaniel Morris and Benjamin Smith have recently argued, the modernization that propelled the Mexican miracle forward is deeply implicated in the history of the drug trade and the role of the state in alternately promoting, protecting, or combatting it.[51] As Morris put it, drug-trafficking networks that linked rural Durango to US cities like Chicago served to "consolidate the political, social and economic modernization of parts of Durango that would otherwise have been left behind by the licit side of the 'Mexican Miracle.'"[52] As the drug war continues today under the auspices of Mexico's military, lack of access to its historical files will surely impede scholarly understandings of how drugs have shaped the development of contemporary Mexico.

In today's Mexico, of course, state violence remains a central problem. When Jaime Pensado and Enrique Ochoa published their volume *México beyond 1968* in 2018, they argued that it was explicitly written to "provide some of the historical context for understanding current violence and repression."[53] In much the same way that historians living through the terror of the late 1960s and early 1970s revised their histories of the revolutionary period, today's inequality, insecurity, and repression continue to fuel a revision of the so-called golden age of the *milagro mexicano*. The history revealed through the files of state security agencies has made increasingly clear that as students, journalists, campesinos, labor militants, Indigenous activists, and others questioned the miracle's bitter ends—in the dual sense of both its modernizing objectives and its eventual descent into crisis—they faced increasingly violent forms of repression. And this repression, historians have argued, was not incidental to the history of Mexico's economic miracle and its aftermath but part and parcel of the state project to manage modernization. Surveying this history reveals, as Aviña and Smith have recently written, that "the government guarded the edges of the politically possible"—and, as the scholarship makes clear, the economically possible—"with the barrel of a gun."[54] Today, as historians, advocates, and truth commissioners now reckon with the violence endemic to the miracle and its aftermath, much more than historiography is at stake.

Christy Thornton is associate professor of history at New York University. She is author of *Revolution in Development: Mexico and the Governance of the Global Economy* (2021), which won the 2022 Luciano Tomassini Latin American International Relations Book Award from the Latin American Studies Association.

Notes

1. See, for example, Lustig, *Mexico*.
2. Ranis, "*¿Se está tornando amargo el milagro mexicano?*," 22. Translations are mine unless otherwise noted.
3. For a recent summary, see Sherman, "The Mexican 'Miracle' and Its Collapse." For a contemporaneous account, see Baer, "Import Substitution and Industrialization in Latin America."
4. Moreno-Brid and Ros, *Development and Growth in the Mexican Economy*, 86; Aggarwal, *Debt Games*, 335.
5. Cline, "Mexico's Crisis, the World's Peril," 107.

6. The term *guerra sucia* remains controversial for implying a war with two equal sides, when in fact the scale of state violence far outstripped that of the armed resistance in Mexico. The debate within Mexico is addressed in Comisión Nacional de los Derechos Humanos, "Informe sobre la violencia política de Estado en México."

7. On forced disappearance, see Vicente Ovalle, *Tiempo suspendido*, who argues that forced disappearances in Mexico were beginning already in the 1930s and 1940s.

8. See, for example, the discussion of the *pax priísta* in Knight, "Myth of the Mexican Revolution."

9. Aviña and Smith, "Mexico's Dirty War," 1.

10. Herrera Calderon and Cedillo, "Introduction: The Unknown Mexican Dirty War," 7. On the struggle over what was permissible within the Mexican press, see Freije, *Citizens of Scandal*; and Rodríguez Munguía, *La otra guerra secreta*.

11. Aguilar Camín and Meyer, *In the Shadow of the Mexican Revolution*, 251.

12. Aguilar Camín and Meyer, *In the Shadow of the Mexican Revolution*, 200.

13. Gilly, *La revolución interrumpida*. See also Knight, "Mexican Revolution."

14. Padilla, *Rural Resistance in the Land of Zapata*, 15.

15. Herrera Calderon and Cedillo, "Unknown Mexican Dirty War," 1. For an early investigation of the state security services, see Aguayo Quezada, *La Charola*.

16. Trevizo, "Political Repression and the Struggles for Human Rights"; Carey and Román Gaspar, "Carrying on the Struggle"; Carey, "Transcending Violence."

17. Ramírez Garrido, "68: Crónica de los archivos bajo llave."

18. Doyle, "Official Report Released on Mexico's 'Dirty War.'" See also Doyle, "Tlatelolco Massacre."

19. See, for example, Aguayo Quezada, *1968: Los archivos de la violencia*; Álvarez Garín, *La estela de Tlatelolco*; and García Medrano, *El 2 de octubre de 1968*.

20. Doyle, "Impunity's Triumph."

21. For the draft version, see Doyle, "Draft Report Documents Eighteen Years."

22. Sotelo Marbán, "El informe del Fiscal." See also López García, "La FEMOSPP y su informe histórico." For the full report, see Fiscalía para Movimientos Sociales y Políticos del Pasado, "Informe histórico a la sociedad Mexicana."

23. Cedillo, "Tracing the Dirty War's Disappeared."

24. Doyle, "Impunity's Triumph."

25. Padilla and Walker, "In the Archives," 5. This new generation included many of the authors of the special issue of the *Journal of Iberian and Latin American Research* edited by Padilla and Walker, "Spy Reports: Content, Methodology, and Historiography in Mexico's Secret Police Archive."

26. Cedillo, "Tracing the Dirty War's Disappeared." Daniela Spenser also organized and produced a guide to the IPS files that circulated as a CD-ROM ("Guerra fría y guerrilla en México").

27. For a description of using the archive in this period, see Padilla and Walker, "In the Archives," 4–5.

28. Key histories produced using this material include Aguayo Quezada, *De Tlatelolco a Ayotzinapa*; Alegre, *Railroad Radicals in Cold War Mexico*; Aviña, *Specters of Revolution*; Carey, *Plaza of Sacrifices*; Condés Lara, *Represión y rebelión en México*; Dillingham, *Oaxaca Resurgent*; Herrera Calderón and Cedillo, *Challenging Authoritarianism in Mexico*; Keller, *Mexico's Cold War*; Montemayor, *La violencia de estado en México*; Padilla, *Rural Resistance in the Land of Zapata*; Rangel Hernández, *La*

Liga Comunista 23 de Septiembre; Pensado and Ochoa, *México beyond 1968*; and Walker, *Waking from the Dream*, among others.

29. Aviña, *Specters of Revolution*, 12; emphasis mine.
30. Padilla, *Rural Resistance in the Land of Zapata*, 15.
31. Aviña, *Specters of Revolution*, 42.
32. Servín, "Los 'enemigos del progreso,'" 83.
33. Padilla, *Rural Resistance in the Land of Zapata*, 2.
34. Padilla, *Rural Resistance in the Land of Zapata*, 23.
35. Aviña, "'We Have Returned to Porfirian Times,'" 107.
36. Herrera Calderon and Cedillo, "Unknown Mexican Dirty War," 6.
37. In addition to Herrera Calderón and Cedillo, *Challenging Authoritarianism in Mexico*, see Oikión Solano and García Ugarte, *Movimientos armados en México*, vol. 2; Castellanos, *México armado*; and Pensado and Ochoa, *México beyond 1968*.
38. On the Henriquista massacre, see Servín, *Ruptura y oposición*.
39. Walker, *Waking from the Dream*, 1.
40. Aviña, *Specters of Revolution*, 14.
41. Piccato, "How to Build a Perspective on the Recent Past," 97. See also Loaeza, "Gustavo Díaz Ordaz."
42. Padilla and Walker, "In the Archives," 7.
43. Paxman, "Crisis at Mexico's National Archive."
44. Paxman, "Can Mexico's National Archive Restore Its Reputation?"
45. Commentary by Tanalís Padilla and Louise E. Walker in Olcott and Mannion, "Open Forum on Archives and Access: The DFS Controversy."
46. Secretaría de Gobernación, "Informe de la Presidencia de la Comisión para la Verdad."
47. Mecanismo para la Verdad y el Esclarecimiento Histórico, "Sedena incumple plazos ordenados por el INAI."
48. Doyle and Dorfman, "Guacamaya Leaks and the Ayotzinapa Case."
49. Lopez and Sheridan, "He's Leading Mexico's Probe of the Dirty War."
50. See, for example, Cedillo, "Operation Condor"; Aviña, "El Norte Chiquito"; and Morris, "Crisis, Corruption and State-Led Development."
51. See Smith, *Dope*.
52. Morris, "Crisis, Corruption and State-Led Development," 39.
53. Pensado and Ochoa, *México beyond 1968*, xii. See also Piccato, *A History of Infamy*.
54. Aviña and Smith, "Mexico's Dirty War," 2.

References

Aggarwal, Vinod K. *Debt Games: Strategic Interaction in International Debt Rescheduling*. New York: Cambridge University Press, 1996.

Aguayo Quezada, Sergio. *De Tlatelolco a Ayotzinapa: Las violencias del Estado*. Mexico City: Proceso, 2014.

Aguayo Quezada, Sergio. *La Charola: Una historia de los servicios de inteligencia en México*. Mexico City: Grijalbo, 2001.

Aguayo Quezada, Sergio. *1968: Los archivos de la violencia*. Mexico City: Grijalbo, 1998.

Aguilar Camín, Héctor, and Lorenzo Meyer. *In the Shadow of the Mexican Revolution: Contemporary Mexican History, 1910–1989*. Austin: University of Texas Press, 1993.

Alegre, Robert F. *Railroad Radicals in Cold War Mexico: Gender, Class, and Memory*. Lincoln: University of Nebraska Press, 2013.

Álvarez Garín, Raúl. *La estela de Tlatelolco: Una reconstrucción histórica del movimiento estudiantil del 68*. Mexico City: Grijalbo, 1998.

Aviña, Alexander. "An Archive of Counterinsurgency: State Anxieties and Peasant Guerrillas in Cold War Mexico." *Journal of Iberian and Latin American Research* 19, no. 1 (2013): 41–51.

Aviña, Alexander. "El Norte Chiquito: From 'Dirty Wars' to Drug Wars in the Guerrero Hotlands." *European Review of Latin American and Caribbean Studies* 112 (2021): 71–89.

Aviña, Alexander. *Specters of Revolution: Peasant Guerrillas in the Cold War Mexican Countryside*. New York: Oxford University Press, 2014.

Aviña, Alexander. "'We Have Returned to Porfirian Times': Neopopulism, Counterinsurgency, and the Dirty War in Guerrero, Mexico, 1969–1976." In *Populism in Twentieth Century Mexico: The Presidencies of Lázaro Cárdenas and Luis Echeverría*, edited by Amelia M. Kiddle and María L. O. Muñoz, 106–21. Tucson: University of Arizona Press, 2010.

Aviña, Alexander, and Benjamin T. Smith. "Mexico's Dirty War: A Reassessment." *Bulletin of Latin American Research* 43, no. 3 (2024): 209–85.

Baer, Werner. "Import Substitution and Industrialization in Latin America: Experiences and Interpretations." *Latin American Research Review* 7, no. 1 (1972): 95–122.

Carey, Elaine. *Plaza of Sacrifices: Gender, Power, and Terror in 1968 Mexico*. Albuquerque: University of New Mexico Press, 2005.

Carey, Elaine. "Transcending Violence: A Crisis of Memory and Documentation." In Herrera Calderon and Cedillo, *Challenging Authoritarianism in Mexico*, 198–210.

Carey, Elaine, and José Agustín Román Gaspar. "Carrying on the Struggle: El Comité 68." *NACLA Report on the Americas* 41, no. 3 (2008): 20–21.

Castellanos, Laura. *México armado, 1943–1981*. Mexico City: Ediciones Era, 2011.

Cedillo, Adela. "Operation Condor, the War on Drugs, and Counterinsurgency in the Golden Triangle (1977–1983)." Kellogg Working Paper 443. Notre Dame, IN: Kellogg Institute for International Studies, 2021.

Cedillo, Adela. "Tracing the Dirty War's Disappeared: The Documents of Operación Diamante." *Journal of Iberian and Latin American Research* 19, no. 1 (2013): 71–90.

Cline, William R. "Mexico's Crisis, the World's Peril." *Foreign Policy*, no. 49 (1982): 107–18.

Comisión Nacional de los Derechos Humanos. "Informe sobre la violencia política de Estado en México." June 2021. https://www.cndh.org.mx/sites/default/files/documentos/2022-07/Informe_Violencia_politica_Estado_2022.pdf.

Condés Lara, Enrique. *Represión y rebelión en México (1959–1985)*. Mexico City: Porrúa, 2007.

Dillingham, A. S. *Oaxaca Resurgent: Indigeneity, Development, and Inequality in Twentieth-Century Mexico*. Stanford, CA: Stanford University Press, 2021.

Doyle, Kate. "Draft Report Documents 18 Years of 'Dirty War' in Mexico." National Security Archive, February 26, 2006. https://nsarchive2.gwu.edu/NSAEBB/NSAEBB180/index.htm.

Doyle, Kate. "Impunity's Triumph: The Failure of Mexico's Special Prosecutor." National Security Archive, June 8, 2006. https://nsarchive2.gwu.edu/NSAEBB/NSAEBB180/doyle_impunity_triumph.pdf.

Doyle, Kate. "Official Report Released on Mexico's 'Dirty War.'" National Security Archive Electronic Briefing Book No. 209, November 21, 2006. https://nsarchive2.gwu.edu/NSAEBB/NSAEBB209/index.htm.

Doyle, Kate, ed. "Tlatelolco Massacre: U.S. Documents on Mexico and the Events of 1968." National Security Archive Electronic Briefing Book No. 99, October 10, 2003. https://nsarchive2.gwu.edu/NSAEBB/NSAEBB99/.

Doyle, Kate, and Claire Dorfman, eds. "Guacamaya Leaks and the Ayotzinapa Case," National Security Archive Electronic Briefing Book No. 823, March 10, 2023. https://nsarchive.gwu.edu/briefing-book/mexico-ayotzinapa/2023-03-10/guacamaya-leaks-and-ayotzinapa-case.

Fiscalía para Movimientos Sociales y Políticos del Pasado (FEMOSPP). "Informe histórico a la sociedad mexicana." Procuraduría General de la República. Mexico City, 2006.

Freije, Vanessa. *Citizens of Scandal: Journalism, Secrecy, and the Politics of Reckoning in Mexico*. Durham, NC: Duke University Press, 2020.

García Medrano, Renward. *El 2 de octubre de 1968, en sus propias palabras*. Mexico City: Rayuela Editores, 1998.

Gilly, Adolfo. *La Revolución interrumpida*. Mexico City: Ediciones El Caballito, 1971.

Herrera Calderón, Fernando, and Adela Cedillo, eds. *Challenging Authoritarianism in Mexico: Revolutionary Struggles and the Dirty War, 1964–1982*. New York: Routledge, 2012.

Herrera Calderón, Fernando, and Adela Cedillo. "Introduction: The Unknown Mexican Dirty War." In Herrera Calderon and Cedillo, *Challenging Authoritarianism in Mexico*, 1–19.

Keller, Renata. *Mexico's Cold War: Cuba, the United States, and the Legacy of the Mexican Revolution*. New York: Cambridge University Press, 2015.

Knight, Alan. "The Mexican Revolution: Bourgeois? Nationalist? Or Just a 'Great Rebellion'?" *Bulletin of Latin American Research* 4, no. 2 (1985): 1–37.

Knight, Alan. "The Myth of the Mexican Revolution." *Past and Present* 209, no. 1 (2010): 223–73.

Loaeza, Soledad. "Gustavo Díaz Ordaz: El colapso del milagro mexicano." In *Una historia contemporánea de México: Actores*, edited by Ilán Bisberg and Lorenzo Meyer, 2:117–55. Mexico City: Editorial Océano, 2003.

Lopez, Oscar, and Mary Beth Sheridan. "He's Leading Mexico's Probe of the Dirty War. Who's Spying on Him?" *Washington Post*, June 3, 2023.

López García, Jonathan. "La FEMOSPP y su informe histórico." Secretaría de Gobernación, Mexico. https://sitiosdememoria.segob.gob.mx/work/models/SitiosDeMemoria/Documentos/PDF/Breve_semblanza_del_Informe_de_la_FEMOSPP.pdf.

Lustig, Nora. *Mexico: The Remaking of an Economy*. Washington, DC: Brookings Institution Press, 2000.

Mecanismo para la Verdad y el Esclarecimiento Histórico. "Sedena incumple plazos ordenados por el INAI para la entrega de documentos sobre los llamados 'vuelos de la muerte.'" Press release, May 7, 2024. https://www.meh.org.mx/comunicacion/comunicados/sedena-incumple-plazos-ordenados-por-el-inai-para-la-entrega-de-documentos-sobre-los-llamados-vuelos-de-la-muerte/.

Montemayor, Carlos. *La violencia de estado en México: Antes y después de 1968*. Mexico City: Debate, 2010.

Moreno-Brid, Juan Carlos, and Jaime Ros. *Development and Growth in the Mexican Economy: A Historical Perspective*. New York: Oxford University Press, 2009.

Morris, Nathaniel. "Crisis, Corruption and State-Led Development in the Making of the Mexican Drug Trade." *Past and Present* 265, no. 1 (2024): 235–73.

Oikión Solano, Verónica, and Marta Eugenia García Ugarte, eds. *Movimientos armados en México, siglo XX*. Zamora: El Colegio de Michoacán and CIESAS, 2006.

Olcott, Jocelyn, and Sean Mannion, eds. "Open Forum on Archives and Access: The DFS Controversy." *Hispanic American Historical Review*, Open Forum, September 2015. https://hahr-online.com/open-forum-on-archives-and-access-the-dfs-controversy/.

Padilla, Tanalís. *Rural Resistance in the Land of Zapata: The Jaramillista Movement and the Myth of the Pax Priísta, 1940–1962*. Durham, NC: Duke University Press, 2008.

Padilla, Tanalís, and Louise E. Walker. "In the Archives: History and Politics." In "Spy Reports: Content, Methodology, and Historiography in Mexico's Secret Police Archive," edited by Tanalís Padilla and Louise E. Walker. Special issue, *Journal of Iberian and Latin American Research* 19, no. 1 (2013): 1–10.

Paxman, Andrew. "Can Mexico's National Archive Restore Its Reputation?" *LASA Forum* 51, no. 2 (2020): 89–93.

Paxman, Andrew. "Crisis at Mexico's National Archive." April 12, 2015. https://andrewpaxman .wordpress.com/2015/04/12/crisis-at-mexicos-national-archive.

Pensado, Jaime M., and Enrique C. Ochoa, eds. *México beyond 1968: Revolutionaries, Radicals, and Repression during the Global Sixties and Subversive Seventies*. Tucson: University of Arizona Press, 2018.

Piccato, Pablo. *A History of Infamy: Crime, Truth, and Justice in Mexico*. Oakland: University of California Press, 2017.

Piccato, Pablo. "How to Build a Perspective on the Recent Past." *Journal of Iberian and Latin American Research* 19, no. 1 (2013): 91–102.

Ramírez Garrido, Jamie. "68: Crónica de los archivos bajo llave—Un viaje a los sótanos del Archivo General de la Nación." *Nexos*, September 1, 1998.

Rangel Hernández, Lucio. *La Liga Comunista 23 de Septiembre 1973–1981: Historia de la organización y sus militantes*. Morelia: Universidad Michoacana de San Nicolás de Hidalgo, 2011.

Ranis, Gustav. "¿Se está tornando amargo el milagro mexicano?" *Demografía y Economía* 8, no. 1 (1974): 22–33.

Rodríguez Munguía, Jacinto. *La otra guerra secreta: Los archivos prohibidos de la prensa y el poder*. Mexico City: Random House Mondadori, 2007.

Secretaría de Gobernación. "Informe de la Presidencia de la Comisión para la Verdad y Acceso a la Justicia del Caso Ayotzinapa." Gobierno de México, August 18, 2022.

Servín, Elisa. "Los 'enemigos del progreso': Crítica y resistencia al desarrollismo del medio siglo." In *Del nacionalismo al neoliberalismo, 1940–1994*, edited by Elisa Servín, 79–127. Mexico City: Fondo de Cultura Económica, 2010.

Servín, Elisa. *Ruptura y oposición: El movimiento henriquista, 1945–1954*. Mexico City: Cal y Arena, 2001.

Sherman, John W. "The Mexican 'Miracle' and Its Collapse." In *The Oxford History of Mexico*, edited by William Beezley and Michael Meyer, 537–68. New York: Oxford University Press, 2010.

Smith, Benjamin T. *The Dope: The Real History of the Mexican Drug Trade*. New York: Norton, 2021.

Sotelo Marbán, José, et al. "El informe del Fiscal omite temas fundamentales incluidos en el Informe ¡Que no vuelva a suceder!, que se le entregó el 15 de diciembre de 2005." National Security Archive, December 12, 2006. https://nsarchive2.gwu.edu/NSAEBB/NSAEBB209 /Reaccion_al_Informe_del_Fiscal.pdf.

Spenser, Daniela. "Guerra fría y guerrilla en México: Guía de acceso al archivo de la Dirección de Investigaciones Políticas y Sociales, AGN." CD-ROM. Mexico City: Centro de Investigaciones y Estudios Superiores en Antropología Social, 2004.

Trevizo, Dolores. "Political Repression and the Struggles for Human Rights in Mexico: 1968– 1990s." *Social Science History* 38, nos. 3–4 (2014): 483–511.

Vicente Ovalle, Camilo. *Tiempo suspendido: Una historia de la desaparición forzada en México, 1940–1980*. Mexico City: Bonilla Artigas Editores, 2019.

Walker, Louise. *Waking from the Dream: Mexico's Middle Classes after 1968*. Stanford, CA: Stanford University Press, 2013.

Turning Values into Value

Archaism and the Launching of China's Economic Takeoff

Rebecca E. Karl

I begin with a question: How can we think historically about our current moment in which the global logics of capitalist governance are wedded, in many places, to the regressive depths of state-sponsored socioeconomic and neotraditional cultural forms? This is not new in historical terms, although it has arisen these days in a freshly virulent form. Here I discuss this question and its form in China, as it is shaped by and through the firm discursive extirpation of the history and practice of socialism in China (1949–79) and globally (1917–89), and as it articulates a claim to an economic "takeoff" (since 1979) that is necessarily linked to the "cultural rejuvenation" of the Chinese nation and people. The current Chinese leader Xi Jinping's culturalist policies of brutal resource extraction, labor suppression, and capital accumulation in a regressively neo-Confucian cultural-ideological mode are certainly not the only example of such a contemporary marriage (one can think of Trump's America, Bolsonaro's Brazil, Modi's India, and a large host of others). Indeed, since his inauguration in 2012, Xi has "consistently promoted China's ancient values and traditions as a means by which to achieve a new 'spiritual civilization,'" while Vice Chairman Xu Jialu of the Standing Committee of the National People's Congress "claims that the 'worldviews, values, ethics, and aesthetics' of China can serve as an antidote to the corrosive effect of modern American culture, which, he avers, 'poses a serious challenge to our traditional values.'"[1]

Radical History Review
Issue 151 (January 2025)   DOI 10.1215/01636545-11506826
© 2025 by MARHO: The Radical Historians' Organization, Inc.

The admixture of regressive culturalism with capitalist brutality and racist governance (exemplified in the militarized, genocidal annihilation of the Palestinian people by an atavistic Zionism embodied today in the Israeli state and its global allies) is not just a problem of the current moment. This tendency names a persistent, latent possibility in modernity and in capitalism, a latency that historically has manifested as fascism and/or colonialism. Harry Harootunian has named this culturalist tendency an "archaism" embedded in "the measure[s] by which capitalism saves itself from the crisis it causes."[2]

This is how I'd like to locate the current mobilization in China of Confucian archaism, a sociocultural form of what also could be called heritage racism, in its elevation of a sedimented culturalist essence claimed by Han Chinese for China as such; this Confucian essence is then extended to argue that the (Han) Chinese are uniquely suited to benefit from the contemporary moment of capitalist accumulation and global conflict, while also shaping it. This linkage is starkly observable, now that the immediate past years of lockdown and dynamic COVID-19 restrictions have been lifted, in the pursuit of what the activist Promise Li calls the "continuation of a logic of governance that prioritizes the preservation of profits for the ruling class over people's livelihoods." This logic, he has noted, is not merely China's but is broadly shared globally.[3]

For the purposes of this brief roundtable comment, I would add to Promise Li's observation that this logic of governance substantiates itself on the persistence of an ahistorical conflation of value (as an economic relation) and values (as a sociocultural relation). In China's case, contemporary neotraditionalists do not see the post-Mao mandated breakup of the socialist collectives and the consequent wholesale privatization of public property as the key mechanism through which capital accumulation and economic "takeoff" in the capitalist mode was violently inaugurated and legitimated throughout the 1980s and 1990s. Instead, they find in supposed enduring and ahistorical Chinese cultural values the central economic, value-producing mode through which the national state and a layer of the recent ultrarich have accrued wealth and power, while also exporting parts of that accumulation to invest in and appropriate scarce resources and exploit labor power the world over.

Of course, this conflation and accumulation are not unique to China. The contemporary Chinese version follows centuries of Euro-American (and Japanese) accumulation accompanied by *their* cultural claims to a unique ability to convert values into value (Protestantism, Christianity, Judaism, Bushido or collective spirit, or whatever culturalist-racist essence du jour is on offer at any given historical moment). It is notable that the Chinese version of converting values to value is happening today at a pace and scale—in both breadth and depth—hitherto unprecedented in human history. And it is being implemented in an environment already fully despoiled by previous rounds of dispossession and extraction, and over swathes of the globe already impoverished through Euro-American-led colonial plundering and postcolonial uneven development. The full-scale entry of Chinese capital— either as a state form or as a private form—into those realms since the late 1990s, as well as the specific appropriations of land, resources, and labor power through the ideology and practice of rapacious developmentalism, are only accelerating the global histories of capitalist domination and displaced degradations. Colonial violence was embedded in the earlier forms of domination by naked design; the ongoing military occupation and genocidal annihilation in Palestine today can be seen as an intensified continuation of this violence into our current era. Yet, despite culturalist disavowals of (neo)colonialism by Chinese actors in the contemporary moment, violence is embedded in today's practices as well, albeit sometimes less nakedly.[4]

Indeed, taking Chinese disavowals of neocolonialism as credible expressions of Chinese cultural difference from Euro-American-Japanese pasts merely obscures the monstrous present of the racialized and gendered extractions proceeding under the guise of Confucian harmony and national rejuvenation. *When Marx Met Confucius*, a mostly risible but also ideologically indicative five-part series developed in 2023 by Hunan TV, articulates starkly the current state of neotraditionalist claims. In one episode, Marx is made to avow his essentially Confucian roots through his abiding commitment to political stability and harmony (*hexie* 和谐). "Xi Jinping thought," that body of ruling political, moral, and economic thinking now enforced in Chinese schools and social life as a foundational philosophy for the twenty-first century, claims to be this very synthesis in the service of a continuous and recognizable (Han) Chineseness that is always specifically Chinese (Confucian) but also adaptive to the world in which it operates.[5] This Chineseness, in its current form, is no passive adapter to global survival, unlike its forebears in the nineteenth and twentieth centuries. Rather, it is an active shaper of contemporary global cultural and capitalist norms. No less an eminent thinker than Wang Hui has given a good deal of academic and philosophical heft to this current set of syncretic claims.[6]

What needs to be said, in the unnuanced way I am using for the purposes of this roundtable, is that the historical evacuation of the distant past—its rendering into a homogenized, vacuous presentism—intends to underwrite ideologically the current moment of wished-for, abstract, infinite accumulation. As Neferti Tadiar has put it, "the past time of dead labor as well as the future time of disposable life" are both concretized "in favor of extractable value in the present."[7] Meanwhile, the immediate past—of the twentieth century's conflictual revolutionary legacies and socialist experiments—is overwritten either as an historical aberration and wrong turn or as the murderous project of a singular madman (Mao Zedong), even as the (admittedly unsuccessful) attempts under socialism to break with the abstractions of capitalist value extraction are now disavowed as having contravened the culturalist essence of "the Chinese ethnos."[8] Whatever the achievements of the post-Mao era in producing and accumulating wealth—and these achievements have been enormous, as well as enormously environmentally destructive and socially unequal—the question of whether economic takeoff (China's or anyone's) can sustain itself must confront the ongoing threat of foundational crises in capitalism globally and locally. China's threats to Taiwan's political, social, and economic autonomy—recently taking on ever more severe forms with military flyovers and verbal assaults on Taiwan's governing party, accompanied by economic sanctions and disciplining of Taiwanese capital investments in the mainland; the real estate bust and attempts to bail out sectors of the economy now collapsing under the weight of their own propulsive but hollow growth; the attempts to rein in sectors of capital and bind them more closely to the PRC state—all of these and more indicate the state of chaos not only in China's capitalist present but in the global capitalist system. Some scholars, such as Pun Ngai, have theorized this form of crisis in the Chinese case as "infrastructural capitalism"; she proposes this new stage of monopoly capitalism premised on the relations between capital and the continual conflicts occasioned by working-class demands on production and reproduction.[9] Pun's wildly optimistic view of the prospects for "the living tradition" of China's radical labor movement notwithstanding (on this, she and I disagree), it seems correct to see "infrastructural capitalism" as a compensatory form intended to absorb, disarm, and deflate labor militancy even while it requires the continual intensification of productivity in digitized, as well as traditional, worker forms.

However, as we consider the prospects for the future—and it is hard for me to see past our current moment of genocidal violence, atavistic reanimation of patriarchy, and treatment of "surplus populations" as redundant and disposable—it seems clear to me that neotraditionalist archaism only feeds the worst of these tendencies, pushing them toward the fascist revivals staring us in the face, rather than providing us any clues for how to exit from our current situation. Economic takeoff—a "miracle" by another name?—underpinned by such archaism cannot solve our problems. As China's recent decades have demonstrated, such developmentalist economism merely deepens our precarious conditions. Meanwhile, neotraditionalism is a social disaster. As Susan Greenhalgh has recently written, the 2021 decision announcing the "three-child policy" in China was articulated in culturalist mode, intended to "promote the traditional virtues of the Chinese nation, respect the social value of childbirth . . . and foster a new culture of marriage and childbearing."[10] Unsurprisingly, the promise of harmony and Confucian values is just one ideologically potent mechanism of would-be state control over the bodily extraction of labor power and progeny in the name of the accumulation of wealth for the few, the power of the nation-state, and the domination of capitalism and patriarchy in this era of derivative, speculative monopolies. China is, of course, just one piece in this puzzle. But it is a very large one.

Rebecca E. Karl is professor of history and teaches on modern China, gender, and social theory at New York University. Her most recent publications include *China's Revolutions in the Modern World: A Brief Interpretive History* (2020) and *The Magic of Concepts: History and the Economic in Twentieth-Century China* (2017).

Notes

1. Smith, *Qing Dynasty and Traditional Chinese Culture*, 1.
2. Harootunian, *Archaism and Actuality*.
3. Li, "Zero-COVID, Reopening, and the Proliferation of State Capitalisms."
4. There is a raging debate among scholars, journalists, and policymakers in and outside China over whether China can be considered a (neo)colonial power in Africa and elsewhere, and whether the Belt and Road Initiative can be seen as an overt or covert (neo)colonial initiative. C. K. Lee efficiently summarizes some of these issues in the introduction to her book *The Specter of Global China*. While I accept Lee's challenge to think seriously about the specificities of Chinese capitalist practices, I think her major point—that China's state-sponsored capitalist form is primarily a political endeavor while private capital's form is primarily economic—is overdrawn.
5. Rana Mitter recently stated, "Bureaucrats, tycoons, and pop stars have been required to endorse it; students now learn it in school; CCP members must use a smartphone app that regularly communicates its precepts" ("Real Roots of Xi Jinping Thought").
6. Although originally published in four volumes in 2004, before Xi Jinping's rise to power, Wang Hui's *Rise of Modern Chinese Thought* was recently condensed and published in one (enormous) English volume translated under the direction of Michael Gibbs Hill, thus giving academic weight and philosophical heft to the idea that Marxism and Confucianism have happily fed on one another from the late nineteenth century onward.
7. Tadiar, *Remaindered Life*, 127.
8. It is important to note the recent shift in vocabulary that references the Chinese as an ethnic people (*minzu* 民族) not a political people (*renmin* 人民). The move to "integrate" the various non-Han ethnicities into an overall "Chineseness" (dictated by and through the Han) indexes this shift as well.
9. Pun, "China's Infrastructural Capitalism," 343.
10. Greenhalgh, "Biopolitics of the Three-Child Policy."

References

Greenhalgh, Susan. "The Biopolitics of the Three-Child Policy." *Made in China*, June 6, 2024. https://madeinchinajournal.com/2024/06/06/the-biopolitics-of-the-three-child-policy/.

Harootunian, Harry. *Archaism and Actuality: Japan and the Global Fascist Imaginary*. Durham, NC: Duke University Press, 2023.

Lee, C. K. *The Specter of Global China: Politics, Labor, and Foreign Investment in Africa*. Chicago: University of Chicago Press, 2017.

Li, Promise. "Zero-COVID, Reopening, and the Proliferation of State Capitalisms." Lausan Collective, January 6, 2023. https://lausancollective.com/2023/zerocovid-reopening -statecapitalisms/.

Mitter, Rana. "The Real Roots of Xi Jinping Thought." *Foreign Affairs*, March/April 2024. https://www.foreignaffairs.com/browse/review-essay.

Pun Ngai. "China's Infrastructural Capitalism and Infrastructural Power of Labor: The Making of the Chinese Working Class." *positions* 32, no. 2 (2024): 341–69.

Smith, Richard J. *The Qing Dynasty and Traditional Chinese Culture*. Lanham, MD: Rowman and Littlefield, 2015.

Tadiar, Neferti X. M. *Remaindered Life*. Durham, NC: Duke University Press, 2022.

Wang Hui. *The Rise of Modern Chinese Thought*. Translated by Michael Gibbs Hill. Cambridge, MA: Harvard University Press, 2023.

In Search of a Story Engine

The Brazilian Economic *Milagre* and the Rise
of the Technocratic Developmental State

Paula Vedoveli

The Brazilian economic miracle has remained at the core of analyses of the military regime that governed the country from 1964 to 1985. Even today, many of those who lived through the period of the *milagre* place the social and economic transformations the country underwent in the late 1960s and early 1970s at the center of their lived experiences under the regime. Economic historians have sought to unveil the magnitude of this transformation with recourse to macroeconomic indicators that we have made a conspicuous part of the knowledge infrastructure mobilized for knowing the economy.[1] During the years from 1968 to 1973, the period commonly associated with the Brazilian *milagre*, the Brazilian economy grew at an average annual rate of 11.1 percent of the GDP, against 4.2 percent in the four preceding years. It was not the first time the Brazilian economy had presented impressive growth rates. During the elected presidency of Juscelino Kubitschek (1956–61), the Brazilian economy grew by about 50 percent of the GDP and 60 percent of industrial production; inflation, however, grew from 11.8 percent in 1955 to 25.4 percent in 1960, alongside a rising balance of payment deficits and debt burden.[2] The period of the *milagre* witnessed for the first time accelerated growth with lower inflation rates (from 25.5 percent in 1968 to 15.6 percent in 1973) and significant balance of payment surpluses (at an average of US$1.1 billion per year between 1968 and 1973), which lowered the ratio of net foreign debt to exports from 2 in

Radical History Review
Issue 151 (January 2025)   DOI 10.1215/01636545-11506798
© 2025 by MARHO: The Radical Historians' Organization, Inc.

1968 to 1.4 in 1973.[3] The period seems even more impressive if we observe that by late 1963, inflation had risen to 80 percent and GDP growth had shrunk to 0.6 percent from 6.6 percent in 1962.[4]

Despite their apparent inherent significance due to their contemporary centrality to assessments of economic performance, numbers are performative instruments that by themselves cannot support narratives of economic miracles without recourse to what Tiago Mata has called a story's "engine," or a source of tension capable of organizing the unfolding of the narrative over time in relation to context, protagonists, and outcome.[5] Narratives of economic miracles have been built on engines mobilized when these transformations took place and later to reinterpret these processes. Jason Petrulis has noted how the narrative of a South Korean miracle was mobilized to support economists' and policymakers' attempts to reify "universalist claims of development economics" while highlighting that today's preferred engine ties the miracle to Koreans' behavior. Despite the differences between these two narrative engines, Petrulis suggests that they both left unexplored the costs of accelerated industrialization under an authoritarian regime.[6] The South Korean and the Brazilian economic miracles have clear parallels, not least in the fact that they unfolded in underdeveloped countries under authoritarian regimes that mobilized technical experts to promote an account of technocratic state management of the economy. Still, these similarities do not presuppose that the proliferation of economic miracle narratives after World War II was predicated on the diffusion of convergent engines, nor do they explain how the unequal distribution of the costs and benefits of the socioeconomic transformations has remained a secondary—or entirely omitted—part of the narrative. What, then, was the story engine of the Brazilian economic miracle?

We can start by defining what a miracle may entail, and consider whether it may be the realization of the *unexpected*. An economic miracle was and is primarily seen as the process of acceleration of economic growth, and there was a time when continuous economic growth was not to be expected.[7] Until the 1930s, the business cycle theory tied the expectation of growth to an ensuing period of economic stagnation.[8] The experience of uninterrupted, self-sustained economic growth was then an anomalous phenomenon and, as Timothy Mitchell has noted, a "potentially destabilizing force."[9] By the 1950s, however, uninterrupted and—in developed countries—self-sustained growth was not only the central component of state action in the economic sphere but an *expected* means and outcome of the development process as established by development and growth economists.[10] A key epistemological transformation facilitated this transition. The production and diffusion of universalist theories of development anchored in the expectation of a takeoff toward steady economic expansion, along with the widespread adoption of the United Nations' 1953 System of National Accounts, helped establish contemporary attempts at quantifying economic growth—such as national income, GNP, and GDP—as what Daniel Speich, following Bruno Latour, has termed "inscription devices" that help economic actors govern the uncertainty connected with a future of continuous growth.[11] At the time of the Brazilian miracle, economic growth was not an unexpected process but rather an *anticipated* result of state-led action that could be quantified in stable inscriptions of the national economy.

If not the unexpected, the Brazilian economic miracle could have been the realization of the *unpredictable*. Here, the key self-proclaimed Brazilian technocrats behind the economic miracle would categorically state that if the miracle was the realization of the unpredictable then there had been no miracle. This was the opinion of the Brazilian minister of the treasury Antônio Delfim Netto (1967–74).[12] For the minister of planning João Paulo dos Reis Velloso (1969–79) as well, it made "no sense to talk about a Brazilian miracle" as a rupture with the past or as a process unexpected or unpredicted.[13] Re-created by the military regime in 1964, the Ministry of Planning was the technocratic institution charged with designing the country's development strategy. Velloso's assessment of the Brazilian experience in 1973 seems to contradict his earlier statement that, given the scarce resources at the disposal of his ministry, promoting development felt "'almost like producing a miracle.'"[14] But here the miracle was not the realization of the unpredictable but an effort to prepare the correct interpretation of possible economic futures presented as an "as if" narrative in a development plan, a reasoning device capable of articulating what could happen through careful and realistic planning.[15] Thus Velloso, a thirty-eight-year-old economist who had studied at Yale, sought to present himself not as a "saint who performs miracles" but as a technocrat who "believes that work— if not faith—indeed moves mountains."[16] Velloso and his ministry are products of what Mitchell has called "economentality"—the systematic inclusion of the future into government through economic policymaking, a process that eventually allowed the state to discipline and govern the potentially destabilizing expectations of future economic expansion, not least through planning.[17] Planners such as Velloso therefore capitalized on the elusive distinction between predictions, projections, estimates, and targets to offer "a view of the performance of the Brazilian economy" that helped support the economic policy of the military regime.[18] It should not be surprising that Velloso rose to prominence after he had publicly contested the "pessimistic projections" made by the futurologist Herman Kahn about Brazil's future in his 1967 book *The Year 2000*, in particular his estimates of the country's national income per capita by 2000.[19] Framing the miracle as a predictable, state-led process of economic engineering helped dissociate it from Brazil's subsequent experiences with economic stagnation and recession during the latter years of the military regime.

The rise of economentality as a dimension of governmentality, and the recourse to techniques of futurity to discipline collective expectations and buttress the legitimacy of the regime—whose authority in economic affairs had been challenged in 1967 after a stabilization program led to a recession[20]—thus meant forfeiting the narrative engine of the unpredictable. Could the Brazilian experience have been structured by a story engine that presented the miracle as a feat of wonder, a process that surpassed expectations of what was then seen as possible? To answer this question, we must explore how contemporaries presented the conditions for accelerated economic growth in underdeveloped countries. Development and growth economics tied the conditions for economic expansion in the 1950s and 1960s to what Mauro Boianovsky has termed "capital fundamentalism."[21] This was the premise that development was predicated on capital accumulation, as expressed in the often-quoted contention by the development economist Arthur Lewis that for development to occur in underdeveloped countries, 10 percent to 15 percent of national income should be allocated toward investment.

Rather than a simple accounting exercise, however, capital fundamentalism depended on an epistemological transformation of how contemporaries conceived capital accumulation and the strategies they employed to measure it. In the early twentieth century, capital accumulation had been assessed through long-term changes in a country's stock of assets as measured in estimates of national wealth.[22] The diffusion of national accounting after World War II, however, made possible the short-term assessment of capital accumulation by equating it with national savings, which was then understood as the accounting difference between what was produced and what was consumed by a country in a given year. Because savings should be allocated as investment to expand the stock of physical capital of a country to support development, growth required the expansion of aggregate production beyond aggregate consumption levels. After World War II, this was a goal made possible by the establishment of national income, GNP, and GDP as tools of short-term economic management rather than as indices of economic welfare—or as indicators of an economy's capacity to respond to the demands of society.

National income estimates were initially envisioned in the early 1930s by the Russian-American economist Simon Kuznets as a measure of a population's economic welfare rather than an economy's "short-term productive capacity."[23] However, Kuznets's mobilization of the accounting framework to assess a country's "economic potential" for production during World War II, and the subsequent diffusion of national accounting, eventually led the economist to recognize, in 1972, the potential of GDP for measuring "short-term changes in current economic performance" of a country.[24] Consequently, if accelerated growth required accelerated savings, this could be achieved in the short run by expanding production and promoting saving as a goal of economic policymaking. The Brazilian military government was not oblivious to the relationship between capital accumulation and economic growth; besides sponsoring the rise of aggregate production, the regime established compulsory savings programs administered by state agencies, thus helping the state channel savings toward investment in strategic economic sectors.[25] In this sense, the miracle was the realization of the possible as engineered by the state.

Perhaps, then, the miracle's narrative engine could be traced to the unfolding of an empirically observable phenomenon that defied rational explanation or required further decoding. A particularity of the Brazilian *milagre* in this sense was the government's capacity to produce high rates of economic growth while also reducing inflation, therefore challenging the short-run Phillips curve. Successive governments since the early 1960s experimented with unsuccessful stabilization programs centered around orthodox monetary and fiscal policies that led to a drastic reduction of economic activity and eventually to workers' striking against the rising cost of living and the reduction of their wages' purchasing power. Throughout the decade, the efficiency of economic policies to control inflation became a common barometer of the government's capacity to manage the economy. Together with Treasury Minister Delfim Netto's conviction that growth required reducing rising prices,[26] the government placed the goal of controlling inflation at the center of economic policymaking after 1969.[27]

In the United States and Western Europe in the preceding decades, growth had been the response policymakers had provided to what had been identified as one of the central causes of inflation—the wage-price spiral, or the argument that rising wages above productivity gains supported the expansion of artificial demand that pressured prices upward.[28] As Charles Maier has expertly demonstrated, in the United States during the 1930s and after World War II, there emerged a shared confidence in the capacity of economic growth to provide a solution to class and distributional conflicts resulting from scarcity produced by unbounded (or unplanned) economic expansion.[29] This gave rise to what Maier has termed the "politics of productivity," the claim that the expansion of productivity as the basis of economic growth would be responsible for raising standards of living.[30] Therefore, rather than raising wage levels to promote welfare, the politics of productivity established that wage gains would be a consequence of society's capacity to increase output and efficiency of production, which would then support self-sustained economic growth. Planning thus emerged as an apolitical instrument "towards productive efficiency,"[31] one that privileged short-term political horizons amenable to narratives of economic miracle. The United States' goal of exporting the politics of productivity as part of its strategy of international economic governance was then bolstered by the postwar experience with economic miracles first in Germany and then in Japan, which had been engineered by US governments as accumulators of capital following the American tenets of the politics of productivity.[32] Abundance turned into an engineering challenge rather than a political outcome of class conflict, and again Germany and Japan served as successful cases of how the politics of productivity converted questions of domestic politics—concerned with resource allocation, distributional conflicts, the design of political institutions, and the configuration of political competition—into questions of output and efficiency, supported by the reality of rising productivity and economic growth in the 1950s and 1960s.[33]

The Brazilian economic miracle was grounded on a local version of the politics of productivity mobilized to solve the inflation-growth conundrum.[34] The public debate among economists connected with the government about the causes of inflation—whether it resulted from artificial demand or rising production costs[35]—concealed the fact that both diagnoses were anchored in an emerging "politics of scarcity" as the necessary companion to the politics of productivity, a process anticipated by Maier when he noted how the latter provided "a substitute for harsh questions of allocation."[36] Thus, when Delfim Netto gave a speech to the commercial class in São Paulo in 1969, he articulated the basis of technocratic policymaking as the public man's responsibility to act according to the principles of realism and rationality; while the former required realizing that resources were finite and scarce, the latter suggested a strategy to apply these resources without imposing further sacrifices on the population.[37] The politics of productivity therefore helped displace an earlier narrative in which abundance was a precondition of economic expansion based on the availability of natural resources, and advanced an alternative narrative according to which abundance is the expected outcome of the state's capacity to engineer efficient allocation of finite resources.

The convergence of the politics of scarcity with the politics of productivity then provided Brazilian economists with a solution to the inflation-growth conundrum: shifting the costs of monetary and fiscal adjustment to the working class in the form of a new wage policy that should solve, according to the military regime, the challenges presented by labor legislation for controlling inflation. According to the economist Mario Henrique Simonsen, the designer of the new policy implemented in 1965, demands for rising wages would be addressed through a simple "arithmetic calculation" that freed the government and business from the pressure posed by organized labor, since wages would now be adjusted according to an index of expected inflation called *correção monetária*, or monetary adjustment.[38] As a result, real wages in 1967 were 71.9 percent of real wages in 1964.[39] Though the military regime in 1968 implemented a new wage formula as an attempt to support growth of demand, the period 1967–73 saw a reduction or stagnation of real minimum wage despite economic growth and rising productivity.[40] Even though skilled workers saw above-average wage increases, in general, wages did not benefit from the expansion of production and productivity, and the state's priority remained to support high levels of investment and profit.[41] Thus the authoritarian nature of the regime allowed the federal government to unilaterally solve the distributive conflict resulting from inflation control policies, thence endorsing the politics of scarcity cum politics of productivity.[42]

The administration of Emílio Garrastazu Médici (1969–74) mobilized the narrative of an economic *milagre* to identify the period with previous experiences in Germany, Japan, and South Korea.[43] In this process, the politics of scarcity cum politics of productivity was indeed recognized and mobilized by contemporaries as a story engine of the Brazilian narrative. It was therefore with recourse to "the coefficients of productivity" that Delfim Netto justified his prediction in early 1973 that wages would incorporate the benefits of growth.[44] This widespread narrative engine was adopted even by those who resisted the effects of the regime's economic policies. In late 1973 an organization of industrial workers published its own report on productivity in the steel industry as part of national conferences to "provide knowledge about the socio-economic reality of the several sectors that form this category [of workers]."[45] The report mobilized annual indices of productivity—measured as the number of ingots produced per the number of workers in the industry—to argue that an increase in productivity of 30 percent between 1968 and 1972 had not translated into wage increases, and thus lending support to strikes in the sector.[46]

This story engine supported a narrative of economic miracle as the multiplication of scarce resources in the Brazilian case. This narrative framed the authoritarian state as an institution that engineered plenty by addressing the threat of scarcity through the technocratic allocation of resources.[47] It should therefore be unsurprising to see how this narrative of the rise of the developmental state in Brazil seemed to endorse the authoritarian institutions that the military regime had put in place to concentrate capacity and the authority to collect and allocate resources at the local and national levels. The military regime had prohibited the Brazilian Parliament from raising expenditures during the discussion of the budget and endowed the federal executive with control over public expenditure and the mechanisms to finance it; these prerogatives were later expanded to include concentration of tax power at the expense of the state and municipal units of the federation.[48]

These authoritarian reforms situated the federal government as the only authorized resource collector and allocator, prerogatives expanded by its capacity to set price and tax rate controls and distribute subsidies, and fostered by its emergence as the central promoter of savings and of investment in the private sector, making the latter increasingly more dependent on incentives and subsidies provided by the state.[49] Indeed, the role of the state as the main collector and allocator of resources was early on enshrined in the re-creation of the Ministry of Planning and Economic Coordination in 1964 and recognized by its technocratic spokesmen, who identified the main function of the government's involvement in the economy to be the distribution of resources and the implementation of policy priorities through a system of incentives, rather than the adoption of restrictive legislation.[50] Coordination was then a necessary function of the reality of the politics of scarcity *cum* productivity. Because of the recognized trade-off between consumption and production, which had been made visible through national accounting,[51] the new technocratic developmental state should coordinate the divergent "interests of producers and consumers" by, for example, establishing price tables that determined the rate of profit for producers and the costs of goods for consumers.[52] Similarly, the new wage policy could then be presented not as a policy that shifted the costs of stabilization onto workers, but as a technical decision that sought to reduce collective uncertainty caused by inflation—or at least the expectation of inflation—thus helping channel savings through the financial system to finance public spending and private investment in order to support capital accumulation. Critics of the regime would sarcastically remark that the true miracle would have been if the miracle had *not* happened under such circumstances.[53]

The transformation of economic growth into a key metric of "temporal change"[54] supporting assessments of economic performance that have endorsed narratives of economic miracles thus relied on normalizing expectations that the national economy should be the object of state-led technocratic management. This enabled the government to coordinate the competing claims of business, labor, and capital to ensure a constant expansion of aggregate output in the face of scarce and finite resources, thus realizing the promises of the developmental state.[55] But these promises were predicated on the argument that economic growth, through increasing productivity, would support rising living standards. Even before steelworkers contested the truth claim of these promises, the 1970 census revealed rising income concentration and inequality by showing that the income of the richest 20 percent had grown by about 67 percent during the previous decade, whereas the income of the poorest 10 percent had grown by only 28 percent. Numbers for changes in *relative* income, however, told a much grimmer story: whereas the relative income of the richest 10 percent had grown by 22 percent during the same period, the relative income of the poorest 10 percent had shrunk by 13 percent. Changes in the distribution of the national income again corroborated the pessimistic conclusion that growth had not raised living standards for all, as only the richest 10 percent had seen a growth in their participation in national income, which reached 47.8 percent in 1970.[56]

Income concentration might have been the result of reforms implemented in the first years of the military regime, but rising inequality was a consequence of the very miracle often touted by contemporaries.[57] In newspaper articles censored in Brazil, the international press remarked how "workers are not sharing in the growth experienced by the country" and highlighted—often with numbers from the 1970 census—how Brazil's "admirable economic miracle" had favored the rich.[58] Responding to criticisms, the government's self-proclaimed technocrats would argue that continuous economic growth depended on the government's capacity to resist adopting policies of redistribution.[59] The young Brazilian economist the government appointed to provide a technical justification for income concentration would explain that to better distribute income it would be necessary to "sacrifice" (future) economic growth to "transfer" to the population part of what was then allocated as investment, an unfeasible option given the government's unwillingness to renounce high rates of growth. Carlos Langoni, a recent graduate from the University of Chicago, argued that rising inequality was the necessary by-product of development in its first stages, when the government had to choose between investment in the expansion of physical capital (as advocated by development economists) and investment in education—and thus opted for the former.[60]

While it unfolded, the Brazilian experience was framed as a conviction narrative that sought to mobilize people to act in an uncertain world out of their belief in the truth content of the *milagre*.[61] Maier notes that the politics of productivity was supported by the empirical reality of rising productivity and prosperity.[62] In Brazil, the lived experience of an economic miracle was epitomized by changing consumption patterns among certain groups. Frank Trentmann has pointed out how stories of boom are tied to experiences of consumption—thus presenting the material justification of witnessing a miracle and believing in one.[63] For contemporaries, the Brazilian economic miracle was one of rising consumption that unraveled not *in spite of* income concentration but *because* of growing inequality. Whereas Brazilian structuralists had argued that accelerated economic growth was impossible without structural transformations of Brazilian society to expand the internal market, income concentration, as engineered by a technocratic developmental state, supported the rise of a middle class capable of acquiring goods of high aggregate value provided by the leading sectors of the Brazilian miracle.[64] Concentration—of income, capital, expertise, and political power—was thus the empirical (rather than the narrative) engine of the Brazilian experience.

As a narrative of conviction, the Brazilian economic miracle mobilized as a story engine the emergence of a technocratic developmental state capable of engineering abundance in a world of scarcity through the technical collection and allocation of resources to define, plan, and implement the empirical realities of the *milagre*. Adopting this story engine as a descriptor of the transformations the country experienced in the late 1960s and early 1970s, however, leads us to miss the opportunity to heed Petrulis's warning about the costs of accelerated economic transformations under an authoritarian regime. Rather than corroborating the picture of the Brazilian state as an impartial technical manager of the economy, as the state tried to claim during the *milagre*, we should reframe the narrative of economic miracle as a strategic form of governmentality that sought to justify increasingly authoritarian forms of concentration in service of the contemporary universalist paradigm of development as accelerated economic growth. The association of miracle narratives with profound transformations in the nature of the state and its instruments of governance over society thus helps us understand why these stories seemed to have traveled easily in the decades following World War II amid rising inequality and political violence and instability. It may also allow us to explore whether we will see new narratives of miracles emerge as tools of governmentality in response to the environmental governance challenges we currently face.

Paula Vedoveli is assistant professor of international history at the School of International Relations at the Fundação Getulio Vargas. She is currently working on her first book manuscript, "Brokering Capital: Sovereign Creditworthiness and the Making of Global Finance, 1851–1914." Her next project will examine the making of economic knowledge regimes through macroeconomic indicators in the Global South in the twentieth century.

Notes

I would like to thank Enrico Recco for his research assistance for this essay and Oto Montagner for his invaluable feedback. All errors are my own.

1. Mitchell, "Economentality"; Angeletti, "La formation de l'économie française"; Desrosières, "Managing the Economy."
2. Mesquita, "Inflação, estagnação e ruptura."
3. Veloso, Villela, and Giambiagi, "Determinantes do 'milagre' econômico brasileiro."
4. Mesquita, "Inflação, estagnação e ruptura."
5. Mata, "Economics as a 'Story Engine'"; Mata, "Economic Narratives at Work."
6. Petrulis, "'Country of Hair,'" 3.
7. On growth, see, for example, Borowy and Schmelzer, *History of the Future of Economic Growth*; Schmelzer, *Hegemony of Growth*; Collins, *More*; Yarrow, *Measuring America*; O'Bryan, *Growth Idea*; Cook, *Pricing of Progress*; Macekura, *Mismeasure of Progress*; and Bivar, "Historicizing Economic Growth."
8. Mitchell, "Economentality."
9. Mitchell, "Economentality," 497. During the interwar years, economic growth remained secondary to the adoption of stabilization programs in countries attempting to rise in the contemporary ethnoracial international hierarchy supported by the League of Nations. Jóhannesson, "Engineering the Economy through Austerity."
10. See, for example, Alacevich, "Birth of Development Economics"; Alacevich and Boianovsky, "Writing the History of Development Economics"; Boumans and De Marchi, "Models, Measurement, and 'Universal Patterns'"; and Macekura, "Development and Economic Growth."
11. Speich, "Use of Global Abstractions," 12. See also Speich, "Travelling with the GDP."
12. *O Estado de S. Paulo*, "O milagre."
13. Velloso, "Continuidade foi uma das causas do êxito." All translations are my own unless otherwise indicated.
14. Weis and Rocha, "Êles planejam o nôvo Brasil," 50.
15. For a discussion of "as if" narratives in economics, see Morgan and Stapleford, "Narrative in Economics."
16. Weis and Rocha, "Êles planejam o nôvo Brasil," 50, 46.
17. Mitchell, "Economentality."
18. *O Estado de S. Paulo*, "Velloso faz estimativa otimista para o Brasil"; see also *O Estado de S. Paulo*, "Em 1973, as metas de 1974." This elusive distinction was criticized in the highly censored press at the time. See, for example, *O Estado de S. Paulo*, "Diretrizes da política monetária."
19. Weis and Rocha, "Êles planejam o nôvo Brasil," 46. Kahn updated his estimates during the miracle. *O Estado de S. Paulo*, "Kahn reforma conceitos"; *O Estado de S. Paulo*, "Kahn: nem terrorismo pára êste País."
20. Mesquita, "Inflação, estagnação e ruptura."
21. Boianovsky, "Beyond Capital Fundamentalism."

22. See Vedoveli, "Brokering Capital." For a contemporary discussion of the purposes of national wealth estimates, see Shimizu, "Wealth Surveys in Japan"; and Goldsmith, "Synthetic Estimate of the National Wealth of Japan."
23. Syrquin, "GDP as a Measure of Economic Welfare," 3.
24. Syrquin, "GDP as a Measure of Economic Welfare," 4. See also Syrquin, "Quantifying Economic Development."
25. On how Celso Furtado, an influential Brazilian economist, explored this relationship, see Boianovsky, "View from the Tropics."
26. Mário Mesquita has argued that the government's incapacity to justify choices of economic policymaking during the period 1961 to 1964 such as the need for stabilization plans—which in 1961, 1963, and 1964 focused on constraining demand—produced a deterioration in the management of macroeconomic factors such as inflation ("Inflação, estagnação e ruptura").
27. Macarini, "A política econômica da ditadura militar." For contemporary perspectives, see Delfim Netto, "Perspectivas monetárias para o segundo semestre"; *O Estado de S. Paulo*, "Alcançados os objetivos"; and *O Estado de S. Paulo*, "Diretrizes da política monetária."
28. On how the wage-price spiral influenced economic policymaking after World War II, see, for example, Tomlinson, "Managing the Economy."
29. Maier, "Politics of Productivity." As Stephen Macekura shows, this claim was supported by the League of Nations ("Whither Growth?"). For a history of scarcity, see Jonsson and Wennerlind, *Scarcity*, especially chap. 7.
30. Maier, "Politics of Productivity." See also Alacevich, "World Bank."
31. Maier, "Politics of Productivity," 130.
32. Maier, "Politics of Productivity."
33. Maier, "Politics of Productivity."
34. See especially *O Globo*, "Simonsen acha que atual política econômica garante desenvolvimento"; *O Estado de S. Paulo*, "Atualidade econômica"; and *O Estado de S. Paulo*, "O consumo de energia elétrica."
35. Macarini, "A política econômica da ditadura militar." For a contemporary assessment, see *O Estado de S. Paulo*, "O milagre."
36. Maier, "Politics of Productivity," 128. The politics of scarcity has a long genealogy. Margherita Zanasi argues that an unprecedented deterioration of economic conditions in late eighteenth-century imperial China led Chinese scholars and officials to seek "economic growth as a strategy for fighting scarcity and lifting the population of the empire out of poverty." The recognition of the imperatives of "economic scarcity" led them to advocate for greater state intervention in the economy through planning and state-directed allocation of resources ("Globalizing Development," 18; 20).
37. *O Estado de S. Paulo*, "Alcançados os objetivos."
38. Resende, "Estabilização e reforma," 210; *O Globo*, "Simonsen acha que atual política econômica garante desenvolvimento."
39. Resende, "Estabilização e reforma," 200–201.
40. Lago, "A retomada do crescimento," 235.
41. Lago, "A retomada do crescimento," 235.
42. Resende, "Estabilização e reforma," 211.
43. Araujo, "A macroeconomia do governo Médici." See also *O Estado de S. Paulo*, "O milagre."
44. *O Estado de S. Paulo*, "Salário superará parcela do BNH."

45. *O Estado de S. Paulo*, "Política salarial motiva encontro de metalúrgicos."

46. *O Estado de S. Paulo*, "Para [] salário."

47. As note 36 shows, earlier narratives according a prominent role to the state as a promoter of plenty and prosperity against scarcity can be found, for example, in late imperial China. Margherita Zanasi, "Globalizing Development."

48. Lago, "A retomada do crescimento."

49. Lago, "A retomada do crescimento."

50. Velloso, "Continuidade foi uma das causas do êxito."

51. Maier, "Politics of Productivity." On how this trade-off was recognized by the management of the World Bank and shaped their investment priorities, see Alacevich, "World Bank."

52. *O Globo*, "Delfim admite inflação de 14 porcento em 73."

53. De Mendonça, *A industrialização brasileira*.

54. Mitchell, "Economentality," 484.

55. On national accounting as an instrument of governmentally, see Mitchell, "Economentality." For economic growth as the response to French policymakers' realization that decolonization brought the reality of finite resources to the core of French economic policymaking after World War II, see Angeletti, "La formation de l'économie française."

56. Araujo, "A macroeconomia do governo Médici," 60.

57. Lago, "A retomada do crescimento," 237.

58. *O Estado de S. Paulo*, "Jornais ingleses comentam situação dos trabalhadores"; see also *O Estado de S. Paulo*, "Órgão londrino aponta riscos do autoritarismo."

59. *O Globo*, "Simonsen acha que atual política econômica garante desenvolvimento." For a contemporary profile of Mario Henrique Simonsen, future minister of the treasury (1974–79) during the Geisel administration, see Simonsen, "Fazenda."

60. Amorim, "Reflexões para melhor distribuir nossa renda," 58. Langoni's argument was further developed in *Distribuição da renda e desenvolvimento econômico do Brasil*.

61. For conviction narratives, see Morgan and Stapleford, "Narrative in Economics."

62. Maier, "Politics of Productivity."

63. Trentmann, "Rise and Fall."

64. Macarini, "A política econômica da ditadura militar"; Lago, "A retomada do crescimento"; Araujo, "A macroeconomia do governo Médici."

References

Alacevich, Michele. "The Birth of Development Economics." *History of Political Economy* 50, no. S1 (2018): 114–32.

Alacevich, Michele. "The World Bank and the Politics of Productivity: The Debate on Economic Growth, Poverty, and Living Standards in the 1950s." *Journal of Global History* 6, no. 1 (2011): 53–74.

Alacevich, Michele, and Mauro Boianovsky. "Writing the History of Development Economics." *History of Political Economy* 50, no. S1 (2018): 1–14.

Amorim, Paulo Henrique. "Reflexões para melhor distribuir nossa renda." *Realidade*, January 1973, 58–63. https://memoria.bn.gov.br/DocReader/docreader.aspx?bib=213659 &pesq=&pagfis=32743.

Angeletti, Thomas. "La formation de l'économie française: Émergence et stabilisation d'une entité collective." *Politix* 133, no. 1 (2021): 55–78.

Araujo, Victor Leonardo de. "A macroeconomia do governo Médici (1969–1974): Uma contribuição ao debate sobre as causas do 'milagre' econômico." *Revista Economia Ensaios* 33, no. 1 (2019): 41–70.

Bivar, Venus. "Historicizing Economic Growth: An Overview of Recent Works." *Historical Journal* 65, no. 5 (2022): 1470–89.

Boianovsky, Mauro. "Beyond Capital Fundamentalism: Harrod, Domar, and the History of Development Economics." *Cambridge Journal of Economics* 42, no. 2 (2018): 477–504.

Boianovsky, Mauro. "A View from the Tropics: Celso Furtado and the Theory of Economic Development in the 1950s." *History of Political Economy* 42, no. 2 (2010): 221–66.

Borowy, Iris, and Matthias Schmelzer, eds. *History of the Future of Economic Growth: Historical Roots of Current Debates on Sustainable Degrowth.* London: Routledge, 2017.

Boumans, Marcel, and Neil De Marchi. "Models, Measurement, and 'Universal Patterns.'" *History of Political Economy* 50, no. S1 (2018): 231–48.

Collins, Robert M. *More: The Politics of Economic Growth in Postwar America.* Oxford: Oxford University Press, 2000.

Cook, Eli. *The Pricing of Progress: Economic Indicators and the Capitalization of American Life.* Cambridge, MA: Harvard University Press, 2017.

De Mendonça, S. R. *A industrialização brasileira.* São Paulo: Moderna, 1996.

Delfim Netto, Antônio. "Perspectivas monetárias para o segundo semestre." *Jornal do Brasil*, July 6, 1969. https://memoria.bn.gov.br/DocReader/DocReader.aspx?bib=030015_08&hf=memoria.bn.gov.br&pagfis=136832.

Desrosières, Alain. "Managing the Economy." In *The Cambridge History of Science*, edited by Theodore M. Porter and Dorothy Ross, vol. 7, 553–64. Cambridge: Cambridge University Press, 2003.

Goldsmith, Raymond. "A Synthetic Estimate of the National Wealth of Japan, 1885–1973." *Review of Income and Wealth* 21, no. 2 (1975): 125–51.

Jóhannesson, Sveinn M. "Engineering the Economy through Austerity: The Influence of International Economic Expertise in Iceland after the First World War." *Contemporary European History*, published online, April 30, 2024. https://doi.org/10.1017/S0960777324000110.

Jonsson, Fredrik Albritton, and Carl Wennerlind. *Scarcity: A History from the Origins of Capitalism to the Climate Crisis.* Cambridge, MA: Harvard University Press, 2023.

Lago, Luiz Aranha Correa do. "A retomada do crescimento e as distorções do 'milagre,' 1967–1974." In *A ordem do progresso: Dois séculos de política econômica no Brasil*, edited by Marcelo de Paiva Abreu, 213–39. Rio de Janeiro: Elsevier Editora, 2014.

Langoni, Carlos. *Distribuição da renda e desenvolvimento econômico do Brasil.* Rio de Janeiro: Editora Expressão e Cultura, 1973.

Macarini, José Pedro. "A política econômica da ditadura militar no limiar do 'milagre' brasileiro: 1967/69." *Texto para Discussão*, no. 99 (2000): 1–34.

Macekura, Stephen. "Development and Economic Growth: An Intellectual History." In *History of the Future of Economic Growth: Historical Roots of Current Debates on Sustainable Degrowth*, edited by Iris Borowy and Matthias Schmelzer, 110–28. London: Routledge, 2017.

Macekura, Stephen J. *The Mismeasure of Progress: Economic Growth and Its Critics.* Chicago: University of Chicago Press, 2020.

Macekura, Stephen. "Whither Growth? International Development, Social Indicators, and the Politics of Measurement, 1920s–1970s." *Journal of Global History* 14, no. 2 (2019): 261–79.

Maier, Charles S. "The Politics of Productivity: Foundations of American International Economic Policy after World War II." In *In Search of Stability: Explorations in Historical Political Economy*, 121–52. Cambridge: Cambridge University Press, 1987.

Mata, Tiago. "Economic Narratives at Work." In "Forum: Economic Narratives," edited by Laetitia Lenel and Alexander Nützenadel." *Journal of Modern European History* 21, no. 4 (2023): 6–9.

Mata, Tiago. "Economics as a 'Story Engine': John D. McDonald and Business as Game and Gamble." *History of Political Economy* 55, no. S1 (2023): 103–30.

Mesquita, Mário M. C. "Inflação, estagnação e ruptura, 1961–1964." In *A ordem do progresso: Dois séculos de política econômica no Brasil*, edited by Marcelo de Paiva Abreu, 176–96. Rio de Janeiro: Elsevier Editora, 2014.

Mitchell, Timothy. "Economentality: How the Future Entered Government." *Critical Inquiry* 40, no. 4 (2014): 479–507.

Morgan, Mary S., and Thomas A. Stapleford. "Narrative in Economics: A New Turn on the Past." *History of Political Economy* 55, no. 3 (2023): 395–421.

O'Bryan, Scott. *The Growth Idea: Purpose and Prosperity in Postwar Japan*. Honolulu: University of Hawaii Press, 2009.

O Estado de S. Paulo. "Alcançados os objetivos." January 28, 1969. https://acervo.estadao.com.br/pagina/#!/19690128-28774-nac-0026-fem-26-not.

O Estado de S. Paulo. "Atualidade econômica: Armas de combate contra a carestia." January 4, 1973. https://acervo.estadao.com.br/pagina/#!/19730104-29989-nac-0032-999-32-not.

O Estado de S. Paulo. "Diretrizes da política monetária." May 24, 1974. https://acervo.estadao.com.br/pagina/#!/19740524-30415-nac-0003-999-3-cen.

O Estado de S. Paulo. "Em 1973, as metas de 1974." December 20, 1972. https://acervo.estadao.com.br/pagina/#!/19721220-29976-nac-0001-999-1-not.

O Estado de S. Paulo. "Jornais ingleses comentam situação dos trabalhadores." [archive of censored articles] December 6, 1973. https://acervo.estadao.com.br/pagina/#!/19731206-30274-nac-0014-999-14-cen.

O Estado de S. Paulo. "Kahn: Nem terrorismo pára êste País." August 28, 1970. https://acervo.estadao.com.br/pagina/#!/19700828-29261-nac-0005-999-5-not.

O Estado de S. Paulo. "Kahn reforma conceitos." August 27, 1970. https://acervo.estadao.com.br/pagina/#!/19700827-29260-nac-0001-999-1-not.

O Estado de S. Paulo. "O consumo de energia elétrica." April 15, 1973. https://acervo.estadao.com.br/pagina/#!/19730415-30075-nac-0003-999-3-not.

O Estado de S. Paulo. "O milagre: Novo rumo e continuidade." March 31, 1974. https://acervo.estadao.com.br/pagina/#!/19740331-30371-nac-0024-999-24-not and https://acervo.estadao.com.br/pagina/#!/19740331-30371-nac-0025-999-25-not.

O Estado de S. Paulo. "Órgão londrino aponta riscos do autoritarismo." [archive of censored articles] March 29, 1973. https://acervo.estadao.com.br/pagina/#!/19730329-30060-nac-0005-999-5-cen.

O Estado de S. Paulo. "Para [] salário." [archive of censored articles] December 6, 1973. https://acervo.estadao.com.br/pagina/#!/19731206-30274-nac-0014-999-14-cen.

O Estado de S. Paulo. "Política salarial motiva encontro de metalúrgicos." December 6, 1973. https://acervo.estadao.com.br/pagina/#!/19731206-30274-nac-0032-999-32-not.

O Estado de S. Paulo. "Salário superará parcela do BNH." January 4, 1973. https://acervo.estadao.com.br/pagina/#!/19730104-29989-nac-0001-999-1-not.

O Estado de S. Paulo. "Velloso faz estimativa otimista para o Brasil." December 20, 1972. https://acervo.estadao.com.br/pagina/#!/19721220-29976-nac-0033-999-33-not.

O Globo. "Delfim admite inflação de 14 percent em 73." December 19, 1973.

O Globo. "Simonsen acha que atual política econômica garante desenvolvimento." November 10, 1973.

Petrulis, Jason. "'A Country of Hair': A Global Story of South Korean Wigs, Korean American Entrepreneurs, African American Hairstyles, and Cold War Industrialization." *Enterprise and Society* 22, no. 2 (2021): 1–41.

Resende, André Lara. "Estabilização e reforma, 1964–1967." In *A ordem do progresso: Dois séculos de política econômica no Brasil*, edited by Marcelo de Paiva Abreu, 197–211. Rio de Janeiro: Elsevier Editora, 2014.

Schmelzer, Matthias. *The Hegemony of Growth: The OECD and the Making of the Economic Growth Paradigm.* Cambridge: Cambridge University Press, 2016.

Shimizu, Yataka. "Wealth Surveys in Japan." In *Measuring the Nation's Wealth*, edited by the Wealth Inventory Planning Study, 277–90. Washington, DC: U.S. Government Printing Office, 1964.

Simonsen, Mário Henrique. "Fazenda." *O Estado de S. Paulo*, February 22, 1974. https://acervo.estadao.com.br/pagina/#!/19740222-30339-nac-0009-999-9-not.

Speich, Daniel. "The Use of Global Abstractions: National Income Accounting in the Period of Imperial Decline." *Journal of Global History* 6, no. 1 (2011): 7–28.

Speich, Daniel. "Travelling with the GDP through Early Development Economics' History." Working Papers on the Nature of Evidence: How Well Do 'Facts' Travel?, no. 33/08 (2008): 1–33. Department of Economic History, London School of Economics and Political Science, London.

Syrquin, Moshe. "GDP as a Measure of Economic Welfare." ICER Working Paper No. 3/2011. http://dx.doi.org/10.2139/ssrn.1808685.

Syrquin, Moshe. "Quantifying Economic Development." *History of Political Economy* 50, no. S1 (2018): 211–30.

Tomlinson, Jim. "Managing the Economy, Managing the People: Britain c. 1931–70." *Economic History Review* 58, no. 3 (2005): 555–85.

Trentmann, Frank. "Rise and Fall: The Power and Morality of Economic Narratives." In "Forum: Economic Narratives," edited by Laetitia Lenel and Alexander Nützenadel. *Journal of Modern European History* 21, no. 4 (2023): 5–6.

Vedoveli, Paula. "Brokering Capital: Sovereign Creditworthiness and the Making of Global Finance, 1851–1914." Manuscript in progress.

Velloso, João Paulo dos Reis. "Continuidade foi uma das causas do êxito." *O Estado de S. Paulo*, March 18, 1973. https://acervo.estadao.com.br/pagina/#!/19730318-30051-nac-0056-999-63-not.

Veloso, Fernando A., André Villela, and Fabio Giambiagi. "Determinantes do 'milagre' econômico brasileiro (1968–1973): Uma análise empírica." *Revista Brasileira de Economia* 62, no. 2 (2008): 221–46.

Weis, Luis, and Marco Antônio Rocha. "Êles planejam o nôvo Brasil." *Realidade*, February 1970, 44–50. https://memoria.bn.gov.br/DocReader/docreader.aspx?bib=213659&pesq=&pagfis=8391.

Yarrow, Andrew L. *Measuring America: How Economic Growth Came to Define American Greatness in the Late Twentieth Century.* Amherst: University of Massachusetts Press, 2010.

Zanasi, Margherita. "Globalizing Development: A View from Late Imperial China." In *Perspectives on the History of Global Development*, edited by Corinna R. Unger et al., 15–36. Boston: De Gruyter Oldenbourg, 2022.

Economic Miracle or Dream State?

West Berlin as Postwar Tourism Destination

Aimée Plukker

Economic miracle! *Wirtschaftswunder*! You'll be hearing that phrase
mentioned everywhere in Germany, referring, of course, to the prosperity of
this country.
—*Cook's Pocket Travel Guide to Europe* (1963)

There are no miracles in economics.
—Lucio Magri, *The Tailor of Ulm*

In the 1950s the Berlin Tourism Office and the Berlin Chamber of Industry and
Trade published the booklet *West-Berliner Qualität* (*West Berlin Quality*). This collection of photographs of industries and products made in West Berlin—such as
machines, pianos, soap, and shoes—encouraged the reader to buy and order these
products to aid in "the struggle for freedom and Western World democracy."[1] The
brochure included a photograph of a faceless man with a leather bag, his suede-
gloved hands holding a Pan Am ticket for a flight from New York to Berlin (fig. 1).
The photograph of what appears to be a US traveler illustrates the intertwinement
of postwar tourism in West Berlin with selling the city's economic recovery in the
context of the Cold War. Advertising Berlin as a tourist destination and its products
("Berlin Quality—a Household Word") justified US military presence and economic
aid to West Germany, such as provided by the Marshall Plan (also known as the
European Recovery Program, or ERP, which was implemented from 1948 to
1952).[2] This article demonstrates how after the Second World War a renewed

Radical History Review
Issue 151 (January 2025)   DOI 10.1215/01636545-11506854
© 2025 by MARHO: The Radical Historians' Organization, Inc.

Figure 1. Man with Pan Am
ticket. *West-Berliner Qualität*
(1950s), Box 1, Berlin West
Verkehrsamt 1945–60. Courtesy
of Historisches Archiv zum
Tourismus, Technische
Universität, Berlin.

"dream-filled sleep" came over West Berlin, and through it, a "reactivation of mythic forces" that advanced the idea of the *Wirtschaftswunder*, or economic miracle, of capitalism: the rapid economic reconstruction from the ruins of the war.[3] The magic of advertising sold the illusion of the city's recovery, seducing its audiences, from potential US tourists to domestic and local visitors, to believe in the achievements of the capitalist West as opposed to the communist East.[4] The tourism industry, operating within a never-ending realm of reification as an influential "image-machine," was the perfect vehicle to promote West Berlin as a showcase city of capitalism and its promise of economic miracles.[5] Tourism advertising enticed potential US tourists to travel and engage in consumerism while it simultaneously underscored the recuperating German industrial prowess; these two ideological narratives reinforced each other and worked in tandem to hide the tensions of the city's economic realities.

  This article argues that the narrative of the economic miracle of recovery, which West Berlin tourism promotion efforts produced during the 1950s, played a key role in the political aims of the Marshall Plan. It reassesses the impact of tourism in the economic boom, extending the view of tourism as a diplomatic tool or form of propaganda to a crucial element of the economic, military, and cultural *dispositif* of

Berlin and the Cold War.[6] As the "official art of capitalist society," advertisements produced imagery and promoted values that are essential to understanding the origins and spread of the idea of the economic miracle.[7] The analysis of visual sources in this article helps to demystify the fetishistic illusions that they created and therefore sheds light on how aesthetics shaped the economic and vice versa.[8] In his *Arcades Project*, Walter Benjamin compared living under capitalism to living in a dream beyond reality and explained how this dream state operates through advertising.[9] Capitalist commercial advertising tries to sell a facade, creating a reality that does not really exist. This article emphasizes that ultimately, the idea of the economic miracle reflects one of the many false promises of capitalism. Miracles in economics don't exist, Lucio Magri claimed for postwar Italy, as the capitalist economy is a "spiral of endlessly expanding accumulation" with crisis waiting around the corner.[10] In the case of Berlin, the unemployment, low wages, and subsidies that facilitated the "miracle" had to be concealed, while the West German industrialists were the main economic and social beneficiaries, some of them former Nazi supporters and war criminals.[11]

Although the size and revenue of tourism and its impact on the total postwar economy of the Federal Republic of Germany (FRG) weren't as large as those of other industries, such as iron and steel, the hospitality industry did contribute to the FRG's economic reconstruction, even though a modest amount in the case of West Berlin, due to its geographical location and war damages.[12] A source reveals that international tourism to Germany almost quintupled between 1950 and 1959, from 102,600 tourists in 1950 to 498,900 tourists in 1959; total receipts from US and Canadian tourists made up 25 percent of the total amount of $444 million dollars in 1957 and almost 40 percent in 1959.[13] These numbers mirrored the growth in German private consumption, which was mostly absent during the 1950s and only grew during the end of the 1950s and in the 1960s. This article highlights the unique symbolic status of Berlin during the Cold War, illustrated well by tourism, which entailed its own economic infrastructure, such as transportation facilities and the reconstruction of hotels.[14] Although tourism did have a material impact on postwar reconstruction, especially through the increased circulation of capital and transatlantic exchange, the focus of the article is on the visual and ideological production of the economic miracle, and how it created a self-fulfilling system of beliefs that entailed material consequences. The idea of the economic miracle of West Berlin was fabricated through three overlapping themes in the tourism promotion of the city. First, the miracle entailed recovery from the Nazi past and the ruins of war through the reconstruction of the city with US aid. Second, it simultaneously stimulated and sold capitalism as the ideal economic system for the Cold War present. Third, it projected a vision for the future, a seductive capitalist dreamworld. These themes can be explained with attention to how, after the war, US tourism to Western Europe was promoted to aid in the economic recovery of war-torn Europe and to fill the dollar gap, the imbalance of imports and exports between the United States and Europe.[15] Advertising locally made products to travelers from the United States in tourism promotion materials such as the booklet *West-Berliner Qualität* became a key feature in transferring US dollars to Europe to boost the circulation of money and commodities. The promotion of West Berlin was of utmost symbolic importance within this early Cold War context, as it became a showcase city of capitalism, and more broadly of "the West" as opposed to the Communist "East."[16] Although not yet a closed entity before the construction of the Berlin Wall in 1961, right after the war Berlin was divided into four sectors: the US, French, and British sectors made up West Berlin while the USSR controlled the eastern part of the city. Due to Berlin's geographical location in the eastern part of Germany, the establishment of the FRG (led by the Western occupation powers) in 1949 and the German Democratic Republic (GDR, led by the USSR) changed the western sectors of Berlin into an "island city" within the Soviet sector. Fostered by politicians, policymakers, and businessmen, making Berlin part of "the West" was a central element of the integration of the FRG. Perceived as the "workshop of Europe," it was widely believed that the reconstruction of the German economy was central to boosting the economy of Europe as a whole. To fulfill the political aims of the Marshall Plan to save capitalism and combat Communism, the narrative of the economic miracle was used to propagate a transatlantic alliance and shared identity between the United States and Western Europe.[17] The currency reform on June 20, 1948, that introduced the deutsche mark to the FRG is usually perceived as the start of the economic miracle. However, it is interesting to note here that the term *economic miracle* was already used by the Nazi regime for the economic success of the Third Reich in the 1930s.[18] In the case of Cold War West Berlin, the miracle entailed a specific economic mode of production, spatial integration, and shared views, such as a liberal notion of freedom, mostly defined as the freedom to buy.

The first section of this article explores how the tourism promotion of West Berlin, largely distributed through the German Tourist Association offices in New York, Chicago, and San Francisco, travel bureaus, and travel agents, presented the city to an US audience as risen from ruins, its reconstruction made possible with help from the Marshall Plan. It discusses how in this process, Berliners were welcomed as hardworking "old friends," justifying US economic aid and intervention while also concealing the Nazi past. The second section explains how the narrative of recovery in tourism was explicitly tied to saving and selling capitalism as an economic system to both locals and foreigners, with a focus on the yearly industrial exhibitions that took place in Berlin. The third section ties together the themes of tourist consumerism and recovered production in exploring the recurring "buy in Berlin" theme, and the ways in which shopping and consumer items became attached to capitalist fictions and projections for the future.[19] As a shop window of the West, the perception of Berlin exemplified liberal notions of freedom, especially the freedom to buy.

The article complements economic histories that have critically reassessed the so-called *Wirtschaftswunder* of West Germany and offers a visual and cultural perspective on the fabrication of the economic miracle narrative through the lens of tourism and how it was fundamental to the political project of the Marshall Plan and integrating Berlin as part of "the West."[20]

Risen from Ruins

Who traveled to Berlin, an island in the Soviet zone? The first "tourists" were soldiers, as in most Western European countries right after the war. Universal Newsreels from 1945 depicted British and Canadian troops on leave visiting the German chancellery for a souvenir of Hitler's former office, and US GIs dancing in Berliner nightclubs.[21] Only toward the end of the 1940s would the first nonmilitary tourists appear, primarily people who had to visit Berlin for work-related reasons; from the 1950s onward efforts were made to attract tourists more widely.[22] The booklet *Berlin at a Glance* (1959), kept as a memento by the US psychologist and psychedelic drugs advocate Timothy Leary, who traveled in Europe in the 1950s, stated that "the tourist business is one of the most important branches of Berlin's economy," with 61,600 foreign overnight guests in 1950 and 330,700 in 1958.[23] A visitor could reach Berlin by road, train, or air, though all aircrafts to Tempelhof Airport had to fly from Hamburg, Hannover, or Frankfurt, and only aircrafts carrying Allied flags were allowed. In 1961 these included Pan American Airways, British European Airways, Air France, and Allied chartered aircrafts.[24] The most popular sight in Berlin was the Cold War and the border between East and West, even before the wall was built. During the early Cold War period tours to East Berlin were organized by US soldiers, and border tourism across the Iron Curtain became an integral part of the postwar tourism industry in Berlin and beyond.[25] Viewing the promotion of West Berlin through the lens of the economic miracle, it appears that East Berlin was only presented through tropes marking it as a "dark," "undemocratic," and "unfree" space, thereby accentuating the accomplishments of the western parts of the city.

After the Second World War Berlin was a city of rubble and ruin. One of the main recurring motifs in the promotion of West Berlin was reconstruction, presenting Berlin as risen from the ashes. Underscoring the successful postwar recovery of the city abroad justified US aid, such as that provided through the Marshall Plan. Many tourism pamphlets started by highlighting the destruction of Berlin during the war to compare it with the city's contemporaneous situation. The new city center consisted mostly of newly built and modernized buildings such as hotels, a center designed by "the exigencies of free enterprise."[26] The booklet *Sight Seeing Tour Berlin* (1957) is a perfect example of the narrative of progress in tourism publications as it explained that around 85 percent of the city's industries were wiped out and 342,000 dwellings were destroyed. The booklet noted hopefully that "thanks to the energy of the Berliners and also thanks to the help given by the Federal Government and foreign countries—in spite of being partitioned into four sectors and in spite of lying like an island in the Soviet Zone—the city has risen like a phoenix from the ashes!"[27] This quote not only emphasizes the influence of aid but also reveals two other important themes reflected in the tourism promotion of the city: a positive description of Berliners as hardworking and therefore worthy of aid, and the unexpected recovery of the city, highlighting Berlin's symbolic importance due to its geographical location.

The tourist industry tried to create sympathy for Berliners to justify the Marshall Plan and underscore the new political and economic ties between West Berlin and the United States. It presented the inhabitants of West Berlin as "old friends," hardworking people who want to become part of "the West," to replace the image of Berliners (or Germans) as the enemy.[28] See, for instance, this quote from the 1952 edition of *Fielding's Travel Guide to Europe*: "No one would deny that the Germans are among the most efficient and industrious workers to be found anywhere. Regardless of any personal prejudice we may still carry, if we are frank and honest we must accord great respect and admiration for the way the German worker has tackled the back-breaking problems of reconstruction—and succeeded."[29] It shows how tourism was used to integrate Berlin, and West Germany more generally, into a new community of capitalist and democratic nations and cultures on both sides of the Atlantic.

A similar upward narrative that promoted Berlin as ready to receive tourists appeared in an article titled "Cosmopolitan Berlin" in the *German Review*, a monthly magazine published by the German Tourist Association in German, English, and French for an intended audience of both domestic and foreign tourists, including from the United States. The article's writer was "flabbergasted to find that this [Berlin] is not a sand-bagged waste of ruins," describing Berlin as "risen from ruins," "ultra-smart," "remarkable," and "cosmopolitan." Berlin made the author feel like a "twentieth century man" of leisure and consumption: "Above all I prefer relaxing in a sidewalk café, sipping wine or nibbling an ice, watching the life of the city pass before my eyes, feeling like nobody in particular at all." Mentioning the new Hotel Kempinski as an example of the many sleeping facilities in the city for foreign visitors, the author concluded that "Berlin is a very good, very old friend." The article promoted Berlin as a model twentieth-century city, including its tourist facilities and quick recovery. It underscored West Berlin as ally, an "old friend," obscuring the Nazi past, the only historical reference being the disappearance of the rubble and ruins caused by Allied bombings.[30]

These examples illustrate the two goals of the narrative of reconstruction: to demonstrate the successful and rapid recovery of the city, and to establish a view of Berlin's past that concealed the recent Nazi past.[31] A possible explanation for the special concern with the latter is provided by Annabel Wharton, who notes:

"The East German government was made up almost exclusively of acknowledged antifascist exiles. The West Berlin government included, in contrast, many de-Nazified National Socialists. The willingness to eliminate most of the past in the West perhaps suggests that they had more to forget than their counterparts in the East."[32] Rarely was the Nazi past directly confronted. An exception is the 1959 travel book *Fun in Europe*, which stated: "Berliners I met and observed also seemed determined to forget the dread cry that first announced their nation's Walpurgis Nacht that began with hope, led to horror, and ended in such devastation and bitter humiliation, preferring now the pursuit of happiness in harmony with the other free peoples of the world."[33] It indicates that even when the Nazi past was mentioned in travel writing, the narrative was immediately reframed to welcome Berliners as friends, as they purportedly shared the same life goals as other people belonging to the free world, including inhabitants of the United States.

Hotel Kempinski and its location on the shopping street Kurfürstendamm (fig. 2) were both often promoted in brochures, booklets, magazines, and postcards as symbols of the economic miracle.[34] Promoting hotels was a great way to attract tourists, especially the upper-middle-class US tourist who usually stayed at first-class hotels, and to portray the postwar recovery of a city where most hotels were destroyed. The Kempinski already existed before the Second World War but was completely in ruins after. It was the first luxury hotel that would reopen in July 1952. Its reconstruction was partly financed through the Marshall Plan, which was also depicted on a banner at the construction site.[35] Friedrich Unger, the last heir of the Jewish Kempinski family, returned from the United States to oversee the construction of the new Kempinski Hotel starting in 1951.[36] A German newspaper wrote about the building of the hotel that "the enclave behind the iron curtain is to receive Europe's most modern hotel, and it is being planned and built by an American."[37] With the ERP funds available, Unger commissioned the hotel to be built "in line with the standards applicable at the time for the hotels in major American cities."[38] The book *Ku'damm No. 27*, which tells the history of the Kempinski Hotel, emphasizes the symbolic value of the opening of the new Kempinski Hotel on the Kurfürstendamm right after the war. Newspapers wrote that "Kempinski shows that Berlin is ready for the future!" and that its building showed the "comeback of Berlin." The book notes that each phase of the construction of the building was seen as proof that Berlin was on its way back, and on almost a daily basis newspaper articles reported about the progress of the building of the hotel.[39]

Hotel Kempinski was not the only hotel that received support through Marshall Plan funds. In Berlin, West Germany, and throughout Europe, many other hotels were reconstructed with US aid, with various Hilton Hotels as the most famous examples.[40] Although the luxurious Hotel Kempinski could only be visited by a select few, notably the wealthy US tourist, it became an important symbol of the recovery of West Berlin and home of the Western traveler, and it often popped up in

Figure 2. Postcard of the Kurfürstendamm by night, with Hotel Kempinski in the background. Courtesy of the Berlin-Brandenburgisches Wirtschaftsarchiv, Berlin.

the city's tourism promotion.[41] In one brochure, for example, only the staircase of the Kempinski was depicted with the words "Stetig Aufwärts" (steady upward). Here, the building of the hotel was literally used as exemplary of the postwar recovery of Berlin.[42] Kempinski was also featured in the Economic Cooperation Administration (ECA) film *Air of Freedom* (1951), which started with the reconstruction of the city with help from the Marshall Plan. The Kempinski sign was shown in a segment that depicted Berlin as "the great and glittering city it had been in the old days," emphasizing Berlin as "Western world center" and "outpost of democracy."[43] The film rebranded the perception of the city's past with an emphasis on happier times before Nazism, while simultaneously presenting the new role of the city with a focus toward the future. The promotion of the hotel not only served the goal of attracting US tourists but also highlighted the success of the Marshall Plan, and capitalism more generally.

   The building of the hotel with Marshall Plan aid, however, also received predictable criticism; the East Berlin newspaper *BZ am Abend* wrote that the city had no need for a hotel: "The number of unemployed is steadily increasing. Businesses are going bankrupt daily. But on the Kurfürstendamm, Reuter [Ernst Reuter, mayor of West Berlin] is building another luxury shop window to detract from the deprivation in West Berlin."[44] These words sharply contrast with the depiction of Reuter's

Berlin in a film of the series *1,2,3 A Monthly Review from Europe* (1952). Produced by the Mutual Security Agency, the film stated that "under Mayor Reuter West Berliners are achieving miracles of effort."[45] It shows how hotels were used as grand symbols of the Marshall Plan, although a contested one in the eyes of some locals, as it did not necessarily benefit many local Berliners, which was especially clear in the case of the Hilton Hotel.[46] "Nine days after the original announcement of a Berlin Hilton, Berlin hoteliers complained to the city's Senate about the construction of the Berlin Hilton," writes Annabel Wharton.[47] In a letter to Mayor Otto Suhr, the Association of Hotel and Restaurant Owners wrote that the new hotel would bankrupt them.[48] The inflated promises of capitalist prosperity offered by the narrative of recovery in the West Berlin tourism promotion are evident when compared to some of the economic realities that the "island city" was facing. Because of the Cold War, 364 companies had left between 1947 and 1949. By 1950 Berlin only reached 19 percent of its prewar production levels, and almost a third of the population received social benefits. The city continued to receive extensive subsidies from the United States and later from West Germany.[49] Thus the recovery had to be promoted as successful to justify the subsidies the city was receiving. A 1949 pamphlet explicitly asked for a halt to the dismantling of German industries as part of postwar reparations by Allied forces and framed the policy as "incompatible with the intentions of the European Recovery Program." The pamphlet emphasized the importance of Western Germany in relation to other European countries, stating that "the recovery of Europe is closely connected with the reconstruction of the German economy." It warned of the demoralization caused by the dismantling of industry and the rising danger that "the German masses be driven into the open arms of *bolschevism* [*sic*]."[50] Besides the dismantling of industries, scientific and technological knowledge was also deliberately transferred from Germany to the United States as part of intelligence programs, as John Gimbel showed.[51] It is important to keep these events in mind to place in perspective the propagandistic narrative of recovery as told in tourism promotion, and to understand why the narrative of recovery was presented in this particular way. As the author of the pamphlet pointed out, in the early Cold War period, there was always the lure of bolshevism, and even more so in West Berlin, where Communism was literally around the corner.

Workshop of Europe

Berlin To-day (1957), published in English by the Berlin Tourism Office, informed the reader that "without the American credits made available to Berlin after 1949 it would have been impossible to set the economy of the former capital of Germany on its legs again and make it productive."[52] Besides convincing a US audience of the fruits of the Marshall Plan, the quote illustrates how policymakers advanced the idea that integrating West Berlin into the global capitalist economy depended on the city's productive efforts. This explains the frequent depiction in tourism promotion of the Kraftwerk West, or the Power Station West in Spandau, one of the westernmost districts of the city.[53] The power plant was rebuilt in a great spectacle with money derived from the Marshall Plan during the Berlin Blockade of 1948, when importing goods through the Soviet Zone was forbidden.[54] The material for the power plant was flown in with assistance from the US general Lucius D. Clay, and equipment for the power plant arrived in 580 flights. Concrete and other building materials also arrived by air. The power plant opened in 1949, making West Berlin and its industries independent of the electric grid in East Berlin, which explains its symbolic significance. One tourism brochure declared how several West Berlin industries, such as AEG and Siemens, could regain their high standard of production thanks to the power plant. Companies, after losing their markets in the East, were now "increasingly dependent on the West."[55] Making use of the industries in West Berlin will "strengthen its power of resistance. As long as West Berlin industry has work, nobody need worry about the fate of Berlin."[56]

The emphasis on the importance of West Berliner production for the city's recovery served as a tool to simultaneously save and sell the "free economy" of capitalism. According to the research and policy committee of the Committee for Economic Development, an advisory organ consisting of several US businessmen, this consisted of an "exchange of goods and services among competing individuals and businesses—technically known as the market."[57] A closer look at the promotion of the annual Deutsche Industrie-Ausstellung (German Industrial Exhibition), one of the most extensively featured events among the many exhibitions, congresses, and festivals that took place in the city, illustrates this point.[58] Located in Charlottenburg, a neighborhood in West Berlin, the exhibition attracted locals (including visitors from the GDR until the building of the Berlin Wall in 1961), as well as Germans from other places and foreigners. Although the exhibition grounds were a pile of rubble in 1945, soon after the war the area was reconstructed, again with the help of the Marshall Plan. At the time of the first industrial exhibition in 1950 it consisted of eleven halls, a building named after George C. Marshall, multiple national pavilions, and Berlin's famous radio tower, the Funkturm.[59] At the exhibit, different industries and industrial products were displayed, from raw materials to consumer goods, including steel, rubber, photography equipment, textiles, paper, and sporting goods. Machines were presented as museum objects to be looked at, surrounded by rope so that nobody could touch them.[60] The German Industrial Exhibition can be placed in the older tradition of international exhibitions, such as the famous world's fairs that started in the nineteenth century, where diverse objects (and in some cases people) were presented as "achievements" and nationalistic and colonial ideologies were emphasized through international competition in science and technology.[61] Exhibitions like the German Industrial Exhibition were obvious sites of political contestation and became well-known, nonviolent Cold War battlegrounds, with the most famous example being the Kitchen Debate between Nixon and Khrushchev that took place at the American National Exhibition at Sokolniki Park in

Moscow in 1959.[62] As S. Jonathan Wiesen rightly writes about the German Industrial Exhibition, "it was the display of industrial and consumer goods that gave life to the idea that the Economic Miracle was both real and, indeed, vital to the survival of capitalism and the personal welfare of German families."[63] A tourism brochure explained that the first edition of the industrial exhibition was a showcase for the "free" economy of West Berlin and "the West," as opposed to the Communist eastern part of the city; it stated: "The free world meets in free Berlin."[64] It shows how the political goals of the exhibition also appeared in the realm of tourism.

Just like the exhibition where the Kitchen Debate took place, the German Industrial Exhibition of 1950 displayed an American model house (and a model man, "Mr. Smith"), which promoted the fruits of American consumer capitalism.[65] The booklet *Amerika zu Hause* (*America at Home*) explained the concept of prefabricated houses to the German visitor. It stressed that the US government aimed to let all US citizens own a house and explained how Mr. Smith, an average American, managed to buy the presented model house, with three bedrooms. The booklet reminded the reader that this dream can only become reality with a "healthy free economic system" and the "efficiency of an excellent industry." The rest of the booklet depicted all aspects of the US economy as a great story of progress; it included many graphs showing growth and displayed the high standard of living of the average American, such as the amount of clothing owned by a woman who lives in the city. Mr. Smith, like other potential consumers, is a happy man who does not have to worry about the future.[66] The fact that this American model house was part of the German Industrial Exhibition is significant, because it presented the United States as the model that German industries, and Germany more broadly, had to follow. The booklet advertised the perks of capitalist consumerism centered around the idea that fulfillment and happiness derive from homeownership and the buying of objects.[67] It thus sought to seduce its audiences to believe in an ideology of accomplishment ruled by commodities: a reaffirmation for visitors from the United States, a future goal for visitors from Germany. The dreamlike image of Mr. Smith served as a lesson that miracles are possible if one adopts the right economic policies.[68] It is worth noting that not only the model house but the exhibition itself was a representation serving to lure its visitors into a dreamworld, as trade fairs were also recognized by the US government as a "marketing technique" for the promotion of international trade to close the dollar gap.[69]

The propagandistic aim of "showcasing economic success" at the fair was present in tourism promotion materials, such as in a flyer from 1951 inviting industries to participate in the exhibition that would help the "activation of the West Berlin economy."[70] The exhibition was applauded for its function as "a unique demonstration of the power and achievement of the free world." The economic, political, and psychological functions of the exhibition were emphasized throughout the brochure: "The free world has confidence in Berlin. Capital is once more invested here. The city not only looks back on a great past, it has a future to look forward to as well."

Here, it was not explained what "great past" was being referred to (probably not the recent past), but it is clear that the flyer presented the exhibition and Berlin as a marketplace where "old friendships" and "new relations" meet, where suppliers are "efficient," and consumers are "interested" and have "accumulated requirements."[71] Capital investment was the driving force of this progress, the only way to secure a bright future for the city and its inhabitants.

The focus on recovery and industry in the tourism promotion materials of West Berlin can be explained by the particular economic policies that were implemented in the city, especially the Marshall Plan counterpart funds that were largely controlled by the United States.[72] As Armin Grünbacher notes, because the United States had a final say in how Germany's counterpart funds were used, it "allowed them, usually against German resistance, to redirect funds into areas that they thought important," such as the electricity industry; this provides another explanation for why the rebuilt power plant in Berlin pops up so frequently in tourism promotion.[73] The release of counterpart funds in 1950 was explicitly focused on promoting German goods abroad, especially because of the economic crisis caused by outbreak of the Korean War.[74] The fact that the German Industrial Exhibition happened at the same time as the release of these funds is therefore no coincidence. West Berlin received an unusually high amount of financial aid in comparison to the rest of West Germany. By March 1953, for instance, more than a third of the total sums of counterpart funds spent were used in West Berlin. Special measures to rebuild industrial Berlin, such as cheaper loans for industrial reconstruction or start-up credits for expellees and "political" refugees from the GDR, were necessary to turn Berlin into the "shop window of capitalism deep in the Soviet zone."[75] Promoting tourism in West Berlin clearly shored up not only Cold War economic policies but also the political agenda of the United States.

Buy in Berlin

"Buy in Berlin" was part of a wide-ranging Marshall Plan advertising campaign.[76] The German Industrial Exhibition was included in the campaign, and millions of German marks were used to promote products from Berlin. After the Marshall Plan ended, "Buy in Berlin" continued to be one of the main campaigns to attract tourists to the city. In 1960 the *German Review* published the article "Lufthansa's New Service Aloft."[77] The article described the new "Senator service" onboard the German airlines on the North Atlantic route: lager beer is now "drawn from the cask during flights for the first time in the history of aviation." A photograph showed the cask on the plane and two passengers enjoying a beer. The focus in the photograph is on the item of consumption and its consumers; of the flight attendant pouring the beer we only see a hand.[78]

Beer was one of the many products depicted in the West Berlin tourism advertising. The brochure *Shopping in Berlin* (1960) highlighted the beer company Berliner Kindl founded in 1872 and included a photograph of a worker in an apron with a wooden beer barrel.[79] The text informed the reader that thanks to Marshall Plan assistance, "the Kindl brewery in West Berlin has become the most modern brewery in Europe." The history of the brewery as told in the brochure emphasized craftsmanship and tradition as key features of Berliner Kindl, while it simultaneously presented the brewery as "modern" because of US financial aid.[80] The brewery, located near one of Berlin's airports, had been heavily damaged by Allied bombing. More than half of the experienced staff had been drafted into the military, and right after the war much of its remaining brewing equipment was confiscated by the Soviet Union; this would later form the basis for a completely new brewery in Moscow. To continue producing beer it operated as a makeshift brewery with the equipment it had. Berliner Kindl probably did not have the most modern equipment available at the time of the brochure's publication, although the brewery did receive US aid in 1955.[81] "The most modern in Europe" was an exaggeration and part of marketing language, a capitalist fiction intended to highlight West Berlin as a tourism destination and the US role in rebuilding it.

The Lufthansa article in the *German Review* also included a photograph of a "courteous and cheerful" Lufthansa flight attendant in front of an airplane (fig. 3). She is not at work but clearly posing, showing off her new uniform designed by the couturier Heinz Oestergaard. After his return from Soviet imprisonment in 1946, Oestergaard was one of the first designers to start making clothes again.[82] He used old army uniforms, curtains, and flags, and in a short amount of time he was able to open his own salon in West Berlin. His first designs made fun of the shortages in Berlin with names such as "the black market" and "power shortage." His first clients were wives of Soviet officers who paid him in fabrics, furs, cigarettes, or whiskey. He quickly made a name in Berlin high society, attracting clients like the actress Romy Schneider, and became one of the most influential German designers of the postwar era.[83] Oestergaard's personal story fits well with the recovery narrative of West Berlin. His designs for Lufthansa were ubiquitous; US audiences were drawn to German products like his as they read tourism magazines in the comfort of their homes. Failing that, they would encounter his products aboard a Lufthansa flight.

The Lufthansa article, with photographs that promoted travel, German beer, and fashion, can be seen as early signs of what Vanessa Schwartz calls "the jet age aesthetic," an aesthetic of fluid motion and communication, "which dematerialized experience into a system of circulating spaces, people, and images." According to Schwartz, systems of transport and image production and reception show ties between transport technology, media, and their aesthetic expression as key forces in shaping social formations.[84] In the Lufthansa article, this was apparent in the differentiation between the traveler and the airline service worker. Besides selling products from Berlin, the article sold the city of Berlin as well. The flight became an attractive medium that promoted the "free" (capitalist) flow of people, goods, and ideas between the US and West Germany and contributed to the integration of West Germany into "the West."

In tourism advertising, Berlin was presented as a showcase of capitalism. There is no better example of this than the frequent depiction of the window displays of the department store KaDeWe (Kaufhaus des Westens) (fig. 4). The brochure *Shopping in Berlin* explained how the rebuilding of the famous department store, financed by the Marshall Plan, became a symbol of Berlin's optimism right after the war. Its large shop windows, lit up at night, were often featured in magazines, brochures, and postcards.[85] The lights and displays of department stores like KaDeWe and Peek & Cloppenburg (featured in the ECA film *City out of Darkness*) were more than just a way to promote its products. As one tourism brochure demonstrated, "For the German population in the East the West Berlin stores are symbolic of the Freedom of the occidental world . . . perhaps even the most impressive symbol. Here they may find what they have almost forgotten: Good qualities in large quantities, excellent service and facilities offered to the customers."[86] Here the shop windows were presented as fulfilling a political task, highlighting the consumer abundance of the liberal capitalism of West Berlin as opposed to the Communist East.[87] When looking at all the references to "freedom" in the promotion of West Berlin, it is worth noting that this "freedom" mostly appears as the freedom to buy in a capitalist society.[88]

The West Berlin tourism promotion literature presented the city as filled with an abundance of consumer goods, experiencing a full recovery through the construction of plenty of new buildings and the blooming of industry. This narrative of recovery underscored the importance of US aid and justified the strong US (military) presence in the city, while also promoting Berlin as a safe and attractive destination for US tourists. It reveals tourism's intertwinement with Berlin as an economic, military, and cultural *dispositif* and the city's symbolic role during the Cold War. Although the tourism advertising of West Berlin propagated the narrative of the economic miracle, to what extent can we speak of such a miracle in West Berlin, and who benefited from it? In postwar capitalist Germany the state played an important role in constructing a competitive market.[89] Ludwig Erhard (who also appeared in a flyer of the German Industrial Exhibition) and his Ministry of Economics was the main figure of this economic policy, which was based on "labor discipline and wage moderation" to boost German exports.[90] Under US hegemony, which put in place a new system of public and private international organizations to forge "a durable transatlantic consensus among governing elites, internationally oriented capitalist owners and reformist trade union leaders," Germany's economic policy mainly aimed at integration into a rapidly expanding world economy.[91] This aim of stimulating export and integration into the global market explains the abovementioned importance of the German Industrial Exhibition and West German industry and goods in tourism promotion materials, as part of international travel to the FRG was business related.[92]

With "the attention of the world . . . focused on Berlin as outpost of the free world," its purportedly fast recovery underscored West Berlin as a city of the future

HAT

Figure 3. Lufthansa flight attendant wearing a uniform designed by Heinz Oestergaard. *German Review*, no. 3 (1960): 22–23. Courtesy of Historisches Archiv zum Tourismus, Technische Universität, Berlin.

Figure 4. Postcard of Kaufhaus des Westens (KaDeWe). Courtesy of the Berlin-Brandenburgisches Wirtschaftsarchiv, Berlin.

and demonstrated the supremacy of "the free West."[93] The repeated references to wealth and abundance in tourism promotion materials make it easy to forget that corporate profits in West Germany were mostly created by specific productivity-enhancing investments. When German manufactures faced low-cost competitors, wage restraint was demanded. This was only possible because of "the decimation and decapitation of the working-class movement under German fascism."[94] Germany's postwar "economic miracle" thus entailed low wages and the repression of labor unions, an element that was already described by the economist Ernest Mandel in the 1960s. Mandel emphasized how low wages and a larger pool of laborers, partly coming from East Germany, alongside large-scale unemployment were main features of economic growth in West Germany, Italy, and Japan. He wrote that the most important factor in these countries' quick economic growth was "the exceptionally high rate of capital accumulation, explained by a very high rate of profit, which in its turn depends upon a much lower level of wages compared with other capitalist countries; and the lower wage levels are to be explained by the much larger reserve army of labour."[95] As Daniel L. Goldy, deputy director of the Marshall Plan's European Labor Division, phrased it, "haunted by the spectre of unemployment," trade unions "have many times chosen to go along with this system."[96] Wages remained low while prices increased. Foreign trade was thus stimulated at the expense of domestic workers.[97]

This other side of the coin was not visible in tourism promotion materials of West Berlin aimed at stimulating foreign trade and bringing US dollars to the city. To attract capital investment, the economic recovery of West Berlin was presented as a success story, but it was only a success for some capitalists, such as the owners of KaDeWe or Hotel Kempinski on the Kurfürstendamm.[98] Concealing the socioeconomic reality of the city and its inhabitants in a dream image of Berlin as a shop window of "the West" was fundamental to Cold War politics. As the Marshall Plan administrator Paul G. Hoffman noted in an outline for a speech in 1949, a "free economy [is] impossible without selling." And as an efficient method of persuasion, the "selling of ideas [is] even more important than [the] selling of goods."[99] The narrative of the economic miracle with its successful recovery, developing industry, and its promise of a future with an abundance of goods in the tourism promotion materials of West Berlin highlighted the victory of capitalism over Communism, even if it was only a facade.

Conclusion

In their efforts to promote tourism to West Berlin, US and West German politicians, policymakers, and businessmen advanced the mythical idea of the economic miracle. With tourism promotion they created a dream image that presented the economic miracle as inherent to the capitalist West as opposed to the communist East. Tourism advertising portrayed the city as risen from the ruins, in which the recent Nazi past was obscured and US aid and military presence were justified. A border city in the Cold War and concurrently a "workshop of Europe," Berlin and its economic recovery, was seen as key to European reconstruction after the war. To boost the West Berlin economy, locally made products and industry such as those displayed at the German Industrial Exhibition were promoted, while simultaneously selling the benefits of the "free economy" of capitalism. According to Henri Lefebvre, it is the nature of "things and products to conceal the truth"; "having become commodities, they lie in order to conceal their origin, namely social labour."[100] Indeed, as we have seen, the emphasis in the tourism promotion of West Berlin is on the commodity; on stories of reconstruction and economic growth; and the "unfree" and "dark" East Berlin. The socioeconomic reality of the city and its inhabitants was concealed in a dream image of Berlin as shop window of the West with inflated projections and hopes for the future. The symbolic importance of the perception of Berlin is perfectly captured in the article "Bridge Between East and West" (1957):

> Though at the moment Berlin cannot fulfill its function as capital of Germany its existence as a *sanctuary of freedom* remains a fact of *supreme political importance*. Berlin is the great obstacle in the way of the complete integration of Middle Germany into the Bolshevist system. Over and above this, "the secret capital of Germany" is the symbol of hope for the 18 million fellow-citizens who are deprived of their rights. Berlin, *"the shopwindow of the West"* as it is so often called, has also the political task of exercising an influence over the oppressed zone, by virtue of independence of its own political life and by demonstrating beyond all doubt the *achievements of the free world.*[101]

The continuous emphasis on West Berlin as "sanctuary of freedom" and "shop window of the West" in the promotion materials for the city should be placed in the economic and political context in which both US and West German policymakers operated during the Cold War. Presenting West Berlin as risen from ruins, as well as focusing on industry and German products, was part of the economic and political goals of the Marshall Plan, which proclaimed the triumph of capitalism and defined the postwar years as an economic miracle. Already in 1949 Paul G. Hoffman talked about "the miracle of recovery" to be achieved by the Marshall Plan through European cooperation and US counsel, encouragement, and material aid.[102] In other words, the narrative of the economic miracle was used at the same time as the economic policy that was supposed to create it was implemented. The way West Berlin was advertised worked as an illusion to convince audiences on both sides of the Atlantic that an economic miracle had already taken place. To integrate Berlin, and the Federal Republic of Germany more generally, as part of the West, West Berlin had to be presented as a success story of progress, freedom, and abundance thanks to US intervention and aid. Within this framing of Berlin, there was no room for the Nazi past. Unemployment and subsidies, actual labor circumstances, and the low wages that facilitated the so-called economic miracle had to be concealed. The freedom to be attained was the freedom of the market defined by competing individuals and businesses, a "free" capitalist economic system in which happiness can only be achieved through the purchase of commodities. Tourism advertising, with its focus on consumption and leisure, offered the ideal dreamworld, a useful smoke screen to promote the superiority of the capitalist and democratic West, turning West Berlin into the perfect showcase of the economic miracle.

Aimée Plukker is a PhD candidate in history at Cornell University and the reviews editor of the *Journal of Tourism History*. Her dissertation examines how Cold War US tourism to Western Europe produced "the West" as a material and imagined space. Her work is published in *Journal of Material Culture* and the anthologies *Transformative Recovery? The European Recovery Program (ERP)/Marshall Plan in European Tourism* (2020) and *Urban Authenticity and Heritage after 1945: Creating Images and Contesting Identities* (forthcoming).

Notes

This article started as a paper presented at a Center for Austrian Studies' Seminar hosted by the University of Minnesota in 2021. I would like to thank the organizers, Sune Bechmann Pedersen, Gundolf Graml, Kevin James, Jess Pearson, and Igor Tchoukarine, and my paper's discussant, Stephanie Eisenhuth. I would also like to thank the participants of the Graduate History Association Colloquium at Cornell University, where I presented a preliminary version of this paper. I am very grateful for the guidance and comments provided by Enzo Traverso and Claudia Verhoeven. Many thanks to the editors of this issue, Ravinder Kaur and Barbara Weinstein, Tom Harbison, Sara Lickey, the two anonymous reviewers, and Harry Churchill, Amr Leheta, Nathan Carlos Norris Cruz, and Daniela Samur, for their help and feedback. A special thanks to Darren Wan for his support and for reading numerous versions of this paper. Last, I would like to thank the staff at the various libraries and archives where I have worked, in particular Hasso Spode, who sponsored my research at the Historisches Archiv zum Tourismus at the Technische Universität in Berlin in 2019. Funding for the archival research used in this article was provided by the Einaudi-SSRC Dissertation Development Program, the German Institute in Amsterdam (DIA), the Harry S. Truman Presidential Library, a Luigi Einaudi Graduate Dissertation Fellowship, and the Max Weber Foundation.

1. Verkehrsamt Berlin and Industrie- und Handelskammer zu Berlin, *West-Berliner Qualität*, D060/11/1/45-60/1 Berlin West, Box 1, Historisches Archiv zum Tourismus, Technische Universität Berlin (hereafter cited as HAT).

2. "Berlin Quality—a Household Word" was the subtitle of a chapter written by a member of the federal parliament (Bucerius, "Berlin"). West Berlin only joined the Marshall Plan in 1949. Earlier aid programs included the United Nations Relief and Rehabilitation Administration (UNRRA) and a special food plan for Germany and Austria designed by Herbert Hoover. Literature on the Marshall Plan is vast; see, for instance, Ellwood, *Rebuilding Europe*; Milward, *Reconstruction of Western Europe*; and Steil, *Marshall Plan*. On the Marshall Plan in Germany, see Hardach, *Der Marshall-Plan*; and Lehmann, *Der Marshall-Plan und das Neue Deutschland*. On the US (military) presence in Berlin, see Eisenhuth, *Die Schutzmacht*; and Stivers and Carter, *City Becomes a Symbol*.

3. Benjamin, *Arcades Project*, 391. See, for instance, Abelshauser, *Wirtschaftsgeschischte*; Abelshauser, *Dynamics of German Industry*; Glossner, *Making of the German Post-war Economy*; Grünbacher, *West German Industrialists*; and Spicka, *Selling the Economic Miracle*.

4. Williams, "Advertising," particularly 199, 208.

5. An example is Garth and Kaufman, *Cook's Pocket Travel Guide to Europe*, 88; Lukács, "Reification and the Consciousness of the Proletariat," 83–110; I borrow the term "image-machine" from Groebner, *Retroland*, 15.

6. For the role of tourism as diplomatic tool, see, for instance, Baranowski et al., "Tourism and Diplomacy"; and Endy, *Cold War Holidays*.

7. Williams, "Advertising," 207.

8. Henri Lefebvre points at the importance of the optical and visual world, images as fragments of space in the creation of illusion, fetishizing abstraction and imposing it as the norm (*Production of Space*, 97). The fetish character of the commodity has been described by Karl Marx as the value of a product that has been masked by its exchange value: "The mysterious character of the commodity-form consists therefore simply in the fact that the commodity reflects the social characteristics of men's labour as objective characteristics of the products of labour themselves, as socio-natural properties of these things (. . .) this fetishism of the world of commodities arises from the peculiar social character of the labour which produces them" (Marx, *Capital Volume I*, 164–65).

9. "The advertisement is the ruse by which the dream forces itself on industry" (Benjamin, *Arcades Project*, 171).

10. Harvey, "Value in Motion," 102; Magri, *Tailor of Ulm*, 141.

11. On how industrialists boosted the myth of the economic miracle, see Grünbacher, *West German Industrialists*. On the change in Allied policy toward the trials of German industrialists from 1947 onward, see Baars, "Capitalism's Victor's Justice?" For an excellent case study on how objects like the Volkswagen became an emblem of the economic miracle despite their Nazi past, see Scholz, "Miraculous Objects."

12. Statistical data of the FRG reveal that until 1950 the total revenue of the hospitality industry (including bars and restaurants) was DM 3,423,207,000, 13.5 percent of the total revenue of the iron and steel industry, or DM 25,271,619,000. In 1970 the total revenue would be DM 25.75 billion. *Die Nichtlandwirtschaftlichen Arbeitsstätten in der Bundesrepublik Deutschland 13.9.1950*, 50, 78. According to Horst Ruediger Johnsen, this can also partly be explained to the fact that the German hospitality industry mostly consisted of small, family-owned businesses, with more international hotel chains only arriving in the 1960s ("Development and Financing," 1–2, 9, 71). West Berlin received from 1.2 percent (in 1952) to 1.6 percent (in 1970) of the total number of tourists in the FRG; this figure includes tourists from Germany (Bernhauer, *Deutscher Fremdenverkehrsverband*, 23). However, this percentage should be placed in perspective compared to other West German cities, as in in 1958 Berlin was ranked fourth in receiving the most visitors, after Munich, Hamburg, and Frankfurt (Wolff, "Berliner Fremdenverkehrsprobleme," 16). For an overview with some empirical data on early postwar foreign tourism to the FRG, see Wilde, "Zwischen Zusammenbruch und Währungsreform," 94–99.

13. Statistical information on tourism remains a topic of debate among policymakers in the immediate postwar years, due to inadequate information and different definitions of tourism. The numbers in this source were based on sources from the Organization of

European Economic Cooperation and state tourist bureaus. The total number of receipts from US and Canadian tourists was $116,000,000 in 1957 and $176,4000,000 in 1959 (total amounts: $444,000,000 in 1957 and $451,400,000 in 1959). "Development of Tourism in Western Europe, 1957–1960," 4, appendix 1 and 2, CECA-ECEN-1009, 1961, Historical Archives of the European Union, European University Institute, Fiesole.

14. On the symbolic role and unique status of Berlin during the Cold War, see Eisenhuth and Krause, "Inventing the 'Outpost of Freedom'"; and Jarausch, Eisenhuth, and Krause, *Cold War Berlin*.

15. US tourists would bring dollars to Europe that in turn would be spent on buying products from the United States (*Travel Restrictions*, 198). On postwar US tourism to Europe and the link between the Marshall Plan and tourism, see, for instance, Endy, *Cold War Holidays*; and Groß, Knoll, and Scharf, *Transformative Recovery?*

16. On the promotion of Berlin for tourist purposes during the Cold War, see Poock-Feller, "Berlin lebt"; Warnke, "Mit dem Baedeker"; and Sedlmaier, "Berlin als doppeltes 'Schaufenster.'" For a focus on West Berlin, see Standley, "From Bulwark of Freedom."

17. Hitchcock writes that the Marshall Plan laid the groundwork for the construction of a community of ideas, economic links, and security ties between Europe and the United States, known as the West ("Marshall Plan"); Jackson, *Civilizing the Enemy*. The (military) alliance between the US and Europe against the USSR (and the underlying fear of Communism) was an important component of the Marshall Plan (Hobsbawm, *Age of Extremes*, 240–41, 275).

18. Scholz, "Miraculous Objects," 104; Wiesen, "Miracles for Sale," 152.

19. As Ericka Beckman writes in her work on capital fictions in literature of Latin America in the late nineteenth and early twentieth centuries, the capitalist economy consists of fictitious dimensions, with the material economy "relying on strategies of representations to make itself intelligible" (*Capital Fictions*, xx). In her work on the branding of India, Ravinder Kaur also offers a useful description of what she calls "the great spectacle," a "zone of contact between the speculative dreamworlds of the future and the material conditions of the present, the encounter between what *is* and what *could be* in the new time." The great spectacle is marked by the drawing of futures that do not only inform but seduce and "mass market a given commodity or worldview" (*Brand New Nation*, 16).

20. Recent works that include critical assessments of the idea of the *Wirtschaftswunder* in Germany include Hesse, "Fact or Fiction?"; and Raphael, *Jenseits von Kohle und Stahl*, especially 102–11, 138–42. There are almost no works on the German economic miracle from a cultural perspective; an exception is Wiesen, "Miracles for Sale."

21. Universal Newsreel, *Occupation of Berlin*, newsreel, vol. 18, 417 (1945), item 3, Moving Image Research Center, US National Archives and Record Administration (hereafter cited as NARA), College Park, Maryland; Universal Newsreel, *Berlin Frolics*, newsreel, vol. 18, 425 (1945), item 5, Moving Image Research Center, NARA, College Park, Maryland. For a general introduction on (military) tourism in Berlin till 1948, see Poock-Feller, "Berlin lebt," 105–8; on tours of US soldiers stationed in West Berlin to East Berlin, see Eisenhuth, "Freizeit beim Feind."

22. Documents in multiple folders: Record Group 469, Box 4 Office of the Special Representative in Europe: Trade Development and Tourism, 48–51, Germany, NARA, College Park, Maryland.

23. The brochure also provided many details on the recovery of the city, including information on the power plant and the construction of new hotels. Verkehrsamt Berlin,

Berlin at a Glance (1959), 29, MssCol 18400, Timothy Leary Papers, 1910–2009, Series 3: 1950–1960, Box 17, Folder 17.2 Travel—Europe—Printed Ephemera 1950s, Manuscripts, Archives and Rare Books Division, New York Public Library, New York City.

24. Wolff, "Communication Center Berlin," 168.

25. Time Inc., March of Time, *Berlin Rift in the Iron Curtain* (1953), March of Time Collection, 200 MT 424.60, Moving Image Research Center, NARA, College Park, Maryland; Eckert, "Greetings from the Zonal Border." See also Standley, "Experiencing Communism."

26. Wharton, *Building the Cold War*, 77.

27. Verkehrsamt Berlin, *Sight Seeing Tour Berlin* (1957), D060/11/1/45-60/1 Berlin West, Box 1, HAT.

28. See also the report of special assistant Clarence Randall on international travel, commissioned by President Eisenhower in 1958: "In the postwar period former animosities have yielded to new friendships as Americans have traveled extensively in such countries as Germany and Japan" (*International Travel*, 5).

29. Fielding, *Fielding's Travel Guide to Europe*, 358. The 1953–54 edition of the guidebook is even more positive about the hard-working Germans: "Here is one of the most industrious and efficient peoples of the world—a statistical fact which cannot be denied. Despite any personal prejudices which might still linger here and there, even the severest critic is forced to have enormous admiration and respect for the way the German worker has tackled the back-breaking problem of reconstruction—and succeeded" (*Fielding's Travel Guide to Europe 1953–54*, 387).

30. Tuma, "Cosmopolitan Berlin," 4, 5, 8.

31. Tourism guidebooks also concealed the Nazi past; see, for instance, the following description of Berlin: "it was looked upon by the world as one of the finest cities in the world until World War II. . . . The natives of the Western sector are very friendly to the Americans, as they are grateful for the help they received. . . . Americans are welcome and they are greeted with kindness and consideration" (Barsness, *Europe Calling*, 204–5).

32. Wharton, *Building the Cold War*, 76.

33. Harrity, *Fun in Europe*, 89.

34. Görlich, "Berlin, die geteilte Stadt," 418.

35. Krueger, "Mit Marshall Plan Geldern baut Kempinski ein neues Hotel am Kurfürstendamm," photograph (1951), F Rep. 290-02-01, Erich O. Krueger, 0000259, Landesarchiv Berlin. The hotel received DM 2 million for the reconstruction. Office of the U.S. High Commissioner for Germany Press Release #1052, "Noted Kempinski Firm to Rebuild Berlin Hotel with ECA Assistance," Record Group 469, Box 4, Office of the Special Representative in Europe: Trade Development and Tourism, 48–51, Germany, NARA, College Park, Maryland.

36. The Kempinski family had fled to the United States during the war. Friedrich Unger was the grandson of the founder of Kempinski.

37. Quoted in *Ku'damm No. 27*, 4.

38. *Ku'damm No. 27*, 4.

39. *Ku'damm No. 27*, 130.

40. Hotels constructed in Berlin, for example, included Hotel am Zoo, Hotel am Steinplatz, the Casino-Hotel of Wannsee, Parkhotel Zellermayer (DM 900.000, opened on August 1, 1957), and Berlin Hilton (DM 27.2m, 1958). Other Hilton hotels included Amsterdam Hilton (1963) and Albergo dei Cavalieri Hilton Rome (ECA funding promised, funded

otherwise, 1963). "Ritornano a Berlino i visitatori stranieri," 34, *Rassegna della Stampa Italiana ed Estera* (December 1–15, 1950), vol. 3, no. 29, Biblioteca ENIT, Rome; "Letter Zellermeyer," June 11, 1964, B Rep. 010, Box 703, Landesarchiv Berlin; "Dwinell (Deputy Chief Travel Development Section) to Zellermayer letter," February 14, 1951, Record Group 469, Box 4, Office of the Special Representative in Europe: Trade Development and Tourism, 48–51, Germany, National Archives and Records Administration (NARA), College Park, Maryland; "Pozzy (Chief of the Travel Development Section) to Cunningham (ECA Special Mission to Germany) memorandum," Record Group 469, Box 4, Office of the Special Representative in Europe: Trade Development and Tourism, 48–51, Germany, NARA, College Park, Maryland; Wolff, "Communication Center Berlin"; Wharton, *Building the Cold War*, 79. For useful accounts of Hilton in Europe, see Adalet, *Hotels and Highways*, especially chap. 5; and Langer, "Hotel on the Hill."

41. Kempinski, for example, is promoted in the brochure *German Industries Exhibition* (1953), D060/11/1/45-60/2 Berlin West, Box 2, HAT.

42. *Berlin in Brennpunkt des Weltgeschehens*, Presseamt des Senats von Berlin, D060/11/1/45-60/2 Berlin West, Box 2, HAT.

43. *Air of Freedom* (ECA, 1951), Record Group 306, 306.6909, Moving Image Research Center, NARA, College Park, Maryland.

44. *Ku'damm No. 27*, 131–32.

45. The Mutual Security Agency (MSA) superseded the Economic Cooperation Administration (ECA), the organization that administered the Marshall Plan. MSA, *1,2,3, A Monthly Review from Europe* (1952), Record Group 306, 306.103A, Moving Image Research Center, NARA, College Park, Maryland. I am grateful to Michael Taylor from NARA for helping me find the publication date of this film.

46. For useful accounts on the symbolical function of the hotel, see Davidson, *Hotel*; and James, *Modern Hotel*.

47. Wharton, *Building the Cold War*, 78.

48. Wharton, *Building the Cold War*, 78.

49. Thanks to Stephanie Eisenhuth (pers. comm., March 29, 2021) for providing me with these specific numbers.

50. Schneider, *Marshall Plan*, 2, 25, 31.

51. Operation Paperclip is the most famous part of the wider "intellectual reparations" program that is the focus of Gimbel's work (*Science, Technology, and Reparations*). It is also worth noting, as Eric Hobsbawm points out, that "former fascists were systematically used by intelligence services and other functions not in the public view" (*Age of Extremes*, 239).

52. Verkehrsamt Berlin, *Berlin Today*, 32.

53. Kraftwerk West appears in the map *Berlin ruft die Welt*, the ECA publication *Berlin baut auf—Berlin am Werk!*, and as a "symbol of economic strength" ("wachsende Wirtschaftskraft") in the booklet *Berlin in Brennpunkt des Weltgeschehens* and another booklet in the same series include photographs of the power plant before and after the recovery. Deutschen Zentrale für Fremdenverkehr and Verkehrsamt Berlin, *Berlin ruft die Welt*, D060/11/1/45-60/1 Berlin West, Box 1, HAT; ECA, *Berlin baut auf—Berlin am Werk!* (1950), D060/11/1/45-60/2 Berlin West, Box 2, HAT; *Berlin in Brennpunkt des Weltgeschehens*, Presseamt des Senats von Berlin, D060/11/1/45-60/2 Berlin West, Box 2, HAT. After 1953 the power plant was renamed Kraftwerk Ernst Reuter, after the mayor of West Berlin.

54. In June 1948 the Soviets blocked the railways, roads, and canals to West Berlin as a response to the new currency that the Western Allies implemented. In return, the Allies introduced the airlift; all the goods that were needed in Berlin were flown in through the Tempelhof Airport. The use of Marshall Plan money for the power plant is explained in the ECA publication *Berlin baut auf—Berlin am Werk!*

55. Although the brochure notes that West Berlin lost markets in the East, Julian Germann writes that "under the slogan of an open global trade policy, Erhard's ministry [of economics] reached for markets far beyond the North Atlantic and across the emerging Cold War divide . . . it involved, most critically, sustained efforts on the part of German industry to revive its traditional markets in the European east and southeast" (*Unwitting Architect*, 75–76). This was contrary to US policy, which was aimed at anchoring Germany within Western Europe to strengthen a transatlantic alliance.

56. "Made in Western Berlin," in *Berlin* (probably published in 1951), 25, D060/11/1/45-60/1 Berlin West, Box 1, HAT.

57. Committee for Economic Development, *Monetary and Fiscal Policy*, 17. Marshall Plan administrator Paul G. Hoffman was one of the founders of the CED.

58. Some of these were the *Berliner Festwochen* (usually translated as Berlin Festival Weeks), the International Film Festival, the agricultural fair and the architecture exhibition. For an advertisement of the German Industrial Exhibition, see, for example, the advertisement "Berlin Is Worth a Voyage," *German Review,* no. 2 (1956): 38, HAT. In particular, the architecture exhibition Interbau and the opening of the Hansaviertel that took place in 1957 has received a lot of scholarly attention; see, for instance, Kellermann, "Future Berlin"; Föllmer, "Anti-totalitarianism"; Wagner-Conzelmann, *Die Interbau 1957 in Berlin*; and Warnke, *Stein gegen Stein*.

59. The brochure describes how in 1949 new buildings were constructed at the fairgrounds, and in May 1950 the first large international exhibition about cars took place, which was visited by four hundred thousand people. *Deutsche Industrie Ausstellung Berlin 1950* (Berlin: Dr. Hans Muschke, 1950), D060/11/1/45-60/1 Berlin West, Box 1, HAT. See also *Berlin baut auf—Berlin am Werk!*, 34. The Funkturm was often depicted in tourism promotion, and in general radio towers in West Berlin became important symbols and tools of intelligence during the Cold War, since the towers could send radio programs and stations such as RIAS (Rundfunk im amerikanischen Sektor) to the Eastern part of the city.

60. *German Industries Exhibition* (1953).

61. For a useful account of the historical links between tourism and exhibitions, see D'Eramo, "La fogna più bella della Terra." The first world's fair during the Cold War era would take place in Brussels in 1958. See, for instance, Molella and Knowles, *World's Fairs in the Cold War*. The Marshall Plan itself was also promoted by a traveling exhibition, the "ERP train," that toured through most of Western Europe and attracted around six million people (Bischof and Petschar, *Marshall Plan*; Grünbacher, "Cold-War Economics," 699). Grünbacher explains how a small part of a special 5 percent clause of Marshall Plan counterpart funds went to this exhibition, the other part went to the CIA (for an explanation of the counterpart funds, see note 72).

62. When Nixon led Khruschev through the model US house, including several US technological devices and gadgets, the two leaders debated the differences between capitalism and Communism (starting with the usefulness of some of the presented gadgets), that mostly took place in the kitchen of the model home. See, for example, Baldwin, *Racial Imaginary of the Cold War Kitchen*; Oldenziel and Zachmann, *Cold War Kitchen*.

63. Wiesen, "Miracles for Sale," 154.
64. "Zum ersten Male nach dem Kriege zeigt die westliche Welt an ihrem östlichsten Vorposten, zu welchen Leistungen eine freie Wirtschaft fähig ist. . . . Hier in Berlin, wo sich die beiden Welten berühren, entsteht eine großartige Schau vom Schaffen der freien Welt"; "Die freie Welt trifft sich im freien Berlin" (*Deutsche Industrie Ausstellung Berlin 1950*).
65. Deutsche Industrieausstellung, *Amerika zu Hause*.
66. Deutsche Industrieausstellung, *Amerika zu Hause*.
67. For an excellent account of the "ideology of happiness and privatization," and the importance of the home in the new postwar political economy of the household see: Ross, *Fast Cars, Clean Bodies*, 11, chap. 2.
68. The 1951 flyer *You Are Being Expected . . . in Berlin!* emphasizes once more the economic goals of the industry exhibition: the "potential" and "capacity of a free economy." According to the flyer, the industry exhibited offers "a survey of the present level of industrial capacity in the free economy of the Western world." Because of its industry, Berlin is even presented as more interesting than how it used to be, a city where "the throb of modern life" could be felt. *You Are Being Expected . . . in Berlin!* (Berlin: H. Wigankow, 1951), Do60/11/1/45-60/1 Berlin West, Box 1, HAT.
69. The Intelligence and Services Division, Office of International Trade, Department of Commerce, "Closing the Dollar Gap by Import Promotion" (1950), 46, Gordon Gray Papers, Box 15, Harry S. Truman Library, Independence, Missouri. For a (Foucauldian) description of exhibitions, reality, and representation, see Mitchell, *Colonising Egypt*, chap. 1.
70. Wiesen, "Miracles for Sale," 167; *Deutsche Industrie Ausstellung Berlin 1951*, Do60/11/1/45-60/1 Berlin West, Box 1, HAT; the flyer is published in English.
71. *Deutsche Industrie Ausstellung Berlin 1951*.
72. Grünbacher provides a good explanation of how the Marshall Plan counterpart funds worked: "The U.S. Government did not give money directly to the participating countries so that they could buy whatever they thought they needed. Instead the U.S. delivered the goods and provided services, mainly transatlantic shipping, to the participating governments, which then sold the commodities to businesses and individuals who had to pay the dollar value of the goods in local currency [counterparts] into so-called ERP Special Accounts that were set up at the country's central bank" ("Cold-War Economics," 698).
73. In the case of Berlin, West German companies and experts had doubts about the high amount of aid provided to the city, because of threats of another Soviet blockade and the high transportation costs to and from the city. Grünbacher, "Cold-War Economics," 710, 714–15.
74. Grünbacher, "Cold-War Economics," 712.
75. Grünbacher, "Cold-War Economics," 709–10.
76. Quoted in *Berlin baut auf—Berlin am Werk!*, 34. The campaign was called "Kauf in Berlin."
77. Although Lufthansa did not fly directly to Berlin, the service was offered on flights to Frankfurt, from which passengers could transfer to a flight to Berlin. "Lufthansa's New Service Aloft," *German Review*, no. 3 (1960): 22–23, HAT.
78. The third photograph does show the face of a flight attendant handing a plate of food to two passengers. The caption promotes the "comfortable seats and attentive service" on board the plane that "enhances the enjoyment of the excellent food."

79. Verkehrsamt Berlin, *Shopping in Berlin* (1960), 11, D060/11/1/45-60/1 Berlin West, Box 1, HAT.
80. *Shopping in Berlin*, 10–11.
81. Glaser, "125 Jahre Berliner Kindl." A wooden beer barrel is depicted because the Berliner Kindl brewery made beer in the pilsner style, invented in the Bohemian city of Pilsen in 1842 using the then ubiquitous wooden oak barrels. Other breweries across Europe and later the United States would follow this method, and it became tradition to use wooden barrels for this style of beer, even when other barrel materials were available, since the use of wood also impacts the flavor of the beer. Many thanks to the woodland ecologist and gastronome Artur Cisar-Erlach, who aided me in finding the background information on the Berliner Kindl brewery and the use of wood for beer barrels.
82. Unfortunately, I was unable to find why he was in prison.
83. Wolfgang Altmann writes that manufactured clothing has its origins in Berlin, and this business used to be dominated by Jewish merchants before the war. The fashion shows in Berlin started again in 1949, and in the mid-1950s manufactured clothing reemerged in Berlin with around 350 firms and 60,000 employees. Till the building of the wall, Berlin would be Germany's strongest production location for clothing ("Spirit of Optimism," 14, 38, 40).
84. Schwarz, *Jet Age Aesthetic*, 14.
85. *Shopping in Berlin*, 36–37; *Berlin baut auf—Berlin am Werk!*, 28–29.
86. "Berlin show case of the Western world," "Berlin" (probably published in 1951), p. 26, D060/11/1/45-60/1 Berlin West, Box 1, HAT; ECA, *City out of Darkness* (1950), Record Group 306, 306.3578, Moving Image Research Center, NARA, College Park, Maryland. *Europe in Color*, 114–15, depicts merchandise in glass cases at the Hardenberger Strasse.
87. Some authors challenge the "shortage paradigm" in the history of the Soviet Union, especially during the early years of the Cold War. See, for instance, Susan Reid's article on the qualitative changes that took place in Soviet popular consumer culture during the 1960s–70s ("Cold War binaries"). Alexey Golubev argues that the study of material conditions in the Soviet Union has to shift its focus away from consumption and the Soviet commodity. By looking at how the material structured the social and how socialist practices of selfhood were object-centered he offers a different perspective (*Things of Life*). Toby Manning criticizes the description of food shortages in East Germany of the 1960s in his discussion of John le Carré's popular novel *The Spy Who Came in from the Cold* ("'Breeze Blocks and Barbed Wire'"). It is also worth noting here that even in the 1980s US soldiers went on extensive shopping tours in East Berlin, which "reached such proportions that a positive image of the US servicemember in East Berlin is threatened" (quoted in Eisenhuth, "Freizeit beim Feind," 21–22).
88. For a useful account of notions of "freedom" under capitalism, see D'Eramo, *Dominio*, 164–65. As Magri also points out, postwar consumerism in Italy "cultivated a new lifestyle tendency already present in the American model, to give the individual priority over the collective, to raise status symbols over real needs," e.g., owning a car instead of decent public transportation (*Tailor of Ulm*, 147–48).
89. This form of capitalism has also been called social market economy or ordoliberalism.
90. Germann, *Unwitting Architect*, 70; see also 68–69.
91. Germann, *Unwitting Architect*, 61, 70; see also 64 on American hegemony.
92. Johnsen, "Development and Financing," 25.
93. *Sight Seeing Tour Berlin*.

94.   Germann, *Unwitting Architect*, 65.

95.   Mandel, "Economics of Neo-capitalism." The low wages in West Germany, Italy, and Japan, in combination with a high export rate, are also shown in a comparative table (also comparing France, the UK, and the United States) in the work of Ludger Lindlar, who writes that the export boom in West Germany can be traced back to the "favorable" development of the wage prices per product and the export prices (*Das mißverstandene Wirtschaftswunder*, 256–57, 283). Similarly, Magri writes about that case of postwar Italy that "the true engine of the 'miracle' . . . lay in . . . a combination of technological leap and very low wages." He continues: "The second and decisive growth factor, however, was the permanent wage freeze and the capacity of the proletariat for both sacrifice and initiative. This aspect of the 'miracle,' though often noted, has not been sufficiently analyzed. . . . But everyone had to pay for accumulation, and the powers-that-be-decided that workers and farmers should be the first to pay and the last to profit" (*Tailor of Ulm*, 142, 144).

96.   ECA, "Labor Information," August 13, 1951, ECA Office U.S. Special Representative in Europe, LI-667, Daniel L. Goldy Papers, Box 54, Harry S. Truman Library, Independence, Missouri.

97.   Germann notes that there "was a slow decline of unemployment" and that "wages did not keep up with productivity gains until the late 1960s." He also points at a secret working paper of Erhard that anticipated that the currency reform of 1948 wiped out the public and private debt of the Nazi era, "sparing property owners and employers, at the expense of workers and savers" (*Unwitting Architect*, 65, 69).

98.   A notable exception, outside the realm of tourism promotion, is the book *A Geography of Europe*, which was written for American students by a European professor teaching and working in both Europe and the United States. First published in 1950, the 1962 edition noted: "The actual 'boom' and prosperity that developed in the late 1950s and early 1960s in West Germany seemed quite miraculous for a county that started reconstruction only fifteen years ago. This prosperity is, of course, only a relative one. The average standard of living remains far below what it is in such countries as the United States, Canada, and Switzerland, or even Great Britain and Sweden. The mass of the labor force receives somewhat less in terms of wages and benefits than in several other European countries, but the West Germans are gradually catching up" (Gottmann, *Geography of Europe*, 445).

99.   Hoffman, "Outline Sales Executives Club of New York," September 13, 1949, Paul G. Hoffman Papers, Box 117, Harry S. Truman Library, Independence, Missouri.

100. Lefebvre, *Production of Space*, 80–81.

101. *Berlin Today*, 3; emphasis added.

102. Hoffman, "Effect of the European Recovery Program," 5.

References

Abelshauser, Werner, *The Dynamics of German Industry: Germany's Path toward the New Economy and the American Challenge*. New York: Berghahn, 2005.

Abelshauser, Werner. *Wirtschaftsgeschischte der Bundesrepublik Deutschland, 1945–1980*. Frankfurt: Suhrkamp, 1983.

Adalet, Begüm. *Hotels and Highways: The Construction of Modernization Theory in Cold War Turkey*. Stanford, CA: Stanford University Press, 2018.

Altmann, Wolfgang. "A Spirit of Optimism." In *German Fashion Design (1946–2012)*, edited by Nadine Barth, 14–41. Berlin: Distanz, 2011.

Baars, Grietje. "Capitalism's Victor's Justice? The Hidden Stories Behind the Prosecution of Industrialists Post-WWII." In *The Hidden Histories of War Crimes Trials*, edited by K. J. Heller and G. Simpson, 163–92. Oxford: Oxford University Press, 2013.

Baldwin, Kate A. *The Racial Imaginary of the Cold War Kitchen: From Sokol'niki Park to Chicago's South Side*. Hanover, NH: Dartmouth College Press, 2016.

Baranowski, Shelley, Lisa Pinley Covert, Bertram M. Gordon, Richard Ivan Jobs, Christian Noack, Adam T. Rosenbaum, and Blake C. Scott. "Discussion: Tourism and Diplomacy." *Journal of Tourism History* 11, no. 1 (2019): 63–90.

Barsness, Edward E. *Europe Calling: A Minnesota Newspaperman's New Adventures in the Old World*. New York: Exposition Press, 1959.

Beckman, Ericka. *Capital Fictions: The Literature of Latin America's Export Age*. Minneapolis: University of Minnesota Press, 2013.

Benjamin, Walter. *The Arcades Project*. Translated by Howard Eiland and Kevin McLaughlin, 1982. Cambridge, MA: Belknap Press of Harvard University Press, 2002.

Bernhauer, Ernst. *1902–1972 Deutscher Fremdenverkehrsverband (DFV)*. Bonn: Boldt, 1972.

Bischof, Gunter, and Hans Petschar. *The Marshall Plan: Saving Europe, Rebuilding Austria*. New Orleans: University of New Orleans Press, 2017.

Bucerius, Gerd. "Berlin: The Largest Industrial City in Germany." In *Berlin at the Crossroads of Europe, at the Crossroads of the World*, edited by Ernst Lemmer, 38–45. Berlin: Haupt & Puttkammer, 1960.

Committee for Economic Development. *Monetary and Fiscal Policy for Greater Economic Stability*. New York: Committee for Economic Development, 1948.

Davidson, Robert A. *The Hotel: Occupied Space*. Toronto: University of Toronto Press, 2018.

D'Eramo, Marco. *Dominio: La guerra invisibile dei potenti contro i sudditi*. Milan: Feltrinelli, 2020.

D'Eramo, Marco. "La fogna più bella della Terra." In *Il selfie del mondo: Indagine sull'età del turismo*, 27–37. Milan: Feltrinelli, 2017.

Deutsche Industrieausstellung. *Amerika zu Hause: Zur Erinnerung an die Deutsche Industrieausstellung Berlin 1950, 1–15 Oktober*. Berlin: Deutsche Industrieausstellung, 1950.

Die Nichtlandwirtschaftlichen Arbeitsstätten in der Bundesrepublik Deutschland nach der Zählung vom 13.9.1950, vol. 1. Statistik der Bundesrepublik Deutschland. Stuttgart-Köln: W. Kohlhammer, 1952.

Eckert, Astrid M. "Greetings from the Zonal Border: Tourism to the Iron Curtain." In *West Germany and the Iron Curtain: Environment, Economy, and Culture in the Borderlands*, 85–123. Oxford: Oxford University Press, 2019.

Eisenhuth, Stefanie. *Die Schutzmacht: Die Amerikaner in Berlin 1945–1994*. Göttingen: Wallstein, 2018.

Eisenhuth, Stefanie. "Freizeit beim Feind: US-amerikanische Soldaten in Ost-Berlin." *Zeithistorische Forschungen / Studies in Contemporary History* 15 (2018): 11–39.

Eisenhuth, Stefanie, and Scott H. Krause. "Inventing the 'Outpost of Freedom': Transatlantic Narratives and the Historical Actors Crafting West Berlin's Postwar Political Culture." *Zeithistorische Forschungen / Studies in Contemporary History* 11 (2014): 188–211.

Ellwood, David W. *Rebuilding Europe: Western Europe, America, and the Postwar Reconstruction*. London: Longman, 1992.

Endy, Christopher. *Cold War Holidays: American Tourism in France*. Chapel Hill: University of North Carolina Press, 2004.

Europe in Color. Philadelphia: Curtis Publishing Company, 1957.

Fielding, Temple. *Fielding's Travel Guide to Europe*. New York: William Sloane Associates, Inc., 1952.

Fielding, Temple. *Fielding's Travel Guide to Europe, 1953–54 Edition*. New York: William Sloane Associates, Inc., 1953.

Föllmer, Moritz. "Anti-totalitarianism, Domesticity, and Ambivalent Modernity." In *Individuality and Modernity in Berlin: Self and Society from Weimar to the Wall*, 240–94. Cambridge: Cambridge University Press, 2013.

Garth, S. H., and W. I. Kaufman. *Cook's Pocket Travel Guide to Europe*. New York: Pocket Books Inc., 1963.

German Review. "Berlin Is Worth a Voyage." No. 2 (1956): 38.

Germann, Julian. *Unwitting Architect: German Primacy and the Origins of Neoliberalism*. Stanford, CA: Stanford University Press, 2021.

Gimbel, John. *Science, Technology, and Reparations: Exploitation and Plunder in Postwar Germany*. Stanford, CA: Stanford University Press, 1990.

Glaser, Willi. "125 Jahre Berliner Kindl." *Berlinische Monatschrift*, no. 4 (1997): 84–89.

Glossner, Christian. *The Making of the German Post-war Economy: Political Communication and Public Reception of the Social Market Economy after World War II*. London: I. B. Tauris, 2010.

Golubev, Alexey. *The Things of Life: Materiality in Late Soviet Russia*. Ithaca, NY: Cornell University Press, 2020.

Görlich, Christopher. "Berlin, die geteilte Stadt: Ein Topos in deutschen Reiseführern des 20. Jahrhunderts." *Zeithistorische Forschungen / Studies in Contemporary History* 4 (2007): 408–21.

Gottmann, Jean. *A Geography of Europe*. New York: Holt, Rinehart and Winston, 1962.

Groebner, Valentin. *Retroland: Geschichtstourismus und die Sehnsucht nach dem Authentischen*. Frankfurt am Main: S. Fischer, 2018.

Groß, Robert, Martin Knoll, and Katharina Scharf, eds. *Transformative Recovery? The European Recovery Program (ERP)/Marshall Plan in European Tourism*. Innsbruck: Innsbruck University Press, 2020.

Grünbacher, Armin. "Cold-War Economics: The Use of Marshall Plan Counterpart Funds in Germany, 1948–1960." *Central European History* 45, no. 4 (2012): 697–716.

Grünbacher, Armin. *West German Industrialists and the Making of the Economic Miracle*. London: Bloomsbury, 2017.

Hardach, Gerd. *Der Marshall-Plan: Auslandhilfe und Wiederaufbau in Westdeutschland 1948–1952*. Munich: Deutscher Taschenbuch, 1994.

Harrity, Richard. *Fun in Europe: The Cosmopolitan Traveler's Grand Tour of the Continent*. New York: Duell, Sloan and Pearce, 1959.

Harvey, David. "Value in Motion." *New Left Review*, no. 126 (2020): 99–116.

Hesse, Jan-Otmar. "Fact or Fiction? Complexities of Economic Inequality in Twentieth-Century Germany." In *The Contradictions of Capital in the Twentieth-First Century: The Piketty Opportunity*, edited by Pat Hudson and Keith Tribe, 87–108. Newcastle upon Tyne: Agenda, 2016.

Hitchcock, William I. "The Marshall Plan and the Creation of the West." In *The Cambridge History of the Cold War*, edited by Melvyn P. Leffler and Odd Arne Westad, vol. 1, 154–74. Cambridge: Cambridge University Press, 2010.

Hobsbawm, Eric. *The Age of Extremes: A History of the World, 1914–1991*. New York: Vintage Books, 1996.

Hoffman, Paul. "Effect of the European Recovery Program on Marketing Management." In *Economic Factors in Market Planning*, Marketing Series Number 77, 3–9. New York: American Management Association, 1949.

Jackson, Patrick Thaddeus. *Civilizing the Enemy: German Reconstruction and the Invention of the West*. Ann Arbor: University of Michigan Press, 2006.

James, Kevin J. *Histories, Meanings, and Representations of the Modern Hotel*. Bristol: Channel View Publications, 2018.

Jarausch, Konrad H., Stefanie Eisenhuth, and Scott H. Krause, eds. *Cold War Berlin: Confrontations, Cultures, and Identities*. London: Bloomsbury, 2022.

Johnsen, Horst Ruediger. "Development and Financing of the German Hospitality Industry." Master's thesis, Cornell University, 1985.

Kaur, Ravinder. *Brand New Nation: Capitalist Dreams and Nationalist Designs in Twenty-First-Century India*. Stanford, CA: Stanford University Press, 2020.

Kellermann, Heinz H. "The Future Berlin." *German Review*, no. 1 (1957): 25–29.

Ku'damm No. 27. Munich: Maria Faber; Kempinski Hotel Bristol Berlin [1998].

Langer, Alexander. "The Hotel on the Hill: Hilton Hotel's Unofficial Embassy in Rome." *Diplomatic History* 46, no. 2 (2022): 375–96.

Lefebvre, Henri. *The Production of Space*. Translated by Donald Nicholson-Smith. Oxford: Blackwell Publishing, 1999.

Lehmann, Axel. *Der Marshall-Plan und das Neue Deutschland: Die Folgen amerikanischer Besatzungspolitik in den Westzonen*. Münster: Waxmann, 2000.

Lindlar, Ludger. *Das mißverstandene Wirtschaftswunder: Westdeutschland und die westeuropäische Nachkriegsprosperität*. Tübingen: Mohr Siebeck, 1997.

Lukács, Georg. "Reification and the Consciousness of the Proletariat." In *History and Class Consciousness*, translated by Rodney Livingstone, 83–222. Cambridge, MA: MIT Press, 1971.

Magri, Lucio. *The Tailor of Ulm: Communism in the Twentieth Century*. Translated by P. Camiller. London: Verso, 2011.

Mandel, Ernest. "The Economics of Neo-Capitalism." *Socialist Register* 1 (1964): 56–67.

Manning, Toby. "'Breeze Blocks and Barbed Wire': The Berlin Wall and *The Spy Who Came in From the Cold*." In *John le Carré and the Cold War*, 51–74. London: Bloomsbury, 2018.

Marx, Karl. *Capital Volume I*, 1867. London: Penguin Classics, 1990.

Milward, Alain S. *The Reconstruction of Western Europe, 1945–51*. Berkeley: University of California Press, 1984.

Mitchell, Timothy. *Colonising Egypt*. Berkeley: University of California Press, 1988.

Molella, Arthur P., and Scott Gabriel Knowles. *World's Fairs in the Cold War: Science, Technology, and the Culture of Progress*. Pittsburgh: University of Pittsburgh Press, 2019.

Oldenziel, Ruth, and Karin Zachmann, eds. *Cold War Kitchen: Americanization, Technology and European Users*. Cambridge, MA: MIT Press, 2009.

Poock-Feller, Ulrika. "Berlin lebt—Berlin ruft: Die Fremdenverkehrswerbung Ost- und West-Berlins in der Nachkriegszeit." In *Goldstrand und Teutonengrill: Kultur- und Sozialgeschichte des Tourismus in Deutschland 1945 bis 1989*, edited by Hasso Spode, 104–16. Berlin: Werner Moser, 1996.

Randall, Clarence B. *International Travel: Message from the President of the United States Transmitting a Report on the Barriers to International Travel and Ways and Means of*

Promoting, Developing, Encouraging, and Facilitating such Travel. Washington, DC: Government Printing Office, 1958.

Raphael, Lutz. *Jenseits von Kohle und Stahl: Eine Gesellschaftsgeschichte Westeuropas nach dem Boom*. Berlin: Suhrkamp, 2019.

Reid, Susan E. "Cold War Binaries and the Culture of Consumption in the Late Soviet Home." *Journal of Historical Research in Marketing* 8, no. 1 (2016): 17–43.

Ross, Kristin. *Fast Cars, Clean Bodies: Decolonization and the Reordering of French Culture*. Cambridge, MA: MIT Press, 1995.

Schneider, Wolfgang. *The Marshall Plan and the Dismantling of Industries in Western Germany*. Frankfurt am Main: Kommentator-Verlag/Kurt Allmayer, 1949.

Scholz, Natalie. "Miraculous Objects: The Volkswagen as Imperial Debris." In *Redeeming Objects: A West German Mythology*, 69–114. Madison: University of Wisconsin Press, 2023.

Schwarz, Vanessa R. *Jet Age Aesthetic: The Glamour of Media in Motion*. New Haven, CT: Yale University Press, 2020.

Sedlmaier, Alexander. "Berlin als doppeltes 'Schaufenster' im Kalten Krieg." In *Selling Berlin: Imagebildung und Stadtmarketing von der preußischen Hauptstadt bis zur Bundeshauptstadt*, edited by Thomas Biskup and Marc Schalenberg, 227–44. Stuttgart: Franz Steiner, 2008.

Spicka, Mark E. *Selling the Economic Miracle: Economic Reconstruction and Politics in West Germany, 1947–1957*. New York: Berghahn, 2007.

Standley, Michelle A. "Experiencing Communism, Bolstering Capitalism: Guided Bus Tours of 1970s East Berlin." In *Tourism and Travel during the Cold War: Negotiating Tourist Experiences across the Iron Curtain*, edited by Sune Bechmann Pedersen and Christian Noack, 61–76. London: Routledge, 2020.

Standley, Michelle A. "From Bulwark of Freedom to Cosmopolitan Cocktails: The Cold War, Mass Tourism, and the Marketing of West Berlin as a Tourist Destination." In *Divided, but Not Disconnected: German Experiences of the Cold War*, edited by Tobias Hochscherf, Christoph Laucht, and Andrew Plowman, 105–18. New York: Berghahn, 2010.

Steil, Benn. *The Marshall Plan: Dawn of the Cold War*. New York: Simon and Schuster, 2018.

Stivers, William, and Donald A. Carter. *The City Becomes a Symbol: The U.S. Army in the Occupation of Berlin, 1945–1949*. Washington, DC: Center of Military History, 2017.

Travel Restrictions: Hearings before a Subcommittee on the Committee on Interstate and Foreign Commerce United States Senate on S. Res. 111. Washington, DC: Government Printing Office, 1947.

Tuma, Robert A. "Cosmopolitan Berlin." *German Review*, no. 3 (1955): 3–8.

Verkehrsamt Berlin. *Berlin Today*. Berlin: Brüder Hartman, 1957.

Wagner-Conzelmann, Sandra. *Die Interbau 1957 in Berlin: Stadt von Heute—Stadt von Morgen*. Petersberg: Michael Imhof, 2007.

Warnke, Stephanie. "Mit dem Baedeker nach Ost-Berlin? Baustellen-Tourismus im Kalten Krieg." In *Selling Berlin: Imagebildung und Stadtmarketing von der preußischen Hauptstadt bis zur Bundeshauptstadt*, edited by Thomas Biskup and Marc Schalenberg, 211–26. Stuttgart: Franz Steiner, 2008.

Warnke, Stephanie. *Stein gegen Stein: Architektur und Medien im geteilten Berlin, 1950–1970*. Frankfurt: Campus, 2009.

Wharton, Annabel Jane. *Building the Cold War: Hilton International Hotels and Modern Architecture*. Chicago: University of Chicago Press, 2001.

Wiesen, S. Jonathan. "Miracles for Sale: Consumer Displays and Advertising in Postwar West Germany." In *Consuming Germany in the Cold War*, edited by David F. Crew, 151–78. Oxford: Berg, 2003.

Wilde, Alexander. "Zwischen Zusammenbruch und Währungsreform: Fremdenverkehr in den westlichen Besatzungszonen." In *Goldstrand und Teutonengrill: Kultur- und Sozialgeschichte des Tourismus in Deutschland 1945 bis 1989*, edited by Hasso Spode, 87–103. Berlin: Werner Moser, 1996.

Williams, Raymond. "Advertising: The Magic System." In *Culture and Materialism*, 190–219. London: Verso, 2020.

Wolff, Ilse. "Berliner Fremdenverkehrsprobleme nach 1945." *Jahrbuch für Fremdenverkehr*, no. 2 (1958): 10–16.

Wolff, Ilse. "Communication Center Berlin—Yesterday, Today, and Tomorrow." In *Berlin at the Crossroads of Europe, at the Crossroads of the World*, edited by Ernst Lemmer, 166–74. Berlin: Haupt & Puttkammer, 1960.

Toward a Soviet Future?

Anticolonial Communism in Syria and Lebanon

Ellis Garey

In 1928 Fu'ad al-Shamali, a tobacco worker born in Ottoman Mount Lebanon and cofounder and general secretary of the Communist Party of Syria and Lebanon (CPSL), traveled to Moscow as a delegate to the Sixth Comintern Congress.[1] He had just been released from prison for participating in the 1925–27 anticolonial Syrian Revolt against French colonial rule. Four years later he published an account of the trip under the title *Madha Ra'aytu fi Moscow* (*What I Saw in Moscow*) in the satirical socialist newspaper *al-Sahafi al-Ta'ih* (*The Errant Journalist*).[2] *What I Saw in Moscow* is unique in form and content. Written for an audience assumed to be at minimum ignorant of and more likely antagonistic toward the politics and lived realities of the Soviet Union, it is split between his own experience in 1928 and a fictionalized journey a bourgeois tourist named "Henry" takes to Moscow. Through the blending of fictional narrative and documentary reportage, al-Shamali attempts to bring his readers closer to a Soviet future. His trip to Moscow was undertaken clandestinely from Lebanon against the dictates of the French mandatory administration, which denied his request for a passport. His published reflections on the trip are virtually absent from the historiography on Arab communism and Arab communist engagement with the Soviet Union. This absence is curious, given that al-Shamali's account is likely the earliest published account of an Arab communist's trip to the Soviet Union.[3]

In this article, I provide a close examination and contextualization of al-Shamali's text. Rather than presenting *What I Saw in Moscow* as emblematic of

Radical History Review
Issue 151 (January 2025)   DOI 10.1215/01636545-11506805
© 2025 by MARHO: The Radical Historians' Organization, Inc.

early communist politics in Syria and Lebanon, I propose that its existence and contradictions help elucidate the complicated position anticolonial communists occupied in relation to the Soviet Union in the interwar period. The argument of this article is twofold and builds on recent interventions in the history of Arab communism.[4] First, I argue that the ideological and political development of communists in interwar Syria and Lebanon was profoundly shaped by local conditions, and in particular by the struggle against colonialism, rather than by the Soviet-led Communist International's (Comintern) dictates. Second, I show that the Soviet Union's perceived economic miracle did shape early communist political imaginaries, and that transregional communist infrastructure was central to this process. I see this imaginary as part of a broader set of what Manu Goswami has termed "colonial internationalism" which "improvised a distinct future-oriented politics" in the interwar period.[5]

In both the experiential and fictionalized sections of *What I Saw in Moscow*, al-Shamali presents social life in the Soviet Union as egalitarian and classless, particularly in comparison to French-ruled Lebanon and Syria. In his account, the transformation of Soviet society is largely portrayed in terms of social changes. Yet the underlying proposition in *What I Saw in Moscow* is that this social equality was made possible by the Bolshevik Revolution and the economic miracle it represented. Al-Shamali demonstrates this through anecdotes that portray social positions that are typically unequal or oppositional in a noncommunist society—for example man and woman, aristocrat and peasant, military general and common soldier—as equal in the Soviet Union. He makes explicit reference to the Bolshevik Revolution as a total rupture in Russian society in which workers revolted against capitalists, peasants revolted against feudal lords and usurers, and the people shook off the aristocracy. He also makes passing reference to changes instituted under the New Economic Policy, including currency reform and the use of the gold standard.[6] Yet, rather than focusing on the mechanics of what he sees as the economic miracle ushered in by this rupture, he highlights the transformation in social life that it made possible. In conversations with a range of people living in the Soviet Union, al-Shamali underlines how this equality was unimaginable for someone coming from a "bourgeois" country—especially one suffering under colonial control and what he identifies as the local cultural conservatism responsible for perpetuating capitalist alienation and oppressive gender relations in Syria and Lebanon. Throughout *What I Saw in Moscow*, al-Shamali indicates that Syrian and Lebanese attitudes toward the Soviet Union in the interwar period were ambivalent, misguided, or hostile.

In the first section, I give a brief overview of the emergence of communist politics in Lebanon and Syria. The second section details Lebanese and Syrian communists' participation in and subsequent imprisonment during the 1925–27 anticolonial Syrian Revolt against French colonial rule. The third and final section provides a close reading of *What I Saw in Moscow,* situating al-Shamali's perspectives on Soviet life—and particularly on gender, internationalism, and class in the Soviet Union—in their broader contexts. I ultimately read al-Shamali's utopian representations of social relations in the Soviet Union as both an attempt to counter the colonialist propaganda widespread in French Mandate Syria and Lebanon at the time, and as a genuine expression of an optimistic orientation toward the transformative capacity of communism in the wake of a crushed anticolonial revolt. In doing so, I propose that al-Shamali's text offers new ways of understanding the role of the Soviet Union in the political orientation of anticolonial interwar communists.

The Emergence of Communist Politics in Lebanon and Syria

The emergence of communism in the Global South was long depicted as an essentially imported phenomenon. Communist parties in the interwar period, in turn, were often understood as simply following the dictates of the Soviet Comintern. Recent interventions have contested this by demonstrating that the relationship between the Soviet Union and communists in the Middle East was not unilinear, and by reframing communism in the Middle East as a response to local conditions including anticolonial struggle.[7] Building on these interventions, this section attends to the transregional roots and composition of early communist politics in Syria and Lebanon. By focusing on the biography of Fu'ad al-Shamali, I show how communism as a personal political orientation and communist parties as political organizations were imaginable and possible only in the context of social transformations and transregional political networks that predated the Bolshevik Revolution, even if communist parties did not emerge until the post–World War I period.

From Alexandria to Beirut: Transregional Communism

On January 9, 1923, Fu'ad al-Shamali published a letter to the editor of the Cairo daily newspaper *al-Ahram.* He ended the letter with the following: "My last word goes to the socialist leaders [*zu'ama' al-ishtirakiyya*] of Egypt: Leave the workers to take control of their affairs, because socialism is from the workers, to the workers, and of the workers—not the traders, the landowners, or the lawyers."[8] The letter emerged out of a dispute within the Communist Party of Egypt, but it speaks to two important dimensions of communist politics in the interwar Eastern Mediterranean. First, communist politics often spread through the physical movement and migration patterns of communist organizers. Beginning in the mid-nineteenth century, the Ottoman state began to undertake a variety of infrastructural projects, including port expansion and railway construction, aimed at centralizing state control and encouraging capital investment. These projects often required hundreds to thousands of workers, many of whom migrated from rural areas—where successive debt crises made it harder for peasants to sustain themselves—to cities, particularly port cities, where the majority of the projects took place. Other regional industries, such as silk and tobacco production, were also industrialized in the mid-nineteenth century as some aspects of home production transitioned to factory production.[9] While forms of socialist thought circulated in reformist intellectual circles around this period, it was in industrialized workplaces that many Ottoman workers were first exposed to socialist and anarchist ideas.[10]

Al-Shamali's own trajectory maps closely onto this. Born in Ottoman Lebanon in 1894, he moved to Cairo around 1910 in search of work.[11] By the age of eighteen, al-Shamali had worked in cigarette factories in both Cairo and Alexandria. It was in Alexandria that he was first exposed to both trade unionism and communism. Alexandria in the early twentieth century was known for its migrants, many of whom had emigrated from southern Europe in search of work, and some of whom had multigenerational attachments to anarchism, communism, and socialism. He joined the Egyptian Socialist Party soon after it was founded in 1921 and took on a leadership position in the party shortly thereafter. The following year, al-Shamali cofounded the Party of Lebanese Workers in Egypt, which advocated for better working conditions for migrant Lebanese workers and for an independent Lebanon.[12] For reasons that remain contested, al-Shamali returned to what had become the French-ruled mandates of Lebanon and Syria in 1923. It was at the port of Beirut, upon his ship's arrival from Egypt, that al-Shamali first encountered the socialist intellectual Yusuf Yazbik. Yazbik was working as a translator and secretary in the immigration control department at the port and was responsible for registering the names of departing and arriving passengers.[13] Yazbik's recollections, written decades later, note that he recognized al-Shamali's name from an Arabic daily periodical that had published news of the expulsion of a Bolshevik organizer.

The second dimension of communist politics in the Eastern Mediterranean that al-Shamali's letter to the editor in *al-Ahram* highlights is the tension over the question of the role of workers and worker organizing. Should communists focus on labor organizing or on communist propagandizing more broadly? This was a question that dominated communist debates in the interwar period. For al-Shamali, the answer was clear: he supported a worker-centric communist politics. This ideological commitment emerged out of his experience of being organized into the Communist Party of Egypt via tobacco workers' unions, which led him to an absolute commitment to the power of trade unionism. Indeed, both in al-Shamali's political pamphlets printed during his time as an organizer and in his memoir and autobiographical works published after his expulsion from the CPSL, his articulation of communism is tied solely to his experience as a worker.[14] With the exception of the Soviet political figures he encounters in Moscow, he does not mention communist or Marxist theorists in his writings. According to his opponents, this commitment superseded his commitment to communist revolution itself.[15] In practice, this worker-centrism meant that during the period of his leadership in the various iterations of the Communist Party in Syria and Lebanon, a central focus was the establishment and organizing of labor unions.

According to al-Shamali, he began to organize communist cells across the branches of a tobacco workers' union he had founded in 1924. Around this time, Yazbik wrote a eulogy for the French socialist Anatole France.[16] The eulogy caught the attention of Joseph Berger, a prominent Comintern activist and a Jewish leader of the Palestine Communist Party (PCP). At that time, Berger was in charge of the PCP's relationship with the Comintern.[17] According to Yazbik, Berger traveled to Beirut and contacted him under the pretense that he was a Polish journalist curious about the article. The two set up a meeting in which Berger questioned him about his political beliefs. In addition to inquiring about Yazbik's own relationship to socialism, Berger asked if Yazbik had any other socialist contacts in Lebanon. Yazbik introduced Berger to al-Shamali and invited him to join them for a founding meeting for a Communist Party. While al-Shamali informed them that he had already begun organizing workers into communist cells, he was compelled to come to this new founding Communist Party meeting. According to both Yazbik and al-Shamali, Berger was not interested in al-Shamali's experience and efforts. Nonetheless, al-Shamali joined the party, first named the Lebanese People's Party (LPP), and attempted to gear the party's focus toward organizing workers in Lebanon and Syria.

On May 1, 1925, the LPP held its first May Day celebration. That May Day, an Armenian communist organization in Beirut, Spartak, officially merged with the nascent LPP. Spartak itself was a product of transregional radical networks and the migration, forced and voluntary, of individual communist organizers, including Artin Madoyan, an Armenian born to a shoemaker in Adana in 1904.[18] Unaware of any other communist organization in Beirut, Madoyan and his fellow Spartak members had made contact with the Central Committee of the Communist Party of Armenia in early January 1925 to express their intention to follow Comintern policy. At this point they had already been in touch with the French Communist Party.[19]

French intelligence reports reveal that the French mandatory state deeply feared the potential spread of communism. While sometimes these fears were paranoid, the state did rightly understand that it was transregional communist networks and contacts that facilitated the spread of communist politics. Since the early 1920s, French colonial authorities had been undertaking investigations into the cross-border movement of Communist Party organizers. Of particular concern to the mandatory Intelligence Service was the potential infiltration of communists or communist propaganda from Palestine, about which French authorities maintained regular contact with British authorities, as well as from Adana and Cilicia, from which French troops had only withdrawn in 1922 as they were incorporated into the new Republic of Turkey. French colonial authorities closely surveilled Comintern organizers known to reside in Palestine, Adana, and Cilicia, regularly compiling lists of organizers and their contacts.[20] Cross-border movement became all the more significant during the 1925–27 Syrian Revolt against French colonial rule.

Communists in the 1925–27 Syrian Revolt

The policy of military occupation, of the exploitation and provocation of the population of Syria, which characterises the methods of French imperialism in the colonies, aims at actually annexing Syria to France and maintaining a firm hold on the positions held by French imperialism in the East of the Mediterranean. This policy of enslavement has driven the masses in Syria who had already pronounced themselves in favour of independence, to resort to arms in order to free themselves from French oppression.

Down with the colonial mandates! Down with the League of Nations! Down with French and English imperialism! Long live Syria's independence! Long live the alliance of the international proletariat with the victims of oppression in the colonies![21]

This was the resolution of the Interparliamentarian Communist Conference that met in Brussels on November 10–12, 1925, printed in that week's *International Press Correspondence* (known as *Inprecor*), a Comintern publication aimed at circulating news of communists and communist parties globally. It characterizes Comintern propaganda in the interwar period, which was constantly inflected with support for anticolonial struggles. But what was the anticolonial struggle to which the Comintern was responding, and how did news of it reach Comintern militants outside Syria?

In July 1925, Druze farmers shot down a French surveillance plane in Jabal Hawran.[22] Soon, Sultan al-Atrash, who had led a revolt against French colonial rule in 1922, assembled guerrilla forces that managed to temporarily exert control over the countryside of Jabal Hawran. The Syrian Revolt of 1925–27 had begun, and it quickly struck a chord in other rural areas and urban centers of Syria and Lebanon.[23] When the revolt broke out in July 1925, communist party members were quick to support it and join. French intelligence reports detail frequent encounters with communist flyers supporting the revolt pasted around Beirut, Damascus, and Tyre in particular. Communist posters implored Syrian workers and peasants to support the revolt. By the winter of 1925, French colonial authorities began to arrest communist party organizers in Syria and Lebanon for their participation in the Syrian Revolt.

Recent scholarly interventions have highlighted how communist participation in the Syrian Revolt was formative for the emergence of anticolonial communist politics there, and how these revolts contributed to anti-militarist and anti-imperial communist politics outside of Lebanon and Syria.[24] I am interested in bringing these twin insights together. This section considers how transregional communist networks allowed for the circulation of anticolonial and communist propaganda to, from, and within Greater Syria over the course of the revolt. I pay particular attention to the role of imprisoned Lebanese and Syrian communists in these networks. Communist networks uniquely facilitated the spread of news on the Syrian Revolt outside Syria, and perhaps most important, to France, which in turn promoted the continuation of anticolonialism as a key tenet of interwar communism internationally.

"It should be noted that the prisoners drew the Soviet arms [hammer and sickle]." Thus commented French Colonel Pichot-Duclos on his inspection of a group of stone houses used to detain political prisoners over the course of the Syrian Revolt in the town of Qadmous.[25] Fu'ad al-Shamali was the first communist to be arrested for his involvement in the revolt in December 1925. French occupation forces sent al-Shamali to Arwad, an island off the coast of Syria, that the French Mandate used for the imprisonment of political prisoners during the revolt. Over the next several months, nearly all prominent CPSL organizers were arrested and sent to one of three places. Arwad was the most common location, but some imprisoned communists were sent to the northern Syrian town of Qadmous, and still others were put into forced residence in rural areas throughout Greater Syria. In the case of forced residence, French colonial authorities seem to have generally placed political prisoners in regions where they were socially disconnected from the other inhabitants. Conditions were dire, with prisoners lacking basic necessities including food, clean water, and heat.[26] Seized communist letters also indicate that French prison guards often relied on extreme violence when interrogating prisoners; in one case, two Armenian children (aged fifteen) were beaten so brutally for distributing anti-French materials and refusing to admit communist ties that one went deaf.[27]

Not long after their imprisonment, seven of the communist prisoners went on a hunger strike to protest conditions on Arwad; Fu'ad al-Shamali's brother Nasim was among the strikers. In a seized letter that Nasim attempted to send to their brother Najib in Cairo, he implores him not to send money for medication or medical treatment. Nasim explains that the prison authorities have made clear that they will forcefully intervene medically if necessary, though he states: "I prefer death, which would place the responsibility on those who oppress me and deprive me of my rights."[28]

While imprisoned, communists relied heavily on print media to circulate ideas within and outside the prison walls. Prison authorities regularly seized communist literature sent from abroad to various imprisoned communists. Most commonly seized were issues of *Inprecor*. But imprisoned communists also attempted to write and circulate their own print materials. In September 1927, the prison inspector at Qadmous alerted the central Intelligence Service that imprisoned communists had created a journal titled *La nouvelle Bastille* (The New Bastille) apparently dedicated to literature, humor, and history.[29] Fu'ad al-Shamali, his brother Nasim al-Shamali, Zohran Ghorayeb, Muhi al-Din Kaissa, and Artin Madoyan were identified as responsible for *La nouvelle Bastille* by fellow prisoners, who informed prison authorities of the journal. The group behind *La nouvelle Bastille* intended to circulate it to fellow prisoners weekly. The copy of the journal seized by prison authorities seems to have been a ten-page notebook. According to Jacques Couland, an August edition of *La nouvelle Bastille*, which featured articles in Armenian and Arabic, did manage to circulate in the town of Qadmous and was the subject of police investigations.[30]

Communist activity outside prison and forced exile lessened over the course of the revolt due to fact that the majority of communists in Syria were imprisoned, but it did not stop completely. This is evident in the number of communist tracts reported by police and French intelligence in cities like Beirut, Damascus, and Tyre over the course of the revolt, and it is further detailed in an intercepted August 1926 letter from a communist organizer in Beirut intended for a communist organizer in Palestine. In the letter, the organizer, whose code name is Negib Fayez, first reports on the imprisonment of Nasim al-Shamali, Zohran Ghorayeb, and Georges Azar, all of whom had been recently deported to the island of Arwad. He notes that communists in Syria were attempting to assist them materially and urged the letter's recipient to do the same. The letter also provides a report on communist attempts to organize workers during the revolt; this was successful in some cases, including their encouragement and support of a tramway workers' strike in July 1926, and less successful in others, such as an attempt to organize watchmakers into a union.

The most valuable insights of the letter are perhaps Fayez's description of a day in the life of a communist in August 1926 Beirut. After noting that his main day-to-day efforts were focused on organizing workers into unions, he described a typical day as follows:

Here's how I proceed: I first talk with a few workers, those who are the easiest to win over. When I see them again, I invite them to drink with me at the café, and I repeat this invitation several times. I propagandize for an hour in the morning, before going to work. After lunch, I give free Arabic lessons to Armenian workers, because I intend to organize a "nucleus" in this *milieu* where the spirit of anarchy prevails. In the evening, I leave work after 7 o'clock and visit some friends. From 10 p.m. to midnight, I study literary Arabic.[31]

There are several noteworthy aspects of his description. First, the attempt to form communist nuclei in workplaces was a central early communist strategy. Second, and related, his day-to-day activity during the revolt was focused on organizing workers and not taking part in anticolonial activities as such. Third, the letter's emphasis on Arabic as a practical tool of communist organizing and also as an intellectual pursuit—here evident in his provision of Arabic lessons to Armenian workers and his study of literary Arabic, but elsewhere in the letter demonstrated through his lack of interest in learning French—calls into question the notion that Communist Party intellectual activities in the period were all westward facing.

Fayez goes on to provide an account of the logistical undertaking of distributing communist literature. He notes that he found it most useful to either spread boxes containing leaflets throughout the city, or to post flyers and tracts directly on walls. In both cases, he explains that he did so after midnight, with the help of unemployed workers, when the electricity was off and the chances of being caught were lower.

Communist networks also allowed for anticolonial propaganda to be printed outside Lebanon and Syria and sent back. One example of this is a tract calling on French soldiers to refuse to join the fight in Syria, to lay down their weapons, and to recognize that their interests—as members of the working class—aligned with those revolting. The tract reads, in part:

And why all this? Because the French bankers want to see the privileges they have on Syrian soil continue, because the French bourgeoisie wants to seize the wealth of Syria; she wants to steal it, loot it, exploit, silence the Syrian people . . .
    In the struggle between French imperialism and the working populations of Syria, young workers and young peasant soldiers, stand alongside the Syrian workers![32]

Outlining an anticolonial communist position, the tract draws a clear connection between French capitalism at home and French colonial rule abroad. The producers of this tract relied on transregional communist connections to send it to Syria: it was printed by the French Communist Party, sent to the Palestine Communist Party for distribution, and then smuggled into Syria for additional distribution there.

Imprisoned Syrian and Lebanese communists also managed to use international communist networks to transmit local information on the Syrian Revolt and distribute calls for help and solidarity to audiences abroad. An appeal by four communists in a 1926 issue of *Secours Rouge* (a publication of the French section of International Red Aid) speaks to this.[33] The communists Artin Madoyan, Boyadjian, Bardizbanian, and Kh. Papazian spoke to their conditions in forced residence in the desert of Rakka. The appeal came at the height of the Syrian Revolt and was directed toward French communists. They explained that after being imprisoned for five months at Qadmous, they were sent on an arduous thirteen-day trip to Rakka for forced residence. While the prison authorities had promised them material support, they were given none and were thus forced to spend money from their own pockets with no hope of securing jobs in Rakka. They conclude the letter with a direct appeal to the French comrades: "Comrades, without exaggerating, we are starving. We are now in economic prison which is much harder. If you don't send help immediately, we will starve. Imagine, comrades, while we write this letter, that we are already hungry. And if we can't borrow six dollars now, we will have to go into debt to send the letter. We have no other words. Our final appeal is: help, comrades!" The letter is accompanied by a photo of the four imprisoned communists. The copy of *Secours Rouge* in which the letter is featured was included among other communist publications seized by French mandatory prison authorities, which had been sent from abroad to imprisoned communists in Greater Syria. CPSL members resumed party activities immediately following their release from Arwad in January 1928.[34]

Communist Internationalism and the Sixth Comintern Congress

If it is clear that anticolonial struggle in Syria impacted the contours of communist politics, what can be said about the role of the Soviet Union in shaping the political imaginary of anticolonial communists in Syria in this period? In this section, I examine al-Shamali's focus on, and depictions of, gender, internationalism, and class in the Soviet Union through a close reading of his serialized account of his trip to Moscow, *What I Saw in Moscow.*

 What I Saw in Moscow is subdivided into twelve sections, half of which focus on al-Shamali's lived experience in Moscow and the Sixth Comintern Congress itself. The other half of the series focuses on the status of women and gender relations in the Soviet Union, with an emphasis on love, sexual relationships, and marriage. As I detail below, al-Shamali deals with questions of gender largely by recourse to a fictionalized account of a trip to the Soviet Union taken by a bourgeois tourist whom al-Shamali names "Henry." The boundaries between fact and fiction in *What I Saw in Moscow* are porous, and intentionally so. Through al-Shamali's own recorded experiences, many of which he has likely exaggerated or fabricated, and those of his fictionalized bourgeois tourist, a clear attempt to juxtapose social relations in the Soviet Union and in Mandate Lebanon and Syria emerges. According to *What I Saw in Moscow*, while the Bolshevik Revolution and the economic miracle it facilitated led to equality and progress in nearly all areas of life in the Soviet Union, French colonial control as well as local cultural conservatism perpetuated capitalist alienation and oppressive gender relations in Lebanon and Syria. These depictions not only reflect utopian visions of communist society but also speak to his assessments of Syrian and Lebanese attitudes toward the Soviet Union in this period.

 Al-Shamali begins *What I Saw in Moscow* by acknowledging that while he has promised the newspaper in which the text was originally published that he won't write "Communist propaganda," his own motivations for writing the text stem from the limited availability of reliable information on life in the Soviet Union for the average person in Lebanon and Syria. Comparing the impression most Lebanese and Syrians have of the Soviet Union to the one they have of "Waq al-Waq,"[35] a fictional island in medieval Arabic literature, al-Shamali emphasizes the texture of daily social life in a communist country his text will provide. Thus from the outset he positions the text as having the potential to replace existing imaginaries of the Soviet Union and, more important, how life has been transformed by communism. Al-Shamali's utopian portrayal is striking given that, by the late 1920s, material conditions in Moscow were deteriorating.[36] According to CPSL members who had conversations with him, al-Shamali was not blind to this reality. He discussed the difficult conditions he witnessed in the Soviet Union, but viewed them as a natural part of a society in transition, losing no faith in the transformative capacity of communism.[37] That these difficulties do not appear on the pages of *What I Saw in Moscow* indicates that it was an audience ambivalent or hostile toward communism for which he wrote.

Before the substantive sections of the serialized text begin, al-Shamali addresses some of the logistical questions the reader might have: How was the trip paid for? How did he get there? Did the French colonial administrators know? The trip, al-Shamali explains, was paid for by a combination of funds from the Palestine Communist Party and the Comintern; he traveled from Beirut to Aleppo by car, and from Aleppo to Istanbul and beyond via the Orient Express; he requested a passport from the French mandatory authorities (which was denied), but made his request under the fabricated guise of traveling to Istanbul as a worker representative for a meeting in Istanbul of tobacco workers.

"Henry" the Bourgeois Tourist

"There is no doubt that, before anything else, the reader wants to know about the life of Soviet women and the status of the family there," writes al-Shamali in the first article of the series.[38] The text is clearly aimed at a male audience. He exclusively uses the masculine singular when addressing his audience, and often points out how imaginations of sexually open Soviet women might appeal to his (presumably male) audience. He addresses the impressions his Lebanese and Syrian audience might have of Soviet women by writing to their supposed expectations, claiming that, as his readers know, Soviet women are "open to all," constantly harassed by men, and unable to refuse the advance of any of them. Yet in the second article of the series, al-Shamali returns to this account of Soviet women, asking his readers: "Did my description of the absolutely debauched life in the Soviet Union bother you, or not, dear reader? Are you a conscript of this delicious, debauched life, or one of its spoilers?" Noting the fact that his audience likely believed the Bolshevik Revolution had destroyed any virtuousness in the Soviet Union, al-Shamali warns his readers against believing any aspect of the description of debauched life that he has just provided. This description was nothing more than "satire of statements bourgeois writers make, those who speak about what they do not know and propagate false rumors about social life under the Soviet regime."[39] He implores his readers not to believe that Soviet women are "open to all" in "Bolshevik countries" or that marriage and family life are lost there. He sets out to demonstrate this in the following entries. Rather than dismissing the focus on gender relations in bourgeois critiques as irrelevant, al-Shamali acknowledges from the outset that gender relations are key to understanding how life has been transformed following the Bolshevik Revolution for committed communists like himself as well.

Al-Shamali illustrates what he claims is the true status of gender relations in the Soviet Union through a series of imagined encounters between his fictitious bourgeois tourist, Henry, and various Soviet women. The fictionalized account allows al-Shamali to criticize bourgeois perspectives, which he assumes his readers hold as well, without directly insulting the reader. Henry, rather than the reader, becomes the object of derision. This strategy also allows al-Shamali to build in utopian monologues by fictionalized Soviet women on the status of gender and social relations in the Soviet Union. The purpose of both of these narrative moves is to bring his potentially hostile audience along with him toward a Soviet future.

Immediately after arriving in Moscow, Henry leaves the hotel in search of a sex worker he can hire. Henry is unsuccessful in his search, despite having looked in the places one might find a sex worker in Beirut, according to al-Shamali. At this point, al-Shamali breaks Henry's narration to inform the reader that prostitution has been abolished in the Soviet Union.[40] Perhaps, al-Shamali surmises, the reader might think that prostitution isn't necessary in a country where women are already "open to all." Henry goes back to the hotel disappointed in his inability to find a sex worker and attempts to seduce a maid at his hotel. The maid refuses him, and responds:

> I will excuse your belief, because you live in a bourgeois country where the master—the hotel guest—can lure the hotel maid with the power of money. The maids you have—and I am not saying all of the maids, but the overwhelming majority of them—are tempted by money, so she sells herself because money is of import to her—in the first degree—to gather the "dowry" and buy a husband with it. But here, a girl has no need for a dowry, because her dowry is her health, her beauty, her morals, her knowledge, and her work. In your society, you degrade maids and you disrespect her dignity. But in our view, she respects herself and everyone respects her. People view her like they view a doctor, or a chief justice, or the manager of a workshop. Here, there isn't "her majesty," "slave," "mistress," "manufacturer," but rather women working in jobs which are appropriate for her qualifications, knowledge, intelligence, and standards.[41]

Directly counterposing the status of women in a "bourgeois country" with that of women in a communist country, al-Shamali paints a picture of how transformed class relations facilitate the transformation of gender relations. Despite the idealized nature of the striking claims al-Shamali makes through the fictionalized maid, the function of her speech is to help his reader (who is also, like Henry, trapped in a "bourgeois country") reimagine society, one without capitalist class relations.

Significantly, the sole discussion of the Bolshevik Revolution in *What I Saw in Moscow* focuses on gender and gender relations. Al-Shamali claims that when workers and peasants rose up against the Russian monarchy, their combined admiration and hatred for the monarchy led to mass use of force against female members of the royalty, including in the form of rape. While quick to define these acts as atrocities, al-Shamali just as quickly dismisses them as a routine part of revolution. As evidence of the transformative power of communist revolution for gender relations, al-Shamali notes that while the Bolsheviks may not have been able to prevent violence against women during the revolution, the postrevolutionary Soviet state has put in place the strictest rape laws in the world.[42]

Al-Shamali in Moscow

In the discussion of his own experience of staying in Moscow, al-Shamali focuses largely on the internationalist infrastructure of communism, the internationalist exchange that it facilitates, and the complete reorganization of social relations in a communist society. He accomplishes this largely through routine examples and anecdotes. I take the fact that many of these anecdotes are fabricated as a given, and am instead interested in what their construction tells us about al-Shamali's worldview, and the place of the Soviet Union in it.

Upon arriving at the train station in Moscow, for instance, al-Shamali is recognized by a Comintern worker who has been sent to pick him up along with several other newly arrived delegates, including one from China, one from Senegal, and one from Morocco. Driving to their hotel in the center of Moscow, "the car loaded with this internationalist group," al-Shamali notes to his reader: "I can't describe to you my feelings when I passed through the streets of Moscow for the first time without disseminating Communist propaganda."[43]

In other passages, the internationalist dimensions and the infrastructures that have facilitated them—colonial, communist, and otherwise—are largely reflected through linguistic ability and communication across linguistic divides. While registering a form for his conference identification card, al-Shamali notes to the Comintern employee that he has a basic knowledge of French in addition to his native language, Arabic, thus allowing him to complete the paperwork in French. He reveals that he acquired his knowledge of French imprisoned in a French colonial prison during the 1925–27 anticolonial revolt.[44] Conference discussions themselves are made possible by live translations: "[Each] speaker stands on the platform, with a sound amplification device before him, delivering his speech in Chinese, Hindi, Arabic, or Senegalese—and how many languages the conference members speak!—before he is even done delivering his speech, the translation of it is arriving to the ears of every member in the language that he knows."[45] Al-Shamali describes the mechanics of the translation in detail. Each delegate has a desk equipped with receivers, there is a room for translators to transmit live translations, and there are five language options for delegates to choose from: Russian, German, French, Eng-lish, or the language in which the speech is being delivered. Al-Shamali explains that, because the Chinese delegates generally did not know any of the languages of the conference, a special area with Chinese translation was provided for them.[46]

Al-Shamali mobilizes three other anecdotes from his time in Moscow to emphasize the new social realities and the new structure of class relations in the Soviet Union. All three of them take place outside the conference setting and are presented as a look into the true, newly equalized Soviet life: a Red Army celebration for soldiers who have finished their service, a chance meeting with Soviet Union head of state Mikhail Kalinin on the public tramway, and a discussion with a faculty mem-ber at a medical college.

At the Red Army celebration, al-Shamali is struck by witnessing an army gen-eral play a game of sports with his subordinates. When al-Shamali is introduced to the general, the general notices his shock, and asks him what is so surprising. Al-Shamali comments that it is the first time in his life that he's shaken hands with a general, but that what has most surprised him is watching the general partake in leisure time with the other ranks. The general responds to al-Shamali by explaining: "In the Red Army all of us are brothers, and the leader doesn't adopt his official status until he is carrying out his job; at that point the leader is a leader, the officer is an officer, and the soldier is a soldier, but when [we aren't] carrying out [our jobs] it is as you see."[47] By choosing a social institution—the army—which is in many ways the archetype of hierarchy, al-Shamali signals to his audience the totalizing forms of transformation possible. He does so not by relying on a moral or ethical argument about social interactions within an army setting, but rather by emphasizing the role that work and jobs play in the postrevolutionary Soviet Union. People are not their jobs; the general becomes a general when work calls for it, but he is otherwise just another citizen. The social order al-Shamali and his audience are accustomed to is one in which the jobs people occupy limit their interactions and opportunities out-side work. Al-Shamali presents a utopian vision of social realities made possible by a communist economic miracle.

Walking down the street in Moscow, al-Shamali and his friend "the Comrade 'Doctor Hamdi'" see Mikhail Kalinin. Although not directly stated, Doctor Hamdi is Muhamed Ahmed Said (Hamdi Salam), an Egyptian communist who attended the Communist University of the Toilers of the East (KUTV) and gained medical train-ing at Moscow State University.[48] Curious about where he might be headed, the two follow him to the public tramway system. That Kalinin is riding the tramway system with the rest of the public is a large enough shock to al-Shamali, but equally signif-icant is the trust-based approach to fare paying. He notes that the conductor does not make sure that every passenger has paid their fare. Al-Shamali asks Doctor Hamdi what happens if a passenger doesn't purchase a ticket. Hamdi responds: "The tramway is property of the people, administered by the government. As in, it does not belong to a private company. So, if one of the workers doesn't have money with him at the point of departure and his house is on the outskirts of Moscow, what do you want him to do, my dear? Walk three or four hours? No, he should ride the train without paying, and no one will oppose him."[49] Here, al-Shamali has positioned himself as the bourgeois tourist. His reconstruction of Hamdi's response makes obvious that the question itself comes from the experience of living in a capitalist country; the tramway is not owned by a private company, but if it was, the worker would have to walk an unmanageable distance home. Is this what al-Shamali himself would want?

Like Henry, al-Shamali outlines in the text how his imagination is not immediately reoriented upon learning more about the structure of Soviet society. In response, al-Shamali asks Hamdi if people are also allowed to eat what they want from government restaurants without paying. It is through Doctor Hamdi's response that al-Shamali makes reference to the history of currency in the Soviet Union. Hamdi acknowledges that people eating in government restaurants without paying had indeed become a problem around the time that the government returned to a cash system, at which point anyone who entered a government restaurant was asked to pay upon entry a set price based on what they planned to eat.[50]

Seemingly satisfied with what he has learned about public goods in the Soviet Union, al-Shamali turns to the question of special privileges high-ranking members of the Soviet state have. Hamdi emphasizes that they all ride public transport, rent apartments, and live life like all other people do. In the course of their discussion on hierarchy and privilege in the Soviet Union, Hamdi describes how salary is partially dependent on whether one is a member of the Communist Party or not; those who are members of the Communist Party have a cap on how much they can earn, whereas non–Communist Party members make money according to their profession and its use to the state.[51]

Al-Shamali outlines transformations in class relations most directly through a conversation he has with a doctor on the faculty at a medical college. He does so through a description of how medical training has become accessible to all only in the wake of the revolution, and through a summary of how pay scales are established. Student fee rates are set on the basis of a student's prerevolutionary class background, with elite families paying a much higher cost of attendance. The doctor explains to al-Shamali that this fee structure is made possible by the fact that "medicine isn't a business here, but it is a public job, in other words the doctor doesn't earn his wages from the people but rather from the state, and medical care is free."[52] Doctors' pay rates, in turn, are determined according to the desirability of their location, with the lowest salaries going to those who wish to work in the most desirable location (Moscow) and the highest salaries going to those willing to work in the least desirable locations (the Republic of Tajikistan).[53]

In the final scene of al-Shamali's *What I Saw in Moscow*, he attends a party hosted by a Russian woman and once again uses utopian representations of gender relations to shed light on the social transformations made possible by communist revolution. The scene of the party also affords him the opportunity to outline a brief moment of anticolonial internationalism, in which he phonetically teaches fellow partygoers a Syrian nationalist anthem in Arabic from the Syrian Revolt of 1925–27. A performer at the party promises him that she will present it at a theater in Moscow soon.

He then describes a flirtation he has with a woman at the party, in which he claims that "love, flirtation, and desire were all created in Arab countries."[54] After recounting the flirtatious exchange, al-Shamali reveals to the reader that all of the women at the party—including the woman with whom he had just described having a flirtatious conversation—were married, and most of their husbands were in attendance, too. The woman with whom he was flirting asks him if women in his country have the same degree of social freedom. Al-Shamali tells her: "Our poor women, my dear, are oppressed. Our men—the vast majority of men—think that they are the masters of women who are absolutely at their disposal, and that women were created only to be obedient slaves to men."[55] In contrast, he notes how she describes to him the forms of marriage that exist in the Soviet Union. This transformation in private life, according to al-Shamali's interlocutor, is made possible by the fact that in the postrevolutionary period women and men have become equal in their rights and duties in public life. In both the Soviet Union and Syria and Lebanon, interwar communists' rhetorical commitment to transforming gender relations fits uncomfortably with the reality that gender was often a secondary concern.[56]

What I Saw in Moscow concludes abruptly with a note from al-Shamali explaining that the publisher chose to end it. In the final installment, al-Shamali assures his reader that he will publish a second part in which he will be totally independent and thus able to "describe to the reader the truth of what I saw in the country of (*Waq al-Waq*), yes, in Red Russia."[57] It does not seem that al-Shamali ever published a second installment. *What I Saw in Moscow* offers an unusual opportunity to consider how ideas about the Soviet Union and communists themselves moved across borders in the interwar period.

Conclusion

What can an early Arab communist travelogue tell us about the social history of interwar Lebanon and Syria? And what does it reveal about the ideological development of communism on a global scale in this period? This article has attempted to sketch the contours of early anticolonial communist politics and the transregional networks that facilitated and sustained these politics in the interwar period.

Central to anticolonial communist worldviews and political imaginaries, as evident in al-Shamali's *What I Saw in Moscow*, was the Soviet Union's purported economic miracle and the social transformations it facilitated. For al-Shamali, the Soviet Union represented an alternative future, one he presents in utopian terms to a Lebanese and Syrian audience whose knowledge of the Soviet Union would mainly have come from sources antagonistic toward communism. Al-Shamali's focus on social life, and his reliance on sarcasm and fictionalized accounts, should be read in part as an attempt to appeal to a general audience. But to read it exclusively in this light ignores the centrality of total social transformation to al-Shamali's vision of communist revolution, and misses the influence that material struggle against colonialism in Lebanon and Syria—and the violent repression of this struggle—had had on his worldview by the time he traveled to Moscow. In other words, the goal of economic revolution for al-Shamali and other anticolonial communists was not an economic one as such but a social one, one visible in the daily examples he forwards in *What I Saw in Moscow*: access to education, to public transportation, and to public space and position regardless of gender.

Scholars of the Comintern generally agree that 1928, and the Sixth Comintern Congress in particular, marked a turning point toward the Stalinization of the Comintern. Perhaps more important, for communists actively involved in anticolonial struggle, it also marked a turn away from a more flexible politics compatible with anticolonial national liberation movements.[58] While the Comintern had previously advanced a "united front" approach in the colonized world, at the 1928 Comintern Congress this changed to a "class against class" approach.[59] In the Middle East this position practically translated to the disavowal of alliances with non-communist anticolonial forces.[60]

The CPSL went through significant internal strife between al-Shamali's return to Greater Syria in 1928 following the conclusion of the congress and his expulsion from the party in 1932 for supposed collaboration with colonial authorities.[61] It is most probable that al-Shamali was expelled because of Stalinizing forces in the party, and in particular the desire to bring the party's politics more closely in line with the shifting policies of the Comintern. Yet his expulsion, and his subsequent position as a committed communist barred from party activity, is likely what made the 1934 publication of the text possible. *What I Saw in Moscow* opens a window onto a brief moment of internationalist communist politics and the transregional networks that facilitated and sustained these politics in the interwar period.

Ellis Garey is an intellectual and social historian of labor, communism, and anticolonialism in the modern Middle East. She is the 2024–2026 Postdoctoral Fellow in Labor History at Brown University. Garey's research has appeared in *Journal of the Ottoman and Turkish Studies Association*. Garey is currently working on a manuscript which attends to the emergence of "the worker" as both a social concept and as a historical actor in late-Ottoman and French Mandate Lebanon and Syria.

Notes

1. As I discuss later in this article, multiple communist parties emerged in Lebanon and Syria in the early 1920s (the Lebanese People's Party, or the LPP, and the Armenian party Spartak). Spartak and the LPP merged in 1925 and became the Lebanese Communist Party (LCP). It was not until 1928 that the LCP was recognized by the Comintern as a branch separate from the Palestine Communist Party, and it was then that it became the Communist Party of Syria and Lebanon (CPSL). I have chosen to use the name CPSL for simplicity except for in direct discussion of one of its predecessor parties, in which case I refer to the party by its contemporaneous name.
2. The founder of *al-Sahafi al-Ta'ih*, Iskandar al-Riyashi, while a self-described socialist, was supportive of French colonial rule. See Tannoury-Karam, *The Making of a Leftist Milieu*, 45.
3. Kirasirova, *Eastern International*, 256n69; Budeiri, "Reflections on a Silenced History."
4. For recent interventions on entanglements between Arab communists and the Soviet Union, and in particular the importance of anticolonialism to interwar communism, see Kirasirova, *The Eastern International*; Louro et al., *League against Imperialism*; Sayım, "Communist Anti-militarism in France;" Tannoury-Karam, "A Cornerstone for Building a New World." Tannoury Karam's article engages directly with the question of the Soviet Union as future, particularly during World War II. Al-Shamali's text, and my discussion of it here, represents an earlier iteration of Soviet futurism.
5. Goswami, "Imaginary Futures and Colonial Internationalisms," 1462.
6. For more on the social significance of the NEP, see Sanchez-Sibony, "Global Money and the Bolshevik Authority."
7. Kirasirova, *Eastern International*; Tannoury-Karam, "A Cornerstone for Building a New World"; Sayım, "Communist Anti-militarism in France."
8. "Al-Shuyu'iyya fi Misr," *al-Ahram*, January 9, 1923.
9. Khater, *Inventing Home*, 19–48; Labaki, "'La filature de la soie.'"
10. Dumont, "Jewish, Socialist, and Ottoman Organization"; Khuri-Makdisi, *Eastern Mediterranean*, 152; Sayım, "Communist Center in Thessaloniki."
11. Muruwah, *Al-Shuyu'iyin al-arba'a al-kibar fi tarikh lubnan al-hadith*, 160.
12. Hanna, *al-Haraka al-'ummaliyya*, 328–29; Tannoury-Karam, "Making of a Leftist Milleu," 53; "Letter from the Party of Lebanese," in Walter Browne, *The Political History of Lebanon*, 51–52.
13. Yazbik, *Hikayat 'awwal nawwar*, 62.
14. See al-Shamali, *'Asas al-harakat al-shuyu'iyya*; al-Shamali, *Niqabat al-'ummal*.
15. Dakrub, *Judhur al-sindiyana al-hamra'*; Hanna, *al-Haraka al-'ummaliyya*.
16. This story, widely accepted in the literature, seems to be at least partially inaccurate. Anatole France did not die until the fall of 1924.
17. Ismael and Ismael, *Communist Movement in Syria and Lebanon*, 16–17.
18. Madoyan's family was forced to leave Adana due to the Armenian genocide and the ensuing forced relocation of Armenians from Cilicia by 1922. Madoyan, *Hayat 'ala al-mitras*, 67.
19. Madoyan, *Hayat 'ala al-mitras*, 67.
20. See, for example, intelligence bulletin from Gaillard to Ponsot, November 13, 1926, Centre des Archives Diplomatiques de Nantes (hereafter cited as CADN), 1SL/1/V/1056.
21. Bold in original text. "Resolution on Syria," *International Press Correspondence*, 5, 83, 26 November 1925, 1257.

22. Provence, *Great Syrian Revolt*, 27–29.

23. Bailony, "Transnational Rebellion," 3.

24. For more on communist participation in the Syrian Revolt and its influence on communist anticolonial politics locally, see Tannoury-Karam, "Long Live the Revolutionary Alliance Against Imperialism," 115–19; for more on how the anticolonial revolts in Syria influenced French anti-militarism, see Sayım, "Communist Anti-militarism in France."

25. Note on inspection by Colonel Pichot-Duclos, June 6, 1927, CADN, 1SL/1/V/849.

26. CADN, 1SL/1/V/849.

27. Intelligence report and seized letter written by Comintern organizer Eli Teper to a French communist listed by colonial authorities as "Louis Desclade Clemence." Both were imprisoned at the time of the letter's writing. April 17, 1926. CADN/1SL/1/V/1056.

28. Seized letter from imprisoned communist Nasim al-Shamali to his brother Najib in Egypt. June 24, 1926. CADN, 1SL/1/V/849.

29. Kalil to General Security Director, September 22, 1927, CADN, 1SL/1/V/849.

30. Couland, *Le mouvement syndical*, 147–48n2.

31. See security bulletin on communist correspondence, August 17, 1926. CADN, 1SL/1/V/1056.

32. Communist tract printed in French and Arabic, 3 March 1927, CADN 1/SL/1/V/1056.

33. Security bulletin with enclosed copy of *Secours Rouge*, September 9, 1926, CADN, 1SL/1/V/849.

34. "Confidential rapport sur l'activite communiste en territoires sous mandat Français pendant le mois de Fevrier 1928," CADN 1SL/1/V/1057.

35. Commonly written as "al-Waq Waq," it is rendered here by the alternate designation that al-Shamali uses.

36. Kirasirova, *Eastern International*, 72.

37. Al-Hilu, *Awraq min tarikhuna*, 387.

38. Al-Shamali, *Madha ray'utu*, 2.

39. Al-Shamali, *Madha ray'utu*, 3.

40. Al-Shamali, *Madha ray'utu*, 4. While laws prohibiting prostitution in the Soviet Union did not come into effect until the late 1980s, the notion that women did not need to engage in sex work there was a popular one. In reality, prostitution was a major anxiety for Soviet officials, who often tied the problem of domestic workers' material instability to their potential to become prostitutes. See Klots, "Just Like Any Other Worker?"

41. Al-Shamali, *Madha ray'utu*, 4.

42. Al-Shamali, *Madha ray'utu*, 13.

43. Al-Shamali, *Madha ray'utu*, 13.

44. Al-Shamali, *Madha ray'utu*, 14.

45. Al-Shamali, *Madha ray'utu*, 17.

46. Al-Shamali, *Madha ray'utu*, 17–18.

47. Al-Shamali, *Madha ray'utu*, 20.

48. See Kirasirova, *Eastern International*, 19–20 and 78–81.

49. Al-Shamali, *Madha ray'utu*, 23. I have translated "one of the workers" literally here as I have interpreted *ahad al-'ummal* as an intentional reference to an existing collective body of workers, as opposed to a single worker.

50. Al-Shamali, *Madha ray'utu*, 24.

51. Al-Shamali, *Madha ray'utu*, 23.

52. Al-Shamali, *Madha ray'utu*, 25.
53. Al-Shamali, *Madha ray'utu*, 26.
54. Al-Shamali, *Madha ray'utu*, 28.
55. Al-Shamali, *Madha ray'utu*, 30.
56. For more on the Soviet context, see Goldman, *Women, the State and Revolution*. A political pamphlet of al-Shamali's on labor unions begins by imploring male workers to organize with their female counterparts, yet his actual organizing seems to have been largely among male workers. For more on women and the CPSL see Tannoury-Karam, "The Making of a Leftist Milieu."
57. Al-Shamali, *Madha ray'utu*, 31.
58. See Sayım, "Transregional by Design"; and Drachewych and McKay, "Introduction: Left Transnationalism."
59. Kirasirova, *Eastern International*, 96. Kirasirova also notes the ethnic implications of this policy: the Comintern issued a directive to "Arabize" Communist parties in the Middle East as part of the "class against class" approach.
60. Sayım, "Transregional by Design," 4.
61. Kirasirova, *Eastern International*, 96; al-Hilu, 420–21.

References

Al-Ahram. Al-Shuyu'iyya fi Misr," January 9, 1923.

Al-Hilu, Yusuf Khattar. *Awraq min tarikhuna*. Beirut: Dar al-Farabi, 1988.

Al-Shamali, Fu'ad. '*Asas al-harakat al-shuyu'iyya fi-l-bilad al-Suriyya/al-Lubnaniyya. (The Establishment of Communist Movements in Syria and Lebanon)*. Aleppo, Syria, 1935.

Al-Shamali, Fu'ad. *Madha ray'utu fi Moscow (What I Saw in Moscow)*. Beirut, Lebanon, 1934.

Al-Shamali, Fu'ad. *Niqabat al-'ummal (Workers' unions)*. Beirut, 1929.

Bailony, Reem. "Transnational Rebellion: The Syrian Revolt of 1925–1927." PhD diss., University of California, Los Angeles, 2015.

Budeiri, Musa. "Reflections on a Silenced History: The PCP and Internationalism." *Jerusalem Quarterly*, no. 49 (2012): 68–78.

Couland, Jacques. *Le mouvement syndical au Liban 1919–1946*. Paris: Editions sociales, 1970.

Dakrub, Muhammad. *Judhur al-sindiyana al-hamra': hikayat nushu' al-hizb al-shuyui'i al-lubnani 1924–193*. Beirut: Dar al-Farabi, 1974.

Drachewych, Oleksa, and Ian McKay. "Introduction: Left Transnationalism? The Communist International, the National, Colonial, and Racial Questions, and the Strengths and Limitations of the 'Moscow Rules' Paradigm." In *Left Transnationalism*, edited by Oleksa Drachewych and Ian McKay, 3–46. Montreal: McGill-Queen's University Press, 2019.

Dumont, Paul. "A Jewish, Socialist, and Ottoman Organization: The Workers' Federation of Salonica." In *Socialism and Nationalism in the Ottoman Empire, 1876–1923*, edited by Mete Tunçay and Erik Jan Zürcher, 49–88. London: British Academic Press, 1994.

Goswami, Manu. "Imaginary Futures and Colonial Internationalisms." *American Historical Review* 117, no. 5 (2012): 1461–85.

Hanna, 'Abdullah. *Al-Haraka al-'ummaliyya fi Suriyya wa-Lubnan, 1900–1945. (The Workers' Movement in Syria and Lebanon, 1900–1945)*. Damascus: Dar Dimashq, 1973.

Ismael, Tareq Y., and Jacqueline S. Ismael. *The Communist Movement in Syria and Lebanon*. Gainesville: University Press of Florida, 1998.

Khater, Akram Fouad. *Inventing Home: Emigration, Gender, and the Middle Class in Lebanon, 1870–1920*. Berkeley: University of California Press, 2001.

Khuri-Makdisi, Ilham. *The Eastern Mediterranean and the Making of Global Radicalism, 1860–1914*. Berkeley: University of California Press, 2010.

Kirasirova, Masha. *The Eastern International: Arabs, Central Asians, and Jews in the Soviet Union's Anticolonial Empire*. Oxford: Oxford University Press, 2024.

Klots, Alissa. "Just Like Any Other Worker? Class and Gender in the Regulation of Domestic Service in the Early Soviet Period." *Journal of Social History* 56, no. 1 (2022): 114–43.

Labaki, Boutros. "'La filature de la soie dans le sandjak du Mont-Liban': Une expérience de croissance industrielle dépendante (1840–1914)." *Arabica* 29 (1982): 80–90.

"Letter from the Party of Lebanese Workers in Alexandria to U.S. Ambassador in Cairo, July 5, 1922." In *The Political History of Lebanon, 1920–1950*, vol. 1, edited by Walter Browne, 51–52. Salisbury, NC: Documentary Publications, 1976.

Louro, Michele, Carolien Stolte, Heather Streets-Salter, and Sana Tannoury-Karam, eds. *League against Imperialism: Lives and Afterlives*. Leiden University Press, 2020.

Madoyan, Artin. *Hayat 'ala al-mitras: dhikrayat wa-mushahadat. (A Life on the Barricade: Memories and Testimonies)*. Beirut: Dar al-Farabi, 2011.

Muruwah, Karim. *Al-Shuyu'iyin al-arba'a al-kibar fi tarikh Lubnan al-hadith (The Four Prominent Communists in the History of Modern Lebanon)*. Beirut: Dar al-Saqi, 2008.

Provence, Michael. *The Great Syrian Revolt and the Rise of Arab Nationalism*. Austin: University of Texas Press, 2005.

Provence, Michael. "Ottoman Modernity, Colonialism, and Insurgency in the Interwar Arab East." *International Journal of Middle East Studies* 43, no. 2 (2011): 205–25.

"Resolution on Syria." Interparliamentarian Communist Conference. *International Press Correspondence* 5, no. 83 (November 26, 1925).

Sanchez-Sibony, Oscar. "Global Money and Bolshevik Authority: The NEP as the First Socialist Project." *Slavic Review* 78, no. 3 (2019): 694–716.

Sayım, Burak. "Communist Anti-militarism in France and Anti-colonial Wars in Morocco and Syria." *Twentieth Century Communism* 24, no. 24 (2023): 17–42.

Sayım, Burak. "A Communist Center in Thessaloniki at the Junction of Mediterranean and Post-Ottoman Spaces." *Mashriq & Mahjar* 9, no. 2 (2022): 31–41.

Sayım, Burak. "Transregional by Design: The Early Communist Press in the Middle East and Global Revolutionary Networks." *Journal of Global History* 18, no. 2 (2023): 216–35.

Tannoury-Karam, Sana. "A Cornerstone for Building a New World: The Soviet Union and the Futurity of Leftist Arab Intellectuals, 1920–1948." *Middle East Journal of Culture and Communication* 17 (2024): 9–28.

Tannoury-Karam, Sana. "Long Live the Revolutionary Alliance Against Imperialism: Interwar Anti- Imperialism and the Arab Levant." In Louro et al., *League against Imperialism*.

Tannoury-Karam, Sana. "The Making of a Leftist Milieu: Anti-colonialism, Anti-fascism, and the Political Engagement of Intellectuals in Mandate Lebanon, 1920–1948." PhD diss., Northwestern University, 2017.

Yazbik, Yusuf Ibrahim. *Hikayat 'awwal nawwar fi al-'alam wa-fi Lubnan: Dhikrayat wa tarikh wa nasus (The Story of May Day in the World and in Lebanon: Memories, History, and Texts)*. Beirut: Dar al-Farabi, 1974.

The Silence of Numbers

Revisiting the Political Economy of the
Chilean "Miracle"

Johanna Gautier Morin

In July 1982, the video artist Lotty Rosenfeld disturbed the normal operations of the Santiago Stock Exchange by projecting two video installations onto the monitors, displaying her protest sign "NO+," which stood for "No más" (no more). This sign had been designed by the Colectivo Acciones de Arte (CADA), a group of activist artists who used theatrical, video, and art performances that disrupted everyday life to resist Pinochet's dictatorship (1973–90). Their visual actions soon became a symbol of political resistance adopted by other opposition movements.[1] Simultaneously, she projected the inscription "LOTTY ROSENFELD *Una herida americana* / 1982" (an American wound) onto the facade of the stock exchange. She wanted to draw attention to the real spectacle unfolding inside: the regime's entire rhetoric, which sought to justify political repression in the name of its economic revolution to foster miraculous growth, collapsed as the financial markets plummeted.[2]

Rosenfeld targeted the stock market because, of all the economic sites that symbolized the regime's glitz, it most embodied global integration and free markets. Until the financial bubble burst with the collapse of the fixed exchange rate system in June 1982, the regime's supporters could boast that they were driving the country full speed ahead on the road to First World prosperity. They believed that the adoption of a model of outward growth backed by military force would be the miraculous recipe for resurrecting the economy from the ashes of socialism. In the aftermath of

Radical History Review
Issue 151 (January 2025)   DOI 10.1215/01636545-11506777
© 2025 by MARHO: The Radical Historians' Organization, Inc.

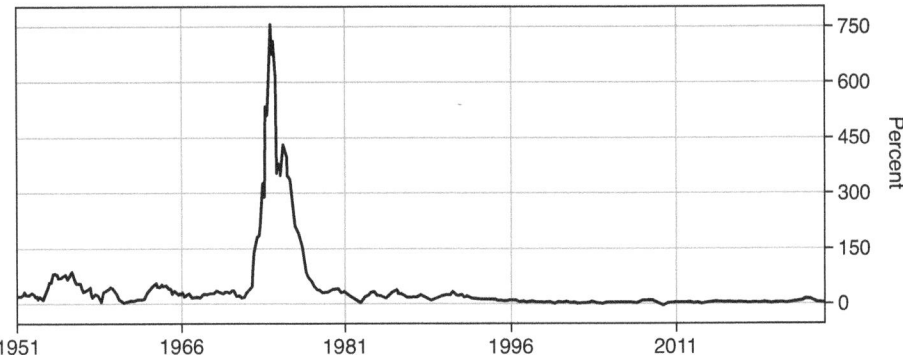

Figure 1. Chile inflation rate. Source: National Institute of Statistics, Chile.

the 1975 global recession, financial stabilization and austerity programs effectively curbed inflation, boosted output, and significantly expanded domestic capital markets. This success was reflected in the growing gross domestic product (GDP) and the taming of inflation—both indicators used to claim that Pinochet's policies had planted the seeds of an economic "miracle."

The term *miracle* was commonly used in conservative and neoliberal milieus to portray Chile's economic expansion as a model for other developing countries.[3] This metaphor was borrowed from the recovery and growth of West Germany and Japan following World War II. The magical connotation of the term reflected the unforeseen rise from the ashes of the war. Applied to Chile, the term was associated with an economic revolution that used "shock therapy" to overcome two severe crises that the regime and its supporters considered to be as damaging to Chilean society as war destruction had been to the German and Japanese economies and societies: namely hyperinflation (fig. 1) and Salvador Allende's socialism.[4]

By late 1981, however, statistical abstractions began to deteriorate again.[5] Financial intermediaries faced a surge in nonperforming assets, necessitating intervention and bailouts by the Central Bank. Classical accounts of the crisis translated it into grim figures that were at odds with the rhetoric of economic success: inflation soared from 10 percent in 1982 to 27 percent in 1983, real per capita GDP fell by 20 percent between 1981 and 1983, and unemployment rose to more than 20 percent despite the proliferation of emergency programs.[6] Notwithstanding the extreme violence of political and social repression, this crisis triggered a wave of protests unprecedented since the 1973 coup. Beginning with the "hunger marches" and massive strikes of the copper miners, the movement lasted for years and hastened the 1988 presidential referendum that put an end to the military regime.[7]

The 1982 crisis alarmed observers who were convinced that Chile was a model debtor. The *Washington Post* lamented that Chile had gone from being a prosperous country in 1981, finally recovered from the severe crisis of the early 1970s, to one where, by 1985, one-third of children relied on foreign aid food programs to avoid starvation. Yet the market for luxury goods such as video recorders and color televisions was thriving—evidence that the middle class was enjoying the benefits of an affluent society.[8] Heidi Tinsman's work also shows how women working in the fruit industry could benefit from job creation in the export sector. They had benefited the least from earlier agrarian reforms that excluded them from land redistribution and could finally earn wages that contributed to a degree of female autonomy at home.[9]

"Two Chiles" thus cohabited, as Peter Winn underscored in highlighting the growing antagonisms of a fractured society: one benefiting from growth, the other becoming its exploited victim.[10] The steady expansion of shantytowns provided contingents of underpaid, undeclared workers who massively joined the ranks of resistance to the regime in the wake of the financial downturn.[11] More recently, Patricia Richards showed how structural racism also systematically discriminated against Indigenous populations, who suffered from the effects of economic reforms during and after the dictatorship.[12] At the national level, it became clear that increasing wealth accumulation coexisted with new highs in poverty that did not appear in aggregate statistics.

But the myth of the Chilean "miracle" did not die with the crisis. The economy eventually recovered, and the GDP rose steadily from the mid-1980s onward. By 1990, GDP had returned to its 1981 level, proving to free-market enthusiasts that the reforms had ultimately proved successful (fig. 2). In the 1990s, as privatization and deregulation gained global traction, the center-left coalition government known as the Concertación maintained the economic organization and legislation inherited from the Pinochet dictatorship. This surprising continuity inspired Sebastián Edwards to reassess the economic miracle according to two criteria: since GDP increased during the post–dictatorship years, and, according to his analysis, the economic model developed by Pinochet's neoliberal advisors, the "Chicago Boys," was "maintained, improved, and deepened" for decades, it proved that Pinochet's indicators of success and his reforms had won the "war of ideas."[13]

Moving beyond the traditional debate over the rehabilitation or the anathematization of the dictatorship era, recent literature has posed new questions to assess whether Chile's growth was due to adherence to laissez-faire economics or, conversely, to government intervention in the economy. Some economists argue that elected governments have consistently implemented industrial policies and provided government support to leading industries to support growth.[14] Others have reexamined the past economy to determine if the Chilean road to economic success was a "miracle" or a "mirage."[15] But in general, the efforts to reconstruct a comprehensive balance sheet of the regime and its aftermath have focused

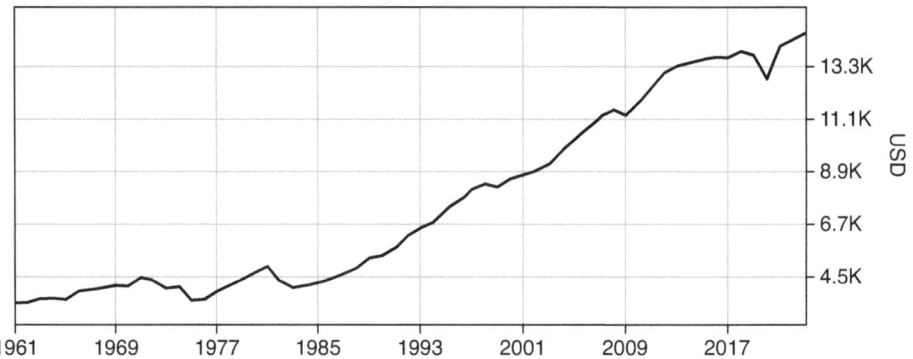

Figure 2. GDP per capita in Chile (1960–2022). Source: World Bank, https://tradingeconomics.com /chile/gdp-per-capita (accessed November 1, 2023).

strictly on policymaking and economic ideas—that is, on policymakers and their economic advisors.

This article proposes to change the terms of the problem. Instead of questioning Chile's macroeconomic record or reevaluating the policies of successive governments, it aims to reflect on the definitions and measurement tools used to nurture the myth of the "Chilean miracle." It views this phenomenon as a chimera of modern times—a metaphorical creature that stands on three pillars. The first was the elimination of those who opposed the reforms: in the "war of ideas," economists who predicted a bleak future, contrary to the alluring narrative of the regime's economic revolution, were silenced, exiled, or assassinated. The second was the support of international financial institutions that contributed to the glowing praise for the Chilean growth model.[16] The IMF and the World Bank directly provided financial assistance and oversaw Pinochet's reforms to service Chile's external debt following the 1982 financial crisis, despite severe human rights violations. The third was the set of econometric indicators that national and international observers used to assess economic growth. Any economic life not represented by these indicators was therefore not accounted for in the political economy of the miracle. By examining the materiality of the production and conceptualization of economic and statistical abstractions, this article proposes an alternative history of economic knowledge in Chile through the lens of the feminist critique that emerged in the 1970s to point out the silence of national accounts and growth indicators on unpaid domestic work, the informal economy, and environmental externalities. Most of the feminist thinkers studied here were affiliated with the United Nations Economic Commission for Latin America (CEPAL in Spanish and Portuguese). Drawing on CEPAL documents, publications from other international organizations, newspaper clippings, and economists' debates, this article revisits the political economy of the myth of the miracle and argues for a comprehensive critique of Chile's development and economic integration.

Silencing Heresy

Pinochet's rule, like the neighboring anticommunist dictatorships of Juan María Bordaberry in Uruguay (1972–76) and the junta in Argentina (1976–83), sought to justify its illiberal policies with an economic project that was considered legitimate by the international community of the Western bloc.[17] He presented his coup as the only solution to the social, moral, and economic crisis facing Chile.[18] The regime he created was ideologically coherent, motivated by a desire to eradicate the "Marxist cancer," defend national security, strengthen fundamentalist Catholic values, restore the classist social order, and recover private property by any means necessary.[19] The "New Right," which supported the coup, sought an economic revolution and advocated a social refoundation.[20] It found in Pinochet's authoritarian rule the means to manage the country's economy independently of the democratic whims of the people.[21]

The fiercest repression targeted communists, socialists, and community organizers who had played a central role in reorganizing the national economy under Allende's statist policies.[22] Following the end of the dictatorship, the National Commission for Truth and Reconciliation investigated the crimes of the regime and compiled lists of victims who were murdered or disappeared. Among the most famous cases were agrarian reformer Marta Ugarte Román and her colleagues from the Juntas de Abastecimiento y Control de Precios (Supply and Price Control Boards), which had overseen the distribution of goods and controlled their prices to combat inflation and redistribute wealth among the general population. These public figures, who defended a different vision of economic management, went underground immediately after the coup and tried to find refuge in embassies to flee the country, but many were arrested, tortured, murdered, or deported.[23] By fighting and destroying all political, trade union, and intellectual dissent, the junta left no standing opposition to its reforms and attempts to transform society.[24]

Through the repression of individuals, the regime sought to stifle ideas that did not support its vision of the economy, even in exile. The most emblematic example was the assassination of the economist Orlando Letelier, the former Chilean ambassador to the United States, and his young colleague Ronni Moffitt, a twenty-five-year-old development specialist, in Washington in 1976. Arrested with other members of the Allende government after Pinochet's coup in 1973, Letelier had been deported to the Dawson Island concentration camp, a torture site in Kawésqar territory, from which he escaped only through international support and diplomatic pressure on the condition that he leave Chile forever. In exile, Letelier continued to oppose the junta with all his might. He published his sharp criticism of the dictatorship's authoritarian, neoliberal economic reforms in major international newspapers such as the *Nation* and *Le Monde Diplomatique*.[25] In retaliation, the Chilean authorities stripped him of his citizenship, violating the Geneva Convention against

Statelessness. Letelier was driving with Moffitt to make a public statement to the *New York Times* when their car exploded.[26]

The FBI soon discovered that the junta's intelligence agency, the Dirección de Inteligencia Nacional (DINA), was responsible for this act of state-sponsored terrorism.[27] Failed assassination attempts had repeatedly targeted Letelier since he had fled to the United States.[28] But he was not the only economist to be murdered. Fernando Olivares Mori, an activist with the Movimiento de Izquierda Revolucionaria (MIR-Chile), who worked at the Centro Latinoamericano de Demografía (CELADE) of CEPAL, was arrested in his Santiago office on October 5, 1973; his body was found fifteen years later.[29] Carmelo Soria, another CEPAL employee and Spanish communist refugee, was tortured and murdered by the same DINA official involved in Letelier's case, Eugenio Berrios.[30] Immediately after the coup, Pinochet had indeed accused CEPAL of being an internationalist socialist organization that harbored dissidents seven kilometers from the Palacio de la Moneda, where he ruled.[31] Chilean police issued arrest warrants that forced many of the CEPAL staff into exile. Supported by other dictatorships, especially in Paraguay (1954–89), Brazil (1964–85), Uruguay (1973–85), and Argentina (1976–83), the DINA hunted down and eliminated opposition figures who had fled abroad, using the interstate terrorist network infamously known as "Operation Condor."[32] In response, several countries severed diplomatic relations with Chile and welcomed CEPAL economists as political refugees.[33] However, the international community was greatly divided over the legitimacy of the regime's economic reforms and the means to enforce them.[34]

Money Doctors or Money Thaumaturges? The Miracle Workers

Pinochet's autocracy combined physical elimination and forced exile of political opponents with neoliberal economic reforms carried out with the help of experts, "money doctors" trained in the latest econometric methods at top-tier US universities.[35] In 1995, Juan Gabriel Valdés, who had been Letelier's young research assistant at the Institute for Policy Studies in Washington—a progressive think tank advocating for peace, human rights, and the environment, where Valdés, Letelier, and Moffit were research fellows—published the first comprehensive prosopography on the role of Chilean economists trained at the University of Chicago. These economists, known as the "Chicago Boys," held influential positions in the Pinochet administration.[36] Not only did his work highlight Pinochet's pioneering role in imposing neoliberal policies conceived in monetarist terms, but his reflections triggered a complete reframing of global historiography on the transnationalization of economics and the role of economists as "meddlers" and "globalists."[37] The technocratic support of the Chicago Boys provided an intellectual rationale to their economic shock doctrine.[38] Orlando Letelier, from exile, publicly and adamantly campaigned against these reforms and the intellectual hegemony of monetarist theories over Latin American economic policy.[39]

The conjunction of political repression and economic liberalization appeared all the more compatible since the latter justified the former. The scientist turn of economics and its apparent separation from the realm of politics and society endowed Chile with a legitimate, "objective" project in the eyes of the international expert community.[40] From then on, Chile enjoyed international recognition for its commitment to developing a free market economy. Margaret Thatcher and Ronald Reagan, in particular, admired Pinochet's reforms as the living proof of the free market "economic miracle."[41] In defense of Pinochet's reforms, the internationally renowned economists and Nobel laureates Friedrich Hayek and Milton Friedman traveled twice to Chile and advocated the autocratic state of emergency imposed by the military as a necessary transitional dictatorship to free markets.[42] In a 1981 interview with the Chilean newspaper *El Mercurio*, Hayek claimed: "A dictatorship may be a necessary system for a transitional period. . . . It is possible for a dictator to govern in a liberal way. And it is also possible for a democracy to govern with a total lack of liberalism. Personally, I prefer a liberal dictator to democratic government lacking in liberalism."[43] The Sveriges Riksbank awarded the Prize in Economic Sciences in Memory of Alfred Nobel to Milton Friedman on October 14, 1976, three weeks after the assassination of Orlando Letelier. In their memoir, *Two Lucky People*, Milton and Rose D. Friedman recalled that they were unable to visit Stockholm when they came to Sweden to receive the prize. They remained under round-the-clock police protection because of demonstrations and newspaper attacks protesting Milton Friedman's alleged involvement as an advisor to General Pinochet.[44] One demonstrator disrupted the ceremony with shouts of "Down with capitalism, freedom for Chile." Friedman repeatedly denied these accusations and referred to the mob of Chilean students as "hoodlums," equating them with Nazis who suppressed free speech.[45] The role and influence of Hayek and Friedman on neoliberal reforms in Latin America are still controversial, but neither of them ever condemned the dictatorships that have used and misused their ideas. If nothing else, they were guilty of silence.[46]

Trapped in their own ambivalence, the International Monetary Fund (IMF) and the World Bank also collaborated with the Pinochet regime and provided the financial backing necessary to facilitate his reforms, notwithstanding the resulting human rights controversies.[47] The technical "trick" they put forward was their self-proclaimed "economic neutrality," which allowed them to ignore domestic politics—although they had systematically denied loans to Allende's socialist government.[48] This axiological "neutrality" had permitted the IMF and World Bank to endorse a neoliberal agenda in many military regimes since the early years of the Cold War.[49]

In a 668-page report concluding a mission that visited Chile in 1977 to observe its economic "transition," the World Bank praised the reforms introduced by the Pinochet administration as being "consistent with advice long offered Chile by the World Bank and other international institutions."[50] These recommendations centered on three principles: decentralization, privatization, and open market policies aimed at achieving a GDP growth rate of 5.5 to 6.0 percent per year, reducing the debt service ratio, and building international reserves. The report warned that the success of Pinochet and his advisors' strategy depended on their ability to reconcile efficient resource allocation and accelerated growth with a "reasonably equitable" distribution of income and the alleviation of "absolute poverty."[51] These two loose concepts were never clearly defined in the report. Poverty itself was not a concern of the World Bank until the 1970s, when the organization gradually linked the concept to that of development. Its definition and monetization also evolved over time. In 1975, the bank set an arbitrary threshold of US$50 per year to define "absolute poverty," and its alleviation was conceived as a mechanism to increase national GDP.[52]

These recommendations echoed the policies proposed in *El ladrillo* (*The Brick*), an economic manifesto coauthored by the Chicago Boys and businesspeople in 1973 that advocated the restructuring of Chilean society on the basis of free market principles, decentralization, the reduction of government controls, the expansion of capital markets, and a guaranteed income for families living below the "extreme poverty line" (undefined).[53] These guidelines were not always followed to the letter, not least because the Chicago Boys had a fluctuating influence on the government and often found themselves in competition with other groups of reformers from the upper echelons of the army or the business sector.[54] But the military implemented most of them, and these reforms had a significant impact on sectors such as labor legislation, the educational system, social security and health care, the judiciary, and governmental administration.[55] The implementation of the reforms took place amid an atmosphere of "triumphalism," as all dissenting opinions had been silenced.[56] The conformity of such reforms with the World Bank's recommendations allowed the bank to approve a US$33 million loan for Chile in 1976. World Bank president Robert McNamara justified the decision by stating, "There is no room for political considerations in that type of situation."[57] The divorce between politics and economics was finally achieved.

Likewise, upon returning from a visit to Chile in the same year, US secretary of the treasury William Simon commended the "economic freedom" he observed in the regime, while noting that Pinochet claimed "progress was being made" on addressing human rights concerns.[58] International opinion did matter sufficiently for the Chilean government to resort to a public relations firm to enhance its public image, as recently demonstrated by Pablo Pryluka in his original study on the contract signed between the military regime and the J. Walter Thompson advertising company in 1974.[59]

However, the outcomes of the reforms failed to meet the government's desired success; the 1982 crisis hindered the expected GDP takeoff. But once again, the IMF extended financial aid to service the foreign debt. The standby agreement they negotiated implied another orthodox stabilization program, to which the government diligently adhered. In particular, the negotiations focused on fiscal reforms aimed at reducing expenditures, such as the elimination of wage indexation, the introduction of new income and property taxes, the raising of public sector tariffs, and the sale of public sector assets. Regarding monetary policy, the abandonment of the fixed exchange rate was expected to reduce capital outflows and increase the availability of domestic savings. The IMF welcomed the easing of restrictions on international transactions and payments.[60] All the reforms converged on boosting output growth, as measured by the country's GDP.

Scarce and Biased Data: Unraveling the Numbers

Beyond direct collaboration with international actors, the third pillar of the myth of the Chilean miracle was the set of measurement tools that national and international observers employed to assess economic growth. The two main indicators typically cited to discuss the miracle were the growing GDP and the declining poverty index. One issue that can be raised here relates to the origin and consistency of the data used to formulate these indicators—a problem that was at the heart of institutional concerns, as CEPAL has pointed out the limitations or unreliability of regional data in most of its publications (Table 1).

Although Chile has maintained one of the most consistent data collections in Latin America since the establishment of the National Statistics Institute in 1843, there have been intermittent discontinuities over time. The economists Christian Caamaño-Carrillo, Sergio Contreras-Espinoza, and Orietta Nicolis lamented the absence of quarterly information prior to 1986 in their attempt to reconstruct the Chilean GDP from 1965 to 2009. They emphasized that the calculation frequency of GDP is of "particular interest since the low number of data (for example, yearly) could cause serious problems in terms of the quality of quantitative analysis."[61] Their proposed reevaluation estimates a "clean" GDP and reveals that classical accounts of the period before 1986, referred to as "dirty GDP," have overestimated the GDP (fig. 3).

The economic miracle was thus lauded with scarce and biased data. Aware of these shortcomings, even the 1977 World Bank report had warned against any pretense of proposing economic projections, "given the difficulties with the data base."[62] The dearth of precise data from this period is particularly noteworthy when examining the living conditions of marginalized populations. Poverty rates were not evaluated during the Pinochet regime, as the National Institute of Statistics could not provide the relevant data before the late 1980s (Table 2). To address discrepancies in the national population censuses within the region, the United Nations Economic and Social Council had assisted in creating the Latin American and Caribbean Centre for Demography (CELADE) in Santiago in the 1950s. CELADE and CEPAL statisticians and demographers jointly conducted field interviews to gather gender-disaggregated primary data. Both staffs identified several

Table 1. Statistics available on Regional Gross Product in Chile and other Latin American countries (1953–77). Source: CEPAL, "Distribución regional del product interno bruto sectorial en los países de América Latina," *Cuadernos Estadísticos de la CEPAL*, 1981, E/CEPAL/G.1115, 6.

	Estimates			
	Periodic			
	Argentina		*Brazil*	*Chile*
1. Levels of Gross Product Measurement				
Gross	X	X		X
Net			X	
At factor cost	X		X	
At market prices		X		X
2. Activity Coverage	All		All	All
3. Temporal Coverage	1953, 1958 and 1959	1961-1976ᶜ	1959 and 1970	1960-1976
4. Valuation				
At current prices	X	X	X	
At constant prices				1965

ᵃ Calculations made for the entire country.
ᵇ All, referring to industries, which include all establishments producing goods and services for sale in the market, at a price covering production costs (see the national accounts system, SYST/STAT/5.1/Rev. 3, paragraph 57.3 to 5.14 and 5.39. In other words, all establishments producing goods in a systematic manner, regardless of the activity code in the CIUU they decide).
ᶜ In recent years, data updated for some provinces.

issues when dealing with data that included undercounting, age-related omissions, and a considerable proportion of "not specified" or "not reported" responses to census questionnaires. Inaccurate information provision also resulted from insufficiently trained enumerators.[63]

Data on the living standards, economic participation, and health conditions of women, migrant populations, and Indigenous people were significantly limited. The research, conducted by the demographer Fresia Donoso, who collaborated with CEPAL and CELADE in Chile during the 1960s and 1970s, exposes the deficiencies in Chilean censuses and the difficulties she faced in obtaining information regarding the fertility and health of migrant women.[64] The gender aspect of the problem was, however, not limited to Chile, but was a global tendency in the production and compilation of national and international data.

Table 1. (*Continued*)

				Estimates		
				Sporadic		
Bolivia	*Colombia*	*Ecuador*	*Mexico*	*Panama*	*Peru*	*Uruguay*
X	X	X	X	X	X	X
		X				X
X	X		X	X	X	
Some	All	All	All	All	All[b]	All
1965-1969	1960-1975	1965	1960, 1965 and 1970	1960 and 1968	1970-1977	1961
X			X	X		X
	1970			1960	1973	

Lives beyond Numbers

When the Danish economist Ester Boserup published *Women's Role in Economic Development* in 1970, she ignited an international debate among feminists in multilateral organizations regarding the data's silence on women's lives.[65] In the following years, the UN Commission on the Status of Women launched the series World Conferences on Women, to meet every five years, starting in Mexico City in 1975. These international meetings persistently stressed the egregious macroeconomic ignorance regarding the exact living conditions of women around the world. Public or private, national or international organizations leveraged inadequate statistics that obscured the reality of women's lives. As a result, most policies and development programs were likely to fail to meet women's needs.[66] CEPAL addressed the issue in preparation for the Mexico conference, followed by the Regional

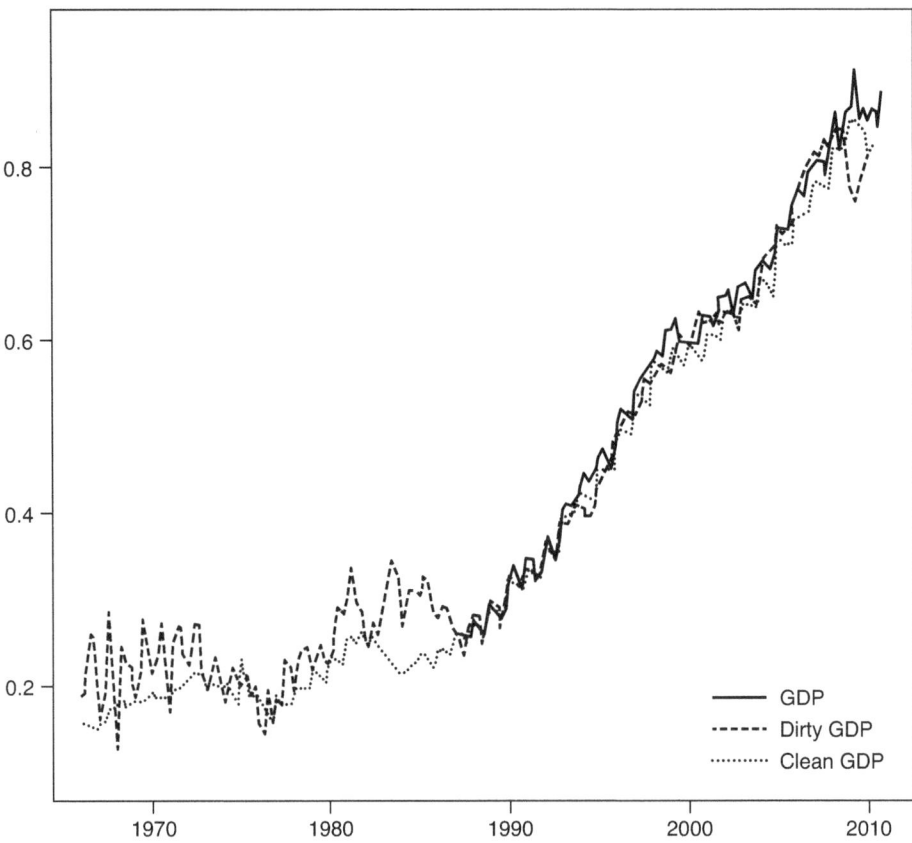

Figure 3. Comparison of estimated "clean" GDP versus "dirty" GDP, and quarterly GDP calculated by the Central Bank of Chile after 1986. Source: Caamaño-Carrillo, Contreras-Espinoza, and Nicolis, "Reconstructing the Quarterly Series of the Chilean Gross Domestic Product," 1837.

Conference on the Integration of Women into the Economic and Social Development of Latin America held in Havana in 1977. Women delegates at these conferences expressed dissenting opinions in a multilateral environment primarily focused on trade development and global integration. Since the 1960s, governments in leading Latin American economies had demonstrated mounting interest in national statistics to formulate public policies for economic organization and growth planning. In this, their focus had been directed toward outward-looking and growth-oriented aspects of the economy systematically translated into GDP measures, therefore neglecting the gendered division of labor, the informal economy, and environmental degradation.[67]

The critique of the silence of the data converged with the increasingly widespread feminist critique of the accuracy of GDP measurements during the 1970s. Such criticisms were not new. The Chicago economist Margaret Reid had already brought to light in the 1930s the consequences of neglecting unpaid domestic labor

Table 2. Income distribution and poverty in Latin America. Source: Hojman, "Poverty and Inequality in Chile," 75, based on data from UNDP (1994) and World Bank (1993, 1995).

Country	1	2	3	4
Argentina	na	na	20	13
Chile	-	-	25	15
Chile 1989	10.5	17.0		
Chile 1992	10.2	18.3		
Venezuela	14.3	10.3	58	9
Colombia	12.7	13.3	45	29
Mexico	11.9	13.6	51	26
Brazil	7.0	32.1	73	23
Peru	14.1	10.5	75	29

Key:

1 = Income share of the lowest 40 percent of households, percent, 1980–91 (except for Chile, 1989 and 1992).
2 = Ratio between the income shares of the highest 20 percent and lowest 20 percent of households, 1980-91 (except for Chile, 1989 and 1992).
3 = Absolute poverty in rural areas, percent, 1980–90.
4 = Rural population as percent of total, 1992.
na = not available.

for the overall economy.[68] Feminist thinkers have persistently addressed the matter and, within the realm of international organizations, linked it to the underevaluation of women's contributions to development.[69] This critique acquired an international dimension in the late 1960s, when representatives from Latin America, the Caribbean, and India at the United Nations drew attention to the persistence of the colonial statistical system in the international accounting system.[70] In an organization such as CEPAL, particularly convinced for decades that economic growth would be the driving force behind social and human development, criticism of economic indicators could only come from the growing presence within its staff of people with different profiles and interests, increasingly linked to grassroots activist and nongovernmental organizations.[71]

In line with these critiques, Chilean women economists proposed alternative calculating methods to address the shortcomings of the classical account of national economies. In 1983, Lucía Pardo suggested reevaluating the Chilean GDP to incorporate domestic housework, which she estimated to amount to over 30 percent of the total GDP. She used the wage data provided by the June 1981 Survey of Employment and Unemployment in Gran Santiago to calculate the value of household work hours using benchmark hourly wages paid in the market for food industries, commercial laundries, childcare centers, and all activities equivalent to household activities.[72] Her work highlighted how the indicators used to define the so-called Chilean miracle introduced a serious gender bias in the representation of economic reality.

The failure of traditional economic measures to account for women's unpaid work intersected with the shortcomings in tracking the informal economy, both of which disproportionately affected women. Investigations conducted by the International Labor Organization in the early 1990s highlighted how women from rural areas with limited education were informally employed on a seasonal basis within the agro-industry. The 1993 ILO visit revealed, for instance, how a fruit and vegetable processing plant situated outside Curicó in the central valley of Chile officially reported twenty workers (all men, mostly engineers, clerical staff, and security personnel) but actually employed an additional hundred undeclared women workers to process vegetables during the high season.[73] No general statistics exist for this period. Nowadays, the global network Women in Informal Employment: Globalizing and Organizing (WIEGO) estimates that informal employment in Chile constitutes around 27 percent of total employment and evaluates that women are more likely to be employed informally, where they are more vulnerable to economic downturns.[74]

The issue becomes even more pronounced when addressing sex work, illegal and persecuted by the military regime yet thriving in the 1980s. The share of prostitution in Chilean economic activity has been a subject of moral and social concern for conservative elites and workers' organizations alike since the end of the nineteenth century. As more women entered low-paying industrial jobs throughout the twentieth century, prostitution became more widespread as a way to compensate for insufficient income. This link between female prostitution and the capitalist workplace led labor activists to use the image of the working-class prostitute to advocate for class struggle.[75] Women's bodies and queer bodies have thus become focal points in the ultra Right's crusade for law and order. Civil organizations such as the Gremialist movement of Jaime Guzmán; El Poder Femenino, led by María Correa Morandé and Elena Larraín; the extreme right-wing paramilitary movement Frente Nacionalista Patria y Libertad; and the Unidad Nacional Femenina supported all forms of repression with the aim of eradicating deviance from their norms.[76] Their influence was such that they were able to ensure that Chile retained one of the world's most repressive and illiberal abortion laws; voluntary termination of pregnancy remained completely illegal under any circumstances until 2017.[77] Any group or individual deemed to be incompatible with the new society that emerged following the 1973 military coup was thus at great risk of elimination or invisibilization. The reportage conducted during the dictatorship by the photographer Paz Errázuriz on transgender sex workers in the impoverished neighborhoods of Santiago is quite revealing in this regard. Invisible in aggregated statistics, they were key actors in a parallel economy that the military regulated or sustained as clients and oppressors.[78]

The invisibility of lived experiences was equally severe for Indigenous populations. A recent study on the spatial distribution of poverty in Chile demonstrates that the poorest areas are not even included in the National Socioeconomic Characterization Survey (Encuesta de Caracterización Socioeconómica Nacional, Casen) carried out by the Ministry of Social Development and Family. For example, no data is available for the southernmost region. This region corresponds to the land of the Kawésqar people, one of the most targeted Indigenous groups during the dictatorship due to their transhumant lifestyle. Information about their living conditions is mostly provided by artists and activists who documented the displacement and economic disorganization they experienced.[79]

In Chile, the discrimination and invisibilization of Indigenous ways of life have always been intimately connected to the legal and economic management of the environment. One of the solutions that the government found to revive the economy and credit flows after the 1982 crisis was the privatization and internationalization of the country's forestry. Starting in 1985, the government lured indirect foreign investment in the stock market through debt-for-equity swaps in forestry companies. This financial vehicle boosted the expansion of the sector, in particular the expansion of radiata pine and eucalyptus logs.[80] Gradually during the 1980s and 1990s, the international export of forest-related products became the second economic driver of the country behind copper production, to the detriment of native forests and Indigenous lands.[81] The rapid and sometimes illegal expansion of forest plantations into the Araucanía region provoked deadly conflicts with Mapuche people who were dispossessed of their lands and resources.[82]

In 2019, when the largest democratic debate the country ever witnessed opened with the formation of a constituent assembly of 155 delegates, including 17 Indigenous people, to draft a new constitution, the issue of native forest protection was part of a broader discussion about the protection of the environment and natural resources against private appropriation and monopolization.[83] Article 134 declared as "natural common goods" "the territorial sea and its seabed; beaches; waters, glaciers, and wetlands; geothermal fields; air and the atmosphere; high mountains, protected areas, and native forests; the subsoil, and others declared by the Constitution and the law."[84] International proponents of the economic "miracle" accused the assembly and its first elected president, Elisa Loncón, a Mapuche from the Araucanía region, of threatening "chaos" in the "world's most successful emerging markets."[85] In any case, the social divide and the persistence of the myth of the miracle defeated the radicalism of this new constitution, and the majority of voters rejected its adoption in 2022.

Conclusions

The mass protests in 2019, demanding change, took most of Chile's economic elite by surprise, as they believed in the success of the Chilean socioeconomic model. During these demonstrations, Lotty Rosenfeld's "NO+" reappeared on signs as people protested the pension system, patriarchal oppression, discrimination against Indigenous peoples, and environmental destruction. Millions of people rallied around the central demand to revise the 1980 constitution and dismantle the neoliberal regime inherited from the Pinochet era. These protesters defied the national and international enthusiasm for the so-called miracle and rose up against the inequality and corruption they perceived as deeply embedded in the legal and economic system in which many felt trapped and disillusioned.[86] While Chile's economy thrived in aggregate terms, perceptions of inequalities and resentment of the dictatorship's legacy eventually led people to disregard economic indicators.[87]

The emergence and persistence of the myth of the Chilean economic miracle can be attributed to the intersection of three factors: the spreading popularity of monetarist ideas among business circles and military elites, the growing confidence in the inherent success of free markets, and the unwavering faith, broadly shared by international organizations, in the reliability of economic indicators. This phenomenon flourished in the Cold War context, providing a legitimizing narrative for a dictatorship under the banner of economic revolution. This chimera, combining both populist and technocratic elements, shaped the debates about a new constitution to replace the one inherited from the dictatorship. Despite a lack of consensus on the success of the Chilean economy in quantifiable terms, economic discussions often revolve around a clash of statistics. Conversely, the constituent assembly of 2022 faced criticism for including only one economist and proposing economic reforms deemed unrealistic, driven more by ideals than rigorous macroeconomic analysis.

This article seeks to shift the terms of this debate by challenging the perceived certainties of economic knowledge, and accounting for the material and ideological biases that have led both national and international experts to overlook certain lived realities—human and nonhuman—within Chile. This new analytical approach calls for a complete reconsideration of the meaning of economic success, particularly within the narrow confines of international competition and rankings.

Johanna Gautier Morin is a historian of capitalism and economic knowledge from a global and intersectional perspective. She is currently Research Fellow in the Open Society Hub for the Politics of the Anthropocene at Central European University, where she works on the critical history of international economic indicators. She has published on the debt crisis, economic reforms, and the history of economic ideas in Algeria, Chile, and Mexico.

Notes

Support for this article came from ECOINT, a program that has received funding from the European Research Council (ERC) under the European Union's Horizon 2020 research and innovation programme (grant agreement No. 885285).

1. Katunaric, "CADA: Un ejemplo de la resistencia," 306.
2. On Rosenfeld's intervention, see Herzberg, *Historias recuperadas*, 31–69; Parkos Arnall, "Lotty Rosenfeld"; and Rosenfeld, "Una herida americana."
3. Peppelenbos, "Chilean Miracle," 1–4; French-Davis, "Is Chile a Role Model for Development?"
4. For a conservative and neoliberal critic of Allende's policies and a celebration of growth induced by the free-market policies adopted by the Pinochet regime, see Hojman, *Chile*; Bosworth, Dornbusch, and Labán, *Chilean Economy*; Kaiser, "Fall of Chile"; and Roberts and Araujo, *Capitalist Revolution in Latin America*.

5. On the impact of the oil shock on the Chilean economy in the 1970s and the austerity program introduced by the government in 1975, see Edwards, "Economic Policy," 2–4; and Caputo and Saravia, "The Monetary and Fiscal History of Chile," 14–15. On the critic of economic indicators as "abstractions," see Speich Chassé, "Use of Global Abstractions."

6. Naudon and Pérez, "Unemployment Dynamics in Chile"; Arellano, "El financiamiento del desarrollo"; Arellano, "De la liberalización a la intervención"; Velasco, "Liberalization, Crisis, Intervention"; Margitich, "1982 Debt Crisis"; Caputo and Saravia, "Monetary and Fiscal History of Chile."

7. Valdés, "El movimiento de pobladores"; Quiroga, "Las jornadas de protesta nacional"; Bravo, "Etnografía histórica de la protesta urbana"; Durán, "Los pobladores y la política"; Hoppe Guiñez, *Plebiscito en Chile*; Ulianova, Santoni, and Nocera, "Los años de la protesta."

8. Rowe, "Rise and Fall of Chile." Neoliberal thinkers praised the increase in consumption of household appliances such as TV sets, refrigerators, cars, washing machines, as a marker of prosperity for the many. See Kaiser, "Fall of Chile," 687.

9. Tinsman, *Partners in Conflict*, 9; Tinsman, *Buying into the Regime*, 76–77.

10. Winn, *Victims of the Chilean Miracle*, 56.

11. Schneider, *Shantytown Protest in Pinochet's Chile*, 153–90.

12. Richards, *Race and the Chilean Miracle*, 1–32, 70–100.

13. Edwards, *Chile Project*, 19.

14. Hausmann and Rodrick, "Economic Development as Self-Discovery"; Agosin and Bravo Ortega, "Emergence of New Successful Export Activities"; Agosin, Larraín, and Grau, *Industrial Policy in Chile*.

15. Escalante, "Influence of Pinochet"; Lebdioui, "Chile's Export Diversification"; Orihuela et al., "Decentralizing the Chilean Miracle."

16. Oakes, *Case of Chile*; Chawla, "Chilean Model of Development."

17. Teichman, *Politics of Freeing Markets*; Dezalay and Garth, *Internationalization of Palace Wars*; Bulmer-Thomas, *Economic History*; Compagnon, "L'Affaire Pinochet"; Solimano, "Three Decades"; Guillén Romo, "De Chicago à Santiago."

18. First declaration of the junta broadcasted on the Magallanes radio channel right after the coup, later signed by the four putschists, and published in *El Mercurio*, September 13, 1973, 3.

19. The expression "Marxist cancer" comes from General Gustavo Leigh, Pinochet's army commander who participated in the *pronunciamento*. It targeted the most criticized Allende's reforms, such as the series of nationalization of the financial and industrial sectors, land expropriations, and price control. See Gunson, "Obituary." For a discussion on the legitimacy-building of the Pinochet regime, see Valdivia Ortiz de Zárate, "Construction du pouvoir"; Lagos, Hounshell, and Dickinson, *The Southern Tiger*.

20. Cristi and Ruiz, "Conservative Thought"; Brava Lira, "Pueblo y Representación"; Silva, "Technocrats and Politics in Chile"; Silva, "Intelectuales"; Martínez and Díaz, *Chile*; Pollack, *New Right*; Boisard, *L'émergence*.

21. Silva, "Los tecnócratas y la política en Chile."

22. On the main targets of Pinochet's repression, see Amat, "State Repression," 517. On Allende's planning of the economy, see Stallings and Zimbalist, "Political Economy of the Unidad Popular," 70–71.

23. Frens-String, *Hungry for Revolution*, 193; Calderón Opazo, *Marta Ugarte*; Estrada Arellano, "Marta Ugarte."

24. Austin, "Armed Forces, Market Forces"; Boisard, Enders, and Verdo, "L'Amérique latine des régimes militaires"; Calvo, *La doctrina militar*; Huneeus, "Technocrats and Politicians"; Canelo, "La politique sous la dictature argentine."

25. Letelier, "Economic 'Freedom's' Awful Toll"; Letelier, "Economic 'Freedom' and Political Repression"; Letelier, "Les techniques économiques ne sont pas neutres." See a discussion of Letelier's publications in Lawner and Soto, *Orlando Letelier el que lo advirtió.*

26. Letelier, "Testament." Juan Gabriel Valdés later became Chile's ambassador to the United States and shared his memory of the event with the *BBC News* twenty years later: *BBC News*, "Chile's US Ambassador Remembers DC Car Bomb That Killed His Boss," June 16, 2014, YouTube video, 3:44, https://www.youtube.com/watch?v=K31QXHHKdjE&ab_channel=BBCNews. See also Saul Landau's testimony: Institute for Policy Studies, "IPS and the Letelier-Moffitt Assassinations," streamed live on February 26, 2013, YouTube video, 1:14:21, https://www.youtube.com/watch?v=FmXSWqMIJ9A&ab_channel=InstituteforPolicyStudies.

27. FBI Vault Archives, Memorandum from J. G. Deegan to R. J. Gallagher, "Bombing of Former Chilean Ambassador to US Massachusetts Avenue, Washington, D.C.," September 21, 1976; FBI General Investigation Division, Mr. Leavitt, September 23, 1976 (automatically declassified on November 17, 2021); FNI Unclassified EFTO, "Chilbom: PFO-Murder-Subversive," September 24, 1976.

28. FBI Vault Archives, Communication Section, FM Baltimore (174-2905) to Director Priority (185-789), EFTO "Chilbom; Protection of Foreign Officials—Murder; Explosives and Incendiary Devices—Subversive; 00:WFO," September 22, 1976.

29. CEPAL, "Defensor de los derechos humanos: homenaje a Raoul Wallenberg," 2013-03, LC/L.3597.

30. UN Department of Public Information, UN Secretary-General Boutros-Ghali, Boutros, "Secretary-General hopes impending judicial decision on 1976 murder of ECLAC staff member in Chile will facilitate long-awaited resolution of case: [statement, 14 Dec. 1994]," December 14, 1994, [ST/DPI/PRESS]ECLAC/337.

31. The Palacio de la Moneda is the seat of the president of the Republic of Chile in Santiago. It became infamous internationally when it was bombed during the 1973 coup. CEPAL's headquarters are located 7.7 km from the Palacio, in an upscale neighborhood now surrounded by golf courses and branches of US Ivy League universities.

32. McSherry, "Tracking the Origins of a State Terror Network"; McSherry, *Predatory States*; Dinges, *Condor Years*; Godoy, *Popular Injustice.*

33. Intervención de Alicia Bárcena, Secretaria Ejecutiva de la CEPAL, con ocasión del conversatorio: "CEPAL: Memorias del 73," CEPAL, November 8, 2016; Pozo Artigas, *Exiliados, emigrados y retornados.*

34. Kornbluh, *Pinochet File*, 83–87.

35. Drake, *Money Doctors*; Glaser, "Chile's Monetarist Money Doctors"; Boisard and Heredia, "Laboratoires de la mondialisation économique."

36. Valdés, *Pinochet's Economists.*

37. Biglaiser, "Internationalization of Chicago's Economics"; Fourcade, "Construction of a Global Profession"; Fourcade, *Economists and Societies*; Mirowski and Plehwe, *Road from Mont Pèlerin*; Lanteri and Vromen, *Economics of Economists*; Slobodian, *Globalists*; Saith, *Cambridge Economics in the Post-Keynesian Era*; Martin, *Meddlers.*

38. Fontaine Aldunate, *La historia no contada*; Délano and Traslaviña, *La Herencia de los Chicago Boys*; Sgard, *L'économie de la panique*, 29; Klein, *Shock Doctrine*; Silva, *In the*

Name of Reason; Fischer, "Influence of Neoliberals in Chile"; Guillén Romo, "De Chicago à Santiago."

39. Biglaiser, "Internationalization of Chicago's Economics"; Barder, "American Hegemony Comes Home."

40. Dezalay and Garth, *Global Prescriptions*; Ihl, "Objetividad de Estado."

41. Beckett, *Pinochet in Piccadilly*; Evans, "Pinochet in London"; Morley and McGuillon, *Reagan and Pinochet*; Livingstone, *Britain and the Dictatorships of Argentina and Chile*; Appelbaum, *Economists' Hour*; Saith, *Cambridge Economics in the Post-Keynesian Era*.

42. Farrant, McPhail, and Berger, "Preventing the 'Abuses' of Democracy"; Caldwell and Montes, "Friedrich Hayek."

43. Hayek, interview.

44. Friedman and Friedman. *Two Lucky People*, 400–402.

45. Weinraub, "Friedman, in Nobel Lecture."

46. Caldwell and Montes, "Friedrich Hayek," 304–5; Edwards and Montes, "Milton Friedman in Chile."

47. Sharma, "United States, the World Bank, and the Challenges of International Development"; Sharma, "Between North and South"; Kedar, "Economic Neutrality during the Cold War"; Kedar, "International Monetary Fund and the Chilean Chicago Boys."

48. Kedar, "World Bank-United States-Latin American Triangle."

49. Urzúa, "Five Decades of Relations"; Kofas, "Politics of Foreign Debt"; Kofas, "Stabilisation and Class Conflict"; Kofas, "IMF, the World Bank, and US Foreign Policy"; García Heras, *El Fondo Monetario y el Banco Mundial en la Argentina*; Kedar, "Beginning of a Controversial Relationship"; Kedar, "Chronicle of an Inconclusive Negotiation."

50. World Bank, *Chile: An Economy in Transition*, v.

51. World Bank, *Chile: An Economy in Transition*, 257.

52. Konkel, "Monetization of Global Poverty," 293–94.

53. De Castro, *El ladrillo*.

54. Gautier Morin and Rossier, "Interaction of Elite Networks."

55. Fernández Jilberto, "Chile: Burocracía militar"; Edwards, *Chile Project*, 82–85.

56. Silva, "Technocrats and Politics in Chile," 395.

57. Robert McNamara, quoted in *Philippines Daily Express*, Manila, May 21, 1976.

58. Wicker, "Two-Faced Policy for Chile."

59. Pryluka, "Advertising Pinochet."

60. IMF, *Minutes of Executive Board Meeting*, on "Chile – 1982 Article IV Consultation; Stand-By Arrangement; and Purchase Transaction – Compensatory Financing Facility," January 10, 1983, 83/8, 3–40. IMF online depository, https://archivescatalog.imf.org /Details/archive/125069905.

61. Caamaño-Carrillo, Contreras-Espinoza, and Nicolis, "Reconstructing the Quarterly Series of the Chilean Gross Domestic Product," 1827.

62. World Bank, *Chile: An Economy in Transition*, 258.

63. Azorín and Cavallini, "Estudio sobre la asignación de recursos"; Lopes, "Los censos como fuentes de datos"; Donoso, "Situación de las estadísticas vitales"; Preger, "Variables socio-económicas."

64. Donoso, "Analisis de la fecundidad diferencial de inmigrantes y nativas"; Cortés et al., *Investigación e información sociodemograficas*; Donoso, "Aplicaciones del modelo de Coale-Trussell"; Golini, "Fiftieth Anniversary of CELADE."

65. Boserup, *Women's Role in Economic Development*. For the debate this book triggered, see Benería and Sen, "Accumulation, Reproduction, and Women's Role in Economic Development."
66. UN Women, *Report of the World Conference*.
67. UNECLA, "Report of the Regional Conference on the Integration of Women."
68. Reid, *Economics of Household Production*.
69. Benería, "Accounting for Women's Work."
70. Raychaudhuri, "On Some Estimates of National Income"; Speich Chassé, "Use of Global Abstractions"; Avaro and Gautier Morin, "Uncovering the Hidden Value."
71. Nieves Rico, *Hacia la institucionalización del enfoque de género*; Daeren, "Enfoque de género en la política económica-laboral."
72. Pardo, "La dueña de casa y su aporte al PGB"; Pardo and Cruz, *La dueña de casa en sus actividades de trabajo*.
73. Thomas, "Decent Work in the Informal Sector," 8.
74. Luján Salazar and Vanek, "Informal Workers in Chile."
75. Hutchison, "El fruto envenenado del árbol capitalista," 133.
76. Cristi, *El pensamiento politico de Jaime Guzmán*; Correa Morande, *La guerra de las mujeres*; Power, *Right-Wing Women in Chile*, 217–47.
77. Palacios and Martínez, "Liberalism and Conservatism in Chile," 2.
78. Errázuriz, *La manzana de Adán*.
79. See, for example, the series of solemn portraits of Kawésqar people realized by photograph Paz Errázuriz from 1994 to 2002 (*Kawésqar*), and Patricio Guzmán's documentary *El Botón de Nácar* in 2015.
80. Clapp, "Creating Competitive Advantage," 287–88.
81. Christian, "Chile Promotes Forestry Industry."
82. Comisión Verdad Histórica, "Informe de la Comisión Verdad Histórica." For a general account of conflicts around forest expansion, see Reyes and Nelson, "Tale of Two Forests," 384; and Richards, *Race and the Chilean Miracle*.
83. Burgess, "Environmentalists and Glacier."
84. "Propuesta: Constitución Política de la República de Chile."
85. Raisbeck, "Chile's Proposed Left-Wing Constitution Could Spell Chaos"; *Financial Times*, "Chile's Draft Constitution Is Seriously Flawed."
86. Peña and Silva, *Social Revolt in Chile*; Palacios-Valladares, "Chile's 2019 October Protests"; Pozzi et al., "2019–2020 '*Chile despertó*' protests."
87. Edwards, *Chile Project*, 2. For pre-2019 evaluations of inequality in Chile, see OECD, *In It Together*, 291–332; UNDP, *Desiguales*.

References

Agosin, Manuel R., and Claudio Bravo Ortega. "The Emergence of New Successful Export Activities in Latin America: The Case of Chile." Inter-American Development Bank Working Paper 552, IADB, Washington DC, 2009.

Agosin, Manuel, Christian Larraín, and Nicolás Grau Veloso. *Industrial Policy in Chile*. Serie Documentos de Trabajo, Repositorio Académico de la Universidad de Chile, 2009. https://repositorio.uchile.cl/handle/2250/144090.

Agostini, Claudio A., Philip H. Brown, and Diana Paola Góngora. "Distribución especial de la pobreza en Chile." *Estudios de Economía* 35, no.1 (2008): 79–110.

Amat, Consuelo. "State Repression and Opposition Survival in Pinochet's Chile." *Comparative Political Studies* 57, no. 3 (2023): 506–45.

Appelbaum, Binyamin. *The Economists' Hour: False Prophets, Free Markets, and the Fracture of Society*. New York: Little, Brown and Company, 2019.

Arellano, José Pablo. "De la liberalización a la intervención: El mercado de capitales en Chile, 1974–1983." *El Trimestre Económico* 52, no. 207 (1985): 721–72.

Arellano, José Pablo. "El financiamiento del desarrollo." In *Reconstrucción económica para la democracia*, edited by Alejandro Foxley et al., 189–236. Santiago: Editorial Aconcagua and CIEPLAN, 1983.

Austin, Robert. "Armed Forces, Market Forces: Intellectuals and Higher Education in Chile, 1973–1993." *Latin American Perspectives* 24, no. 5 (1997): 26–58.

Avaro, Maylis, and Johanna Gautier Morin. "Uncovering the Hidden Value of Unpaid Work: A Global History of Marginalized Metrics." SocArXiv. May 3, 2024. https://doi.org/10.31235/osf.io/h8q6s.

Azorín, Francisco, and Carlos Cavallini. "Estudio sobre la asignación de recursos para el mejoramiento de las fuentes de estadísticas demográficas en los paises de América latina." CEPAL, División de Estadística, May 1974, 74-7-1385.

Barder, Alexander D. "American Hegemony Comes Home: The Chilean Laboratory and the Neoliberalization of the United States." *Alternatives: Global, Local, Political* 38, no. 2 (2013): 103–21.

Beckett, Andy. *Pinochet in Piccadilly: Britain and Chile's Hidden History*. London: Faber and Faber, 2002.

Benería, Lourdes. "Accounting for Women's Work: The Progress of Two Decades." *World Development* 20, no. 11 (1992): 1547–60.

Benería, Lourdes, and Gita Sen. "Accumulation, Reproduction, and 'Women's Role in Economic Development': Boserup Revisited." *Signs* 7, no. 2 (1981): 279–98.

Biglaiser, Glen. "The Internationalization of Chicago's Economics in Latin America." *Economic Development and Cultural Change* 50, no. 2 (2002): 269–96.

Boisard, Stéphane. "L'émergence d'une nouvelle droite: Monétarisme, conservatisme et autoritarisme au Chili (1955–1983)." PhD diss., Toulouse 2, 2001.

Boisard, Stéphane, Armelle Enders, and Geneviève Verdo, eds. "L'Amérique latine des régimes militaires." *Vingtième Siècle: Revue d'histoire*, no. 105 (2010): 3–209.

Boisard, Stéphane, and Mariana Heredia. "Laboratoires de la mondialisation économique. Regards croisés sur les dictatures argentine et chilienne des années 1970." *Vingtième Siècle: Revue d'histoire*, no. 105 (2010): 109–25.

Boserup, Ester. *Women's Role in Economic Development*. New York: St Martin's Press, 1970.

Bosworth, Barry P., Rudiger Dornbusch, and Raúl Labán, eds. *The Chilean Economy: Policy Lessons and Challenges*. Washington, DC: Brookings Institution, 1994.

Bouter, Artie C. "Residents of an Economy." In *The IMF's Statistical System in Context of Revision of the United Nations' System of National Accounts*, edited by Vincente Galbis, 3–19. Washington, DC: International Monetary Fund, 1991.

Brava Lira, Bernardino. "Pueblo y representación en la historia de Chile." *Revista Chilena de Derecho* 17, no. 1 (1990): 7–20.

Bravo, Viviana. "Etnografía histórica de la protesta urbana: Las jornadas nacionales contra la dictadura, Santiago de Chile, 1983–1986." *Revista Antropologías del Sur* 6, no. 12 (2019): 129–48.

Bulmer-Thomas, Victor. *The Economic History of Latin America since Independence*. New York: Cambridge University Press, 2003.

Burgess, Daniel. "Environmentalists and Glacier Activists Are Poised to Rewrite Chile's Constitution." *State of the Planet*, Columbia Climate School, July 9, 2021. https://news .climate.columbia.edu/2021/07/09/environmentalists-and-glacier-activists-are-poised-to -rewrite-chiles-constitution/.

Caamaño-Carrillo, Christian, Sergio Contreras-Espinoza, and Orietta Nicolis. "Reconstructing the Quarterly Series of the Chilean Gross Domestic Product Using a State Space Approach." *Mathematics* 11, no. 8 (2023): 1827–41.

Calderón Opazo, René. *Marta Ugarte: La vida por justicia; Vida y obra (1934–1976)*. Santiago: René Calderón Opazo, 2023.

Caldwell, Bruce, and Leonidas Montes. "Friedrich Hayek and His Visits to Chile." *Review of Austrian Economics* 28, no. 3 (2014): 261–309.

Calvo, Roberto. *La doctrina militar de la seguridad nacional: Autoritarismo político y neoliberalismo económico en el Cono Sur*. Caracas: Universidad Católica Andrés Bello, 1979.

Canelo, Paula. "La politique sous la dictature argentine: Le processus de réorganisation nationale ou la tentative inachevée de refonte de la société (1976–1983)." *Vingtième Siècle: Revue d'histoire*, no. 105 (2010): 81–92.

Caputo, Rodrigo, and Diego Saravia. "The Monetary and Fiscal History of Chile, 1960–2016." University of Chicago Working Paper, January 2019.

de Castro, Sergio, ed. *El ladrillo: Bases de la política económica del gobierno militar chileno*. Santiago: Centro de Estudios Publicos, 1992.

Chawla, R. L. "Chilean Model of Development." *India Quarterly* 59, nos. 1–2 (2003): 155–80.

Christian, Shirley. "International Report: Chile Promotes Forestry Industry." *New York Times*, October 31, 1988.

Clapp, Roger Alex. "Creating Competitive Advantage: Forest Policy as Industrial Policy in Chile." *Economic Geography* 71, no. 3 (1995): 273–96.

Comisión Verdad Histórica y Nuevo Trato con los Pueblos Indígenas. *Informe de la Comisión Verdad Histórica y Nuevo Trato con los Pueblos Indígenas*. Santiago: Comisionado Presidencial para Asuntos Indígenas, 2008.

Compagnon, Olivier. "L'Affaire Pinochet (1990–2006): La justification à l'épreuve des changements d'échelle." In *Affaires, scandales, et grandes causes: De Socrate à Pinochet*, edited by Luc Boltanski, Nicolas Offenstadt, Elisabeth Claverie, and Stéphane Van Damme, 347–64. Paris: Stock, 2007.

Correa Morande, María. *La guerra de las mujeres*. Santiago: Editorial Universidad Técnica del Estado, 1974.

Cortés, Fernando, Fresia Donoso, Mario Kaminsky, Adriana Marshall, Mónica Preger, Susana Torrado, and Luis Zuñiga. *Investigación e información sociodemograficas: Hacia un sistema integrado de estadísticas en América Latina*. Buenos Aires: CLACSO, 1977.

Cristi, Renato. *El pensamiento politico de Jaime Guzmán: Autoridad y libertad*. Santiago: Ediciones Lom, 2000.

Cristi, Renato, and Carlos Ruiz. "Conservative Thought in Twentieth Century Chile." *Canadian Journal of Latin American and Caribbean Studies* 15, no. 30 (1990): 27–66.

Daeren, Lieve. "Enfoque de género en la política económica-laboral: El estado del arte en Amérique Latina y el Caribe." Proyecto CEPAL-GTZ "Institucionalización del Enfoque de Género en la CEPAL y en Ministerios Sectoriales," LC/L.1500-P. Santiago, Chile, 2001.

Délano, Manuel, and Hugo Traslaviña. *La herencia de los Chicago Boys*. Santiago: Ornitorrinco, 1989.

Dezalay, Yves, and Bryant G. Garth, eds. *Global Prescriptions: The Production, Exportation, and Importation of a New Legal Orthodoxy*. Ann Arbor: University of Michigan Press, 2002.

Dezalay, Yves, and Bryant G. Garth. *The Internationalization of Palace Wars: Lawyers, Economists, and the Contest to Transform Latin American States.* Chicago: University of Chicago Press, 2002.

Dinges, John. *The Condor Years: How Pinochet and His Allies Brought Terrorism to Three Continents.* New York: New Press, 2005.

Donoso, Fresia. "Analisis de la fecundidad diferencial de inmigrantes y nativas, por provincia y area de residencia, Chile, 1960, trabajo final de investigación." Santiago: CEPAL/CELADE, 1965.

Donoso, Fresia. "Aplicaciones del modelo de Coale-Trussell para ajustar tasas por edad de fecundidad matrimonial." Santiago: Centro Latinoamericano de Demografía, 1979.

Donoso, Fresia. "Situación de las estadísticas vitales en América Latina." Documento de Referencia No. 4, presented to the Comité de Expertos para el Mejoramiento de las Fuentes de Estadísticas Demográficas, Buenos Aires, May 25–29, 1974.

Drake, Paul W., ed. *Money Doctors, Foreign Debts, and Economic Reforms in Latin America from the 1890s to the Present.* Lanham, MD: SR Books, 1994.

Durán, Mario Garcés. "Los pobladores y la política en los años ochenta: Reconstrucción de tejido social y protestas nacionales." *Historia* 396, no. 1 (2017): 119–48.

Edwards, Sebastián. *The Chile Project: The Story of the Chicago Boys and the Downfall of Neoliberalism.* Princeton, NJ: Princeton University Press, 2023.

Edwards, Sebastián. "Economic Policy and the Record of Economic Growth in Chile in the 1970s and 1980s." UCLA Working Paper no. 283 (1983): 1–34.

Edwards, Sebastián, and Leonidas Montes. "Milton Friedman in Chile: Shock Therapy, Economic Freedom, and Exchange Rates." *Journal of History of Economic Thought* 42, no. 1 (2020): 105–32.

Errázuriz, Paz. *Kawésqar, hijos de la mujer sol.* Santiago: Lom Ediciones, 2019.

Errázuriz, Paz. *La manzana de Adán.* Santiago: Zona, 1990.

Escalante, Edwar E. "The Influence of Pinochet on the Chilean Miracle." *Latin American Research Review* 57, no. 4 (2022): 831–47.

Estrada Arellano, Sergio. "Marta Ugarte: Entre dos tumbas y memorias; Reflexiones sobre el cuerpo y la muerte en los detenidos desaparecidos chilenos." *Antrópica: Revista de Ciencias Sociales y Humanidades* 4, no. 7 (2018): 57–74.

Evans, Rebecca. "Pinochet in London—Pinochet in Chile: International and Domestic Politics in Human Rights Policy." *Human Rights Quarterly* 28, no. 1 (2006): 207–44.

Farrant, Andrew, Edward McPhail, and Sebastian Berger. "Preventing the 'Abuses' of Democracy: Hayek, the 'Military Usurper,' and Transitional Dictatorship in Chile?" *American Journal of Economics and Sociology* 71, no. 3 (2012): 513–38.

Fernández Jilberto, Alex E. "Chile: Burocracia militar, oposición política y transición democrática." *Afers Internationals*, no. 9 (1986): 73–107.

French-Davis, Ricardo. "Is Chile a Role Model for Development?" In *Rethinking Development Strategies after the Financial Crisis*, volume 2, *Country Studies and International Comparisons*, edited by Alfredo Calcagno, Sebastian Dullien, Alejandro Márquez-Velázquez, Nicolas Maystre, and Jan Priewe, 81–92. New York: United Nations, 2016.

Financial Times. "Chile's Draft Constitution Is Seriously Flawed." August 30, 2022.

Fischer, Karin. "The Influence of Neoliberals in Chile before, during, and after Pinochet." In *The Road from Mont Pèlerin: The Making of the Neoliberal Thought Collective*, edited by Philip Mirowski and Dieter Plehwe, 305–46. Cambridge, MA: Harvard University Press, 2009.

Fontaine Aldunate, Arturo. *La historia no contada de los economistas y el president Pinochet.* Santiago: Zig-Zag, 1988.

Fourcade, Marion. "The Construction of a Global Profession: The Transnationalization of Economics." *American Journal of Sociology* 112, no. 1 (2006): 145–94.

Fourcade, Marion. *Economists and Societies: Discipline and Profession in the United States, Britain and France, 1890s to 1990s.* Princeton, NJ: Princeton University Press, 2009.

Frens-String, Joshua. *Hungry for Revolution: The Politics of Food and the Making of Modern Chile.* Oakland: University of California Press, 2021.

Friedman, Milton, and Rose D. Friedman. *Two Lucky People: Memoirs.* Chicago: University of Chicago Press, 1998.

García Heras, Raúl. *El Fondo Monetario y el Banco Mundial en la Argentina: Liberalismo, populismo y finanzas internacionales.* Buenos Aires: Lumiere, 2008.

Gautier Morin, Johanna, and Thierry Rossier. "The Interaction of Elite Networks in the Pinochet Regime's Macroeconomic Policies." *Global Networks* 21, no. 2 (2021): 339–64.

Glaser, Elisabeth. "Chile's Monetarist Money Doctors, 1850–1988." In *Money Doctors: The Experience of International Financial Advising, 1850–2000*, edited by Marc Flandreau, 166–89. London: Routledge, 2005.

Godoy, Angelina Snodgrass. *Popular Injustice: Violence, Community, and Law in Latin America.* Stanford, CA: Stanford University Press, 2006.

Golini, Antonio. "The Fiftieth Anniversary of CELADE." *Genus* 63, nos. 3–4 (2007): 9–17.

Guillén Romo, Héctor. "De Chicago à Santiago: Le modèle économique chilien." *Revue Internationale et Stratégique* 91, no. 3 (2013): 107–15.

Hausmann, Ricardo, and Dani Rodrik. "Economic Development as Self-Discovery." *Journal of Development Economics* 72, no. 2 (2003): 603–33.

Hayek, Friedrich. Interview. *El Mercurio*, April 12, 1981, 8–9.

Herzberg, Julia P. *Historias recuperadas: Aspectos del arte contemporáneo en Chile desde 1982.* New York: Centro Latino de Arte y Cultura; Rutgers: State University of New Jersey, 1993.

Hojman, David E. *Chile: The Political Economy of Development and Democracy in the 1990s.* Pittsburgh: University of Pittsburgh Press, 1993.

Hojman, David E. "Poverty and Inequality in Chile: Are Democratic Politics and Neoliberal Economics Good for You?" *Journal of Interamerican Studies and World Affairs* 38, nos. 2–3 (1996): 73–96.

Hoppe Guiñez, Álvaro. *Plebiscito en Chile, 1988.* Santiago: Haikén Ediciones and Galeria Zebra, 2020.

Huneeus, Carlos. "Technocrats and Politicians in an Authoritarian Regime. The 'ODEPLAN Boys' and the 'Gremialists' in Pinochet's Chile." *Journal of Latin American Studies* 32, no. 2 (2000): 461–501.

Hutchison, Elizabeth Q. "'El fruto envenenado del árbol capitalista': Women Workers and Prostitution of Labor in Urban Chile, 1896–1925." *Journal of Women's History* 9, no. 4 (1998): 131–51.

Ihl, Olivier. "Objectividad de Estado: Sur la science de gouvernement des Chicago Boys dans le Chili de Pinochet." *Revue Internationale de Politique Comparée* 19, no. 3 (2012): 67–88.

Kaiser, Axel. "The Fall of Chile." *Cato Journal* 40, no. 3 (2020): 685–700.

Katunaric, Cecilia. "CADA: Un ejemplo de la resistencia del poder cultural chileno bajo dictadura." *Pandora: Revue d'études hispaniques*, no. 8 (2008): 306.

Kedar, Claudia. "The Beginning of a Controversial Relationship: The IMF, the World Bank and Argentina, 1943–46." *Canadian Journal of Latin American and Caribbean Studies* 35, no. 60 (2010): 201–30.

Kedar, Claudia. "Chronicle of an Inconclusive Negotiation: Perón, the International Monetary Fund, and the World Bank (1946–1955)." *Hispanic American Historical Review* 92, no. 4 (2012): 637–68.

Kedar, Claudia. "Economic Neutrality during the Cold War: The World Bank, the United States, and Pinochet's Chile, 1973–1977." *Cold War History* 18, no. 2 (2018): 149–67.

Kedar, Claudia. "The International Monetary Fund and the Chilean Chicago Boys, 1973–7: Cold Ties between Warm Ideological Partners." *Journal of Contemporary History* 54, no. 1 (2019): 179–201.

Kedar, Claudia. "The World Bank-United States-Latin American Triangle: The Negotiations with Socialist Chile, 1970–1973." *International History Review* 39, no. 4 (2017): 667–90.

Klein, Naomi. *The Shock Doctrine: The Rise of Disaster Capitalism.* New York: Metropolitan Books, 2007.

Kofas, Jon. "The IMF, the World Bank, and US Foreign Policy in Ecuador, 1956–1966." *Latin American Perspectives* 28, no. 5 (2001): 50–83.

Kofas, Jon. "The Politics of Foreign Debt: The IMF, the World Bank, and US Foreign Policy in Chile, 1946–1952." *Journal of Developing Areas* 31, no. 2 (1997): 157–82.

Kofas, Jon. "Stabilisation and Class Conflict: The State Department, the IMF, and the IBRD in Chile, 1952–58." *International History Review* 21, no. 2 (1999): 352–85.

Konkel, Rob. "The Monetization of Global Poverty: The Concept of Poverty in World Bank History, 1944–90." *Journal of Global History* 9, no. 2 (2014): 276–300.

Kornbluh, Peter. *The Pinochet File: A Declassified Dossier on Atrocity and Accountability.* New York: New Press, 2013.

Lagos, Ricardo, with Blake Hounshell and Elizabeth Dickinson. *The Southern Tiger: Chile's Fight for a Democratic and Prosperous Future.* New York: St. Martin's Press, 2012.

Lanteri, Alessandro, and Jack Vromen, eds. *The Economics of Economists: Institutional Setting, Individual Incentives, and Future Prospects.* Cambridge: Cambridge University Press, 2014.

Lawner, Miguel, and Hernán Soto. *Orlando Letelier el que lo advirtió: Los Chicago Boys en Chile.* Santiago: LOM Ediciones, 2011.

Lebdioui, Amir. "Chile's Export Diversification since 1960: A Free-Market *Miracle* or *Mirage*?" *Development and Change* 50, no. 6 (2019): 1624–63.

Letelier, Orlando. "Chile: Economic 'Freedom' and Political Repression." *Race and Class* 18, no. 3 (1977): 247–60.

Letelier, Orlando. "Economic 'Freedom's' Awful Toll: The 'Chicago Boys' in Chile." *Review of Radical Political Economics* 8, no. 3 (1976): 44–52.

Letelier, Orlando. "Les techniques économiques ne sont pas neutres." *Le Monde Diplomatique*, October 1976, 16–17.

Letelier, Orlando. "A Testament." *New York Times*, September 27, 1976.

Livingstone, Grace. *Britain and the Dictatorships of Argentina and Chile, 1973–1982: Foreign Policy, Corporations, and Social Movements.* Cham: Palgrave Macmillan, 2018.

Lopes, Valdecir F. "Los censos como fuentes de datos demográficos en América latina." *Notas de Población* (1974): 49–62.

Luján Salazar, José de Jesús, and Joann Vanek. "Informal Workers in Chile: A Statistical Profile." WIEGO Statistical Brief no. 30 (2022): 1–19.

Margitich, Michael. "The 1982 Debt Crisis and Recovery in Chile." Chile in Transition: Perspectives on Business and Economics, Lehigh University Working Paper 5, 1999.

Martin, Jamie. *The Meddlers: Sovereignty, Empire, and the Birth of Global Economic Governance.* Cambridge, MA: Harvard University Press, 2022.

Martínez, Javier, and Álvaro Díaz. *Chile: The Great Transformation*. Geneva: UNRISD, 1996.

McSherry, J. Patrice. *Predatory States: Operation Condor and Covert War in Latin America*. Lanham, MD: Rowman and Littlefield, 2005.

McSherry, J. Patrice. "Tracking the Origins of a State Terror Network: Operation Condor." *Latin American Perspective* 29, no. 1 (2002): 38–60.

Mirowski, Philip, and Dieter Plehwe, eds. *The Road from Mont Pèlerin: The Making of the Neoliberal Thought Collective*. Cambridge, MA: Harvard University Press, 2009.

Morley, Morris, and Chris McGuillon. *Reagan and Pinochet: The Struggle over US Policy toward Chile*. Cambridge: Cambridge University Press, 2015.

Naudon D., Alberto, and Andrés Pérez M. "Unemployment Dynamics in Chile: 1960–2015." *Economía Chilena* 21, no. 1 (2018): 4–33.

Nieves Rico, María. *Hacia la institucionalización del enfoque de género en las políticas económico-laborales en América Latina*. Informe del seminario regional, Unidad Mujer y Desarrollo, LC/L.1667-P. Santiago: CEPAL, 2001.

Oakes, Pamela. *The Case of Chile: Export Orientation as a Model for Development in Latin America*. Miami: University of Miami, 1994.

OECD. *In It Together: Why Less Inequality Benefits All*. Paris: OECD Publishing, 2015.

Orihuela, Javier Cortés, Juan D. Díaz, Pablo Gutiérrez Cubillos, Alexis Montecinos, Pablo A. Troncoso, and Gabriel I. Villarroel. "Decentralizing the Chilean Miracle: Regional Intergenerational Mobility in a Developing Country." *Regional Studies* 57, no. 5 (2023): 785–99.

Palacios, Margarita, and Javier Martínez. "Liberalism and Conservatism in Chile: Attitudes and Opinions of Chilean Women at the Start of the Twenty-First Century." *Journal of Latin American Studies* 38, no. 1 (2006): 1–34.

Palacios-Valladares, Indira. "Chile's 2019 October Protests and the Student Movement: Eventful Mobilization?" *Revista de Ciencia Política* 40, no. 2 (2020): 215–34.

Pardo V., Lucía. "La dueña de casa y su aporte al PGB." *Revista de Economía* 15 (1983): 34–45.

Pardo V., Lucía, and Pablo Cruz N. *La dueña de casa en sus actividades de trabajo: Su valoración en el mercado y dentro del hogar*. Documento Serie Investigación 59, Santaigo: Universidad de Chile, Departamento de Economía, 1983.

Parkos Arnall, January. "Lotty Rosenfeld." *Radical Women: Latin American Art, 1960–1985*, Archives of Women Artists, Research, and Exhibitions, https://awarewomenartists.com/en/artiste/lotty-rosenfeld/ (accessed November 18, 2023).

Peña, Carlos, and Patricio Silva, eds. *Social Revolt in Chile: Triggering Factors and Possible Outcomes*. New York: Routledge, 2022.

Peppelenbos, Lucian Peter Christopher. "The Chilean Miracle: Patrimonialism in a Modern Free-Market Democracy." PhD dissertation, Wageningen University, 2005.

Pollack, Marcelo. *The New Right in Chile, 1973–97*. New York: St Martin's Press, 1999.

Power, Margaret. *Right-Wing Women in Chile: Feminine Power and the Struggle against Allende, 1964–1973*. State College: Pennsylvania State University Press, 2010.

Pozo Artigas, José del, ed. *Exiliados, emigrados y retornados: Chilenos en América y Europa, 1973–2004*. Santiago: RIL Editores, 2006.

Pozzi, Maura, Stefano Passini, Maria Chayinska, Davide Morselli, Adriano Mauro Ellena, Anna Włodarczyk, and Carlo Pistoni. "'Coming Together to Awaken Our Democracy': Examining Precursors of Emergent Social Identify and Collective Action among Activists and Non-activists in the 2019–2020 'Chile despertó' Protests." *Journal of Community and Applied Social Psychology* 32, no. 5 (2022): 830–45.

Preger, Mónica. "Variables socio-económicas relacionadas con estadísticas vitales e información censal sobre migraciones en América latina." Communication to the Working Group "Sistema integrado de Estadísticas Demográficas y Socio-Económicas." Comisión de Población y Desarrollo (CLACSO), Mexico, December 2–6, 1974.

"Propuesta: Constitución Política de la República de Chile." July 4, 2022. https://www.colegiodeprofesores.cl/wp-content/uploads/2022/07/Texto-Definitivo-CPR-2022-Tapas.pdf (accessed November 22, 2023).

Pryluka, Pablo. "Advertising Pinochet: The Cold War Limits to a Neoliberal Crusade." *International History Review* 45, no. 2 (2023): 416–30.

Quiroga, Patricio. "Las jornadas de protesta nacional: Historia, estrategias y resultado (1983–1986)." *Revista Encuentro XXI* 4, no. 11 (1998): 42–60.

Raisbeck, Daniel. "Chile's Proposed Left-Wing Constitution Could Spell Chaos." *Reason*, August 26, 2022.

Raychaudhuri, G. S. "On Some Estimates of National Income: Indian Economy, 1858–1947." *Economic and Political Weekly* 1, no. 16 (1966): 673–79.

Reid, Margaret. *Economics of Household Production*. New York: J. Wiley and Sons, 1934.

Reyes, R., and H. Nelson. "A Tale of Two Forests: Why Forests and Forest Conflicts Are Both Growing in Chile." *International Forestry Review* 16, no. 4 (2014): 379–88.

Richards, Patricia. *Race and the Chilean Miracle: Neoliberalism, Democracy, and Indigenous Rights*. Pittsburgh: University of Pittsburgh Press, 2013.

Roberts, Paul Craig, and K. Lafollete Araujo. *The Capitalist Revolution in Latin America*. New York: Oxford University Press, 1997.

Rosenfeld, Lotty. "Una herida americana." In *Desacato: Sobre la obra de Lotty Rosenfeld*, edited by María Eugenia Brito. Santiago: Francisco Zegers, 1986.

Rowe, James L., Jr. "The Rise and Fall of Chile." *Washington Post*, August 18, 1985.

Saith, Ashwani. *Cambridge Economics in the Post-Keynesian Era: The Eclipse of Heterodox Traditions*. Cham: Palgrave Macmillan, 2022.

Schneider, Cathy Lisa. *Shantytown Protest in Pinochet's Chile*. Philadelphia: Temple University Press, 1995.

Sgard, Jérôme. *L'économie de la panique. Faire face aux crises financières*. Paris: La Découverte, 2002.

Sharma, Patrick. "Between North and South: The World Bank and the New International Economic Order." *Humanity* 6, no. 1 (2015): 189–200.

Sharma, Patrick. "The United States, the World Bank, and the Challenges of International Development in the 1970s." *Diplomatic History* 37, no. 3 (2013): 572–604.

Silva, Patricio. *In the Name of Reason: Technocrats and Politics in Chile*. State College: Pennsylvania State University Press, 2009.

Silva, Patricio. "Intelectuales, tecnócratas y cambio social en Chile: Pasado, presente y perspectivas futuras." *Revista Mexicana de Sociología* 54, no. 1 (1992): 139–66.

Silva, Patricio. "Los tecnócratas y la política en Chile: pasado y presente." *Revista de Ciencia Política* 26, no. 2 (2006): 175–90.

Silva, Patricio. "Technocrats and Politics in Chile: From the Chicago Boys to the CIEPLAN Monks." *Journal of Latin American Studies* 23, no. 2 (1991): 385–410.

Slobodian, Quinn. *Globalists: The End of Empire and the Birth of Neoliberalism*. Cambridge, MA: Harvard University Press, 2018.

Solimano, Andrés. "Three Decades of Neoliberal Economics in Chile: Achievements, failures and dilemmas." WIDER Research Paper, 37 (2009): 1–33.

Speich Chassé, Daniel. "The use of global abstractions: national income accounting in the period of imperial decline." *Journal of Global History* 6, no.1 (2011): 7–28.

Stallings, Barbara, and Andy Zimbalist. "The Political Economy of the Unidad Popular." *Latin American Perspectives* 2, no. 1 (1975): 69–88.

Teichman, Judith A. *The Politics of Freeing Markets in Latin America: Chile, Argentina, and Mexico*. Chapel Hill: University of North Carolina Press, 2001.

Thomas, Jim. "Decent Work in the Informal Sector: Latin America." Working Paper on the Informal Economy. Geneva: International Labor Organization, 2002.

Tinsman, Heidi. *Buying into the Regime: Grapes and Consumption in Cold War Chile and the United States*. Durham, NC: Duke University Press, 2014.

Tinsman, Heidi. *Partners in Conflict: The Politics of Sexuality, Gender and Labor in the Chilean Agrarian Reform, 1950–1973*. Durham, NC: Duke University Press, 2002.

Ulianova, Olga, Alessandro Santoni, and Raffaele Nocera. "Los años de la protesta, 1983–86." In *Un protagonismo recobrado: La Democracía Cristiana chilena y sus vínculos internacionales (1973–1990)*, 149–68. Santiago: Ariadna Ediciones, 2021.

UN Women. *Report of the World Conference of the International Women's Year, Mexico City, 19 June–2 July 1975*. E/CONF.66/34. New York: United Nations.

UNDP (United Nations Development Program). *Desiguales: Orígenes, cambios y desafíos de la brecha social en Chile*. Santiago: Programa de las Naciones Unidas para el Desarrollo, 2017.

UNECLA. "Report of the Regional Conference on the Integration of Women in the Economic and Social Development of Latin America." Havana, Cuba, June 13–17, 1977, E/CEPAL/1042/Rev.1, November 21, 1977.

Urzúa, Carlos. "Five Decades of Relations Between the World Bank and Mexico." In *The World Bank: Its First Half Century*, vol. 2, *Perspectives*, edited by Devesh Kapur, John Lewis, and Richard Webb, 49–108. Washington, DC: Brookings Institution Press, 1997.

Valdés, Juan Gabriel. *Pinochet's Economists: the Chicago School of Economics in Chile*. Cambridge: Cambridge University Press, 1995.

Valdés, Teresa. "El movimiento de pobladores, 1973–1985: La recomposición de las solidaridades sociales." In *Descentralización el Estado: Movimiento social y gestión local*, edited by Jordi Borja, Teresa Valdés, Hernán Pozo, and Eduardo Morales, 263–319. Santiago: FLACSO, 1987.

Valdivia Ortiz de Zárate, Verónica. "Construction du pouvoir et régime militaire sous Augusto Pinochet." *Vingtième Siècle: Revue d'histoire*, no. 105 (2010): 93–107.

Velasco, Andrés. "Liberalization, Crisis, Intervention: The Chilean Financial System, 1975–85." In *Banking Crises: Cases and Issues*, 113–74. Washington, DC: International Monetary Fund, 1991.

Weinraub, Bernard. "Friedman, in Nobel Lecture, Challenges a Tradition." *New York Times*, December 14, 1976.

Wicker, Tom. "A Two-Faced Policy for Chile." *Spokesman Review*, June 16, 1976, 4.

Winn, Peter, ed. *Victims of the Chilean Miracle: Workers and Neoliberalism in the Pinochet Era, 1973–2002*. Durham, NC: Duke University Press, 2004.

World Bank. *Chile: An Economy in Transition*. Washington DC: World Bank, 1980.

Living with Inflation

Policymaking and Popular Practices in Search of Price Stability after Brazil's Economic Miracle

Melissa Teixeira

"Be a woman, bargain" became official economic policy in Brazil in 1973 (fig. 1). In newspapers and magazines, the military government ran its "Say No to Inflation" campaign encouraging women to be flirty and thrifty so that they could "buy more things," spinning this counterintuitive logic into a strategy for how to sustain economic growth as inflation undermined consumers' purchasing power.[1] Between 1968 and 1973, Brazil's economy grew at an impressive average annual rate of 11 percent. Inflation also fell from 82 percent in 1963 to 16 percent by 1973.[2] This so-called economic miracle coincided with the most repressive years of the twenty-one-year military dictatorship (1964–85), the *anos de chumbo* (years of lead).[3] Taking credit for the double-digit growth rates coupled with low inflation, something that once seemed unattainable, the military regime shored up support from its key constituents—industrialists, middle-class consumers, and producers—by weaving a narrative that democracy was bad for economic stability, and blaming prior inflationary spirals on profligate democratic governments and workers' demands for higher wages.

This article explores the role of inflation in making and dismantling Brazil's economic miracle. From 1973 to 1993, the world, according to the historian Eric Hobsbawm, "lost its bearings and slid into instability and crisis."[4] This crisis proved so demoralizing because it extinguished a remarkable period of postwar expansion

Radical History Review

Issue 151 (January 2025)   DOI 10.1215/01636545-11506847

© 2025 by MARHO: The Radical Historians' Organization, Inc.

Figure 1. "Seja mulher, pechinche" (Be a woman, bargain). *Jornal do Brasil*, September 10, 1973. Image courtesy of Jornal do Brasil Acervo.

for nations like France, Spain, Japan, Mexico, and Brazil. Soaring inflation announced the end of these miracles, and economists were forced to rethink their growth models.[5] Yet as "stagflation" became an intractable problem for countries worldwide, Brazil charted its own course. Rather than try to tame inflation, Brazilian officials configured it into a manageable tradeoff with continued high growth rates, and this strategy allowed the military regime to prolong the illusion of its economic triumphs.

Following the 1973 oil shock, inflation spiraled upward in Brazil to become a leading indicator for how the military's economic feats might be more mirage than miracle. Throughout the 1970s, regional inequalities widened, debt ballooned, and workers saw their purchasing power eroded by inflation, especially those employed in informal sectors. Even as the shortcomings of the military's economic planning became apparent, Brazilian policymakers doubled down on their magical formulas, accounting tools, and economic models to repackage their failures into deliberate strategies for growth. Leading officials might have voiced loyalty to austerity prescriptions from the International Monetary Fund (IMF) and other classically trained economists, but they also spurned the conventional wisdom that fiscal and monetary restraint was the only way to achieve price stability. Brazilian policymakers instead opted for a strategy of living with, rather than eradicating, inflation. They designed price controls and indexed wages and financial assets to keep pace with inflation.[6] They also mobilized consumers—especially women—to negotiate prices and report retailers who disregarded price controls to authorities, while still urging them to keep spending.[7] The military's miracle depended on debt-fueled government spending, with austerity limited to severe wage repression for workers—and even that was no match for inflation.[8] Thus, this regime ultimately abandoned its promise of low inflation and instead tried to convince the public (and themselves) that high inflation was a driver of sustainable development that would bear fruit in the near future.

Economic policymaking during and after Brazil's miracle allows us to reconstruct how Brazilians experienced the intense and persistent inflation that defined daily life in the 1970s and 1980s. Looking beyond macroeconomic trends and statistics, I ask how economists, policymakers, and consumers understood and tried to fix (or live with) inflation. While inflation conditioned everyday hardships for Brazilians, there is relatively little research on anti-inflation policies or how citizens navigated dramatic swings between government-imposed price freezes and the inflationary spirals that persisted in spite of them. By examining some of their strategies, petitions, and predictions, I recover the economic thinking that shaped Brazil's spectacular postwar boom and bust, beginning with the military regime's reforms in the 1960s and concluding with the Plano Cruzado in the 1980s. My aim is not to explain the causes of inflation or to evaluate policy best practices. Rather, I explore how "living with inflation" became official policy as the military attempted to maintain high growth rates and, more important, why government officials tackled inflation with even bolder experiments during the country's democratization after 1985. In this drawn-out aftermath of Brazil's miracle, we see how inflation continued to anchor seductive myths about future prosperity.

In Brazil, the unconventional and heterodox policies tested to tackle inflation across these decades are often the target of ridicule; economics has its iron laws, many will insist, and prices rise and fall in predictable ways. For economists within and beyond Brazil, the country is a cautionary tale. Despite the efforts of its technocrats to freeze, forecast, and regulate prices, chronic inflation persisted and turned hyperinflationary as the country steered its democratic transition. Such conclusions, implicitly or explicitly, inform how economists explain the "success" of the 1994 Plano Real in "finally" taming inflation by celebrating its embrace of market-based strategies. By focusing on its "success," however, some scholars overlook how the Plano Real was itself unorthodox in pegging Brazil's currency to a nonmonetary currency that eventually transitioned into a new currency, the *real*. Even the best scholarship on inflation, the anthropologist Federico Neiburg notes, will "ignore the heterodox experiments, or merely subsume them (based on anachronic projections) into the 'predecessors of the neoliberal era.'"[9] Recent scholarship, however, has emphasized the tendency of Brazil's postwar governments (both authoritarian and democratic) to bend economic rules in order to highlight the intellectual continuities across these decades of policy experimentation in Brazil. This article builds on these observations by exploring the institutional legacies, economic beliefs, and political ambitions that shaped the design and implementation of anti-inflation plans from the 1960s to the 1980s.[10] These experiments may have failed, but they also made it possible for Brazilians to cope with decades of crisis.

Brazilian citizens also shaped these decades of policy experimentation by imposing their evolving expectations about government's responsibility in guaranteeing fair prices and a decent standard of living. Brazilian retailers, producers, and consumers had to constantly update their strategies to deal with wildly fluctuating prices and frequently changing rules. The question of what is a fair price and who decides has been central to political struggles in Brazil since the early twentieth century, with poor and working classes mobilizing for government protections against the rising cost of living.[11] Recently, historians of Latin America have approached consumption, especially to meet basic needs, as an issue of the political and social struggle to expand the meanings and practices of citizenship.[12] For Brazil in the 1970s and 1980s, workers' strikes, women's associations, and other pro-democracy movements seized on cost-of-living issues to protest military rule and to advocate for the rights of citizens and consumers. In less overtly political—but still forceful—ways, consumers also channeled complaints about rising prices to state agencies and police precincts, exposing the gaps between government promises for renewed prosperity and their fulfillment. As inflation accelerated throughout the century, it transformed price from a standard-of-living issue into a question of government accountability and, consequently, a cornerstone of democracy itself. In Brazil, the history of inflation is also the history of how its economic miracle collapsed into a protracted process of democratization.

Miracle or Mirage: Inflation and the Military's Economic Plan

The economic history of twentieth-century Brazil can just as easily be written as a story of booms, development, and progress as one of busts, crises, and hardships. From 1968 to 1973, military generals and their economic advisors celebrated the economic miracle not only for high growth rates but also for their triumph over past disappointments. Following decades, if not centuries, of anticipation of the country's industrialization, some Brazilians found evidence that Brazil had finally transformed into the *país do futuro* (country of the future), a phrase made famous by the Austrian-Jewish writer Stefan Zweig while he was exiled in Brazil during World War II. From 1929 to 1945, industry increased its share of Brazil's output from 20.3 percent to 28.6 percent, while agriculture fell from 36.9 percent to 28 percent.[13] By 1964, agriculture accounted for only 16 percent of national GDP and industry for 32 percent.[14] Upon seizing power in 1964, the military committed itself to accelerating this trend. To many, Brazil's ascent to the ranks of wealthy, industrialized, modern nations was not only evident in statistics on industrial production but also in infrastructure feats like the Trans-Amazonian Highway or in middle-class homes now equipped with televisions. As one journalist explained in 1971, "This is Brazil, which is getting stronger day by day, leaving behind the stigma of underdevelopment. . . . Today's Brazil, which yesterday was the country of the future, is now a nation of the present."[15]

Yet whereas some considered it prophetic that Brazil was the *país do futuro*, others could not help but find irony in how economists were always so eager to project the country's successes far into the future. Despite Brazil's rapid industrialization in postwar decades, some economists pointed to why it remained improbable that the country would achieve the standard of living of France or the United States. At best, one Brazilian economist said derisively in 1968, Brazil might assume "merely the position of arrogant leader to the luminous Third World."[16]

Despite past defeats and persistent skepticism, the military regime nonetheless attempted, in the words of the historian Carlos Fico, to "reinvent optimism" and thereby staked its legitimacy on promises of economic prosperity and political stability.[17] Taming inflation was key to both objectives. Alongside programs to promote industrialization, Brazilian officials also initiated bold reforms to bring down inflation and simultaneously enlisted conservative women's groups to patrol price controls and denounce offending retailers. With both tactics, the military regime celebrated its triumphs over inflation while detaching the issue from workers' struggles for higher wages.

To offer some context, by the mid-1960s, chronic inflation had become the troubling counterpart to Brazil's fast-paced development. Since the late 1930s, rising prices, especially for food, presented social and political problems for Brazil's governments, as workers in industrializing cities demanded higher wages. Under Getúlio Vargas, Brazil's dictator turned populist president from 1930 to 1945 and again from 1951 to 1954, the federal government created agencies to issue price controls for essential goods and oversee the distribution of food from countryside to city. Such measures did not fix inflation, but they did recognize government protections for fair prices as an essential component of social citizenship—and revealed the extent to which inflation would remain a liability for postwar governments attempting to drive industrialization and maintain social peace. Organized labor pushed for higher wages and more government controls to deal with *carestia*, or the rising cost of living.[18] Juscelino Kubitschek, president from 1956 to 1961, coordinated an impressive state-led drive for development, promising fifty years of growth in just five. Brazil experienced high growth rates of 9 percent to 10 percent, while middle-class consumers enjoyed greater access to automobiles and televisions.[19] Critics, however, pointed to Brazil's ballooning debt and its worsening balance of payments, blaming Kubitschek for fifty years of inflation in five. Once he left office, worsening economic conditions fueled political instability.

In postwar Brazil, inflation became the target of political conflicts and fierce intellectual debate. Brazilian economists often fell into one of two camps: monetarists, who recited economist Milton Friedman's assertion that "inflation is always and everywhere a monetary phenomenon" and argued that fiscal and monetary discipline was essential for price stability; and structuralists and dependency theorists, who argued that inflation was a consequence of underdevelopment because of domestic bottlenecks and the worsening terms of trade.[20] This latter group emphasized concerning trends: while, on average, industrial output increased annually by 9 percent between 1945 and 1973, agriculture increased by only 4 percent. The growing gap between industrial and agricultural sectors posed a challenge to long-run stability. First, Brazil remained dependent on agricultural exports, especially coffee, to cushion its balance of payments and cover the importation of capital goods to support industrialization. Second, food production could not keep up with the demands of an industrializing nation. Food prices increased by 338 percent between 1939 and 1950 and by 465 percent between 1950 and 1960. This trend worsened in the 1960s, with food prices rising by an astonishing 1,706 percent between 1960 and 1967.[21] Neither economists nor consumers could deny that the greater ease with which middle-class households acquired automobiles had not eradicated the challenges they faced to meet basic needs.

While it is an oversimplification to argue that inflation triggered the 1964 coup in Brazil, it is equally impossible to explain popular and political support for dictatorship without accounting for the rising cost of living and general sense of economic instability.[22] By March 1964, annual inflation approached 100 percent, which opposition groups marshalled as proof of the government's failures.[23] The military overthrew João Goulart, president from 1961 to 1964, and consolidated support from conservative movements, including those led by *donas de casa*, or housewives. The Campanha da Mulher pela Democracia (CAMDE) based in Rio de Janeiro, for example, was emphatic in its anticommunist stance and its calls for military intervention. Historians emphasize CAMDE's growing political power and how these women forged transnational connections to similar movements in Chile and the United States.[24] Beyond anticommunism, CAMDE also rallied behind fighting inflation in endorsing the military's promises to restore economic stability.[25]

The challenges that middle-class housewives faced in buying milk or meat amounted to real hardships, which they leveraged to claim their moral authority on economic issues. Consider how CAMDE maneuvered preexisting institutions. Upon seizing power, the military regime kept the elaborate system of price controls used by prior governments. Key was the Superintendência Nacional de

Abastecimento (SUNAB), a federal agency created in 1962 to set price controls on essential goods and regulate the food supply. This agency led inspections nationwide and penalized producers, warehousers, or venders who did not abide by price controls. From its inception, SUNAB depended on consumer denunciations, and this generated official and unofficial channels for *donas de casa* to participate in the battle against inflation. After the 1964 coup, CAMDE routinely met with representatives from SUNAB as well as from the ministries of agriculture, finance, and planning.[26] CAMDE also printed ads in newspapers on how to denounce violators to authorities and issued "blacklists" of retailers who refused to follow SUNAB pricing.

CAMDE (and its counterparts) turned cost-of-living campaigns into a central component of their "work to rebuild democracy," with their definition of democracy inescapably tied to their anticommunist position and their conviction that the populist orientation of prior democratic governments had ceded too much moral and material ground to organized labor.[27] For decades, workers had called on the government to guarantee fair prices, articulating these claims as essential social rights. In the 1960s, CAMDE leveraged women's roles as caretakers and consumers to cast inflation as a problem that interfered with their "daily responsibility to properly nourish their husbands and children."[28] By working with SUNAB, women carved out a public role for themselves in economic planning, but one that reinforced normative gender roles. Groups like CAMDE in Rio de Janeiro or the Campanha da Mulher Contra a Inflação in Curitiba tried to depoliticize inflation by framing it as a family matter, but such arguments also served the military's pro-business and antilabor orientation. Conservative women defended their actions in the name of "democracy," yet their definition of democracy amounted to a dictatorship trying to neutralize social conflicts around economic problems by turning inflation into an "easy understanding between government, business, and consumers."[29]

To tackle inflation and jump-start growth, the military regime launched a new economic program that generally benefited industrialists and consumers, while workers bore the burden of austerity policies. Minister of Planning Roberto Campos promised fiscal and monetary reforms with the aim of restoring price stability. From 1964 to 1967, his Programa de Ação Econômica do Governo (PAEG) took a three-pronged approach: first, eliminate government deficits and restore confidence in government bonds with the Readjustable Obligations of the National Treasury (ORTN), an inflation-indexed bond that made it possible to finance long-term borrowing; second, restrict credit to businesses to tame demand-fueled inflation; and third, use a formula for automatic salary adjustments to align wages with productivity.[30] As much as Campos and his successors professed their commitments to fiscal and monetary discipline, the military regime expanded government spending, largely remaining faithful to the state-led developmentalist programs guiding industrialization since the 1930s.[31] In the late 1960s, IMF mission leaders in Brazil often criticized that the lack of follow-through on pledges to curb government spending would not bring long-term relief for inflation.[32]

Where the military broke with tradition was in its repression of real wages with the PAEG formula to adjust workers' salaries for inflation.[33] The regime systematically underestimated (or even falsified) inflation estimates, which meant that wages progressively lost purchasing power. In Rio de Janeiro, the real minimum wage fell by 38 percent between 1964 and 1970.[34] Falling real wages after 1964 contrasted sharply with the prolabor policies of populist governments from Vargas and Kubitschek to Goulart, with economists noting that real wages in Rio de Janeiro had increased by 26 percent between 1952 and 1964. The Brazilian economist Mário Henrique Simonsen, finance minister from 1974 to 1979 under General Ernesto Geisel, later celebrated the PAEG formula because "it had the advantage of replacing an endless game of striking and protest with a simple arithmetic calculation."[35] In practice, it was not the PAEG formula but the regime's repressive tactics that eliminated workers' strikes. It was no coincidence that Brazil's miracle coincided with the dictatorship's most violent years when students, leftists, and trade unionists endured censorship, arbitrary detentions, and disappearances.

The military celebrated the PAEG for laying the groundwork for its economic miracle. The economy recovered by 1968, with industry growing at average annual rates of 20 percent for the next six years. For Antônio Delfim Netto, finance minister from 1967 to 1974 during the repressive presidency of General Emílio Médici, Brazil's miracle was self-sustaining because of how new sources of credit bolstered consumer demand, which in turn stimulated industrial production and employment.[36] Exports also more than tripled from US$1.9 billion in 1968 to US$6.2 billion in 1973, which turned the balance of payments from a deficit to a surplus. Triumphantly, the regime took credit for bringing down inflation, which fell to 16 percent by 1973. These successes were key to the regime's survival. Despite repression, the military remained in power for twenty-one years partly because it could count on support from a growing middle class that accepted this authoritarian system in exchange for an improved standard of living.[37]

Yet to what extent could the military claim this credit? Critics such as the structuralist economist Maria da Conceição Tavares questioned how quick the regime was to celebrate its own successes, especially on inflation. Rather than restore price stability, the PAEG turned inflation into an instrument for financing industrialization, ultimately benefiting large corporations with access to foreign capital while generating new bottlenecks and increasing the concentration of wealth. Already in 1967 Tavares recognized how turning inflation into a "great defense mechanism against stagnation" would generate artificial profits for industry and banking while inevitably aggravating social tensions.[38] Since her prescient observations, economic historians have further discredited the military's miracle. Was Brazil's performance in these years more recovery than miracle, as the country rebounded from the global recession of the early 1960s?[39] To what extent did the miracle depend on the process initiated with Kubitschek's push for "fifty years in five," or even Vargas's corporatist overhaul of industrial relations?[40] Or was it the expansionary credit policies and foreign direct investment, coupled with ruthless wage repression, that drove rising industrial production?[41] While scholars continue to debate these questions, this last explanation is as essential for explaining Brazil's meteoric rise in the late 1960s as its spectacular downward spiral in the 1970s.

"Growthflation" and the Miracle's Undoing

De repente, tudo como nos velhos tempos—"Suddenly, everything was as it was in the old days."[42] By 1973, the cracks in Brazil's growth model were apparent, even as the military exaggerated its successes and rode the wave of euphoria over Brazil's third World Cup victory in 1970. From 1973 to 1980, the economy continued growing at average annual rates of 8 percent.[43] While the rest of the world slipped into recession, Brazil's generals could still reasonably defend their record. Critics of the military's program, however, questioned if Brazil's miracle was sustainable, pointing to widening income inequality and regional disparities. Another indicator, moreover, ticked upward: inflation. Following the 1973 oil crisis, inflation in Brazil jumped to 35 percent in 1974 and reached 80 percent by 1979 (fig. 2). Rising inflation was, in part, a consequence of higher oil prices. While government technocrats could conveniently blame the exogenous supply-side shock for spiraling inflation, it became increasingly hard to deny that Brazil's economic miracle had sown the seeds for its own undoing.

The economist André Lara Resende notes that as early as 1967, Finance Minister Delfim Netto openly "abandoned the objective of totally conquering inflation, announcing publicly that a yearly inflation of 15 percent would be tolerable."[44] Médici's miracle, Resende summarizes, depended on wage repression and foreign capital infusions in the form of direct investments and loans, and even the severest wage repression was not enough to counteract the inflationary pressures of expansionary policies. From 1968 to 1974, Brazil's external debt ballooned from US$4 billion to US$20 billion.[45] Higher levels of foreign debt made Brazil vulnerable to future shifts in international financial markets.[46] Even the PAEG's celebrated indexation system became a sign of moral if not monetary defeat by ostensibly amounting to an admission by the government of its failure to combat inflation. Bankers and industrialists used the ORTN as the basis for the monetary correction of fixed assets and so it acquired the status of a parallel currency, one that functioned as a better store of value and as a medium of exchange in financial transactions.[47] Even PAEG's architect Campos admitted in 1975, while serving as ambassador to the United Kingdom, that indexation was no "miracle formula" but a "second-best solution, to be resorted to when there is no prospect of restoration of price stability." PAEG reforms, in other words, tried "to neutralize the distortion caused by inflation" but

Figure 2. Inflation in Brazil, 1945–85. Chart by author using data in Table A.3 of *The Economic and Social History of Brazil since 1889*, eds. Luna and Klein.

not to "fight inflation."[48] By the mid-1970s, Brazil was experiencing what economists termed "inertial inflation," or the rise in prices because of the "formal and informal mechanism for indexation, which turns yesterday's inflation into the primary cause of today's inflation."[49]

Brazil's approach to living with inflation became a topic of international debate, too, with some economists praising the regime for its unorthodox policies even as evidence of exhaustion mounted.[50] Even inflation hawks at the IMF noted that Brazil had become "accustomed to chronic and rather heavy inflation."[51] It followed that it did not necessarily make sense for Brazil to use the same strategies as other countries. In the United States, rising inflation led economists to abandon midcentury growth models as irrelevant in the face of "stagflation," but Brazilian officials continued to spin their heterodox indexation schemes into a recipe for "growthflation."[52]

As recession loomed worldwide, Brazilian technocrats applied magical thinking to their macroeconomic calculations; inflation might be endemic to Brazil, but was that *necessarily* bad? By some metrics, Brazil's miracle remained relatively unshaken by the 1973 oil shock.[53] Between 1974 and 1980, annual growth in industry averaged 7 percent, lower than during the miracle years but hardly showing signs of stagnation. With a growing middle class, domestic consumers continued buying Brazilian-made automobiles and televisions.[54] At the same time, chronic inflation posed an inescapable paradox: high inflation fueled consumerism—why save if tomorrow's money will be worthless?—but the spending sprees were themselves inflationary. The military dictatorship used inflation to sustain its economic miracle, and this strategy became its greatest liability.

To live with chronic inflation was hardly simple or straightforward. From the 1970s, Brazilian consumers, workers, industrialists, grocers, and retailers had to constantly update how they bought and sold goods to maximize their profits and purchasing power. For Brazil's incipient but growing middle classes, inflation undermined their ability to satisfy their needs and wants, turning into a daily reminder that the progress that seemed assured just a few years earlier was evaporating.[55] The historian Louise Walker describes how in Mexico, following its own period of "miraculous" growth, there was a palpable sense that the nation was "waking from the dream."[56] Rather than a sudden jolt, the unraveling of Brazil's miracle was a gradual process, hardly perceptible at first. The Austrian-Brazilian economist Paul Singer used the Portuguese expression *"se esgotou"* (has ran out) to describe the slow exhaustion of Brazil's miracle.[57]

Throughout the 1970s, Brazil stood at the tipping point between living with and unraveling from inflation. Buying in bulk became a nearly universal practice among middle-class consumers, turning into a "sporting event" in cities like São Paulo and Rio de Janeiro as daily shopping invited cutthroat competition.[58] When SUNAB temporarily lifted price tables for goods like meat, butchers quickly restocked and *donas de casa* flooded into shops. Scholars of consumption often focus on the acquisitive thrill driving middle-class demand for new fashions to understand the emergence of new ideological and political projects to define what constitutes a decent standard of living.[59] In 1970s Brazil, that euphoria was also palpable in how people acquired cooking oil or flour. Journalists described the frenzied acquisitions with amusement and derision: dozens of tubes of toothpaste, boxes upon boxes of pudding mix, or cases of olive oil in single shopping sprees. Whether or not the acquired goods were practical or necessary seemed to be beside the point; shoppers, at the end of their spree, stood around for "the careful sharing of trophies and expenses." As much for university-trained economists as for bystanders, buying in bulk became both cause and consequence of inflation. What economists discussed in terms of the psychology of future expectations, one *Veja* columnist mockingly called a "collective psychosis of scarcity."[60]

Public campaigns proliferated with instructions to housewives on how to bargain for better prices and economize in their shopping. In 1973, as discussed above, the regime's Conselho Nacional de Propaganda launched its famous "Say No to Inflation" campaign, as if it were a choice (fig. 1). The campaign featured white, middle- and upper-class women, adorned in jewelry and the latest fashions, exhorting fellow *donas de casa* to use their good looks and charm to bargain down prices and stretch their household budgets. The ads reinforced traditional gender norms as much by asserting that a woman's primary responsibility was cooking and caring for the family as by fixating on flirtation as her primary economic strategy. They also glossed over the struggles of working-class women, especially Black and mixed-race women.[61] The "Say No to Inflation" ads quickly became a target of mockery. Journalists stressed the comical mismatch between the compounding economic problems and how the military dictatorship transferred the burden onto small businesses and house-wives. As the editor of a Pernambuco newspaper protested, the *povo*, or people, had only one way to comply with this mandate: *"deixando de comer e de vestir"*—to stop eating and buying clothes.[62]

The military's strategy in these years was precisely to make consumers and retailers responsible for inflation. Even though the regime limited the rights of cit-izens to free association, consumer associations grew in number in the 1970s to channel consumer frustrations into regulatory action, or, perhaps, to distract from the regime's ineffectiveness at lowering inflation. The government's anti-inflation campaigns ran alongside those by consumer associations outlining strategies for women on where to shop and how to confirm whether retailers followed price tables. In Rio Grande do Sul, for example, the Associação de Proteção ao Consumi-dor was established on May 13, 1975, with the date no coincidence as the founder assured that "the Association was created on the anniversary of the abolition of slav-ery in order to liberate the Brazilian consumer from the enslavement they suffer in the hands of unscrupulous industrialists and merchants."[63] Organizations like the Associação Nacional de Defesa do Consumidor were even partially funded by the Ministry of Finance as "a way for the government to defend the popular econ-omy."[64] The category "popular economy" refers to the people's "pocketbook" or to the financial well-being of popular classes. It dates to Vargas-era criminal laws of the 1930s that outlined penalties for economic crimes including usury and price goug-ing. Laws to defend the popular economy evolved in subsequent decades, cement-ing in the popular imagination the idea that fair prices for essential goods was an economic right.[65] Yet the enforcement mechanisms in place to deter speculation had always been threadbare and would remain so.

Behind the public campaigns and consumer associations stood a complex and expanding set of government agencies responsible for controlling the price and dis-tribution of essential goods. The Conselho Interministerial de Preços (CIP), estab-lished in 1968, and SUNAB were two of the main organs responsible for price con-trols for producers and retailers.[66] SUNAB, in particular, was responsible for defending consumers; when someone suspected a crime had been committed, they called SUNAB offices or the local police. SUNAB even launched its own public campaigns calling on consumers to be vigilant against saboteurs: "Defende-se: Ajude a Sunab a Defender Você" ("Defend Yourself: Help SUNAB Help You").[67] As public service announcements exhorted consumers to "exercise your rights," it became increasingly apparent how ineffective this system of price controls was. Con-sumers voiced their frustrations with the "abuses of so many merchants who do not respect the SUNAB tables." Even when SUNAB was able to investigate retailers, its presence was hardly a deterrent, and consumers complained that "at the end of each week, we notice random increases in the price of goods, especially for food."[68]

Consumer complaints turned retailers into internal saboteurs of Brazil's miracle as food prices were subjected to administrative review and criminal investigation. After the 1973 oil crisis, it was not just the price of gasoline or imported goods that threatened to unravel the progress of previous years. Consumers filed complaints against the butchers who ignored SUNAB prices for ground beef and the restaurants that increasingly charged a *couvert* (service fee) for bread and butter, a practice that while not technically illegal departed from the convention that these items should be free of charge.[69] SUNAB tracked the number of denunciations filtering into regional offices, with officials logging the monthly fines.[70] As inflation worsened, the denunciations increased, but so did people's frustration with this system. Felicia de Oliveira, for example, called her precinct multiple times to complain about exorbitant prices, but with little consequence. "The police bureaucracy is very slow to punish a misdemeanor," she lamented.[71] The problem was systemic. SUNAB investigations against repeat offenders were often archived without resolution. In 1979, for example, one official at SUNAB's Bahia office admitted to a series of "irregularities" in how this office processed complaints. In the previous two years, hundreds of criminal investigations into price violations had either been abandoned or dismissed without cause while the "retailers [continued to] act with impunity." The official even noted the "pages ripped from the case files" pertaining to high-profile investigations, seemingly to prevent any resolution. Retailers, moreover, complained about the "fines applied, often in arbitrary ways and contrary to the legislation in place." Some consumers, frustrated by the bureaucratic dead ends, called to disband SUNAB given its "total inefficiency and lack of structure."[72]

Brazilians of all social classes had to keep track of inflation indices, SUNAB tables, wage adjustment schedules, and credit timetables, all of which required a sophisticated literacy in math. And yet the consumer complaints, bargain shopping, and installment purchases were no match for rising inflation. Conservative women's groups like CAMDE receded into the background in the 1970s, perhaps because it became too difficult to reconcile their anti-inflation campaigns with their continued loyalty to the military dictatorship. In their place, progressive social movements emerged to channel people's daily hardships into formal petitions for the government to do more to control prices.

In 1973, for example, women belonging to "clubes de mães," or community mothers' associations, founded the Movimento do Custo de Vida (Cost of Living Movement).[73] Established in poorer and underserved neighborhoods on the periphery of São Paulo, these women spearheaded their movement with a survey comparing the prices for fifteen essential foods in October 1972 and October 1973. At the start of 1973, Finance Minister Delfim Netto had promised that inflation would not surpass 12 percent, and yet this forecast did not capture the everyday struggles of poor and working-class Brazilians. The "mães da Periferia de São Paulo," as the women signed their petition to the president and other public officials, protested the rising cost of living and how it disproportionately impacted working-class communities. From 1972 to 1973, they reported that food prices increased by 69 percent in São Paulo's wealthy central neighborhoods and by 120 percent in the periphery.[74] Income inequality worsened during Brazil's miracle, and inflation exacerbated the consequences of this trend for working-class Brazilians.

Brazil's military regime responded to mounting pressures from civil society by slowly loosening some of its repressive measures and reintroducing limited channels for political competition. The repressive *anos de chumbo* under Médici gave way to the *distensão*, or loosening, under Geisel. In 1974, the regime initiated a process of slow, gradual, and top-down political liberalization by allowing open elections for Congress in which a single opposition party, the Movimento Democrático Brasileiro (MDB), ran against the military's official party. The MDB won far more seats than expected, and it became apparent that Geisel had overestimated the level of popular support for the regime's policies.[75]

Amid this controlled political opening, inflation offered an obvious and everyday example of how the military regime failed to deliver long-term stability and a decent standard of living. The economy became an arena of social conflict and renewed citizen demands for economic rights. By the late 1970s, inflation was the target of lockouts, strikes, and protests organized by workers, producers, and ordinary citizens taking direct action by folding *carestia* into pro-democracy protests.

The Movimento do Custo de Vida remained one of the most important of these groups for how it turned protests against inflation into protests for justice and equality. These women repeatedly petitioned the president and other officials with concrete demands: first, price freezes on goods, followed by salary increases for workers, additional family benefits, and investments in food-growing cooperatives.[76] They justified their demands by citing laws dating to the 1930s and by detailing their everyday struggles. Doing so, they expanded the meaning of economic justice beyond prices and wages to advocate for a range of goods and services. In August 1978, for example, this movement drafted a petition, signed by more than one million people, clarifying that *carestia* was about more than food prices; it encompassed everything spent on housing, schooling, transportation, and health care. The movement highlighted disparities in access to essential goods, infrastructure, and services, noting the lack of running water and sewage in their peripheral neighborhoods and the limited number of schools. Beyond all that, they also insisted that "all of us, as human beings, have the right to recreation, rest, and everything that enriches our lives. And all that costs money."[77]

As social movements intensified their opposition to the military's handling of the economy, Brazilian officials deflected attention from their failures by doubling down on their convictions that democracy remained the real threat to Brazil's progress. Their arguments were reinforced by the rise of military dictatorships in neighboring Latin American countries. While Brazil's military regime never supported the neoliberal policies embraced in Chile after 1973 or Argentina after 1976, each of these dictatorships spun narratives that blamed chronic inflation on the wage-price spiral driven by the pro-labor policies of prior democratic governments. And by the 1970s, political explanations for inflation had become routine in other parts of the world as well.[78] In the United States, for example, social scientists looked to the "vote-maximizing political business cycle" to explain inflation as a rational policy choice for politicians confronted with wage demands from unionized workers.[79] Brazilian officials internalized this logic as they defended their iron grip on policy-making. Campos and Delfim Neto argued that hasty democratization would only make economic matters worse: "Too frequent electoral consultations seem to be incompatible with a coherent and effective anti-inflationary policy, and may indeed lead to 'stop-go' patterns of behavior, with policies being relaxed before they become effective." Economic stability, for Campos, required the "substantial delegation of power to the Executive Branch of government, to enable it to orchestrate monetary, fiscal and income policies."[80]

Brazil's finance ministers, however, had long abandoned their commitments to fiscal and monetary discipline, and workers were not the group driving inflationary policies. PAEG reforms certainly codified winners and losers, but the protections offered with indexation for financial assets in fact generated a climate in which holders of financial capital profited wildly from inflation. In 1970, banking accounted for 5.4 percent of Brazil's GDP; this value had jumped to 7.9 percent by 1980 and would reach 11.9 percent by 1985.[81] Campos and Delfim Netto had generated an attractive investment climate as much by suppressing wages as by protecting foreign and domestic capital from losses. "Growthflation" benefited the banking sector and large corporations, generating all sorts of incentives for the military dictatorship to accept high inflation as a workable development strategy.

The military regime's penchant for debt-led growth might have delayed the effects of the 1973 global recession, but 1978 marked a turning point as interest payments on debt spiked and inflation showed no signs of easing.[82] Brazilians continued their shopping sprees, now motivated more by pessimism about the economic forecast. Out of "desperation," the historian Matthew Nestler argues, Finance Minister Mário Henrique Simonsen launched another anti-inflation advertising campaign, one mocked by the public because it again turned prices into a problem for small businesses and housewives to figure out.[83] The burden of inflation always fell hardest on the poor and working classes, but now Brazil's finance ministers struggled to convince middle-class consumers, industrialists, and even themselves that inflation was under control.

The military celebrated indexation and price controls as rational technocratic solutions, but Brazilians were losing confidence in economists and their *economês*, or economics jargon, if they ever had such faith.[84] Officials demurred or denied wrongdoing when confronted about their failures to predict or contain inflation, and this generated more public distrust. Even Campos eventually admitted the "failure" of economists to predict the "seriousness of inflation" and lamented how "humbly I have come to realize, that there is something, after all, to the infamous objurgation thrown at Brazilian economic technocrats by disgruntled politicians, that 'economics is the art of achieving misery with the aid of arithmetic.'"[85]

The "arithmetic" used by Brazilian officials, however, was not only faulty—it was also fraudulent. In August 1978, more than fifty thousand people, including workers, students, members of the Movimento do Custo de Vida, and other pro-democracy groups, gathered in front of the São Paulo Cathedral. They protested not only the rising cost of living but the government itself because it had forged the official inflation rate used to calculate salary adjustments and other monetary corrections. The government, using the index of the Instituto Brasileiro de Economia (IBRE) at the Fundação Getúlio Vargas, estimated inflation at 12.6 percent in 1973, but the Departamento Intersindical de Estatística e Estudos Sócio-Econômicos (affiliated with labor unions in São Paulo) calculated it at 22.5 percent. Why protest these numbers five years later? The protest erupted following a World Bank report that questioned IBRE numbers, suggesting that the military regime was either willfully lying about inflation or too incompetent to measure it accurately. Debates over numbers, according to Neiburg, mobilized political action.[86] Inflation accounting not only mattered for how Brazilians perceived their well-being, but also for their waning trust in a government that staked its legitimacy on the tradeoff between civil liberties and economic prosperity.

This protest marked a turning point because it exposed the growing sense of economic uncertainty and the military's inability to maintain social peace. Just a few years before, government technocrats had boasted of their clever steering of Brazil's miraculous takeoff, but now their statistics were the target of public ire and ridicule. Years later, in an interview with Delfim Netto broadcast on the television program *Globo Debate*, a reporter cut to interviews with workers, consumers, and politicians polled about the former minister's record. As one interviewee contended: "In '73 he ordered the manipulation of statistical data. That was proven. . . . And '73 was the year when Minister Delfim Netto could not count beyond twelve. He spent the whole year saying that inflation was 12 percent, 12 percent, 12 percent."[87] In fact, inflation not only exceeded 12 percent, it was skyrocketing to unimaginable heights.

With the second oil shock in 1979, the strategies of prior decades became unsustainable. The so-called Volcker shock led interest rates to reach 20 percent in the United States by 1981, increasing the cost of borrowing globally. Across Latin America, debt obligations became unmanageable. The region's so-called lost decade brought debt crisis, high unemployment, anemic growth, and volatile inflation in the 1980s. For Brazil, real GDP tripled from 1965 to 1980, with per capita income doubling and industrial production increasing fourfold. And then Brazil spiraled into its deepest recession in modern history: the GDP showed an absolute decline in 1981 for the first time since 1942. Brazil's growth rate fell from an annual average of 9 percent in the 1970s to 3 percent in the 1980s. The country's capital goods industry also went into serious decline, with production in 1983 barely at 60 percent of 1980 levels. Inflation reached 111 percent in 1980, a trend that worsened as triple-digit inflation became the new normal. In Brazil, the cumulative consequences of the debt crisis were starkest for the standard of living. GDP per capita fell by 15 percent between 1980 and 1983 and did not recover 1980 values until 1987.[88] Between 1981 and 1989, the Gini index, a measure of inequality, rose from 0.57 to 0.63, just as the country prepared for democratization. As unemployment spiked and the cost of living spiraled, other social problems compounded as urban violence proliferated and municipal governments struggled to meet the basic infrastructure and sanitation needs of local communities. The miracle came to a definitive end.

After the Miracle: Democracy and Inflation

In 1984, Brazilians mobilized for their country's transition to democracy. Direitas Já (Direct Elections Now) protests erupted, calling for a direct presidential election to formally end the decades-long dictatorship. The slow and controlled process of liberalizing the military's grasp on power, first *distensão*, or loosening, and then *abertura*, or opening, gave way to a mass movement. Direitas Já protests failed to bring immediate direct presidential elections but succeeded in asserting that Brazil's democratic transition would be open and participatory. The 1988 Constitution epitomized this commitment. A National Constituent Assembly, comprising members of civil society groups and political parties, convened in early 1987 to draft a constitution. Working groups and individuals across the country mailed proposals calling for far-reaching welfare programs such as universal health care alongside those demanding immediate relief from economic hardships.[89] Concerns over inflation permeated these discussions. Citizens called on their government to guarantee fair prices for milk and meat. As aspirations for Brazil's future mounted, a dispiriting question lingered: "*O que poderá acontecer com a economia?*" (What will happen to the economy?)[90]

In 1984, annual inflation stood at 228 percent. By 1988, when Brazil ratified its constitution, it reached 1,118 percent (fig. 3). Brazil's miracle had burst; its gains eroded as accelerating inflation threatened both macroeconomic stability and citizens' well-being. In public debates and in people's everyday complaints, inflation was the economic event of the 1980s—a numerical measure of another boom-bust cycle gone awry.

In the 1980s, economic questions—of fairness, relief, and efficiency—became essential to debates over "what is a democracy?" This question was debated

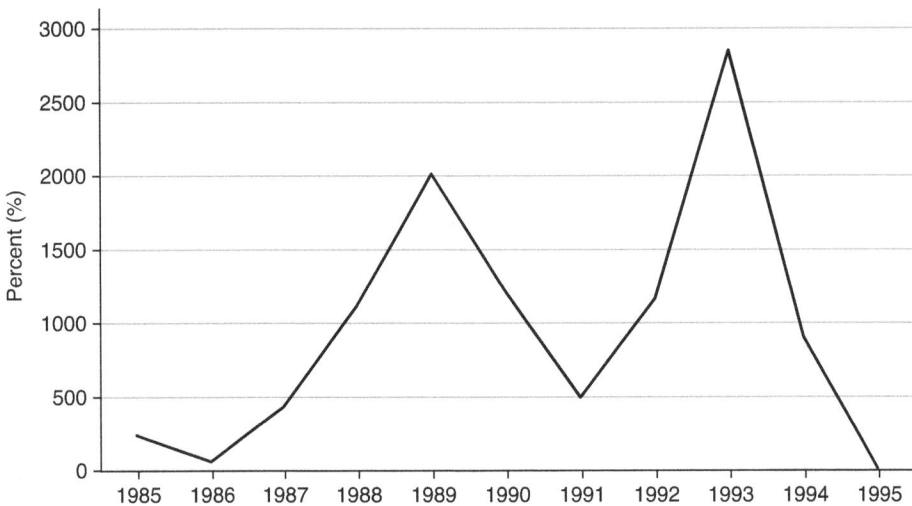

Figure 3. Inflation in Brazil, 1985–95. Chart by author using data in Table A.3 of *The Economic and Social History of Brazil since 1889*, eds. Luna and Klein.

within Brazil and across Latin America, from Mexico to Argentina, as the region struggled with debt, inflation, and rising poverty. By 1982, Brazil was the developing economy with the largest debt, estimated at US$86 billion. Initially, officials were optimistic about their ability to avoid Mexico's fate—a dramatic currency devaluation—but Brazil eventually was forced to restructure its foreign debt and enter painful negotiations with the IMF. As the debt crisis unfolded alongside the country's democratization, the public debated: Would Brazil's first civilian governments following military rule be more accountable to foreign creditors than to its own citizens?[91] IMF-imposed austerity stood at odds with the government's promises to end hunger and improve living conditions. Activists who in the 1970s challenged military rule by mobilizing for improved health care, sanitation, education, and other public services for poor and marginalized communities now had direct influence with their election to public office. But inflation thwarted democratic aspirations as municipal governments went bankrupt and abandoned public services.[92]

The so-called winners of inflation tended to be the large corporations and propertied classes, and yet the assumption that inflation was a political choice driven by working-class demands nonetheless persisted in the 1980s. Banks enjoyed protections through the indexation system and the government itself profited from the monetary financing of budget deficits. The burden of inflation fell hardest on the poorest segments of society, namely the 50 percent of the population without access to formal banking (and thus dependent on paper money to make payments) and workers ineligible for formal wage adjustments.[93] Yet some economists and political scientists still blamed inflation on the electoral calculations that led politicians to accelerate the monetary financing of expansionary budgets.[94] Conveniently forget-ting the military's profligacy, inflation once again quickly turned into a problem endemic to democracies.[95]

Those skeptical that a fledgling democracy could implement prudent reforms found a useful case study in Brazil. In 1986, President José Sarney announced the Plano Cruzado. Sarney's rise to the presidency was unexpected. In 1985, Tancredo Neves had picked Sarney as the vice presidential candidate for the indirect elections. Neves won the election but died before taking office, and so Sar-ney became the first civilian president after two decades of military rule. Sarney had two tasks: to oversee Brazil's democratization by convening the National Con-stituent Assembly and to tackle inflation. When he took office in March 1985, pri-ces were rising by 10 percent each month, with annualized inflation reaching 243 percent by the end of the year. In February 1986, prominent economists working with Finance Minister Dílson Funaro—including Pérsio Arida and André Lara Resende, who later worked on the Plano Real—drafted Decree Law No. 2.283 to outline the Plano Cruzado, the first of many attempts to fix inflation during Sar-ney's and his successor Fernando Collor de Mello's administrations. Sarney's oppo-nents accused him of using the Plano Cruzado as a populist gambit to win popular support for his party.[96] But Sarney's supporters defended his plan as a more egal-itarian and democratic approach to inflation for how it increased real wages and froze prices, a formula that shifted more income and purchasing power to low-income citizens.

The Plano Cruzado (and, with some tweaks, the subsequent plans too) aimed to stop inflation in its tracks by freezing prices. To recall, the Movimento do Custo de Vida and other social movements had petitioned for price freezes in the 1970s and so this measure was met, initially, with popular support. The Plano also replaced Brazil's currency the cruzeiro with the cruzado, worth 1,000 cruzeiros. As simple as the plan seemed—to ban retailers and wholesalers from price increases and issue a new currency to function as a more reasonable unit of exchange—nothing about it was straightforward.

For future commentators and scholars alike, the plans tested in these years—the Plano Cruzado (1986), Plano Cruzado II (1986), Plano Bresser (1987), Plano Verão (1989), and Plano Collor (1990)—were doomed to fail, with the logic and instruments underpinning these plans ridiculed for years to come. The Plano Cru-zado unleashed explosive demand for consumer goods because Brazilians took advantage of price freezes, for food and televisions alike, in anticipation of future increases. The freezes, in turn, generated scarcity and contraband markets. Yet what seems obvious in hindsight is not useful for understanding how these plans func-tioned and altered both public and private understandings of the price mechanism and what constitutes fair market value.

The spectacular failure of inflation planning should not, moreover, overshadow the euphoria in 1986, when it appeared at first that the Plano Cruzado might work. Monthly inflation rates fell from 17.79 percent in January to 0.32 percent by May.[97] Many leaned into the hype over this plan because, in theory, it addressed the hardships of the poor and working classes. The price freezes were a strategy to stop inertial inflation by de-indexing the economy, a heterodox approach indebted to conversations with economists in other countries. In fact, Argentina's Austral Plan and Brazil's Plano Cruzado were designed in tandem and shared many features. Both plans were shaped by democratizing impulses, as Raúl Alfonsín, Argentina's first civilian president following seven years of military rule, also confronted the question "What is democracy?" amid debt crisis and violent inflation. The answer, historian Jennifer Adair shows, was as much about access to food as to the ballot box, with Alfonsín promising to eliminate hunger and shortages.[98]

The Plano Cruzado announced a new minimum salary and automatic adjustments for workers' wages as soon as annual inflation reached 20 percent.[99] Maria da Conceição Tavares, hostile to IMF recommendations and later a supporter of the Workers' Party (Partido dos Trabalhadores [PT]), gave an emotional testimony shortly after Sarney announced the Plano Cruzado to defend its economic logic and advocacy for workers' interests. The Plano Cruzado, for Federico Neiburg, was exceptional for the heterodox ideas it put into practice (rejecting calls for fiscal and monetary austerity) and for how it united structuralist and developmentalist economists such as Tavares and a rising cohort of economists like Resende and Arida trained in new mathematical methods at the Pontifical Catholic University of Rio de Janeiro (PUC-Rio) and universities in the United States.[100] Tavares, during a nationally televised interview in March 1986, claimed that "there are very few times in my professional life that I have been proud of my profession," and added that economics had been sabotaged by the "technocratic abuses committed in those [the military] years." In her view, the Plano Cruzado departed from how the military executed its plans through violent measures to repress workers and with little regard for whether their wages could support a decent standard of living.

Brazilian officials promised transparency and initially praised the Plano Cruzado for how it guaranteed economic fairness with the *tablita*, the conversion table used to calculate the current value of debts and other contracts, as well as the government-issued price tables that listed the legal prices that retailers could charge for goods. While price tables in particular had been a staple of economic life for decades, somehow the Plano Cruzado offered something new—and something consistent with values of popular participation in government and economic fairness. These were the same values that social movements across Brazil foregrounded in debates over the new constitution being drafted as the Plano Cruzado was implemented. This optimism now seems naive at best. In fact, Tavares was later mocked for her praise of the Plano Cruzado, as journalists zeroed in, with their chauvinist overtones, on her emotional and tearful endorsement. Tavares, in turn, continued defending her initial optimism: "I cried because it was the first plan that I saw defending the interests of the poor," she explained years later when criticizing how the Plano Real might have fixed inflation but made workers worse off in the process. In 1996, she lamented: "Today, it is not easy for me to cry for an economic plan."[101]

Despite these erratic times, Brazil's economy initially showed signs of recovery following the debt crisis, with GDP growth at 7.5 percent and industrial growth at 11.3 percent in 1986. This growth was driven by insatiable consumer demand for durable goods, as the reasoning that saving money was the equivalent to throwing it away intensified. One might expect that the debt crisis had extinguished any lingering memories of past prosperity in Brazil, but journalists conjured up the military's miracle in their forecasts. "Brazil seems to have returned to the golden years of the economic miracle," one journalist splashed on the front page of a May issue of *O Jornal do Commercio* to summarize the optimism of industrialists and consumers in the early days of the Plano Cruzado.[102] Others warned that inflation-fueled buying was a recipe for a future crisis. "We are in paradise," Wolfgang Sauer, president of Brazilian Volkswagen, observed, "making money like never before."[103] This euphoria, he warned, was an "illusion" as long as inflation remained out of control and the debt crisis was unresolved, and this illusion was in fact reminiscent of past miracles.

As is well documented, the Plano Cruzado (and its successors) failed to tame inflation—which reached 2,851 percent in 1993—and generated new problems. Perhaps the image that best defined the spectacular unraveling of Brazil's potential as the *país do futuro* was that of supermarkets with empty shelves. In newspapers and ads circulating in the public sphere, the burden of navigating inflation continued to fall on women, responsible for maximizing household budgets in this context of contraband markets, empty shelves, and ersatz substitutions for essential goods.[104]

As scarcity generated creativity, additional paradoxes emerged in Brazil. For example, meat consumption doubled in middle-class households between February and July 1986, all while newspapers reported meat shortages across the country.[105] Meat disappeared from the butcher shops and supermarkets legally required to uphold SUNAB pricing and found its way into contraband markets. Local newspapers tracked the meat supply with meticulous and sensational detail, with investigative reporting on cattle ranching and how intermediaries distorted supply chains by hoarding meat in anticipation of "thaws" in price freezes, alongside anecdotal reporting on the strategies that *donas de casa* used to buy meat. Government reports, in turn, churned over statistics on the number of fines or arrests, with owners of refrigerated warehouses and wholesale distributors arrested by federal police for "charging an *'ágio'* on the sale of meat."[106] Increasingly, Brazilians applied the term *ágio*, or a premium that signifies some usurious transaction, to describe buying goods at the butcher or the open-air food markets. Goods like meat often become targets of speculation and price gouging in wartime and during other national emergencies, but Brazil was not at war in the 1980s.[107] With exceptional economic strategies deployed in peacetime, controversies about price and supply turned into fundamental debates over the role of government in guaranteeing citizens' basic needs.

To prevent speculative behavior, Sarney famously called on citizens to denounce retailers selling above the official price freezes or merchants engaged in illegal activities. The *fiscais de Sarney* (Sarney's inspectors)—largely *donas de casa* doing their routine shopping—issued complaints to police, which led to investigations that sometimes resulted in business closures.[108] Sarney's government seized on the participatory spirit of Brazil's transition to democracy to amass public support for his plans, turning ordinary citizens into agents of public regulatory powers. In fact, the *fiscais de Sarney* were the reinvention of older tactics in Brazil, dating to the 1930s, in which governments issued special decree laws to punish speculators. Such efforts allowed the government to boldly broadcast its efforts to protect citizen well-being, but compliance was too uneven to be effective. Given how fragile the public's trust in government was in the 1980s, consumer denunciations remained more a safety valve than an effective enforcement mechanism.

Opportunities to strategize and hoard were not accessible to all Brazilians, and the Plano Cruzado's impact was highly different across socioeconomic classes. The wage adjustments built into the plan benefited professionals and workers in the formal sector who belonged to powerful trade unions. Those with the means to do so deployed strategies to maximize their purchasing power at the supermarket and invested their wealth in inflation-hedging ways. According to the anthropologist Maureen O'Dougherty, such investments often took the form of consumer durables like refrigerators or automobiles, or what she calls "miniaturization in real-estate investment."[109] For the working poor, however, salary adjustments were irregular and improvised; the poor lacked the means to purchase nonperishables in bulk or store their wealth in household durables. Economic justice was not only a matter of buying food at fair prices but about access to banking services and other tools that would make it possible to anticipate and meet future needs.

Brazil's first civilian government after decades of military rule attempted a radical experiment to defeat inflation with economic tricks that defied the conventional wisdom that fiscal and monetary contractions were the only solution. Sarney's ministers promised the public that price freezes would bring economic recovery—and maybe even another miracle. But the Plano Cruzado turned buying and selling practically anything into an exercise in forecasting the future and thus, ultimately, a gamble. Because this plan, more so than its predecessors, depended on the cooperation of consumers, industrialists, and retailers, its failures led to the erosion of public confidence in democratic governance at this crucial juncture. As Lúcia Pacífico Homem, president of the Movimento das Donas de Casa de Minas Gerais, proclaimed in June 1987: "I will be a watchdog over my own pocketbook. For Sarney, never again."[110]

Amid the dramatic economic reversals of the 1980s, Brazil's miracle became a distant memory, evoked by some in their mocking commentary on how Brazil was still the country of the future. Officials asserted their predictions with arrogance, only to be proven woefully wrong at every turn. When Finance Minister Funaro prophesized that "the year 1987 will have lower inflation than 1986," he would ultimately be off by a factor of seven.[111] In light of inconceivable numbers and accumulating hardships, Brazil cycled through ministers; some had their terms cut short by scandals and others simply admitted defeat. In June 1987, Luiz Carlos Bresser Pereira, finance minister from April to December 1987, defensively retorted: "I'm a minister, not a magician."[112]

As skeptical—and sneering—as Brazilians sounded when asked about how their government handled the inflationary crisis, it becomes even more striking that they remained optimistic about the ongoing project to design a new political system. Writing the 1988 Constitution was a public and participatory event. From 1986 to 1988, Brazilians organized working groups to draft amendments and sent thousands of petitions to delegates. Their letters, preserved at the Museu da República in Rio de Janeiro, reveal citizens' hopes for Brazil's future. Some offered lengthy and highly theorized political manifestos while others wrote rushed letters, sometimes with incomplete sentences or incongruous demands. Working within the limits of the institutions created to govern the democratic transition, petitioners nonetheless expressed their desires to overturn the status quo, to totally reimagine government and its powers. Their proposals spanned the ideological spectrum, including many idiosyncratic suggestions. These letters also documented everyday hardships of poverty, exclusion, and violence. Many letter writers asserted their authority to advise the constitution writers on account of how their firsthand experiences empowered them to articulate the needs of ordinary people. Brazilians worked to define new principles of democracy, which also created spaces to debate Brazil's economic future.

This process of writing the 1988 Constitution provides an unexpected window into the hyperinflation unfolding, as inflation reached 432 percent in 1987 and surpassed 1,100 percent in 1988 (fig. 3). Discussion of the crisis could not be avoided, especially as the initial euphoria of the Plano Cruzado gave way to higher prices, empty shelves, and more conflicts over profits and property. The Plano Cruzado also inspired debates about democratic governance. In August 1986, for example, legal scholars debated proposals to eliminate the decree law and how the executive branch used this instrument to legislate without congress. The Plano Cruzado inspired arguments for and against decree laws. For one law professor, the Plano

Cruzado was "the first time that the decree law was used on behalf of the people," but even so, he warned, "it is a dangerous instrument."[113] For the political scientist Bolívar Lamounier, however, the Plano Cruzado bolstered his argument that the tool should be reformed but not abandoned; otherwise, how could government intervene during a crisis "without the element of surprise with the decree law?"[114] Whereas some debated the possibilities for democracy in technical terms, others offered idealism over and above specific instructions. Pointing to the "failure of the Plano Cruzado," one manifesto from Rio Grande do Sul called on Brazilians to "remember Adam Smith"—not for his advocacy of free trade but for his insistence that "no society can be prosperous and happy if its members are mostly poor and unhappy."[115]

After decades of military rule, and amid another crisis, writing this constitution was imbued with urgency and optimism. Delegates debated all aspects of social and economic life in Brazil, a process reflected in the length of the constitution, with 250 articles. It codified far-reaching promises to protect workers' rights; uphold gender and racial equality; guarantee health care as a human right; defend the cultural, linguistic, and territorial sovereignty of Indigenous peoples; safeguard the environment; and so on. While inflation permeated debates over economic and social rights, no articles about it or protections against it were codified in the constitution, beyond mention of the government's responsibility to defend the popular economy or economic well-being of popular classes, protections carried over from 1930s Vargas-era constitutions.[116]

Delegates advocating for measures to protect workers' rights did push to include articles for automatic monthly adjustments to salaries linked to the cost-of-living index. They also proposed amendments calling for "constitutional and legal mechanisms to protect salaries against the eroding value of the currency."[117] These proposals were rejected. Others called for measures to protect consumers by increasing public powers to regulate weights and measures, prices, advertisements, and "general market conditions." Such protections were to be included alongside other fundamental individual rights.[118] These guarantees were also not codified.

Perhaps to omit concrete protections against inflation was a pragmatic choice. Constitutions are not designed to legislate but to outline fundamental rights and powers of government. Inflation was a matter for ordinary law, more of a technical problem or one too unpredictable to be subordinated to generalizable principles. The delegates might also have implicitly understood that to legislate inflation would invariably result in undemocratic or unfair outcomes. To some, inflation generates a predictable set of winners and losers. But if Brazilians had learned anything over the previous twenty years, it was that the only thing harder than controlling prices was forecasting how individuals respond. To codify inflation into the constitution would be to formally pick winners and losers, to decide which groups deserved protection in a crisis and who would have to make their own loopholes to safeguard their well-being and property. Any measure to hedge against future losses or protect the interests of one group against another would yield new conflicts. The 1988 Constitution affirmed economic rights as essential to Brazilian democracy, but the question of how to guarantee a fair price remained as unsettled and urgent as ever.

Decades of chronic inflation had turned every purchase into a tug of war in which prices determined the winners and losers. The military regime had chosen industrialists, middle-class consumers, and bankers as its winners, but how would Brazil's fledgling democracy decide whose profits or property to protect? What goods and services were essential and how should their prices be regulated? Even as these questions remained in the ongoing debate, what was undeniable in these crisis-ridden decades was that for Brazilians, as the anthropologist Roberto DaMatta notes, "citizenship and inflation had become deeply intertwined."[119]

Conclusion

The Plano Cruzado and its successors did not fix inflation, nor did the 1988 Constitution bring immediate political stability. By then, the once-celebrated economic miracle had become a faint echo of the past, and yet it remained a point of reference in public debates and in the popular imagination. Brazil's economic miracle had two deeply intertwined afterlives. Some Brazilians evoked the past to bolster their hopes that "we will have a new miracle," while others sighed with resignation that Brazil was still struggling as an "emerging power."[120] And for most people, these conjectures about the country's future potential offered little comfort as inflation reached 2,851 percent in 1993.

Prices skyrocketed alongside corruption scandals and political humiliations that further eroded public confidence. The most dramatic of these occurred in March 1990 with the *confisco da poupança*, the colloquial term used to describe when President Collor and Finance Minister Zélia Cardoso de Mello froze 80 percent of personal bank accounts in Brazil for eighteen months, an act that many decried as an arbitrary government seizure of assets. If the military dictatorship had fabricated data to conserve public confidence in its miracle, the irony of Brazil's democratic transition became the farcical extent to which newly elected politicians disregarded the importance of popular support for their economic policies. Then, almost miraculously, the heterodox (and controversial) Plano Real "succeeded" in taming inflation. The economists who designed the Plano Real subsequently wrote books and memoirs to celebrate their radical program as a savvy mix of compliance with neoliberal reforms alongside rebellious commitment to experimentation and transparency.

And this is where histories of Brazil's miracle and the subsequent debt crisis conclude, with the Plano Real. Scholars interrogate its neoliberal emphasis on privatization, open markets, and fiscal discipline, and they debate the social impact. Economists—some with resignation and others with conviction—see the Plano Real as the inevitable answer to the exhaustion of Brazil's state-led and debt-financed developmentalist growth model that prevailed from the 1930s to the 1980s. Postwar inflation is thus either treated like any other macroeconomic variable or narrowly discussed to explain why failures to tame it left no option but eventual conformity to neoliberal praxis in the 1990s.[121] But to understand how neoliberal formulas took hold after decades of heterodox policies, it is important to account not only for why past plans failed but also how they had already turned access to essential goods and services into individualized conquests. The key to how inflation transformed Brazilian society during these crucial decades lies not in debates over its eventual cure but in the seductive promises of all the preceding experiments.

It is easy enough to point out the faulty logic that defined policymaking, as much during the military dictatorship as during the country's democratization, or to emphasize the differences between the military's focus on growth at the expense of working classes and the attempts of democratic leaders to design anti-inflation plans that prioritized social mobility. Yet what connects these decades of experimentation is how policymakers tried to govern by different economic rules. From the 1960s to 1980s, Brazilian officials tested controversial ideas in pursuit of price stability; this, according to the former finance minister Guido Mantega, marked the country's "greatest period of creativity" in generating new economic theories.[122] And this creativity was not limited to government planning, as all Brazilians experimented with how to stretch their purchasing power and savings in these difficult economic times.

Brazil's economic miracle is a story of both relentless optimism in the face of daunting realities and persistent skepticism in citizens' responses to government promises for renewed prosperity. To contend with the consequences, the country's economic performance needs to be evaluated not only with stark indicators—high growth rates, high levels of industrial production, growing inequality, galloping inflation, ballooning debt—but also for the experimental strategies and unconventional thinking of Brazilian economists and consumers alike. How did people deal with the economics of scarcity that accompanied high inflation? How did inflation shape democratic governance and expectations? These questions inspired this article's multidecade analysis of Brazil's miracle and its spectacular collapse. They are also questions that await further research—mine and, hopefully, that of other scholars as well. Inflation is more than a variable to be tracked and forecast. In Brazil, persistent inflation fused with struggles for democratic accountability, social mobility, and economic justice. This was—and remains—the case in Brazil, where inflation was not an exceptional event but a constant challenge that defined people's livelihoods and opportunities for decades.

Melissa Teixeira is assistant professor of history at the University of Pennsylvania. She is a historian of Brazil and Latin America with a focus on intellectual, economic, and legal history. Her first book *A Third Path: Corporatism in Brazil and Portugal* was published in 2024. She is currently working on a new project entitled "Inflation and the Making of Brazilian Democracy."

Notes

I would like to thank Amy Chazkel and Sarah Seo for the invitation to present an early version of this article to the Legal History Workshop at Columbia University, and all the workshop participants for their questions, feedback, and suggestions. Valeria Lopez-Fadul also read and offered invaluable feedback. In addition, I thank the entire *RHR* editorial team and coeditors of this issue Ravinder Kaur and Barbara Weinstein for their feedback and support throughout the revision process, and the anonymous reviewers for their diligence and instrumental comments.

1. Nestler, "Desperation of the Military's Economists."
2. Measurements of Brazil's economic performance in these years will vary. For consistency, I make calculations using data in Klein and Luna, *Economic and Social History of Brazil*, esp. table A.3.
3. Pereira, *Development and Crisis in Brazil*; Skidmore, "Years between the Harvests"; Veloso, Villela, and Giambiagi, "Determinantes do 'milagre' econômico brasileiro."
4. Hobsbawm, *Age of Extremes*, 403.
5. On the intellectual "fracture" in economics during the 1970s crisis, see Rodgers, *Age of Fracture*, chaps. 2–3. See also Maier, "'Malaise.'"
6. On indexation, see Modenesi, *Regimes monetários*, chap. 4.
7. On women and consumer politics, see Cohen, *Consumers' Republic*; O'Dougherty, *Consumption Intensified*; and Tinsman, *Buying into the Regime*.
8. Frieden, "Brazilian Borrowing Experience."
9. Neiburg, "Inflation," 606.
10. Specifically, some scholars emphasize how the Plano Real built on the 1985 "Larrida Plan" in that both featured currency indexation. Neiburg, "Inflation," 621; Modenesi, *Regimes monetários*, chap. 4.
11. Meade, "'Living Worse and Costing More.'"
12. Adair, *In Search of the Lost Decade*; Elena, *Dignifying Argentina*; Frens-String, *Hungry for Revolution*.
13. Klein and Luna, *Economic and Social History of Brazil*, 106.
14. Data from World Bank database for World Development Indicators. Series Code NV.AGR.TOTL.ZS: Agriculture, forestry, and fishing, value added (% of GDP) and Series Code NV.IND.TOTL.ZS: Industry (including construction), value added (% of GDP), https://databank.worldbank.org/reports.aspx?source=2&country=BRA (accessed October 3, 2024).
15. *O Cruzeiro*, "Municípios de maior progresso do Brasil," 50.
16. *Jornal do Brasil*, Lopes, "Como inventar o futuro do Brasil."
17. Fico, *Reinventando o otimismo*.
18. On labor and the politics of *carestia* in the 1940s and 1950s, see French, *Brazilian Workers' ABC*, 201–6, 229–30; and Ioris, "'Fifty Years in Five.'"
19. On Kubitschek's developmentalist state, see Sikkink, *Ideas and Institutions*. See also Wolfe, *Autos and Progress*, chap. 5.
20. On inflation debates in Latin America, see Fajardo, *World That Latin America Created*, chap. 3; and Bielschowsky, *Pensamento econômico brasileiro*, 25–30.
21. Calculated with price indices for food expenses and wholesale food prices in *Anuário Estatístico do Brasil* for relevant years.
22. To explain the 1964 coup, historians highlight the polarization of Brazilian politics during the Cold War. The military was hostile to Vargas and his successors because of their support for labor; opposition to Goulart mounted when he announced progressive

reforms in March 1964. Klein and Luna, *Brazil, 1964–1985*; Skidmore, *Politics of Military Rule in Brazil*.

23. Economic historians have hardly reached a consensus as to when or why the 1964 economic crisis begins, but scholars increasingly emphasize the global economic downturn rather than domestic problems with import-substitution industrialization (ISI) policies. Souza, "A crise política dos anos 1960."

24. Power, "Who but a Woman?"; Fonseca, *O transnacional e o local*.

25. "CAMDE dá chiclete americano," *Jornal do Brasil*, June 4, 1967, Arquivo Nacional do Brasil (hereafter AN), Fundo Campanha da Mulher pela Democracia (CMD), PE.0/0/8/88.

26. Amelia Molina Bastos, Nota official da CAMDE, April 22, 1966, AN, Fundo CMD, PE.0/0/8/6.

27. "A confiança na luta," *O Globo*, April 24, 1965, AN, Fundo CMD, PE.0/0/92/42.

28. "Maus comerciantes em 'listas negras' da CAMDE," *O Jornal*, May 9, 1965, AN, Fundo CMD, PE.0/0/94/12.

29. "A confiança na luta."

30. While the military regime denigrated the policies of past governments as reckless and populist, historians have largely rejected this characterization. Eduardo Bastian emphasizes the similarities between the PAEG and Goulart's Plano Trienal to note that Goulart's government attempted fiscal and monetary reforms to tackle inflation in the early 1960s. The key difference between the two plans was the PAEG's extreme wage repression. Bastian, "O PAEG e o plano trienal."

31. Some economists emphasize that the miracle deepened—rather than overcame—contradictions inherent to the ISI model, namely that the drive to swap imports of manufactured goods for their domestic production increased national dependency on international markets. Furtado, *Formação econômica do Brasil*, 223–32.

32. Jorge Del Campo, Office Memorandum, July 26, 1967, International Monetary Fund Archives, Washington, DC (hereafter IMF), Classification C/Brazil/810 Mission Del Canto and Staff, July 1967.

33. Since the 1930s, workers' salaries depended on negotiations between state-recognized employer associations and workers' *sindicatos* (unions), but now the PAEG formula calculated wages using current inflation and future predictions. Nagasava, *O sindicato que a ditadura queria*, 12–13.

34. Resende, "A política brasileira de estabilização," 779.

35. Simonsen quoted in Resende, "A política brasileira de estabilização," 802.

36. On transformations in consumer credit, see Santanna, "History of Consumer Credit in Brazil."

37. This midcentury pact, as the historian Louise Walker calls it, was not specific to Brazil, and similar dynamics were apparent in Mexico under the Pax Priísta (*Waking from the Dream*).

38. Tavares, "Notas sobre o problema do financiamento," 148.

39. Veloso, Villela, and Giambiagi, "Determinantes do 'milagre' econômico brasileiro."

40. Singer, *A crise do "milagre,"* 10.

41. Resende, "A política brasileira de estabilização."

42. "A goela da inflação," *Opinião*, January 8–15, 1973, AN, Fundo Divisão de Segurança e Informações do Ministério da Justiça, BR.AN.RIO.TT.0.MCP.AVU.30.

43. Tullio and Ronci, "Brazilian Inflation from 1980 to 1993," 637.

44. Resende, "A política brasileira de estabilização," 789.

45. Klein and Luna, *Economic and Social History of Brazil*, 201.

46. As the historian Jeremy Adelman notes, Brazil's policymakers endorsed massive borrowing which created "habits" that endured into the 1980s, fueling debt-led growth ("International Finance and Political Legitimacy," 122).

47. Almost all indexed contracts in Brazil were denominated in ORTNs. Arida and Lara-Resende, "Inertial Inflation and Monetary Reform," 34.

48. Roberto de Oliveira Campos, "A New Scenario for Decision-Making," November 6, 1975, Centro de Pesquisa e Documentação de História Contemporânea do Brasil, Rio de Janeiro (hereafter CPDOC), EUG/CAMPOS pi 1975.11.06.

49. Francisco Lafaiete Lopes, "Reforma monetária e pacto nacional de estabilização: Uma proposta de combate à inflação," November 1984, CPDOC, TN pi LOPES 1984.11.00.

50. *Opinião*, "Ainda a fama do 'milagre.'"

51. "Brazil—Review of Economic Policies and Developments," September 15, 1967, IMF, Classification C/Brazil/810 Mission Del Canto and Staff, July 1967.

52. Campos, "New Scenario for Decision-Making."

53. The economist Carlos Diaz-Alejandro notes that Brazil's "post-1973 performance was regarded with admiration" ("Some Aspects of the 1982–83 Brazilian Payments Crisis," 515).

54. Woodard, *Brazil's Revolution in Commerce*, 290–91.

55. Since the 1990s, scholars of Brazil and Latin America have looked beyond the concerns of midcentury modernization theorists, who saw the rise of a middle class as a precondition for economic growth and democracy; they focus instead on the practices, discourses, and expectations of groups broadly labeled "middle class" and the political consequences for the formation of such identities. See, for example, López-Pedreros, *Makers of Democracy*; Owensby, *Intimate Ironies*.

56. Walker, *Waking from the Dream*.

57. Singer, *A crise do "milagre,"* 11.

58. "Antes, pela verdade nos preços," *Veja*, April 18, 1974, 80–87, in "Fatores que influem na formação da moral social e da opinião pública brasileira," Telecomunicações Brasileiras S/A, July 30, 1974, AN, Fundo Telecomunicações Brasileiras, BR/DFANBSB/CZ/ASI.0.7.

59. Cohen, *Consumers' Republic*; Trentmann, *Empire of Things*; O'Dougherty, *Consumption Intensified*.

60. "Antes, pela verdade nos preços."

61. Nestler, "Desperation of the Military's Economists," 62.

62. *Diário da Manhã*, "Nossa opinião."

63. *Jornal do Brasil*, "Defesa do consumidor."

64. *O Fluminense*, "Fazenda dá apoio a consumidor."

65. On the 1930s and 1940s, see Teixeira, *Third Path*, chap. 5. On postwar decades, see Silva, "Justiça e ditadura militar no Brasil."

66. In theory, the CIP set price guidelines for producers and industrialists while SUNAB issued price tables for essential goods sold to consumers. Mata, "Controles de preços na economia brasileira." How these organs worked in practice, however, awaits future research.

67. *Jornal do Brasil*, "Superesse recomenda."

68. Informação Nº 0020/118/AVS/79, Serviço Nacional de Informações, Agência de Salvador, September 25, 1979, AN, Fundo Serviço Nacional de Informações (SNI), BR DFANBSB. V8.MIC.

69. "Superesse recomenda."

70. Informação Nº 200/17/AC/80, Serviço Nacional de Informações, Agência de Manaus, October 14, 1980, AN, Fundo SNI, BR DFANBSB.V8.MIC.

71. *Diário de Notícias*, "O povo reclama."

72. Informação N° 0020/118/AVS/79, Serviço Nacional de Informações, Agência de Salvador, September 25, 1979, AN, Fundo SNI, BR DFANBSB.V8.MIC.

73. On the rise of mothers' associations and how working-class women participated in community politics in 1970s Brazil, see Alvarez, *Engendering Democracy in Brazil*.

74. The Movimento do Custo de Vida comprised progressive groups linked to the Catholic Church, student groups, leftist underground political parties, and *sindicatos* (labor unions). Monteiro, "Como pode um povo vivo viver."

75. Skidmore, *Politics of Military Rule in Brazil*, 164–73.

76. Alvarez, *Engendering Democracy in Brazil*, 98–102.

77. Cited in "Movimento Custo de Vida Abaixo Assinado" (facsimile), in Monteiro, "Como pode um povo vivo viver," Anexo N° 8. Note that Brazilian authorities disputed the number of signatures on the petition to discredit the movement. Monteiro, "Como pode um povo vivo viver," 98–99.

78. The historian Charles Maier argues that in Latin America, inflation is a political choice arising from a "working-class–bourgeois conflict": resources are redistributed to working classes via wage adjustments while middle-class groups defined as savers and consumers resented such measures (*In Search of Stability*, 196).

79. Gordon, "Demand for and Supply of Inflation," 809.

80. Campos, "New Scenario for Decision-Making."

81. Tullio and Ronci, "Brazilian Inflation from 1980 to 1993," 651.

82. Adelman, "International Finance and Political Legitimacy," 124–25.

83. Nestler, "Desperation of the Military's Economists."

84. DaMatta, "Para uma sociologia da inflação," 17.

85. Campos, "New Scenario for Decision-Making."

86. Neiburg, "La guerre des indices."

87. *Inflação e salários*, Programa "Globo Debate," *TV Globo*, August 17, 1980, CPDOC, EG-74f.

88. Frieden, "Brazilian Borrowing Experience," 96; Klein and Luna, *Economic and Social History of Brazil*, table A.3.

89. Silva, *Poder Constituinte e Poder Popular*.

90. "Direitas-Já e a Economia Nacional," *Folha de São Paulo*, April 23, 1984, in Lopes, *O choque heterodoxo*, 116–17.

91. Scholars note that Brazilian officials tried to conceal the scope of the debt crisis from the public. Diaz-Alejandro, "Some Aspects of the 1982–83 Brazilian Payments Crisis"; Bacha and Malan, "Brazil's Debt."

92. McCann, *Hard Times in the Marvelous City*, chaps. 3–4.

93. Tullio and Ronci, "Brazilian Inflation from 1980 to 1993," 649.

94. Alston et al., *Brazil in Transition*, 72–96; Weyland, *Politics of Market Reform*, 72.

95. To be sure, the assumption that "populist" governments disregard fiscal or monetary constraints is not supported by past case studies, especially for countries with legacies of inflation crises. Kaplan, "Fighting Past Economic Wars."

96. Sola, "Heterodox Shock in Brazil."

97. "Índice geral de preços— Disponibilidade Interna (% a.m. IGP-DI)," Percent change in monthly inflation, from 1944 to August 2024, accessed October 4, 2024, Ipeadata.gov.br.

98. Adair, *In Search of the Lost Decade*, 2.

99. Some economists point to the automatic wage increases as the reason for its failure. Baer and Beckerman, "Decline and Fall of Brazil's Cruzado," 36, 43–44.

100. Neiburg, "Economistas e culturas econômicas," 193.
101. Quoted in *Folha de S. Paulo*, "Conceição não choraria hoje."
102. *Jornal do Commercio*, "Classe média regressa ao paraíso."
103. Quoted in *Jornal do Commercio*, "Sauer teme a euphoria entre as montadoras."
104. *Jornal do Brasil*, "Sarney exalta mulheres e não teme dificuldades."
105. O'Dougherty, *Consumption Intensified*, 67.
106. "Evolução do Programa de Estabilidade Econômica," August 17, 1986, AN, Fundo SNI, BR DFANBSB.V8.MIC.
107. See, for example, Jacobs, "'How About Some Meat?'"; and De, "'Commodities Must Be Controlled.'"
108. O'Dougherty, *Consumption Intensified*, 67–68.
109. O'Dougherty, *Consumption Intensified*, 57.
110. Quoted in *Brasil dia-a-dia*, 134.
111. Annual inflation is not the best measure of economic performance because monthly inflation was so volatile with the freezes. As a broad comparison, annual inflation was 61 percent in 1986 and 432 percent in 1987. See Figure 3.
112. Quoted in *Brasil dia-a-dia*, 135.
113. José Afonso da Silva, quoted in "Queda do decreto-lei fortalece o congresso," Comissão Provisória de Estudos Constitucionais, August 8, 1986, Museu da República, Rio de Janeiro (hereafter MR), CEC MC006CECEF.
114. Quoted in "Queda do decreto-lei fortalece o congresso."
115. Manifesto of *sindicatos* for Rio Grande do Sul journalists and photographers, "Manifesto aos constituintes," July 16, 1987, MR, CEC MC020CPMCSOC.
116. Teixeira, *Third Path*, chap. 5.
117. Parcer, Comissão da Ordem Social, Subcomissão dos Direitos dos Trabalhadores e Servidores Públicos, May 19, 1987, MR, CEC MC011CPMCAN.
118. Parcer, Comissão da Soberania e dos Direitos e Garantias do Homem e da Mulher, Subcomissão dos Direitos e Garantias Individuais, June 17, 1987, MR, CEC MC011CPMCAN.
119. DaMatta, "Para uma sociologia da inflação," 16.
120. *Jornal do Brasil*, "Brasil vai pedir novos empréstimos aos bancos."
121. Weyland, *Politics of Market Reform*, chap. 4.
122. Mantega, "O pensamento econômico brasileiro," 107.

References

Adair, Jennifer. *In Search of the Lost Decade: Everyday Rights in Post-dictatorship Argentina*. Oakland: University of California Press, 2019.

Adelman, Jeremy. "International Finance and Political Legitimacy: A Latin American View of the Global Shock." In *The Shock of the Global: The 1970s in Perspective*, edited by Niall Ferguson, Charles S. Maier, Erez Manela, and Daniel J. Sargent, 113–27. Cambridge, MA: Belknap Press of Harvard University Press, 2011.

Alston, Lee J., Marcus André Melo, Bernardo Mueller, and Carlos Pereira. *Brazil in Transition: Beliefs, Leadership, and Institutional Change*. Princeton, NJ: Princeton University Press, 2016.

Alvarez, Sonia E. *Engendering Democracy in Brazil: Women's Movements in Transition Politics*. Princeton, NJ: Princeton University Press, 1990.

Anúario Estatístico do Brasil – 1951. Vol. XII. Rio de Janeiro: Serviço Gráfico do Instituto Brasileiro de Geografia e Estatística, 1952.

Anúario Estatístico do Brasil – 1964. Vol. XXV. Rio de Janeiro: Conselho Nacional de Estatística, 1964.

Anúario Estatístico do Brasil – 1967. Vol. 28. Rio de Janeiro: Serviço Gráfico do Instituto Brasileiro de Geografia e Estatística, 1967.

Anúario Estatístico do Brasil – 1968. Vol. 29. Rio de Janeiro: Serviço Gráfico do Instituto Brasileiro de Geografia e Estatística, 1968.

Arida, Persio, and André Lara-Resende. "Inertial Inflation and Monetary Reform: Brazil." In *Inflation and Indexation: Argentina, Brazil, and Israel*, edited by John Williamson, 27–45. Washington, DC: Institute for International Economics, 1985.

Bacha, Edmar L., and Pedro Malan. "Brazil's Debt: From the Miracle to the Fund." Texto para Discussão, no. 80. Rio de Janeiro: Pontifícia Universidade Católica do Rio de Janeiro, Departamento de Economia, 1984.

Baer, Werner, and Paul Beckerman. "The Decline and Fall of Brazil's Cruzado." *Latin American Research Review* 24, no. 1 (1989): 35–64.

Bastian, Eduardo. "O PAEG e o plano trienal: Uma análise comparativa de suas políticas de estabilização de curto prazo." *Estudos Econômicos* 43, no. 1 (2013): 139–66.

Bielschowsky, Ricardo. *Pensamento econômico brasileiro: O ciclo ideológico do desenvolvimentismo*. Rio de Janeiro: IPEA/INPES, 1988.

Brasil dia-a-dia: O retrato dos últimos 50 anos, edited by Sheila Mazzolenis. São Paulo: Editora Abril, 1988.

Cohen, Lizabeth. *A Consumers' Republic: The Politics of Mass Consumption in Postwar America*. New York: Alfred A. Knopf, 2003.

DaMatta, Roberto. "Para uma sociologia da inflação: Notas sobre inflação, sociedade e cidadania." In *Na corda bamba: Doze estudos sobre a cultura da inflação*, edited by José Ribas Vieira et al., 15–32. Rio de Janeiro: Relume Dumará, 1993.

De, Rohit. "'Commodities Must Be Controlled': Economic Crimes and Market Discipline in India (1939–1955)." *International Journal of Law in Context* 10, no. 3 (2014): 277–94.

Diário da Manhã. "Nossa opinião: Diga não á inflação." April 25, 1973.

Diário de Notícias. "O povo reclama." February 27, 1973.

Diaz-Alejandro, Carlos F. "Some Aspects of the 1982–83 Brazilian Payments Crisis." *Brookings Papers on Economic Activity* 1983, no. 2 (1983): 515–52.

Elena, Eduardo. *Dignifying Argentina: Peronism, Citizenship, and Mass Consumption*. Pittsburgh: University of Pittsburgh Press, 2011.

Fajardo, Margarita. *The World That Latin America Created: The United Nations Economic Commission for Latin America in the Development Era*. Cambridge, MA: Harvard University Press, 2022.

Fico, Carlos. *Reinventando o otimismo: Ditadura, propaganda e imaginário social no Brasil*. Rio de Janeiro: Editora Fundação Getúlio Vargas, 1997.

Folha de S. Paulo. "Conceição não choraria hoje." February 25, 1996.

Fonseca, Renan Reis. *O transnacional e o local nas revistas Reader's Digest e Seleções: Relações de gênero nos Estados Unidos e no Brasil (1939–1971)*. Rio de Janeiro: Ape' Ku Editora, 2020.

French, John D. *The Brazilian Workers' ABC: Class Conflict and Alliances in Modern São Paulo*. Chapel Hill: University of North Carolina Press, 1992.

Frens-String, Joshua. *Hungry for Revolution: The Politics of Food and the Making of Modern Chile*. Oakland: University of California Press, 2021.

Frieden, Jeffry A. "The Brazilian Borrowing Experience: From Miracle to Debacle and Back." *Latin American Research Review* 22, no. 1 (1987): 95–131.

Furtado, Celso. *Formação econômica do Brasil*. 18th ed. São Paulo: Companhia Editora Nacional, 1982.

Gordon, Robert J. "The Demand for and Supply of Inflation." *Journal of Law and Economics* 18, no. 3 (1975): 807–36.

Hobsbawm, Eric. *The Age of Extremes: A History of the World, 1914–1991*. New York: Vintage Books, 1996.

Ioris, Rafael R. "'Fifty Years in Five' and What's in It for Us? Development Promotion, Populism, Industrial Workers, and *Carestia* in 1950s Brazil." *Journal of Latin American Studies* 44, no. 2 (2012): 261–84.

Jacobs, Meg. "'How About Some Meat?': The Office of Price Administration, Consumption Politics, and State Building from the Bottom Up, 1941–1946." *Journal of American History* 84, no. 3 (1997): 910–41.

Jornal do Brasil. "Brasil vai pedir novos empréstimos aos bancos." January 7, 1987.

Jornal do Brasil. "Defesa do consumidor: Lições de Ralph Nader à moda gaúcha." May 14, 1975.

Jornal do Brasil. "Sarney exalta mulheres e não teme dificuldades." March 8, 1986.

Jornal do Brasil. "Superesse recomenda: Um olho no preço e outro no bolso. Dará certo?" October 7, 1977.

Jornal do Commercio. "Classe média regressa ao paraíso." May 18–19, 1986.

Jornal do Commercio. "Sauer teme a euphoria entre as montadoras." January 10, 1986.

Kaplan, Stephen Brett. "Fighting Past Economic Wars: Crisis and Austerity in Latin America." *Latin American Research Review* 53, no. 1 (2018): 19–37.

Klein, Herbert S., and Francisco Vidal Luna. *Brazil, 1964–1985: The Military Regimes of Latin America in the Cold War*. New Haven, CT: Yale University Press, 2017.

Klein, Herbert S., and Francisco Vidal Luna. *The Economic and Social History of Brazil since 1889*. New York: Cambridge University Press, 2014.

Lopes, Francisco Lafaiete. *O choque heterodoxo: Combate à inflação e reforma monetária*. Rio de Janeiro: Editora Campus, 1986.

Lopes, Lucas. "Como inventar o futuro do Brasil." *Jornal do Brasil*, March 13, 1968.

López-Pedreros, A. Ricardo. *Makers of Democracy: A Transnational History of the Middle Classes in Colombia*. Durham, NC: Duke University Press, 2019.

Maier, Charles S. *In Search of Stability: Explorations in Historical Political Economy*. New York: Cambridge University Press, 1987.

Maier, Charles S. "'Malaise': The Crisis of Capitalism in the 1970s." In *The Shock of the Global: The 1970s in Perspective*, edited by Niall Ferguson, Charles S. Maier, Erez Manela, and Daniel J. Sargent, 25–48. Cambridge, MA: Belknap Press of Harvard University Press, 2011.

Mantega, Guido. "O pensamento econômico brasileiro de 60 a 80: Os anos rebeldes." In *50 anos de ciência econômica no Brasil (1946–1996): Pensamento, instituições, depoimentos*, 107–57. Petrópolis: Vozes, 1997.

Mata, Milton da. "Controles de preços na economia brasileira: Aspectos institucionais e resultados." *Pesquisa e Planejamento Econômico* 10, no. 3 (1980): 911–53.

McCann, Bryan. *Hard Times in the Marvelous City: From Dictatorship to Democracy in the Favelas of Rio de Janeiro*. Durham, NC: Duke University Press, 2013.

Meade, Teresa. "'Living Worse and Costing More': Resistance and Riot in Rio de Janeiro, 1890–1917." *Journal of Latin American Studies* 21, nos. 1–2 (1989): 241–66.

Modenesi, André de Melo. *Regimes monetários: Teoria e a experiência do real*. São Paulo: Manole, 2005.

Monteiro, Thiago William Nunes Gusmão. "'Como pode um povo vivo viver nesta carestia': O Movimento do Custo de Vida em São Paulo (1973–1982)." Master's thesis, Universidade de São Paulo, 2015.

Nagasava, Heliene. *O sindicato que a ditadura queria: O Ministério do Trabalho no governo Castelo Branco (1964–1967)*. Jundiaí: Paco Editorial, 2018.

Neiburg, Federico. "Economistas e culturas econômicas no Brasil e na Argentina: notas para uma comparação a propósito das heterodoxias." *Tempo Social* 16, no. 2 (2004): 177–202.

Neiburg, Federico. "Inflation: Economists and Economic Cultures in Brazil and Argentina." *Comparative Studies in Society and History* 48, no. 3 (2006): 604–33.

Neiburg, Federico. "La guerre des indices. L'inflation au Brésil (1964–1994)." *Genèses* 84, no. 3 (2011): 25–46.

Nestler, Matthew. "The Desperation of the Military's Economists: Advertising as a Way to Fight Inflation in 1970s Brazil." *Journal of Latin American Studies* 53, no. 1 (2021): 53–80.

O Cruzeiro. "Municípios de maior progresso do Brasil." June 23, 1971, 50–53.

O'Dougherty, Maureen. *Consumption Intensified: The Politics of Middle-Class Daily Life in Brazil*. Durham, NC: Duke University Press, 2002.

O Fluminense. "Fazenda dá apoio a consumidor." August 4, 1976.

Opinião. "Ainda a fama do 'milagre.'" March 19–25, 1973.

Owensby, Brian. *Intimate Ironies: Modernity and the Making of Middle-Class Lives in Brazil*. Stanford, CA: Stanford University Press, 1999.

Pereira, Luiz Carlos Bresser. *Development and Crisis in Brazil, 1930–1983*. Translated by Marcia van Dyke. Boulder, CO: Westview Press, 1984.

Power, Margaret. "Who but a Woman? The Transnational Diffusion of Anti-Communism among Conservative Women in Brazil, Chile and the United States during the Cold War." *Journal of Latin American Studies* 47, no. 1 (2015): 93–119.

Resende, André Lara. "A política brasileira de estabilização: 1963–68." *Pesquisa e Planejamento Econômico* 12, no. 3 (1982): 757–806.

Rodgers, Daniel T. *Age of Fracture*. Cambridge, MA: Harvard University Press, 2011.

Santanna, Danielle. "The History of Consumer Credit in Brazil: From the Developmentalist Era to Lula." *International Journal of Political Economy* 49, no. 3 (2020): 203–21.

Sikkink, Kathryn. *Ideas and Institutions: Developmentalism in Brazil and Argentina*. Ithaca, NY: Cornell University Press, 1991.

Silva, Ângela Moreira Domingues da. "Justiça e ditadura militar no Brasil: O julgamento dos crimes contra a economia popular." *Diálogos* 18, no. 1 (2014): 51–73.

Silva, José Afonso da. *Poder constituinte e poder popular: Estudos sobre a Constituição*. São Paulo: Malheiros Editores, 2007.

Singer, Paul. *A crise do "milagre."* Rio de Janeiro: Paz e Terra, 1976.

Skidmore, Thomas. *The Politics of Military Rule in Brazil, 1964–1985*. New York: Oxford University Press, 1989.

Skidmore, Thomas. "The Years between the Harvests: The Economics of the Castelo Branco Presidency, 1964–1967." *Luso-Brazilian Review* 15, no. 2 (1978): 153–77.

Sola, Lourdes. "Heterodox Shock in Brazil: *Técnicos*, Politicians, and Democracy." *Journal of Latin American Studies* 23, no. 1 (1991): 163–95.

Souza, Luiz Eduardo Simões de. "A crise política dos anos 1960." In *Economia brasileira: Da colônia ao governo Lula*, edited by Marcos Cordeiro Pires, 139–59. São Paulo: Editora Saraiva, 2010.

Tavares, Maria da Conceição. "Notas sobre o problema do financiamento numa economia em desenvolvimento—o caso do Brasil (1967)." In *Da substituição de importações ao capitalismo financeiro: Ensaios sobre economia brasileira*, 10th ed., 125–52. Rio de Janeiro: Zahar Editores, 1982.

Teixeira, Melissa. *A Third Path: Corporatism in Brazil and Portugal*. Princeton, NJ: Princeton University Press, 2024.

Tinsman, Heidi. *Buying into the Regime: Grapes and Consumption in Cold War Chile and the United States*. Durham, NC: Duke University Press, 2014.

Trentmann, Frank. *Empire of Things: How We Became a World of Consumers, from the Fifteenth Century to the Twenty-First*. New York: HarperCollins, 2016.

Tullio, G., and M. Ronci. "Brazilian Inflation from 1980 to 1993: Causes, Consequences and Dynamics." *Journal of Latin American Studies* 28, no. 3 (1996): 635–66.

Veloso, Fernando A., André Villela, and Fabio Giambiagi. "Determinantes do 'milagre' econômico brasileiro (1968–1973): Uma análise empírica." *Revista Brasileira de Economia* 62, no. 2 (2008): 221–46.

Walker, Louise E. *Waking from the Dream: Mexico's Middle Classes after 1968*. Stanford, CA: Stanford University Press, 2013.

Weyland, Kurt. *The Politics of Market Reform in Fragile Democracies: Argentina, Brazil, Peru, and Venezuela*. Princeton, NJ: Princeton University Press, 2002.

Wolfe, Joel. *Autos and Progress: The Brazilian Search for Modernity*. Oxford: Oxford University Press, 2010.

Woodard, James P. *Brazil's Revolution in Commerce: Creating Consumer Capitalism in the American Century*. Chapel Hill: University of North Carolina Press, 2020.

Stories of History

Ethiopia between Hope and Despair in *Anbessa* and *Faya Dayi*

Hannah Borenstein

An Explosion Rocked the Stage

On June 23, 2018, a bomb went off in Addis Ababa. In prior years, explosions in the form of mass protests, repressive military responses, and clashes between protestors and police rattled the country, often resulting in deaths and imprisonment of activists and dissenters. But in 2018 someone, allegedly dressed in a police uniform, threw a grenade at a rally being held in Meskel Square for the newly appointed prime minister, Abiy Ahmed, killing two people and injuring over 150.[1]

Tens of thousands of Ethiopians came to the rally to support Prime Minister Abiy, who had taken the political reins a few months earlier and had quickly made a series of sweeping changes seemingly in line with a more liberal style of governance. He wore a lime-green T-shirt to the event with an image of Nelson Mandela holding a raised-fist salute, appearing to emerge out of a silhouette of Africa, and the words "No one is free until the last one is free" in English. At the rally, Abiy sought to instill energy into an Ethiopian population that had rapidly become hopeful, against all odds. "Building an independent nation is not the same as building a free society," Abiy said that day. He continued: "What good is a free country if we don't enjoy freedom? If we are not free from fear? If we don't have freedom of speech and expression? If we build dividing walls rather than bridges." Soon after these

Radical History Review
Issue 151 (January 2025)   DOI 10.1215/01636545-11506812
© 2025 by MARHO: The Radical Historians' Organization, Inc.

remarks, the explosion rocked the stage, Abiy was escorted to safety, and thousands descended into panic. But later that day, Abiy went on television to address the nation, still wearing the same T-shirt; he said somberly and firmly, "Certain groups planned and coordinated to destroy this large gathering."[2] "They have tried very hard but their operation has failed." Less than two days later, Abiy was seen on television donating blood at Tikur Anbessa (Black Lion) Hospital.

If the grenade had momentarily threatened to erode the fervor so many felt for Abiy, his blood donation reversed this course. Estimated approval ratings must have been inordinately high, rising more quickly than the new skyscrapers in the city. That summer in Addis Ababa and beyond, "Abiy mania" took hold, and many residents, including many disenfranchised Oromos, spoke of having new and palpable hope (*tesfa*, Amharic ተስፋ).[3] Abiy mania was intoxicating not just for Ethiopians, and not just because Abiy's young and fresh face drew comparisons to figures from Nelson Mandela, Justin Trudeau, and Mikhail Gorbachev to Barack Obama. T-shirts, posters, and other political paraphernalia sold both at home and abroad alluded to liberal America's 2008 Obama-era hope, with identical color schemes and the Amharic ተስፋ in place of the "HOPE" on Obama's familiar poster. Abiy garnered hope for more than freeing political prisoners, unblocking censored websites, and brokering a peace deal with Eritrea. He also represented a shift to a more liberal economic policy, indicating his willingness to privatize previously state-owned enterprises (notably Ethiopian Airlines and the telecoms sector). Abiy reinvigorated hope for Ethiopia's economic miracle to materialize.

Content and Form

In what follows I trace a few different narratives about Ethiopia's economic miracle, and the politics and discourses of these narratives. To understand how Ethiopia's economic miracle has been reported means contending with other narratives—of Ethiopia's political economy, the discourse and politics of narration of Ethiopian history and historiography, and ethnographic and artistic renderings of life in Ethiopia. Like so much of Ethiopian history, most of the conversation around Ethiopia's economic miracle has focused on macrodevelopmental projects and disputes between international and Ethiopian leadership. Rarely are we given insights into what people living in Ethiopia think and feel about the changing country's political-economic trajectory, which, too, are felt in explosive ways.

I contend that this is a matter of form, which national news coverage and even political theorizing cannot fully capture. In their efforts to create objective and historically informed narratives, these narratives often convey a false notion that Ethiopian historiography is an agreed-on storyline. In this article I argue that hope and despair—the experiential dialectic of Ethiopia's economic miracle—captured in a particular type of filmic capacity, resists a familiar narrative structure and allows for a fruitful purchase on understanding what it means for Ethiopians to live amid the turmoil of a materializing "economic miracle."

Two films—Mo Scarpelli's *Anbessa* (2019) and Jessica Beshir's *Faya Dayi* (2021)—offer compelling and necessary perspectives on the economic miracle. They are both unconventional documentaries that through their form and content offer critical and complementary ways of thinking about how economic miracles fold and unfold. *Anbessa*, set on the peripheries of Addis Ababa in the Amharic language, captures what it means to live in a state of urban dispossession and fear, while trying to imagine and cultivate hope and memory. *Faya Dayi*, a hypnotic monochrome feature set on the outskirts of the city of Harar and in the region of Oromia, follows a community of people whose lives center around khat, an endemic stimulant plant, which people ironically use to both make a living and kill time. The films are different in languages, locations, and colors, but they both show how people generate their own hope in the midst of the despair of dispossession of land and optimism. In addition to showing the lived experience of Ethiopia's material reality, these artistic renderings, which use captured life but edit and blend real images in surreal ways, allow viewers to look at what an economic miracle means in constructive ways. More broadly, the analysis seeks to position creative forms of storytelling as integral to understanding the changing political and economic structural terrain.

In the sections that follow I situate debates about Ethiopian historiography alongside discussion about the material conditions of Ethiopia's economic miracle. I aim to add some context to the idea of Ethiopia's economic miracle by asking *who* gets to tell the stories and histories of Ethiopia's ups and downs. I begin by explaining how Ethiopia came to be an "emerging economy" in developmental discourse, and describe some of the struggles it has faced in realizing its miracle. Then, I situate the Ethiopian "economic miracle" historically in debates about Ethiopian historiography and narrative. Finally, I turn to the two films to present a counterpart to storylines written by academics, policymakers, and politicians, to provide a critical medium to understand and engage with the idea of the "economic miracle" at large. In so doing, I argue that these critical voices—of everyday people—are an essential and often-missed perspective in producing a narrative of economic miracles, which are often discussed on a macro scale.

Cutting an African Lion's Hope

In 2015, a few years before Abiy mania, Ethiopia was dubbed an "emerging economy." The country had experienced substantial growth in GDP over the prior ten years, with projections to keep growing. Ethiopia was considered an "African lion" by the Brookings Institution (an American think tank that conducts research about public policy and economic development), poised to undergo its own sub-Saharan African economic miracle, akin to that of the Asian tigers between the 1950s and 1990s. This was a seductive idea not only for global investors; it also appealed to many Ethiopians because it followed the late prime minister Meles Zenawi's hopes for a developmental state in the federation's early years. Brookings noted that Ethiopia, among a few other African countries, was part of the "last great untapped market, ripe for rapid growth and development," but lacked research and support.[4] Prime Minister Abiy's promise to lead Ethiopia into this new era allowed hope to continue to permeate.

But just as quickly as hope can be sewn, felt, and built, it can be cut. In Amharic, the translation of "hopeless" is *tesfa qoretewal*. "*Qoretewal*" comes from the verb "to cut," which is also used to mean sawing, severing. The anthropologist Daniel Mains titled his 2013 ethnography *Hope Is Cut* to invoke the condition of hopelessness young people feel amid modernization, development, and positive economic projections.[5] Though written before Abiy's appointment, the intensity and sharpness of cutting hope is also a useful analytic to understand the fallout after the fervent and brief Abiy mania. After Abiy's tumultuous arrival abruptly inserted immense optimism into a narrative of progress and growth, hope, again, was cut.

By 2020 Ethiopia had descended into a civil war, with the Tigray People's Liberation Front and the Ethiopian National Defense Forces engaging in deadly conflict. Prime Minister Abiy, who won the Nobel Peace Prize in 2019 for mediating a long-standing conflict with neighboring Eritrea, repressively shut down the telecoms services in Tigray that he promised to privatize, again sent dissenters to prison, and allowed mass violence to occur on his watch. A lack of foreign direct investment (FDI), a continuous problem in Ethiopia, grew ever deeper, and global hope and admiration for Abiy turned, for many, to despair.[6] Most of the mainstream narratives about Abiy's rise and fall, and Ethiopia's economic miracle, tend to be linear. But much like chronicles of Ethiopian history, they discursively lack a sense of irony, timelessness, dreaminess, and nuance that most of the population felt before, during, and after Ethiopia's rise to potential economic prowess. Much like the economic miracle, the story of Abiy's rise and fall is a seductive narrative, but not one that reflects the lived experience of many Ethiopians, who have been experiencing a dispossession of land, autonomy, and hope for much longer.

Memories of Discursivity and Metanarratives

It is difficult to know where to begin when historicizing Ethiopia's economic miracle in part because there is a tendency in Ethiopian historiography to chart a grand periodized narrative that includes a series of pivotal regime changes.[7] Some look all the way back to the Solomonic era, but in more recent analyses scholars often turn back to Emperor Menelik II's victory over Italian invaders during the European Scramble for Africa. From there, they tend to chronicle transitions in the monarchy that led to Emperor Haile Selassie's rule, followed by an account of the brief Italian occupation, then Haile Selassie's return, then a revolution in 1974 which put the Derg—a communist military junta that oversaw the murder of likely hundreds of thousands of Ethiopians—in power. Finally, narratives usually turn to the revolution in 1991 in which the Ethiopian People's Revolutionary Democratic Front (EPRDF) took charge and established Ethiopia as a multiethnic federation.[8]

While Ethiopia came to be hailed as an African exemplar for defeating would-be colonizers as early as the late 1890s, others have called this grand narrative into question.[9] Historians, especially from marginal ethnic groups, often contend that the Ethiopian state was created through conquest, coercion, concessions, and oppression and was thus a dependent colonial state. For instance, rather than seeing Emperor Menelik II's reign as one that merely opposes Italian colonial rule, many Oromo groups in Ethiopia experienced state formation as a violent process that saw an internal conquest and dispossession of land.[10]

In the process of defeating Italian invaders Menelik II rose from being the provincial monarch of Shewa to the emperor of modern Ethiopia and declared the new nation-state's capital to be Addis Ababa ("New Flower" in Amharic). In so doing Menelik II settled on Oromo land. To this day, the city is known to many by indigenous Oromo people as Finfinne—an Oromo name and reference to the city's hot springs in their language, Oromiffa. Establishing the capital as Addis Ababa was thus contested from the outset but helped to construct the city as an ideological core. During this time emphasis was also put on the Amharic language, the Ethiopian Church, and land tenure policies that were advantageous to certain ethnic groups. Because Ethiopia is so culturally and linguistically diverse (there are more than eighty languages actively spoken within the country), creating the capital of the state as a powerful Amhara core centrally tied the city to the global economy, and the early administration transitively tied other parts of Ethiopia to political and economic initiatives in peripheral ways.[11]

This disjuncture of core and periphery was felt through Haile Selassie's rule, which was characterized as one of modernization in the grand narrative, but also remains contested. In *Marxist Modern*, the anthropologist Don Donham made these opposing chronicles and ironies clear in his ethnographic portrait of the Ethiopian Revolution. Donham wrote of a metanarrative of modernity in which the "recurrent dialectic among modernist, anti-modernist, and traditionalist stances" led to the modernization of Ethiopia, with modernist conceptions of the future resting on a particular arrow of technological progress where "the future continually arrives more quickly."[12]

While the grand narrative of modernity was constructed in the capital of Addis Ababa, it was in Maale, where Donham did fieldwork, that he saw a disjuncture. In Maale, people talked about a conception of the future tied to a notion of divine kinship that continually threatened to fall apart; Donham argued that people in Maale had a narrative that was not in sync with the "core" of Ethiopia. Educated people in Addis Ababa, who were seen to "lead Ethiopia out of backwardness—enjoyed unquestioned prestige" and positioned themselves as protagonists in the story of progress. However, Donham notes the student movement's central reform—the nationalization of land—was not a true response to peasants' own agitations, nor was it out of step with Ethiopian modernism.[13] Initially the intellectual Left and the formation of *zemecha*—students who would implement land reform in the countryside—gained prominence, but then the military realized they would be able to form a stronger base in the capital without their leftist resistance. While land reform was restructured to use land ownership to "underpin the stratification of persons into classes" in certain areas in southern Ethiopia, for instance, it was also seen as a chance to reestablish local autonomy from northern Amhara.

In *Ethiopia in Theory: Revolution and Knowledge Production, 1964–2016*, the late political theorist Elleni Centime Zeleke added context to these misunderstandings between the students who refashioned Marxist-Leninist categories to create an Ethiopian understanding of historical materialism. Zeleke sees the attachment that students had to Lenin's writings and ideas about nationalities as important in refashioning certain categories to fit the Ethiopian political landscape. The consequences of some of these teleological renderings meant that they "also used the 'eternal' laws of the social sciences as weapons to silence their opponents."[14] Zeleke offers *tizita*—which means memory in Amharic, but which is also a genre of music in which people invoke memories often alongside loss—as both concept and method. For Zeleke, *tizita* sensorially interrupts a relation of historical contingency.

In a similar vein, the two films I take as objects in subsequent sections offer an alternative account to understand how the contested past is prologue, especially as it pertains to the narrative of Ethiopia's economic miracle. While *Anbessa* sees how Addis Ababa is weaponized against the inhabitants' poor, *Faya Dayi* gives a rare glimpse into how people in the "peripheries" of Ethiopia experience political decisions made by vanguard politicians at its core.

The most recent chapter of this Ethiopian *durée* (how long it is depends on who you ask) that leads to the political economic present is the revolution in 1991. Here, the coalition of the EPRDF, made up primarily of four political parties from Tigray, Amhara, Oromo, and the Southern Nations, joined forces to overthrow the Derg.[15] The Tigray People's Liberation Front, led by Meles Zenawi and steeped in Marxist-Leninist ideology, saw themselves as a vanguard party that should lead the country into a revolutionary democracy. The system of ethnic federalism they introduced drew on Leninist ideas about nationalities, with the outward facing purpose being to accommodate demands and desires for ethnic autonomy.

In the 1990s Ethiopia was then divided into regional states and chartered cities based on ethnicity and language. As of 2024, there are eleven regional states and two chartered cities—Addis Ababa and Dire Dawa. In addition to its economic federalist structure, the new Ethiopia was designed in Prime Minister Meles's vision as a developmentalist state. Despite military assistance from the United States in overthrowing the Derg, for many years Ethiopia diverged from other African states and, much to the chagrin of the United States, opposed most neoliberal reforms and privatized aid.[16] Meles, who died in 2012, asserted that Ethiopia was a "democratic developmental state," meaning that its democratic orientation was as important as its development. Some political scientists argued that this was theoretically different than Asian tiger states, which prioritized development over democracy, and that a divergence between theory and reality occurred in Ethiopia where development, too, was really the priority.[17]

Those who saw value in the Washington Consensus grew frustrated with Ethiopia, which did not readily take loans from the World Bank, IMF, and other Western institutions. But as the country remained one of the world's poorest for years, possibilities for growth and transformation felt far off for quite some time. Thus, when the Brookings Institution designated Ethiopia as an African lion, the roar was a tantalizing prospect.

Tensions over the Right to the City

In creating plans for the Ethiopian developmental state, under Meles's leadership, the Ethiopian government created the first growth and transformation plan in 2010 with the aim of boosting the GDP by 11 to 15 percent in five years. Through targeting over 8 percent annual agricultural growth by enhancing productivity of small-holder farmers and improving participation and engagement of the private sector, the government put forth a public goal to reach middle income status by 2025.[18] By 2011, government officials began developing a project to realize this goal. The Addis Ababa master plan was introduced, which would expand the boundaries of the Ethiopian capital by 1.1 million hectares into the Oromia Special Zone in 2014.[19] This ushered in protests that called into question the 1995 Constitution, which had divided Ethiopia into ethnically based regional states.[20]

The plan would have brought several Oromo cities and towns under the Addis Ababa city administration's purview, likely with the intention of leasing peripheral lands to foreign companies in the interest of generating FDI. However, owing in part to the repeated history of land dispossession, when the plan was introduced in 2014, it was met with widespread dissatisfaction. Oromo people had historically experienced a type of dispossession from their land when the Ethiopian state was formed and Menelik II renamed the capital Addis Ababa. Just as they continued to call that capital Finfinne, they continued to reject the plan.[21]

The master plan was egregious not only because it displaced thousands of Oromo people living on the outskirts of the city, many of whom were farmers, but because it symbolically made clear that the right to self-determination with respect to land was a farce. The right to the city was about more than just Addis Ababa; it was, as David Harvey notes in regard to most mass movements to claim urban space, "far more than the individual liberty to access urban resources: it is a right to change ourselves by changing the city."[22] For Oromos the master plan meant continued land dispossession and also the psychosocial feeling of hopelessness. Unsurprisingly, the expressed discontent mostly occurred in and around the urbanization that was pushing Oromo people out of their homes. However, there were protests around the country that received less news coverage. Demonstrations were nearly always met by violent repression, and death estimates reached into the tens of thousands, as they continued to fight for the city.

An Emerging Economy's Growing Pains

While internal political dissatisfaction grew, narratives about Ethiopia's economic growth elicited positive international responses and pundits positioned the country as an "emerging economy." In 2014 Michael Schuman published an article for *Time* magazine with the title "Forget the BRICs; Meet the PINEs."[23] The BRICS (Brazil, Russia, India, and China) were named by the Goldman Sachs economist Jim O'Neill in 2001 as a group of countries that had, at the time, over 40 percent of the world's population and a quarter of global GDP.[24] With a 2008 economic crisis plaguing the United States and Europe, China stepped up and became a major player in the global economy, developing a stimulus program including worldwide infrastructural programs, some of which were in Ethiopia.

In 2010 South Africa joined the BRICS, and in 2014 the group launched the BRICS Development Bank. But, according to Schuman, that same year indicated that BRICS economic growth was not materializing. The PINES included the Philippines, Indonesia, Nigeria, and Ethiopia, with a combined population of six hundred million at the time. Compared to the others, Schuman noted, "Ethiopia may be even more exciting. Once synonymous with poverty, peace and strong economic management have turned the nation around."

Alongside Addis Ababa expansion plans, ambitious infrastructural plans followed suit. Condominiums on the outskirts of Addis Ababa were constructed rapidly, displacing those in informal housing arrangements (a central objective in *Anbessa*), while a Chinese-funded light rail system was constructed throughout the city.[25] Although the Grand Ethiopian Renaissance Dam was being constructed outside of Addis, iconography celebrating its construction was present throughout the capital. Starting infrastructural projects not only supported growth but, as Mains notes, "secure[d] legitimacy through images of progress and modernity."[26]

It is important, though less often discussed, how other major global powers played a role in Ethiopia's rise and demise. Because of Ethiopia's developmentalist framework, critics often fail to delve into nuanced critiques of privatization and geopolitical strategies pursued by leading parties. However, the anthropologist Christina Tekie Collins has explored how before, during, and after Prime Minister Abiy's rise the state promoted economic growth as a project of state resource management, or a distinctly Ethiopian capitalism—"a system guided by a distinct developmental ideology that addresses the political-economic concerns of the country's ruling elite."[27] The question that people were subtly asking was whether or not an economic miracle of this type could occur in the Ethiopian case.

Even though hope for the African lion to grow occurred alongside demonstrations, the suppression eventually became too bloody to ignore. Internationally, the Oromo protests did not receive significant coverage until the 2016 Olympics in Rio de Janeiro. There, the Oromo marathon runner Feyisa Lilesa raised his hands in an X above his head while finishing second. After the race, silver medal around his neck, he told reporters that the Oromo people were facing brutal discrimination and if he returned to Ethiopia he would be killed. Lilesa sought asylum in the United States and raised his own profile and that of the conflict in the coming months.[28]

A few months later, on October 2, 2016, shortly after Lilesa spoke publicly about the Oromo plight in Washington, DC, hundreds of Oromo people were killed by security forces at a religious festival outside Addis Ababa, and the unrest escalated. The holiday of Irreecha, one of the most important annual celebrations for Oromos, came to be known as the Irreecha massacre. At the event over six hundred festivalgoers were killed by security forces after things somehow "turned chaotic." A few days later, the Ethiopian government announced a six-month state of emergency to quell the protests, which they claimed were coming from "foreign-funded gangs."[29]

Lilesa remained in the United States, and protests in solidarity occurred in 2017 throughout the diaspora. In early 2018, Prime Minister Hailemariam Desalegn resigned, and a few months later, Prime Minister Abiy came to power. He was Oromo and Amhara—the first-ever Ethiopian leader to have Oromo family—and he had a Muslim father and an Orthodox Christian mother. As Abiy embodied not only representation but unity, he developed a hopeful cult of personality, and Abiy mania rapidly took hold.

The Hope and Mania of Abiy Ahmed

For international allies seeking to develop the economic miracle of Ethiopia, Prime Minister Abiy was a promising figure. He was, on paper, more open to liberal economic strategies than any of his Ethiopian predecessors. Because Ethiopia lacked the capital markets to grow their private sector, their relationships to foreign powers remained critical. Many contended before Abiy's leadership that the EPRDF party-state had failed in its promises and served as a model of "illiberal state-building," which by 2018 was increasingly dysfunctional and a source of widespread popular discontent.[30]

In the article "Who Lost Ethiopia?," political scientists Harry Verhoeven and Michael Woldemariam outline Ethiopia's rise and fall in relation to a variety of allies. They note that Abiy's rise was catalyzed by Washington's support of his plans to liberalize the economy, but that the United States also contributed to his downfall by misreading core political realities in Ethiopia. The United States, they contend, saw Ethiopia as an important "anchor state"—involving militaristic and economic interests in which US liberal hegemony sought to operationalize its relationship with Ethiopia—to secure broader control and influence in the Horn of Africa.[31]

By interviewing several policy officials from both Ethiopia and the United States, Verhoeven and Woldemariam observed that key Western officials stressed the lengths to which Abiy went to present himself as "the most pro-American leader Ethiopia has ever had." More substantively, he announced his willingness to liberalize the telecoms sector, privatize Ethiopian Airlines, and buy more "high-quality"—code for non-Chinese—goods. When Abiy met with US officials, he allegedly promised to be a great "new customer," opening an avenue for the United States to compete economically with the Chinese in Africa. Given that the Trump administration green-lit a US$500 million loan to a Vodafone/Safaricom-led consortium—the first private entrant into Ethiopia's massive telecoms market—this strategy initially appeared to be working out.[32] However, Verhoeven and Woldemariam argue that the efforts by the US government to expand its power and influence during the political transition in 2018–20 helped create the conditions for Abiy to wage war with the Tigray region and usher in one of the world's worst humanitarian crises. Consequently, Ethiopia's position in the West as potential lion quickly eroded. The economic miracle, then, must be understood as something that is materially and ideologically produced at the same time, and through concessionary and strategic means.

At the time of writing, some might say Ethiopia's status of potential status as lion still lingers. In 2023, at the Fifteenth BRICS Summit, it was announced that Ethiopia, along with five other emerging market groups, would be admitted into BRICS. However, this exists alongside reports of a continued shortage of FDI, not being very close to middle-income status, and a range of other unknown factors that put Ethiopia's economic future on an uncertain footing.[33] More important, however, this poses a question about how to narrate Ethiopia's economic miracle, and the limits of political analysis and commentary as narrative. Most of the discourse is about public policy and economic governance, or the ethnic tensions that animate so much political discourse around Ethiopia. Many of the debates, which began over claims to the capital city, have expanded to the countryside. Despite regularly occurring violence throughout the country, there is limited news coverage, and the voices of ordinary Ethiopians are rarely profiled. Rarely do we get raw, unfiltered accounts from people being forced to live in the state of dispossession.

Anbessa and *Faya Dayi*—different films that, when taken together, evocatively address these lived experiences of land dispossession amid these recent changes in Ethiopian history—chart a new way of incorporating diverse perspectives into historical and artistic accounts. While they are narrated as epochal and abruptly shifting, they also reveal something else—that this is a slow process of theft and pain, in which people turn to their memories, and continuously sew and cut their hopes.

Anbessa

Anbessa opens as Asalif, a ten-year-old clad in a blue zip-up sweatshirt, opens a flashlight and discovers there are no batteries inside to enable its illumination capacities. Then he picks up a patch on the ground of the old flag of the Ethiopian Empire, which has at the center the Lion of Judah. Staring at the patch he simply says, "*anbessa!*" then starts making roaring noises.

Anbessa means "lion" in Amharic, Ethiopia's national language, which carries with it many cultural and symbolic meanings. Long before it was called an "African lion" by economists at the Brookings Institute, the Lion of Judah (a symbol of the Solomonic dynasty) was positioned on the center of Ethiopia's tricolor flag. The *Kebra Nagast*—a fourteenth-century epic from Ethiopia, written in the ancient script Ge'ez—contains an account of how the Queen of Sheba (Queen Makeda of Ethiopia) met King Solomon in Jerusalem and conceived Menelik I, then brought him and the Ark of the Covenant back to Ethiopia.[34] The historian Nadia Nurhussein asserts that the *Kebra Nagast* then gave textual authority to a narrative of Abyssinia's imperial history.[35] But in modern colloquial parlance, *anbessa* can mean much more. When someone does something impressive or heroic, one might call them, or the act itself, "*anbessa.*" To be a lion is to be cool, capable, and strong. Being *anbessa* means one can take on anything. It is imbued with history, but is also a word and concept that takes on new important meanings in the present.

After we briefly see the mud hut in which Asalif and his mother reside, his friend Kuba urges him to go out and play. The two walk up a hill and look out at the dozens of identical amber and gold condominiums. "The buildings look so nice from here!" Asalif says. "The land where I was born—" and Kuba interjects, "It's all covered by the condominiums now." Then Asalif speculates, "You think there are like seven hundred buildings?"

The condominiums that Asalif and Kuba look out on were there long before the film's 2019 release, and the public release of the master plan. In 2005, the Ethiopian Integrated Housing and Development Plan initiated government plans to build condominium estates to respond to the housing crisis in Addis Ababa.[36] The program was celebrated by some for creating jobs and better housing options for middle-class professionals in the city, but it accompanied a slum clearance plan that contributed to the demolition of informal settlements and the displacement of thousands of poor families.[37] Because the government owns the land, it can evict people with one day's warning.

Film director Mo Scarpelli, who had been working in Ethiopia for over eight years, met Asalif after taking an interest in the social lives surrounding these burgeoning condominiums. In 2015, when they met, condominiums in the eastern part of Addis had become so aesthetically prominent that "Condominium" became the name for a bus stop and neighborhood. Rather than explore this urbanization by centering Asalif in the style of cinema verité, Scarpelli sought to construct the world through Asalif's eyes and interpretations. Although the condominiums displaced him and his family, they also became his place of research and discovery.[38]

The next scene shows Asalif with his mother at home, where she emphasizes the importance of memories in relation to their home. Asalif draws images on scrap paper as she talks about their former home: "You can't forget the palm tree! And the little dam we made to water the garden." She continues, dreaming about their pre-demolition world: "The eucalyptus trees. There were five hundred of them!" It feels fantastical, in the ways Ethiopians often conjure a nostalgia for the future, but she knows these memories have few witnesses, and it is up to the two of them to archive them. The exercise is interrupted when Asalif farts, and they laugh, hysterically, perhaps in part because of the filmmaker's presence. Asalif, is, after all, just a boy.

Asalif brings out such emotional extremes in this scene and others, as children do, often in rapid succession. Even as he is precluded from living in the condominiums, they are also his playground. He and Kuba wander the grounds daily, taking bits of trash and turning them into tools and toys. But the threat of dispossession is always present. In one moment Kuba is playing with a small ball they found in the complex, and Asalif tells him to stop and put it away. "Hide your ball. Or else the condo boys will take it. They'll claim it's theirs. They took my ball last time," he warns.

Even as their possessions are at risk of being taken away by what the condominiums stand for, the boys admire the verticality and bright illumination of the buildings. The structures haunt them as they desire to see the possibilities that the inside of these homes offers. It is here that scholars who write about state infrastructure plans provide useful context; expectations of modernity shape and provide optical spaces for hope, but they rarely materialize into opportunity for middle and lower classes.[39] Asalif and his mom experience this regularly, squatting on what is the edge of the urban and rural. This edge was pushed farther east between the filming, its production, and release. And it has been pushed farther still, now.

"A Lion Can Take on Five Hyenas"

Later in the film, a few characters address the master plan head-on when Asalif sits with older men who are drinking *arake* (a locally fermented alcohol) in a bar. "When they announced the master plan to expand the city into Oromia farmland that really made me mad," one says. "That means all these teff farms will become skyscrapers."[40] Another man adds: "Ah, this government is like a failed car jack. . . . It was supposed to lift the country but instead it fell on itself." One man cautions him to be careful what he says, warning him that he could get arrested, and the rest laugh in confirmation and discomfort. Asalif quietly listens in.

In another scene Asalif finds a broken radio, and as he toys with it, he eventually fixes it and hears a talk radio show come on: "The region is very attractive for investment. The investors will provide sustainable community development, development that will help everyone." The diegetic sound then becomes a faded narration, with images of Asalif's perspective contrasting with what he hears on the radio. "Look, all we see is progress and opportunity here. This investment, it helps everyone. So there is nothing to lose. This development means benefit for all."

Asalif frequently returns to the *arake bet*—where men regularly share stories, myths, and truths in addition to politics. In one scene Asalif sits there as the adults talk about his circumstances. One neighbor mentions that Asalif's father left before the condominiums arose, which explains his delinquent behavior. Another day the men tell stories about killing rats and facing hyenas. In one scene a man tells a story about narrowly escaping an attack of thirty hyenas—clearly a fun imaginative exercise—which scares and haunts Asalif.

Hyenas are a real and mythical threat in Ethiopian life. They live in the high-altitude forests in and around Addis Ababa. Despite their relatively high-pitched howls and yips at night, they are scary and carnivorous creatures. They are said to target smaller people, and especially those alone. Every so often one eats a small child. In Ethiopian myth and folklore humans and hyenas have a complex and at times morphological relationship. Sometimes hyenas can transform into humans, possessing *buda*—the evil eye—scarring people psychologically and socially.[41] In short—they loom large.

What can beat a hyena? A lion, Asalif learns, as he listens to the locals share stories. "A lion can take on five hyenas," one man says. This sparks Asalif's interest as he listens quietly.

"It's Not the Hyenas You Should Fear—It's the Humans"

The filmmakers shot most of *Anbessa* in 2016 and 2017, while the country was undergoing a lot of political upheaval, specifically about Oromo dissatisfaction with the master plan and other long-standing grievances. While this period became associated with Oromo discontent, the disillusionment with the Ethiopian government extended beyond regional and ethnic lines. In *Anbessa*, the language spoken is Amharic, not Oromo, but the context is more broadly about living on the periphery of urban wealth.

Asalif frequently trots up the hill to look at the condominiums that so obviously are ushering in inequality and eroding economic dreams, but he is not the only one. Several in this area are experiencing dispossession, and we see the accumulation literally building and towering beside them. Asalif vocalizes and understands his fears in the form of hyenas, which he hears howling at night. He often talks to animals—birds, horses, and dogs—but hyenas and lions occupy his imagination throughout. Late in the film, Asalif discovers an important material and symbolic armor. While wandering around the condominium we see him discover a piece of yellow plastic, that he strings around his head. The plastic has a thick band, with six-inch strands of thinner strips of plastic hanging down. When he drapes it around his head, he transforms into a lion, roaring, gathering a type of mimetic strength.

The threat to their livelihood is the development and dispossession, yet Asalif fears hyenas most palpably. This is illustrated when a late scene captures some kind of local prospectors who arrive at the house. The scene is shot from a place of hiding—both because Asalif's perspective is one of uncertainty and because the filmmaker likely needed to hide in the house. Two men wearing collared shirts are seen through the door. They come and inquire about buying wood, then ask, "Do you have legal papers to be here?"

"Yes," Asalif's mother says. "Isn't this land the government provided? The government relocated the farmers here when they started condo construction. You're not the first land brokers to ask me about it."

The men continue, "Has anyone offered you a price?"; she responds no. Then she adds, "the real owner lives in Ambo." Ambo is in the Oromia region not far from Addis Ababa. One man asks if the legal owner is there and she says no, but a man who "acts like a lawyer for them" is nearby.

"The way they were asking felt heavy," she says once they leave. Indeed, her tone in the conversation is heavy, too. "It's like they knew my situation already," she says openly, then cautions Asalif: "It's not the hyenas you should fear—it's the humans."

In the final scenes of the film Asalif wanders around empty, unfinished condominiums. He roars and hits the walls of a construction block and *becomes* a lion—fearless and in control. Then he tells a story aloud: "Once upon a time there was a boy, and unfortunately he turned into a lion. Speaking of this, he used to plow the land. And then . . . and then . . . and then . . . " He looks out onto the condominiums from the periphery and music builds and then abruptly takes off his mane. He watches built power lines and clouds shape shift and move in the final scene. A sound of a helicopter hums in the background, which must just be, in fact, the sound of a lion's grumble.

Because the film shows the development of Addis Ababa, the visual projection of Ethiopia's economic miracle, through a child's eyes, it allows viewers to think about the lived experience of this kind of urban development through several registers at once. Fear is palpable throughout, whether symbolized through hyenas or embodied by prospectors. Even as Asalif and the neighbors fear the developments, they also marvel at them and the hope of transformation. Rather than simply critique the structural violence being enacted upon them, the aesthetics allow viewers to imagine the indeterminate experience of living amid government-sanctioned growth and transformation.

Faya Dayi: "The Scent of Coffee Has Changed"

Faya Dayi opens in what feels like a world away from *Anbessa*. Outside of Addis Ababa's burgeoning metropolis, the face of Ethiopia's economic miracle, *Faya Dayi* is situated in the periphery. As the film opens we can scarcely make out the agrarian setting. The lighting is dim, and the time of day is unclear, but eventually we see a boy, arms flailing, running in muddy water in the mist. Here and throughout, director Jessica Beshir allows bodies to move with a perceived weightlessness, emulating how some feel in two related and embodied circumstances: one, a youthfulness living in uncertainty, and two, how people often feel when they chew khat.

If the surreal experience of dispossession in *Anbessa* is filtered through a youthful frame in the eyes of a playful Asalif, in Beshir's black-and-white *Faya Dayi* it is through the production, consumption, and imaginary of khat. Khat is a stimulant in Ethiopia that people chew in the hopes of achieving a state of *mer-khana*, which Beshir has described as a state of grace or a place of calmness and alertness. Sufi Muslims also chew khat to stay awake through the night, praying and chanting in a state of harmony. Khat is also deeply ironic; people see it as a waste of time and productivity even though most people employed in the khat trade are the ones who can find employment. The film focuses on this lived and brutal irony; people want to escape the exile in which they live, and engaging with khat is seen to both enable and prevent them from escaping.

Khat began playing an important role for Ethiopian Muslims in prayer, celebrations, and culture in the late nineteenth century.[42] While in some instances it is understood to be a part of religious life, in others regular khat users are seen as lazy, delinquent, and unemployed. Even as many understand khat to be religious, chewing it is usually seen as an inherent danger to growth and change.

As Mains details in his ethnography about young men in Ethiopia, the men he studied chew khat as a means of passing time. In this way khat functions similarly to the way tea does for unemployed men in Dakar; they use it for entertainment and stimulation, but most formulaically, to "kill time."[43] In Jimma, where Mains did field work, the young men who let "time pass" with khat generally see their condition as one of hopelessness.[44] They cannot take low-waged work because of *yilunnta*—a particular type of social stigma—and like so many young men in and beyond the continent, concerns about the future and excessive amounts of free time are filled with consciousness-altering substances.

As in *Anbessa*, there are no asides by experts on the khat trade to offer statistics about the crop's centrality or the state of Ethiopian agriculture. The scenes transition without a sense of how much time passes between one and the next, or if the film has been edited in chronological order. It is evident that the people living in the region think deeply about their circumstances, an aspect Beshir chooses to highlight by showing how they profoundly and poetically express the conditions of their life. But, in contrast to the wasted time that so often is associated with khat, in the world of *Faya Dayi*, it is also tremendously productive. It is an escape from economic realities and creates them at the same time.

After the opening scene the film transitions to a scene in a home as a fire burns, men pray, and someone grinds coffee. Then, coffee roasts outside. "My father and I used to grow coffee on our land," one man says. "The scent of coffee has changed. It doesn't taste the same. Our coffee is beautiful but it needs a lot of rain. We replaced it with khat." Immediately we float from vicariously experiencing the calmness of this high to the brutal lived experiences of altering one's livelihood to secure survival.

Given that Ethiopia's economy is based primarily on agriculture, the opening sequences reach beyond the experience of only Oromo dispossession to broader agrarian ones as well. That the taste of the coffee and its scent "have changed" is psychosocial. It may be chemically true that the ability to taste coffee has changed, but the structural conditions have, too. And this is a film that addresses those psychosocial impacts on people not typically considered in narratives of Ethiopia's economic miracle.

"Forced into Exile"

With a mere few words, the next scene transitions to young men sorting and processing khat, now a material necessity with climate-induced production problems for coffee. Two young men lie there after a hard day's work, and Mohamed, a young teenager who works the fields, ponders aloud what it would be like to leave Ethiopia for someplace better. He asks his slightly older friend, who went to Egypt, how the process works. His friend explains the process of getting over the border into Egypt, and how it is possible to get to Europe. The fifteen-to-nineteen-day journey at sea also includes a hefty price of 80,000 birr total. Then he explains that he went to Egypt but came back for his mother and the other young boy says his mother left on a similar journey but never came back.

Mohamed's father is one of many who seemingly lives for khat. The plant's irony persists here; khat is both cause and cure; addictive tension and embodied release. In Harar, it seems, khat is boundless; it is the economy and the center of social life. The only way to get beyond it, it seems to Mohamed, is to leave. "Our only wealth is the farm," one woman says, as the boys ponder an elsewhere.

Even as the people invoke mythology, talk about their dreams, and tell tall tales throughout the film, they also bring us back to the specific socioeconomic conditions of Ethiopia's 2010s. Yet, unlike the Oromo protestors around the capital who received mainstream news coverage in 2016, especially following the Irreecha massacre, the residents here offer an additional narrative that adds a seldom-seen dimension to the despair underlying Ethiopia's economic hope.

A little over an hour into the film, a few young men congregate and bring us to the contemporary moment. For a while, we only hear their voices, as montages of the scenery are the focal point: "I remember in 2015, when young people joined the peaceful protests, my friend Tadesse Dendena was shot by a bullet. He bled a lot. So many were injured by tear gas."

Then, another voice narrates, "It is in our own land that we are dying, being imprisoned and forced into exile. All of this because we are Oromo. Nothing else. Our struggle is not new. Our grandparents and great grandparents went through it."

The notion of exile is an important one; this is not a country-based exile but one of temporality, consciousness, and possibility. In his ethnography on migratory imagination and possibility in Togo, the anthropologist Charles Piot writes of Togolese people feeling as if they live in a "nation of exile."[45] A similar sentiment is articulated by the men here, experiencing a fully embodied and psychosocial dispossession. *Merkhana* might be a temporary embodied escape from this sense of exile, even as the lack of choice as to whether they should dwell in that space seems imposed.

Notably, as the people talk in poetic and graceful terms about their condition, Beshir's *Faya Dayi* allows Oromo people to speak in their native language, Oromiffa. In addition to Oromo people being pushed off their land historically, they were also barred from speaking their native language throughout both Haile Selassie's reign beginning in 1941 until 1991. Speaking Oromiffa openly is inherently political.

Finally, in the same scene, we see the faces of a group of young men sitting outside in the fields, revealing who is sharing these thoughts. The wind blows aggressively, and another person adds, "Having to leave school, being imprisoned, beaten, tortured. This is the price we've had to pay for our people. The sacrifice was worth it. The sacrifice we made was worth it. And I am happy. I am not bitter. It's hard for me to express everything I'm feeling right now. That's all. I'm very happy to be here today. This token freedom is not enough for us."

The men sit there, clearly coping with overwhelming emotions. The crops shake in the wind. Elsewhere, across rivers and oceans, uncertainty looms. Unlike in *Anbessa* there are no grand infrastructural reminders of the ruling class. Far away from Addis Ababa, dispossession is both embodied and escaped by and through khat. The hope for elsewhere can be dreamed of while high, just like the reality of lived despair.

Beshir created *Faya Dayi* over ten years of trips to and from Ethiopia, developing deep relationships with the young people living in her grandmother's homeland. She got to know Mohammed well, and his father, whose addiction to khat makes him a volatile and erratic character. But he and the others chew, hoping for a state of *merkhana*.

Faya Dayi kinesthetically and aesthetically renders the sought-after state of *merkhana*—both in attempting to arrive at and dwelling in that state. Beshir decided to produce *Faya Dayi* with a monochrome mise-en-scène with the aim of documenting the interiority of seeking this state of grace. This profound sense of hopelessness and despair runs against a feeling of cautious optimism that people maintain in *Faya Dayi* and the real experience of living in an agriculturally dominant economy.

Stories and Histories

In *Faya Dayi* and *Anbessa* (and in this article) conclusions are awkward. The future is so uncertain. The sequences, as well as the voices of ordinary people who articulate the lived experience of hope and despair, remain turbulent in a tumultuous Ethiopia. The filmmakers no doubt curated a selective collection of pronouncements that are remarkably rich in imagery. But as they reject the desire or purpose to create an authoritative tone, the accounts add a rare and honest narrative seldom seen or heard about how people experience Ethiopia's economic condition.

Here, I think they are both responding, however indirectly, to contestations of narrative dominance by certain ethnic groups, but more often, to politicians and policy "experts" who claim to have a sense of dominion over how to talk about Ethiopia. It is not so much that all these "formal" accounts lack insight; however, the documentary films offer new ways of thinking about how we might get a glimpse of the realities of living through the economic miracle.

By way of analysis I hoped to show here the possibilities that films like these offer new possibilities for story and history. Amharic is a polysemic language, which means that words can have multiple meanings. Like *anbessa*, *tizita*, and countless other words and phrases, meaning is contingent on context. Similarly, *tarik* in Amharic and *seenaa* in Oromiffa mean both "story" and "history."

These films, in resisting narrative structures that contribute to grand historical narratives, respond to literature gaps by attuning their focus to the lived experience of being in an emerging economy. In addition to offering rich insights into the Ethiopian economic miracle, they also provide a literal and figurative lens to think about other forms that we can use to understand the lived experience of economic miracles and economic conditions more broadly.

Hannah Borenstein is assistant professor of anthropology in the Department of Global and Sociocultural Studies at Florida International University. Her first manuscript, in progress, is an ethnography about Ethiopian women distance runners working in a transnational athletics industry. She is interested in the intersections of race, gender, labor, and sport in and beyond East Africa.

Notes

1. Ahmed, "Deadly Attack at Prime Minister's Rally."
2. Al Jazeera, "Ethiopia: Grenade Attack Caused Blast."
3. Marsh, "Why Ethiopians Believe Their Prime Minister Is a New Prophet"; Gardner and Rosser, "'Abiy Ahmed Is Our Miracle.'"
4. Ali, Seid, and Taffesse, "Ethiopia: An Agrarian Economy in Transition."

5. Mains, *Hope Is Cut*, 1.
6. Verhoeven and Woldemariam, "Who Lost Ethiopia?"
7. Clapham, "Rewriting Ethiopian History," 37.
8. See, for example, Henze, *Layers of Time*; Marcus, *History of Ethiopia*; and Pankhurst, *Ethiopians.*
9. See Gebre-Medhin, *Peasants and Nationalism in Eritrea*; and Sorenson, *Imagining Ethiopia.*
10. Holcomb and Ibssa, *Invention of Ethiopia.*
11. Donham and James, *Southern Marches of Imperial Ethiopia.*
12. Donham, *Marxist Modern*, 11.
13. Donham, *Marxist Modern*, 25.
14. Zeleke, *Ethiopia in Theory*, 174–75.
15. Mengisteab, "Federalism in Ethiopia's Transformation."
16. Chang and Hauge, "Concept of a 'Developmental State' in Ethiopia."
17. De Waal, "Theory and Practice of Meles Zenawi," 154.
18. Ministry of Finance and Economic Development, "Growth and Transformation Plan."
19. Tasfaye, "Opposition to Oromia Megacities."
20. Yared Tsegaye, "Ethiopia's Contested Capital."
21. Chimdi, "History of Finfinne Reflects the Way the Oromo People Were Conquered."
22. Harvey, "Right to the City."
23. Schuman, "Forget the BRICs; Meet the PINEs."
24. Green, "BRICS Rivalry."
25. Terrefe, "Infrastructures of Renaissance."
26. Mains, *Under Construction*, 2.
27. Collins, "Meaning and Uses of Privatization," 608.
28. Borenstein, "Feyisa Lilesa's and the Transnational Protest."
29. Schemm, "Ethiopia Imposes State of Emergency."
30. Jones et al., "Africa's Illiberal State-Builders."
31. Verhoeven and Woldemariam, "Who Lost Ethiopia?," 623.
32. In addition to these economic aims, Verhoeven and Woldemariam also show that the United States wanted military hegemony in the Horn and urged Abiy to shift Ethiopia's foreign policy toward new directed relationships to US allies in the Middle East. Abiy, a former intelligence agent, strengthened ties with Israel, which had long collaborated with Addis Ababa on counterterrorism, but now proposed a deepening of relations, especially through closer cooperation between the National Intelligence Security Service, the Mossad, and Israel's National Cyber Directorate.
33. Carien du Plessis, Anait Miridzhanian, and Bhargav Acharya, "BRICS Welcomes New Members in Push to Reshuffle World Order."
34. Ullendorff, *Ethiopia and the Bible.*
35. Nurhussein, *Black Land.*
36. French and Hegab, *Condominium Housing in Ethiopia.*
37. Gardner, "'Addis Has Run Out of Space.'"
38. Close-Up, "'Anbessa' Director Mo Scarpelli On the Impact of Modernisation in Ethiopia."
39. Mains, *Under Construction.*
40. Teff is an endemic grain cultivated in the Horn of Africa and fermented to make *injera*, a central staple in the Ethiopian diet.

41.   Baynes-Rock, "Ethiopian *Buda* as Hyenas."
42.   Gebissa, *Leaf of Allah*.
43.   Ralph, "Killing Time."
44.   Mains, *Hope Is Cut*.
45.   Piot, *Nostalgia for the Future*.

References

Acharya, Bhargav, Miridzhanian, Anait, and du Plessis, Carien. "BRICS Welcomes New Members in Push to Reshuffle World Order." *Reuters*, August 24, 2023. https://www.reuters.com/world/brics-poised-invite-new-members-join-bloc-sources-2023-08-24/.

Ahmed, Hadra. "Deadly Grenade Attack at Ethiopian Prime Minister's Rally." *New York Times*, June 23, 2018. https://www.nytimes.com/2018/06/23/world/africa/ethiopia-explosion-abiy.html.

Al Jazeera. "Ethiopia: Grenade Attack Caused Blast at Rally for PM Abiy Ahmed." *Al Jazeera English*, June 23, 2018. YouTube video, 2:12. https://www.youtube.com/watch?v=gIt6qw4hKjw.

Ali, Seid Nuru, Seid, Yared, and Taffesse, Alemayehu Seyaoum. "Ethiopia: An Agrarian Economy in Transition." In *Africa's Lions—Growth Traps and Opportunities for Six African Economies*, 37–76. UNU-WIDER. Brookings Institution Press, 2016.

Baynes-Rock, Marcus. "Ethiopian *Buda* as Hyenas: Where the Social Is More Than Human." *Folklore* 126, no. 3 (2015): 266–82.

Borenstein, Hannah. "Feyisa Lilesa's and the Transnational Protest of Ethiopia's Most Enduring Olympian." In *Sport and Protest in the Black Atlantic*, edited by Michael J. Gennaro and Brian M. McGowan, 191–215. New York: Routledge, 2023.

Chang, Ha-Joon, and Jostein Hauge. "The Concept of a 'Developmental State' in Ethiopia." In *The Oxford Handbook of the Ethiopian Economy*, edited by Fantu Cheru, Christopher Cramer, and Arkebe Oqubay, 823–41. Oxford: Oxford University Press, 2019.

Chimdi, Tarekegn. "The History of Finfinne Reflects the Way the Oromo People Were Conquered." Advocacy for Oromia, July 19–23, 2004. https://advocacy4oromia.org/articles/the-history-of-finfinne-reflects-the-way-the-oromo-people-were-conquered/.

Clapham, Christopher. "Rewriting Ethiopian History." *Annales d'Éthiopie* 18, no. 1 (2002): 37–54.

Close-Up Culture. "'Anbessa' Director Mo Scarpelli On the Impact of Modernisation in Ethiopia." *Close-Up Culture*, n.d. https://closeupculture.com/2020/04/13/anbessa-director-mo-scarpelli-on-the-impact-of-modernisation-in-ethiopia/.

Collins, Christina Tekie. "The Meaning and Uses of Privatization: The Case of the Ethiopian Developmental State." *Africa* 92, no. 4 (2022): 602–24.

De Waal, Alex. "The Theory and Practice of Meles Zenawi." *African Affairs* 112, no. 446 (2013): 148–55.

Donham, Donald L. *Marxist Modern: An Ethnographic History of the Ethiopian Revolution*. Berkeley: University of California Press, 1999.

Donham, Donald L., and Wendy James, eds. *The Southern Marches of Imperial Ethiopia: Essays in History and Social Anthropology*. Cambridge: Cambridge University Press, 1986.

French, Matthew, and Katherine Hegab. *Condominium Housing in Ethiopia: The Integrated Housing Development Programme*. Nairobi: United Nations Human Settlement Programme, 2011.

Gardner, Tom. "'Addis Has Run Out of Space': Ethiopia's Radical Redesign." *Guardian*, December 4, 2017. https://www.theguardian.com/cities/2017/dec/04/addis-ababa-ethiopia -redesign-housing-project.

Gardner, Tom, and Charlie Rosser. "'Abiy Ahmed Is Our Miracle': Ethiopia's Democratic Awakening." *Guardian*, September 25, 2018. https://www.theguardian.com/global -development/2018/sep/25/abiy-ahmed-miracle-ethiopia-democratic-awakening.

Gebissa, Ezekiel. *Leaf of Allah: Khat and Agricultural Transformation in Harerge, Ethiopia, 1875–1991*. Oxford: James Currey, 2004.

Gebre-Medhin, Jordan. *Peasants and Nationalism in Eritrea: A Critique of Ethiopian Studies*. Trenton, NJ: Red Sea Press, 1989.

Green, Mark. "The BRICS Rivalry." Wilson Center, May 30, 2023. https://www.wilsoncenter.org /blog-post/brics-rivalry.

Harvey, David. "The Right to the City." *New Left Review*, no. 53 (2008): 23–40.

Henze, Paul B. *Layers of Time: A History of Ethiopia*. Hampshire: Palgrave Macmillan, 2004.

Holcomb, Bonnie K., and Sisai Ibssa. *The Invention of Ethiopia*. Trenton, NJ: Red Sea Press, 1990.

Jones, Will, Ricardo Soares de Oliveira, and Harry Verhoeven. "Africa's Illiberal State Builders." Working Paper Series No. 89. Refugee Studies Center, Oxford Department of International Development, University of Oxford, January 2013.

Mains, Daniel. *Hope Is Cut: Youth, Unemployment, and the Future in Urban Ethiopia*. Philadelphia: Temple University Press, 2012.

Mains, Daniel. *Under Construction: Technologies of Development in Urban Ethiopia*. Durham, NC: Duke University Press, 2019.

Marcus, Harold G. *A History of Ethiopia*. Berkeley: University of California Press, 2002.

Marsh, Jenni. "Why Ethiopians Believe Their New Prime Minister Is a Prophet." CNN, August 26, 2018. https://www.cnn.com/2018/08/26/world/abiymania-ethiopia-prime-minister-abiy -ahmed/index.html.

Mengisteab, Kidane. "Federalism in Ethiopia's Transformation." In *The Oxford Handbook of the Ethiopian Economy*, edited by Fantu Cheru, Christopher Cramer, and Arkebe Oqubay, 65–79. Oxford: Oxford University Press, 2019.

Ministry of Finance and Economic Development. "Growth and Transformation Plan 2010/11 2015/6," 2010. https://web.archive.org/web/20131202164408/http://www.mofed.gov.et /English/Resources/Documents/GTP%20English2.pdf.

Nurhussein, Nadia. *Black Land: Imperial Ethiopianism and African America*. Princeton, NJ: Princeton University Press, 2019.

Pankhurst, Richard. *The Ethiopians: A History*. Oxford: Blackwell, 2001.

Piot, Charles. *Nostalgia for the Future: West Africa after the Cold War*. Chicago: University of Chicago Press, 2010.

Ralph, Michael. "Killing Time." *Social Text* 26, no. 4 (2008): 1–29.

Schemm, Paul. "Ethiopia Imposes State of Emergency as Unrest Intensifies." *Washington Post*, April 12, 2023. https://www.washingtonpost.com/world/africa/ethiopia-imposes-state-of -emergency-as-unrest-intensifies/2016/10/10/7825391e-8ee9–11e6-bc00–1a9756d4111b _story.html.

Schuman, Michael. "Forget the BRICs; Meet the PINEs." *Time*, March 13, 2014. https://time .com/22779/forget-the-brics-meet-the-pines/.

Sorenson, John. *Imagining Ethiopia: Struggles for History and Identity in the Horn of Africa*. New Brunswick, NJ: Rutgers University Press, 1993.

Tasfaye, Ermias. "Opposition to Oromia Megacities Echoes Ethiopia's Master Plan Turmoil." *Ethiopia Insight* (blog), April 12, 2023. https://www.ethiopia-insight.com/2023/04/12 /opposition-to-oromia-megacities-echoes-ethiopias-master-plan-turmoil/.

Terrefe, Biruk. "Infrastructures of Renaissance: Tangible Discourses in the EPRDF's Ethiopia / Infrastructures de renaissance: Discours tangible dans l'Éthiopie de le FDRPE." *Critical African Studies* 14, no. 3 (2022): 250–73.

Tsegay, Yared. "Ethiopia's Contested Capital." *Ethiopia Insight,* June 21, 2021. https://www .ethiopia-insight.com/2021/06/21/pushing-boundaries-in-ethiopias-contested-capital/.

Ullendorff, Edward. *Ethiopia and the Bible: The Schweich Lectures of the British Academy 1967.* 1968; repr., Oxford: Oxford University Press, 1997.

Verhoeven, Harry, and Michael Woldemariam. "Who Lost Ethiopia? The Unmaking of an African Anchor State and U.S. Foreign Policy." *Contemporary Security Policy* 43, no. 4 (2022): 622–50.

Zeleke, E. Centime. *Ethiopia in Theory: Revolution and Knowledge Production, 1964–2016.* Chicago: Haymarket Books, 2020.

Believing in (Economic) Miracles in Brazil and Chile

Andre Pagliarini

Japan's economic miracle began in the shadow of a mushroom cloud. So argued Joelmir Beting, the economy editor of one of Brazil's leading newspapers, in July 1970. Beting was intrigued by the former Axis power's sustained postwar economic growth. The kamikaze pilot, "who in the name of the fatherland launched himself at the sides of enemy aircraft carriers," had been replaced by the Japanese worker, "the kamikaze of the economic system, a man who works ten hours a day, has four vacation days per year, whose retirement is only 2.9 dollars per month, merely symbolic, which leads the worker, while still young, to save a third of his salary and invest it in fixed income securities or shares, to have something to live on in his old age."[1] Such discipline and self-sacrifice, Beting suggested, was central not just to Japan's reconstruction following the devastation of World War II but its rise to global economic stardom.[2] Between 1955 and 1973, the Japanese economy grew at roughly 10 percent a year on average, an impressive rate by any standard. Surely Brazilians might learn from the technocratic "samurais in suits."[3]

Beting's Orientalism was interlaced with a subtler, vaguely spiritual notion: that miracles are born of suffering.[4] From this perspective, Japan's rapid industrialization—the engine of its economic miracle—was a kind of deliverance from the fiery judgment of Hiroshima and Nagasaki. No other country experienced the specific horror of nuclear bombardment, of course, but the palliative construct of the economic miracle was frequently invoked elsewhere after profound sociopolitical

Radical History Review
Issue 151 (January 2025)   DOI 10.1215/01636545-11506819
© 2025 by MARHO: The Radical Historians' Organization, Inc.

trauma. West Germany's economic miracle "transformed society and undermined Social Democratic calls for the socialization and planning of the economy," according to Mark E. Spicka.[5] South Korea, destitute after its war with the North, leapfrogged Portugal, Hungary, Mexico, Argentina, and Brazil's GDP by the 1980s, a product of the economic "miracle on the River Han."[6] The creation of the state of Israel, which has enjoyed astronomical economic growth, stemmed to a great degree from the devastation of the Holocaust. As Dan Senor and Saul Singer argued in *Start-Up Nation*, "other small and threatened countries, such as South Korea, Singapore, and Taiwan, can also boast growth records that are as impressive as Israel. But none of them have produced an entrepreneurial culture—not to mention an array of start-ups—that compares with Israel's."[7] One need not agree with the authors' premise to note the common celebration of rapid economic growth in the wake of great tragedy.[8]

Cold War Latin America boasted similar feats, with so-called economic miracles serving to justify dictatorship. Nowhere was this dynamic more evident than in Brazil and Chile. Indeed, even as he admired the Japanese from afar, Beting's own nation was enjoying astronomical growth rates less than a decade into a military regime that would last twenty-one years. In 1973, the elected government of nearby Chile was also toppled by a coup that laid the groundwork for a drastic policy transformation that Milton Friedman would celebrate as "an economic miracle" and "an even more amazing political miracle."[9] Despite such happy talk, however, all was not as it seemed behind the facade of economic growth and development in these societies.

This essay brings to the fore the ideological connotations implied but often missed in the idea of economic "miracles." While increases in employment, foreign investment, and industrialization are tangible facts reflected in data and individual experiences, bundling them together and branding the result a miracle is neither innocuous nor incidental. Emphasizing economic achievements enabled the Brazilian and Chilean dictatorships, as well as friendly foreign governments and international observers, to downplay or obscure the negative aspects of their regimes. To say a particular economic model has produced a miracle is to say essentially that it is working. More than a mere descriptor of hard economic data, an "economic miracle" is an argument for the status quo. In the cases I discuss, the status quo was brutal military rule.

Along with their cadres of icy technocrats, the military dictators of Brazil and Chile insisted that the kind of growth they presided over was only possible because the armed forces had entered the political arena. In a way, there is something to this. As Jennifer Hermann notes of Brazil, it is unimaginable that the economic reforms that purportedly made the miracle possible—a mix of austerity and a sharp turn toward encouraging foreign investment—would have passed a democratic legislature prior to the 1964 coup.[10] Chile's socialist president, Salvador Allende, likewise would never have embraced the policy recipe of Friedman's Chicago Boys. After the coup in Chile, as Juan Gabriel Valdés put it, "one extreme of radical ideology was immediately followed by its very opposite."[11]

But the longer history of Brazilian development in the twentieth century calls into question both the notion that the 1964 coup was an economic imperative and that economic growth under military rule was the result of ingenious policymaking.[12] Inflation had indeed soared under President Juscelino Kubitschek (1956–61) in a way it did not under the generals, from 19 percent in 1956 to over 30 percent in 1960, but the lower post-1964 inflation rate owed much to the fact that the dictatorship deliberately cooled the economy on the backs of the working class.[13] The regime was primarily taken with elitist concerns, as former president Fernando Henrique Cardoso later noted, pointing out that the vast majority of Brazilians saw their real incomes decline during the dictatorship.[14] Whereas Kubitschek had to weigh difficult economic decisions against popular sentiment, the generals simply clamped down on unions and political organizing. They had no popular mandate to concern themselves with.

In the Chilean case, Heidi Tinsman has shown that the agricultural boom that occurred under Pinochet had roots in the pre-1973 period. "The economic miracle for which Chile's military regime would become famous in the 1980s," she writes, "was a product long in the making."[15] Felipe González and Mounu Prem have argued, for their part, that there is a lack of conclusive evidence as to the centrality of the reforms enacted under General Augusto Pinochet for the nominal economic successes of the 1980s.[16] Establishing certainty on the matter one way or another lies beyond the purview of this essay, but the problem of attribution must always be considered when assessing something as nebulous and fantastical as a miracle. In short, we should be wary of those who would claim economic miracle-making entirely for themselves.

In the case of Brazil and Chile, to believe uncritically in miracles is to believe that authoritarian regimes can transcend the circumstances of their creation. As Sebastian Edwards notes, the Chilean miracle was marred by "an original sin: it was put in place by a dictatorship, a regime that violated human rights and systematically persecuted, imprisoned, tortured, and assassinated its opponents."[17] The same was true in Brazil, where the highest rates of economic growth coincided with the harshest repression under President Emílio Garrastazu Médici (1969–74), a period referred to as the *anos de chumbo*, or years of lead. At best, accelerated growth in Brazil and Chile softened the blow of authoritarianism. The implicit conclusion from celebrations of these regimes' economic records, however, is that violent dictatorships can become benevolent or transformative forces for social good. To responsibly assess the Brazilian and Chilean miracles, as this essay aims to do, is to emphasize the violent context in which they emerged—to insist on the prevalence of that grim caveat, "on the other hand . . ."

Making Miracles

Post–World War II Latin America was characterized by several simultaneous transitions away from dictatorship. Structural challenges, however, including a dependency on primary commodity exports and a grossly unequal distribution of wealth, threatened democratic consolidation across the region. Enduring economic disparities produced social unrest, political instability, and military interventions as the global ideological competition of the Cold War escalated. Those involved in the coups and the military governments that followed claimed that their dramatic interventions were necessary to forestall calamity. Aided by "engineers of chaos," Goulart had deliberately sought to ravage the economy so as to introduce "the Trojan horse of political and social subversion," according to Roberto Campos, the Brazilian dictatorship's first minister of planning and economic coordination.[18] The leaders of the Chilean coup decried "the extremely grave economic, social and moral crisis that is destroying the country" and claimed to be "fighting for the liberation of the country from the Marxist yoke."[19] The unconstitutional seizure of power signaled a profound shift in the social, political, and economic life of both nations. A change was coming—for the better, supporters of these interventions insisted.

Brazil's postcoup economic policy focused on curbing inflation, which had been rising since the mid-1950s. Under Goulart, economic growth plummeted from 8.6 percent in 1961 to 0.6 percent in 1963. Brazil's industrial output contracted during his last full year in office, an alarming development that had not happened since the start of World War II.[20] The new military government froze wages to reduce consumer spending power, devalued the Brazilian cruzeiro to increase export competitiveness, and restricted the flow of credit. For the next few years, these measures had a chilling effect on domestic consumption and limited access to capital for businesses. A potent early criticism of the dictatorship focused on its "denationalization" of the country's economy, that is, the relative weakening of domestic businesses against the increasing presence of foreign corporations.[21]

By the end of the decade, however, having stabilized the economy, the regime embarked on an ambitious state-led development plan. Strategic industries like steel and automobiles received significant subsidies to boost production and domestic competitiveness. Massive investments were poured into infrastructure projects like roads, dams, and power plants to create the foundation for renewed industrial growth. Perhaps most emblematic were the regime's efforts in the Amazon, the human toll of which was recounted by the anthropologist Shelton H. Davis in his 1977 monograph *Victims of the Miracle: Development and the Indians of Brazil*. Initiatives such as the Trans-Amazonian Highway and large-scale agribusiness ventures led to extensive deforestation, displacement of Indigenous communities, and environmental degradation.[22] On the tenth anniversary of the 1964 coup, Army Minister Vicente de Paulo Dale Coutinho stressed the regime's commitment to national sovereignty and economic development. In embracing what he called the

"Amazonian challenge"—making the vast rainforest available to commercial interests—the military demonstrated its unmatched aptitude for meeting challenges that previous governments had failed to address.[23] Additionally, the government implemented protectionist trade policies, shielding domestic industries from foreign competition in an attempt to foster domestic production and push back against the charge of denationalization. It also cracked down hard on labor and civil society.

In 1968, student demonstrations, emboldened by global movements of the time, challenged the repressive regime along with artists and intellectuals protesting censorship. Facing stagnant wages, workers joined the oppositional fray with strikes and demonstrations.[24] In response, the regime issued its fifth institutional act, unilateral executive edicts that immediately assumed the force of law. Institutional Act 5 was by far the most draconian step the generals in power would take. It granted the executive branch the power to shutter Congress along with state and municipal assemblies; the ability to suspend habeas corpus in all cases of political crimes against national security, a vast category of infraction; and it mandated that the trial of political crimes be held by military courts with no other judicial recourse.[25] It became a shorthand for the darkest days in Brazil's recent political history. As the 1960s ended, the regime hardened as economic fortunes brightened.

Following its coup in 1973, the Chilean junta quickly set about transforming Chile into a radical free-market economy. Trade liberalization was a central pillar of this approach. Tariffs and import restrictions were slashed, opening the largely closed Chilean economy to foreign competition. Environmental issues under Pinochet may not have been as prominent or widespread as those in the Amazon under the Brazilian dictatorship, but they reflected similar patterns of degradation and exploitation. Large-scale mining operations, such as copper mining in the Atacama Desert, led to habitat destruction, water pollution, and displacement of local communities. The regime weakened or ignored environmental regulations to attract foreign investment and limited public participation and oversight, thus exacerbating environmental inequities.[26]

The new regime also benefited enormously from the goodwill of the Richard Nixon administration, which had worked to destabilize the Chilean economy under Allende.[27] The regime pursued a program of deregulation, privatization, and liberalization of trade and investment. State-owned enterprises were privatized, and market competition was encouraged in various sectors, including banking, telecommunications, and utilities. The government also adopted a floating exchange rate regime, allowing the market to determine the value of the Chilean peso, and removed restrictions on foreign capital flows. Fiscal austerity measures were implemented to reduce government spending and balance the budget, including cuts to social welfare programs and public services. The crackdown on dissent was even more brutal and total than in Brazil, which is to take nothing away from that country's authoritarian violence.[28]

In the years that followed, both regimes used positive economic indicators to contest criticisms that they lacked legitimacy and favored the interests of insular domestic elites and US imperialism. For a while, they apparently had a leg to stand on.[29] Between 1968 and 1973, the Brazilian economy took flight, growing at about 10 percent per year on average. In 1970, the country won its third World Cup title, contributing to a climate of national ebullience carefully choreographed by the regime's propagandists.[30] Results in Chile took longer to emerge, but the effects of its miracle would be arguably more pronounced and long-lasting. In just over a decade and a half, technocrats empowered by Pinochet—the infamous Chicago Boys—"had created a modern capitalist economy that, after some sputtering and a deep currency crisis in 1982, produced an acceleration in efficiency, productivity, and growth. In financial and economic circles there was talk of a budding 'Chilean miracle,'" writes Edwards.[31]

The disconnect between economic growth and political repression is a hallmark of the "miracles" in both Brazil and Chile. Gabriel García Márquez sharply captures this dynamic in *Clandestine in Chile: The Adventures of Miguel Littín*, which recounts in the first person a real exiled Chilean filmmaker's secret reentry into his country more than a decade after the coup. The second chapter, "First Disillusion: The City's Magnificence," captures the titular character's surprise at the Chile he encountered. Leaving the airport, a crestfallen Littín is struck by the apparent peace and prosperity produced by such a vicious regime:

Contrary to what we had heard in exile, Santiago was a radiant city, its venerable monuments splendidly illuminated, its streets spotlessly clean and orderly. If anything, armed policemen were more in evidence on the streets of Paris or New York than here. Starting at the historic Central Station, designed by the same Gustave Eiffel who built the tower in Paris, the endless Bernardo O'Higgins Boulevard flowed before our eyes like a river of light. Even the wan little streetwalkers did not seem as destitute and sad to me as they used to. All at once, the Moneda Palace loomed into view on my side of the taxi like an unwelcome apparition. The last time I saw it, the building was still a burned-out shell covered with ashes in the aftermath of the coup. Restored and once more in use, it now looked like a dream palace at the foot of a French garden. . . . As we approached the center of the city, I stopped admiring the material splendor with which the dictatorship sought to cover the blood of tens of thousands killed or disappeared, and ten times that number driven into exile, and instead concentrated on the people in view.[32]

As García Marquéz implies, the prosperity Littín sees was built on a foundation of violence and fear. Indeed, the Chilean and Brazilian economic miracles can be boiled down to the same essence—spectacular signs of economic growth under-girded by a shadowy repressive apparatus.

Miracles Fade

In late 1972, the new alternative Brazilian newspaper *Opinião* published a long over-view of recent works discussing the country's economic miracle. It highlighted a divide between those economists who believed the government was right to concentrate on sustaining high economic growth even if it meant worsening income inequality in the short term—to grow the cake before divvying it up, as the popular metaphor at the time evocatively put it—and those who argued that the regime's economic model was anathema to redistribution and thus flawed, if not ultimately irredeemable.[33]

Rich as it was, the debate was almost moot. In October 1973—a month after the US-backed coup in Chile—President Richard Nixon provided Israel with fighter jets following a surprise attack by Egypt and Syria. In response, the Organization of Petroleum Exporting Countries (OPEC), led by Saudi Arabia and a coalition of Arab states, put in place an oil embargo on major industrialized countries such as the United States, Canada, Japan, and the United Kingdom. This "Energy Pearl Harbor," as one of Nixon's advisors referred to the move, caused the price of crude oil to quadruple.[34] Such a drastic spike in oil prices sent shock waves across the global economy, ushering in what Karen R. Merrill called "a new era of diminished expectations."[35]

In Brazil, the economic model that produced the miracle went into a tailspin. Confronted with this explosion in the cost of oil and insufficient local supplies to meet petroleum demands, the newly inaugurated General Ernesto Geisel (1974–79) would be forced to either accept lower growth to keep the trade balance from spiraling out of control, or sustain the rates of previous years by sacrificing foreign reserves and taking on higher debt.[36] The government chose the latter, borrowing even more heavily and further ballooning the external debt. This dependence on foreign capital made the economy extremely vulnerable to changes in international interest rates. As interest rates rose, servicing the debt became a significant burden and diverted resources away from productive investments.

Within a decade, the regime's economic policymakers went "from being wonder workers to malingerers" in the eyes of international observers, the *New York Times* reported in 1983.[37] Brazil faced a full-blown debt crisis, unable to meet its financial obligations. The government's attempt to control inflation through wage suppression stifled domestic demand. Coupled with the growing concentra-tion of wealth, this dynamic limited the internal market for manufactured goods. The noxious combination of hyperinflation, recession, and social unrest tarnished the economic miracle, which was by then a distant memory for most. Despite the triumphant narrative that the generals had been able to spin out of the economic miracle, the dictatorship was now presiding over mounting fiscal disaster.

The Brazilian economic miracle serves as a cautionary tale about the dangers of prioritizing short-term growth over long-term sustainability and social equity. While the period did witness significant infrastructural development and industrial expansion, these gains came at a steep price. This reality, at least as much as, if not more than, concerns over human rights and democracy, finally led to the collapse of support for the regime in the business community and among other sectors that had long supported the government. The economic model undergirding the "miracle" exacerbated social inequalities and left the country saddled with a massive debt load that would bedevil subsequent civilian governments once the generals left the political scene in 1985.

Chile's economic miracle took shape for the most part after Brazil's had ground to a halt. The 1980s saw the deepening of neoliberal economic reforms initiated after Allende's ouster and an emphasis on global integration. By opening up to international trade and investment, Chile expanded its export base, diversified its markets, and enhanced its competitiveness in key sectors such as mining, agriculture, and manufacturing. As is discussed from multiple angles in a 2004 edited volume with the inculpatory title *Victims of the Chilean Miracle*, the regime's economic model was also sustained by the violent suppression of labor rights, widening inequality, environmental degradation, and a reliance on foreign debt.

In a wide-ranging review of works dealing with the Chilean economic miracle, Donald G. Richards called into question whether the model is truly a desirable blueprint, as many argued it was throughout the 1990s and beyond.[38] Likewise, Peadar Kirby argued almost thirty years ago that Chile's nominal economic miracle might provide lessons to other nations—a common feature of economic miracles everywhere is that they are frequently feted for their tutelary potential—"but these are as much warnings about what should not be sacrificed in the rush for economic success as they are recipes for successful development."[39] For his part, Angelo Codevilla asserted that the regime's greatest success and its most salient lesson to other countries was the drastic reduction in the size of the state. When Allende fell, he points out, the Chilean government had 650,000 employees. By 1989, the year before Pinochet left power, "the Chilean people had only 157,871 central government employees to support and to obey."[40] A smaller federal workforce may have produced savings in the short term, but it reflected a broader underinvestment in infrastructure, education, and social safety nets that in time would take a toll.[41]

In Washington, selling the Brazilian and Chilean miracles served to burnish US involvement in the creation of military dictatorships that by the early 1970s were garnering increasing domestic attention for their brutality. On his late 1971 tour of Latin America on behalf of the Nixon administration, Finch presented the region's putative economic success stories as triumphs of the Republican approach to the region. He asserted, per the *New York Times*, "that President Franklin D. Roosevelt's Good Neighbor policy and the Alliance for Progress under Presidents

Kennedy and Johnson 'lumped the Latin-American countries together as banana republics.'"

The Nixon government, on the other hand, had no "litmus paper tests as to whether they're democracies or republics or dictatorships. . . . They make decisions on their economic and political systems for themselves."[42] The implication was that the Nixon administration had enabled these regimes to act freely in pursuit of their own economic objectives. The results spoke for themselves. Less than two years after Finch's visit, Allende would fall, establishing conditions for another miraculous Latin American turn. While the 1973 coup marked the beginning of a long national nightmare in the eyes of many, for others it was a blessing that heralded promise and opportunity.

Unlike many of its South American peers, Chile actually did come out of the Cold War in relatively good economic health. But deep issues persisted beneath the surface. A 1992 Oxfam report made the case for the NGO's continued activities in Chile after Pinochet's ouster: "Over the years Oxfam's programme in Chile has been gradually responding to the profound changes that have been taking place in the country. As a result, the emphasis of the programme is no longer on alleviating the effects of human rights violations. Instead it is on the social and environmental costs of Chile's economic transformation." Implicit in the Oxfam report was the argument that despite a democratic political transition, economic measures put into place by unelected technocrats during the Pinochet years would leave lasting social damage whatever their nominal benefits. "A development model such as that employed in Chile, which has a narrow focus on economic growth, is likely to incur social and environmental costs which may make it unsustainable," the report concluded.[43]

Decades later, a Chilean student activist born at the twilight of military rule ran for president on an explicit promise to tackle the noxious legacy of Pinochet's economic policies. "The 'Chilean miracle' was just for the outside world, not for us," Gabriel Boric proclaimed in 2021, adding that "when you talk to people in low-income neighborhoods, they will look around and ask you where this progress can actually be found."[44] By contrast, Boric's opponent once claimed he would have enjoyed Pinochet's support in a presidential race. "If I had met him now we would have had a cup of tea at La Moneda (the presidential palace)," José Antonio Kast asserted.[45] Boric defeated Kast by double digits in 2021, signaling quite clearly that the Chilean electorate favored the candidate promising to bury Pinochet's legacy rather than protect it.[46] Whether he actually can do so remains an open question as of this writing.

Conclusion

Economic miracles are ideological constructs, not products of divine intervention. A cursory glance at notable examples, Brazil and Chile being perhaps the most prominent in Cold War Latin America, suggests a correlation between so-called miracles and drastic policy overhauls almost always carried out under free-market or anticommunist auspices. While these periods of rapid growth by definition yield measurable economic benefits, they frequently come at the expense of social justice, human rights, and democratic governance. As the historian Thomas Skidmore noted, "if repression was the Médici government's gravest liability in international opinion, the economic boom was its greatest asset."[47]

The same could be said of Pinochet in Chile, whose horrid human rights record is still often tempered by laudatory references to the myriad effects of his economic legacy.[48] "In Chile, well, we had the strong government and the strong government was willing to run this risk of freeing the economy and seeing what would happen," one of the Chilean Chicago Boys explained in a euphemistic 2009 interview. "It was clear to us," he continued, "that unless you changed the economic system, the socioeconomic system, we would never have democracy, you see. So the only way to democracy was to change the system and Pinochet in that sense was an instrument of this desire to change the economic system so that eventually we could have a working democracy."[49] More recently, former president Jair Bolsonaro's finance minister has suggested that the legacy of military rule in Brazil is mixed, with economic advances potentially making up for a heavily circumscribed political system.[50] The allure of economic miracles in political debate over time is clearly not easily dismissed.

Despite the shared opinions of their cheerleaders, Brazil's and Chile's economic miracles unfolded through distinct policy approaches and along different time lines. The former experienced a protracted military dictatorship from 1964 to 1985 that pursued import substitution industrialization and state-led development, delivering accelerated growth from 1968 to 1973. As Brazil's finance minister reportedly told then president of the World Bank, Robert McNamara, the goal was "to go for take-off or bust; when that is achieved we can worry about fairer shares."[51] The takeoff came, followed by a spectacular bust. Redistribution was deferred. Chile's coup in 1973, meanwhile, led to the embrace of neoliberal "shock treatment" and the consolidation of a regime known for free-market reforms and privatization under Pinochet's personal authority.[52] "The state literally dismantled itself," as Valdés put it.[53] Economic results took longer to arrive in Chile but arguably proved more enduring. These differences notwithstanding, the Brazilian and Chilean dictatorships shared a basic disregard for democracy and social justice.

Ultimately, even great economic success does not excuse a violent assault on democracy. The consequences of military rule included widespread human rights abuses, suppression of dissent, and a worsening of economic inequalities, underscoring the impossibility of reconciling the arbitrary cruelty and insularity of dictatorship with miracles of any kind. Referring to the Pinochet regime twenty years after its fall, then finance minister Andrés Velasco stated, "that government committed tremendous atrocities that are unforgiveable [which] you cannot justify ever on the basis of this or that economic policy." Velasco, who unsuccessfully sought the presidential nomination for the center-left Nueva Mayoría coalition in 2013, elaborated: "We've worked hard in Chile to make sure that will never happen again. That's why we've been so keen on developing and consolidating the institutions of democracy, not starting from scratch, not reinventing everything everyday [but] by saying this is an achievement, we will keep it, this is a mistake we will change."[54] Velasco notably avoided referring to Pinochet's economic legacy as a "miracle," instead noting prosaically that some of the policies put in place under the former dictator could and should be kept. This, I would argue, is the right discursive approach. It's not that the term *economic miracle* should never be uttered— it is a revealing rhetorical artifact from a fraught historical moment—but it calls out for contextualization, interrogation, and resignification. We should not reflexively refer to these periods of modernization and high economic growth using terms that were intended to bolster the standing of regimes that oversaw enormous suffering.

Sometimes "economic miracles" are best thought of as branding exercises meant to divert attention from unsavory aspects of a particular regime or administration. By focusing on headline statistics and isolated indices of economic growth, such narratives obscure glaring social issues. The cases of Brazil and Chile exemplify this dynamic, but there are more recent examples to consider. Ravinder Kaur, for example, discusses the rebranding, as she puts it, of the Indian economy into an attractive investment destination amid a rising tide of reactionary nationalism.[55] Anne Stevenson-Yang has recently called into question the bases of China's vaunted economic success, arguing that "much of the Chinese economic 'miracle' was powered by American, European and Japanese companies that willingly transferred their technical know-how to their Chinese partners in exchange for what they thought would be access to a permanently growing China market."[56] These economic models serve exclusionary political ends, which makes it all the more important that we be attuned to the language used to justify them. Talk of "miracles" has often served to parry critiques and shore up the status quo, for better or—very often—for worse.

The point is not that wide-ranging economic growth in military Brazil and Chile was an elaborate hoax. Its concrete effects are captured in statistics and reflected in the lives of many ordinary people. But there is specific currency to the "miracle" label so heartily embraced by these regimes. Because people rarely doubt the intentions of miracle workers, that particular superlative served as a tool of legitimation in the eyes of domestic and international opinion. Whether one considers these miracles to have been laudable and unprecedented achievements that laid the groundwork for future growth, or Pyrrhic victories whose fleeting gains were outweighed by their enormous costs, was then and now a largely partisan matter, a legacy of the Cold War's acute polarization. To celebrate the Brazilian and Chilean economic miracles without recognizing the terrible human toll exacted by the regimes that oversaw them is thus to show one's cards. A more holistic vision of economic prosperity should encompass not just growth but also social justice, environmental stewardship, and democratic participation. Only then can we move beyond self-satisfied illusions of miracles and build a more equitable and sustainable future.

Andre Pagliarini is assistant professor of history at Louisiana State University. He has published in *Latin American Research Review*, *Latin Americanist*, *International History Review*, and *Latin American Perspectives* and written widely on Latin American politics in the *New York Times*, the *Guardian*, the *Nation*, *New Republic*, and *Jacobin*. He is a fellow at the Washington Brazil Office, columnist at the *Brazilian Report*, and nonresident fellow at the Quincy Institute for Responsible Statecraft.

Notes

1. Beting, "O milagre japonês," 22.
2. Donald W. Katzner diverges from Beting's analysis in what is basically a recitation of mainstream explanations of Japan's postwar economic success ("Explaining the Japanese Economic Miracle").
3. Beting, "O milagre japonês," 22.
4. Against so many Orientalist analyses of the Japanese miracle, Chalmers Johnson argues that the country's "industrial policy is rooted in Japanese political rationality and conscious institutional innovation, and not primarily or exclusively in Japanese culture, vestiges of feudalism, insularity, frugality, the primacy of the social group over the individual, or any other special characteristic of Japanese society" (*MITI and the Japanese Miracle*, 114).
5. Spicka, *Selling the Economic Miracle*, xi.
6. Harvie and Lee, *Korea's Economic Miracle*, 1–2.
7. Senor and Singer, *Start-Up Nation*, 16.
8. Joseph Zeira challenges many facile assumptions about Israel's economic miracle in *The Israeli Economy*.
9. Friedman, "Free Markets and the Generals," 59.
10. Hermann, "Reformas, endividamento externo e o 'milagre' econômico," 55.
11. Hermann, "Reformas, endividamento externo e o 'milagre' econômico," 7.
12. De Castro Lima, "Da substituição de importações ao Brasil potência," 37.
13. Figures cited in Aarão Reis, *Luiz Carlos Prestes*, 281. Peter Winn suggests the Chilean economic miracle was also built on the backs of working people, in his introduction to *Victims of the Chilean Miracle*, 1–2.
14. Cardoso and Winter, *Accidental President of Brazil*, 115.
15. Tinsman, *Buying into the Regime*, 27.
16. González and Prem, "Legacy of the Pinochet Regime in Chile," 377.
17. Edwards, *Chile Project*, 2.
18. "Diretrizes gerais da política econômico-financeira do govêrno," pp. 1, 6, September 9, 1964, FGV/CPDOC, RC p m 64.08.13.
19. *New York Times*, "Junta in Charge."
20. Fonseca, "Legitimidade e credibilidade," 588.
21. Kinzo, *Legal Opposition Politics*, 252.

22. See especially part 2 of Davis, *Victims of the Miracle*.

23. *O Estado de São Paulo*, "No aniversário, a mensagem dos militares."

24. On Brazilian workers under military rule, see Fontes and Corrêa, "Labor and Dictatorship in Brazil."

25. Maria Helena Moreira Alves offers an overview of the main provisions of Institutional Act 5 (*State and Opposition in Military Brazil*, 95–96).

26. On Pinochet's environmental record, see Klubock, "Labor, Land, and Environmental Change."

27. See Kornbluh, *The Pinochet File*, chap. 2.

28. Anthony W. Pereira has rightly noted that "to compare Brazil's military regime with the more violent and less judicialized regimes in the southern cone is not to attempt to rehabilitate it" (*Political (In)Justice*, 156).

29. Among many others, Júlio Cesar Bellingieri ("A economia no período militar") and Edwar E. Escalante ("Influence of Pinochet on the Chilean Miracle") have called into question some of the assumptions about the economic miracles of Brazil and Chile.

30. See Pagliarini, "'Singers of the Miracle'"; and Fico, *Reinventando o otimismo*.

31. Edwards, *Chile Project*, 2.

32. García Márquez, *Clandestine in Chile*, 16.

33. Those in favor of the regime's model included figures such as Mário Henrique Simonsen, Antônio Delfim Netto, and Carlos Langoni (notably, a Chicago Boy). All three were either serving in government or would later on. On the other side of the debate were economists such as Maria da Conceição Tavares, José Serra, Celso Furtado, and Paul Singer. See *Opinião*, "'Milagre brasileiro'—o grande debate."

34. Cited in Jacobs, *Panic at the Pump*, 3–4.

35. Merrill, *Oil Crisis of 1973–1974*, vii.

36. Baer, *Brazilian Economy*, 87.

37. Hoge, "Brazil's Economy—After the Miracle."

38. Richards, "Political Economy of the Chilean Miracle," 159.

39. Kirby, "Chilean Economic Miracle," 81.

40. Codevilla, "Is Pinochet the Model?," 129.

41. See Long, "Chile Student Protests."

42. Welles, "Finch, on the Eve of Tour," 10.

43. Coote and LeQuesne, *Trade Trap*, 139.

44. Bartlett, "'Fairer Chile.'" See also Davies, "Why Is Inequality Booming in Chile?"

45. Ramos Miranda, "Chile's Kast Channels Pinochet's Ghost."

46. *Economist*, "Chile's New President."

47. Skidmore, *Politics of Military Rule in Brazil*, 138.

48. See, for example, Vergara and Politi, "Half-Century after Pinochet's Coup."

49. Magnus, "Legacy of the 'Chicago Boys.'"

50. See Irajá, "Paulo Guedes relativiza a ditadura"; and Rigamonti, "Guedes relativiza ditadura em aula de economia.'"

51. Clark, "Robert McNamara at the World Bank," 175.

52. Klein, *Shock Doctrine*, 8.

53. Valdés, *Pinochet's Economists*, 4.

54. Magnus, "Legacy of the 'Chicago Boys.'"

55. See Kaur, *Brand New Nation*.

56. Stevenson-Yang, "Rise and Fall of China's Economic 'Miracle.'"

References

Aarão Reis, Daniel. *Luiz Carlos Prestes: Um revolucionário entre dois mundos.* São Paulo: Companhia das Letras, 2014.

Bartlett, John. "'A Fairer Chile': Protest Generation Aims to Reshape Country in Divisive Election." *Guardian*, November 18, 2021. https://www.theguardian.com/world/2021/nov/18/a-fairer-chile-ex-student-leader-bids-to-reshape-country-in-divisive-election.

Bellingieri, Júlio Cesar. "A economia no período militar (1964–1984): Crescimento e endividamento." *Revista Hispeci & Lema* 8 (2005): 8–17.

Beting, Joelmir. "O milagre japonês começou às oito e meia em Hiroshima." *Folha de S. Paulo*, July 26, 1970.

Cardoso, Fernando Henrique, with Brian Winter. *The Accidental President of Brazil.* New York: PublicAffairs, 2006.

Clark, William. "Robert McNamara at the World Bank." *Foreign Affairs* 60, no. 1 (1981).

Codevilla, Angelo. "Is Pinochet the Model?" *Foreign Affairs* 72, no. 5 (1993).

Coote, Belinda, and Caroline LeQuesne. *The Trade Trap: Poverty and the Global Commodity Markets.* London: Oxfam, 1992.

Davies, Richard. "Why Is Inequality Booming in Chile? Blame the Chicago Boys." *Guardian*, November 13, 2019. https://www.theguardian.com/commentisfree/2019/nov/13/why-is-inequality-booming-in-chile-blame-the-chicago-boys.

Davis, Shelton H. *Victims of the Miracle: Development and the Indians of Brazil.* Cambridge: Cambridge University Press, 1977.

de Castro Lima, Saulo. "Da substituição de importações ao Brasil potência: Concepções do desenvolvimento, 1964–1979." *Revista Aurora* 4, no. 1 (2011).

Economist. "Chile's New President Promises to Bury Neoliberalism." December 20, 2021. https://www.economist.com/the-americas/2021/12/20/chiles-new-president-promises-to-bury-neoliberalism.

Edwards, Sebastian. *The Chile Project: The Story of the Chicago Boys and the Downfall of Neoliberalism.* Princeton, NJ: Princeton University Press, 2023.

Escalante, Edwar E. "The Influence of Pinochet on the Chilean Miracle." *Latin American Research Review* 57, no. 4 (2002): 831–47.

Fico, Carlos. *Reinventando o otimismo: Ditadura, propaganda e imaginário social no Brasil.* 2nd ed. Rio de Janeiro: FGV Editora, 2024.

Fonseca, Pedro Cezar Dutra. "Legitimidade e credibilidade: Impasses da política econômica do governo Goulart." *Estudos Econômicos* 34, no. 3 (2004).

Fontes, Paulo, and Larissa R. Corrêa. "Labor and Dictatorship in Brazil: A Historiographical Review." *International Labor and Working-Class History*, no. 93 (2018): 27–51.

Friedman, Milton. "Free Markets and the Generals." *Newsweek*, January 25, 1982.

García Márquez, Gabriel. *Clandestine in Chile: The Adventures of Miguel Littín.* Translated by Asa Zatz. New York: Henry Holt and Co., 1987.

González, Felipe, and Mounu Prem. "The Legacy of the Pinochet Regime in Chile." In *Roots of Underdevelopment: A New Economic (and Political) History of Latin America and the Caribbean*, edited by Felipe Valencia Caicedo, 369–99. Cham, Switzerland: Palgrave Macmillan, 2023.

Harvie, Charles, and Hyun-Hoon Lee. *Korea's Economic Miracle: Fading or Reviving?* New York: Palgrave Macmillan, 2003.

Hermann, Jennifer. "Reformas, endividamento externo e o 'milagre' econômico (1964–1973)." In *Economia brasileira contemporânea: 1945–2010*, edited by Fabio Giambiagi,

André Villela, Lavinia Barros de Castro, and Jennifer Hermann. Rio de Janeiro: Elsevier, 2011.

Hoge, Warren. "Brazil's Economy—After the Miracle." *New York Times*, July 17, 1983.

Irajá, Victor. "Paulo Guedes relativiza a ditadura, por ser 'moldada aos objetivos.'" *Veja*, November 10, 2020. https://veja.abril.com.br/economia/paulo-guedes-relativiza-a-ditadura -por-ser-moldada-aos-objetivos.

Jacobs, Meg. *Panic at the Pump: The Energy Crisis and the Transformation of American Politics in the 1970s.* New York: Hill and Wang, 2016.

Johnson, Chalmers. *MITI and the Japanese Miracle: The Growth of Industrial Policy, 1925– 1975.* Stanford, CA: Stanford University Press, 1982.

Katzner, Donald W. "Explaining the Japanese Economic Miracle." *Japan and the World Economy* 13, no. 3 (2001): 303–19.

Kaur, Ravinder. *Brand New Nation: Capitalist Dreams and Nationalist Designs in Twenty-First-Century India.* Stanford, CA: Stanford University Press, 2020.

Kinzo, Maria D'Alva G. *Legal Opposition Politics under Authoritarian Rule in Brazil: The Case of the MDB, 1966–79.* New York: St. Martin's Press, 1988.

Kirby, Peadar. "The Chilean Economic Miracle: A Model for Latin America?" In *Trócaire Development Review 1996.* Dublin: Trócaire, 1996.

Klein, Naomi. *The Shock Doctrine: The Rise of Disaster Capitalism.* New York: Picador, 2007.

Klubock, Thomas Miller. "Labor, Land, and Environmental Change in the Forestry Sector in Chile, 1973–1998." In Winn, *Victims of the Chilean Miracle*, 337–88.

Kornbluh, Peter. *The Pinochet File: A Declassified Dossier on Atrocity and Accountability.* Updated ed. New York: New Press, 2013.

Long, Gideon. "Chile Student Protests Point to Deep Discontent." *BBC*, August 11, 2011. https://www.bbc.com/news/world-latin-america-14487555.

Magnus, Edie. "The Legacy of the 'Chicago Boys' Lives On in Chile." *Worldfocusonline*, December 9, 2009. YouTube video, 6:14. https://youtu.be/y_ecE5SAoK4 ?si=OCHKYERUnO9JP6gJ.

Merrill, Karen R. *The Oil Crisis of 1973–1974: A Brief History with Documents.* Boston: Bedford/St. Martin's, 2007.

Moreira Alves, Maria Helena. *State and Opposition in Military Brazil.* Austin: University of Texas Press, 1988.

New York Times. "Junta in Charge." September 12, 1973.

O Estado de São Paulo. "No aniversário, a mensagem dos militares." March 31, 1974.

Opinião. "'Milagre brasileiro'—o grande debate." November 27–December 4, 1972.

Pagliarini, Andre. "'Singers of the Miracle': Musical Boosterism and the Marketing of Patriotic Authoritarianism in Dictatorial Brazil." *Latin Americanist* 67, no. 4 (2023): 428–52.

Pereira, Anthony W. *Political (In)Justice: Authoritarianism and the Rule of Law in Brazil, Chile, and Argentina.* Pittsburgh: University of Pittsburgh Press, 2005.

Ramos Miranda, Natalia A. "Chile's Kast Channels Pinochet's Ghost against 'Communist' Left." *Reuters*, December 15, 2021. https://www.reuters.com/world/americas/chiles-kast-channels -pinochets-ghost-against-communist-left-2021-12-15/.

Richards, Donald G. "The Political Economy of the Chilean Miracle." *Latin American Research Review* 32, no. 1 (1997): 139–59.

Rigamonti, Stéfanie. "Guedes relativiza ditadura em aula de economia e diz que havia 'Congresso aberto.'" *Folha de S. Paulo*, September 22, 2023. https://www1.folha.uol.com .br/mercado/2023/09/guedes-minimiza-ditadura-em-aula-de-economia-e-diz-que-havia -congresso-aberto.shtml.

Senor, Dan, and Saul Singer. *Start-Up Nation: The Story of Israel's Economic Miracle*. New York: Twelve, 2009.

Skidmore, Thomas E. *The Politics of Military Rule in Brazil, 1964–1985*. New York: Oxford University Press, 1988.

Spicka, Mark E. *Selling the Economic Miracle: Economic Reconstruction and Politics in West Germany, 1949–1957*. New York: Berghahn Books, 2007.

Stevenson-Yang, Anne. "The Rise and Fall of China's Economic 'Miracle.'" *New York Times*, May 12, 2024.

Tinsman, Heidi. *Buying into the Regime: Grapes and Consumption in Cold War Chile and the United States*. Durham, NC: Duke University Press, 2014.

Vergara, Eva, and Daniel Politi. "A Half-Century after Pinochet's Coup, Some Chileans Remember the Brutal Dictatorship Fondly." *PBS*, September 5, 2023. https://www.pbs.org/newshour/world/a-half-century-after-pinochets-coup-some-chileans-remember-the-brutal-dictatorship-fondly.

Welles, Benjamin. "Finch, on the Eve of Tour, Defends Nixon's Latin Aims." *New York Times*, November 11, 1971.

Winn, Peter, ed. *Victims of the Chilean Miracle: Workers and Neoliberalism in the Pinochet Era, 1973–2002*. Durham, NC: Duke University Press, 2004.

Zeira, Joseph. *The Israeli Economy: A Story of Success and Costs*. Princeton, NJ: Princeton University Press, 2021.

Economic Miracles and Their Hypes

An Africanist Disputation

Abou B. Bamba

In February 1971, Anatole Shub offered to the readers of the *Washington Post* an article on Ivory Coast that could not have been more dithyrambic. Titled "Ivory Coast's Golden Decade," the news report provided a picture that would have made many development planners in the Global South envious. It opened approvingly with a laconic, if catchy, quote attributed to French president Georges Pompidou, who opined that Ivory Coast was now a "model for all Africa." The journalist elaborated: "already black Africa's most prosperous nation after a decade-long 'economic miracle,'" the West African country "continue[d] to gather momentum." Expanding on the portrait, Shub noted: "The air-conditioned skyscrapers, rush-hour traffic and bustling deepwater port of Abidjan are as impressive as the statistics of economic growth. Material standards in the capital, where the population has burgeoned to more than half a million, are already beginning to approach those of Southern Europe a decade ago." Providing statistical evidence to buttress its point on the rising living standard, the contribution emphatically declared: "The gross national product, estimated at $300 per capita, has nearly tripled since independence in 1960, while the initially minute industrial sector has expanded fivefold."[1]

Rosy portrayals like this were not exceptional. Emerging tentatively in the 1950s, such images of Ivory Coast as a poster child of modernization had become a staple in the public discourses by the early 1960s. It was at that time that the label of "economic miracle" was applied to the Ivorian experience of postcolonial

Radical History Review
Issue 151 (January 2025)   DOI 10.1215/01636545-11506791
© 2025 by MARHO: The Radical Historians' Organization, Inc.

development. This think piece attempts to make sense of the mechanism that led to the deployment of the concept of economic miracle to portray Ivory Coast up to the 1980s. In many ways, the essay is about what might be called "the politics of representing economic growth in an African context." In this regard, it concerns itself primarily with the mediated construction of a social reality and proposes that economic miracles be seen as more than a matter of exceptional economic indicators. Rather, I suggest that phenomena that are typically labeled as miracles in economic assessments are actually found in innumerable cases. Yet only a few of those cases are bestowed with the label. Why? How can we account for such a discriminatory rhetorical practice? In other words, why are some instances of rapid economic growth called miracles and others not?

As I seek answers to such questions, I argue that economic miracles are not only manufactured but are also the result of particular processes and procedures to establish a regime of truth in the public arena. To be sure, this makes their deployment a political endeavor of the first order. To flesh out this claim, the article revisits the early post-1945 period, when the use of the concept of economic miracle multiplied across various international contexts, including the Cold War and the reconstruction of several war-torn countries in Europe and Asia. It then shows how the concept came to be applied to the remarkable period of rapid macroeconomic growth that Ivory Coast experienced from the 1960s to the early 1980s. In particular, I underline the active role of the Ivorian authorities in manufacturing the miracle, which they consistently used as a marketing tool. While the era was marked by a significant transformation of the country that certainly propelled Ivory Coast into becoming one of the most prosperous nations in Africa at the time, the Ivorian achievement had its critics. The essay highlights the nature of their criticisms and historically reflects on the reasons they were sidelined during the heyday of the so-called Ivorian miracle.

. . . . .

Although Ivory Coast (and by extension, Africa) is the main focus of this essay, it is helpful to begin this analysis by emphasizing the ubiquity of the phrase "economic miracle" to denote the rapid economic transformation of a country or region, especially in the decades that followed the 1950s. Referred to by contemporaries as *Wirtschaftswunder* (West Germany), *il miracolo economico* (Italy), *les trente glorieuses* (France), or *Kōdo keizai seichō* (Japan), to name a few, it appeared that the phenomenon of extraordinary economic growth was happening on a global scale. Thus, from the standpoint of conceptual history, while the idea of "economic miracle" had been used to describe national economic experiments in the decades that preceded World War II, it was only after the war and its corollaries of devastation, destitution, and hopelessness that the use of the concept proliferated. This insight aligns with Robert Isaak's notion that an "economic miracle seems to start from a disadvantageous situation of war-time destruction, poverty or structural dependence and then rise like a phoenix from the ashes."[2]

Despite the geographic ubiquity of postwar economic growth, the perceptions of economic miracles "became fixated upon certain countries in the second half of the 20th century." In Isaak's estimation, this was "largely due to the reversal of depressed circumstances of nations that lost World War II (such as Germany and Japan) or due to being classified as developing or 'Third World' (such as the "four little dragons" of East Asia)."[3] To this point, one should add the geopolitical context of the Cold War, which not only informed the actions of the historical actors but also predisposed certain observers to appreciate economic realities in particular ways. The stories of West Germany and Japan illustrate well this view. Certainly, the rapid reconstructions of the economies of West Germany and Japan were attributed to the sound choices that the leaders in those countries made in the aftermath of World War II. From liberal economic reforms to boosting the consumer economy or to creating a productive alliance between state bureaucrats and businesspeople, postwar authorities reportedly inspired confidence as they encouraged investment through their industrial supply-side policies and their pragmatism.[4]

The Cold War became an additional factor in fostering a fast-paced economic revival in the West. Several scholars have emphasized this in the case of Japan. From their research, it is clear that Cold War considerations led the United States to reverse course on defeated Japan, especially since Japanese economic recovery became a key tenet of US security policy in Asia. In this context, the US course of action of strict occupation gave way to a new policy that favored the granting of low-interest loans to Japan, the opening of the American market to Japanese goods, and the provision of military protection to Japan.[5] The logic of the Cold War similarly informed the constitution of West Germany as an economic miracle. This was so not only because the East-West antagonism led the Western allies to abandon the policy of dismantling the industrial plants of the zones that they occupied in the divided Germany, but also because the onset of the Marshall Plan gave sufficient financial assistance to reboot West Germany's industrialization.[6]

The geopolitical conjuncture of the Cold War impacted the making of the German miracle in other ways, as demonstrated by the insightful work of Mark Spicka. By turning the reconstruction of Germany into a showdown between the virtues of capitalism and those of communism to deliver the good life, it led West German leaders to "increasingly conceiv[e] of politics as if they were selling a brand name item."[7] Arguably, no other actions encapsulated this vision as well as the political performances of Ludwig Erhard, minister of economic affairs under Chancellor Konrad Adenauer from 1949 until 1963, who would be credited as the architect of the *Wirtschaftswunder*. Spurred by the belief that "'psychology' was an instrument equal in value to traditional economic policies," Erhard engaged in public relations campaigns to sell the idea of German economic growth. In the process, the media was mobilized to create "myths and legends [that] conveyed in an optimistic tone that the reform [initiated by Erhard] had ushered in a new era for German economic recovery."[8]

The role of public relations (PR) and the media in the construction of the German miracle can hardly be overstated. In constructing the Cold War mainly in binary terms, the mass media practically turned East Germany into a foil of its capitalist neighbor. The media also misrepresented economic development in the East even as it celebrated the achievements of the West. For this reason, contemporary coverage of the fraternal antagonism became performative acts that were constitutive of the very reality of the *Wirtschaftswunder*. As early as the 1960s, a perceptive observer had underlined that West Germany's media reports of the "dismal misery" in East Germany tended to be "greatly exaggerated."[9] Exaggeration was not limited to the representation of East Germany, though. In 1962, Peter Alt and Max Schneider had noted that "when we come to physical destruction it is by no means certain that the losses cut much deeper in Western Germany than in other war-torn areas" such as Poland or the Soviet Union. In fact, there was "no catastrophic loss of equipment to prevent the German capitalists from starting up production."[10]

This brief overview suggests that economic miracles are fundamentally mediated affairs—spectacles in which "perceptions, perhaps more than any statistical analysis of the economy, had a critical impact."[11] Isaak put it best in the late 1990s with his statement that "economic miracles are made, not born." Even more significantly, he continued, "national economic achievements that appear to deviate from the laws of nature or so to transcend those laws as to seem that they are brought about through some superhuman agency are 'miracles' mainly in the perception of the beholder."[12] That is exactly why the mobilization of public relations proved so crucial. As I show below, the story of the Ivorian miracle operated within a similar framework in which the Cold War, the dreams of catch-up modernization, and the media use of some of the historical actors all became entangled to create a particular perception of social reality.

. . . . .

Another insight from Isaak's research provides a valuable point of departure: "To be perceived to be an 'economic miracle' it helps to start in a relatively 'down-and-out' position from which it is much easier to double or treble economic growth."[13] Although Ivory Coast is nowhere mentioned in his list of the nation-based economic miracles that occurred in the second half of the twentieth century, Isaak's observation fits a posteriori the Ivorian experience. Consider Anatole Shub's news report that opened this essay. It implicitly takes 1960—the year when Ivory Coast gained independence from France—as ground zero, against which the subsequent development of the country is positively judged. Numerous other works, including journalistic pieces and social science research, resorted to the same discursive strategy to showcase the Ivorian experience in the 1960s and 1970s.[14]

Yet many of the economic indicators and the policy choices that were touted to have ushered in the putative exceptional growth of the Ivorian economy were already in place as early as the 1950s, if not before. One of the undisputed insights of Egyptian economist Samir Amin's pioneering study on the development of capitalism in Ivory Coast was to highlight this historical reality.[15] Significantly, although they usually did not use the term *miracle*, media reports during the late colonial period deployed similar images that ultimately present Ivory Coast as one of France's colonial territories whose economic growth was quite exceptional. This was all the more possible because the opening of the deepwater port of Abidjan in 1951 gave a new lease on life to the Ivorian economy.[16]

At independence, this already decade-long economic boom readily became a "miracle" in the international media, a national exception that contrasted with developments in the rest of Africa. It seems to have been in the French media that the term *economic miracle* emerged in reference to the Ivorian experience. In fact, one of the first publications to use the concept explicitly was an article in *Europe France Outre-mer* in which Robert Taton compared the much-discussed economic expansion of Ivory Coast to the experience of West Germany after 1945. Continuing the comparison, the journalist went on to describe Raphaël Saller—the Martinique-born Ivorian minister of finance and planning—as "Ivory Coast's Erhard."[17] From this time on, it became customary and even ritualistic for other publications to refer to the Ivorian economic expansion as a miracle.[18]

While this is quite remarkable, it should not imply that the idea of the Ivorian miracle was an invention from without; an exclusive ideational construction elaborated in the boardrooms of global media corporations. Much as in the case of West Germany and Japan, the national authorities in Ivory Coast took a leading part in the manufacture of the miracle through both public policy and public relations. For instance, appropriating the theory of comparative advantage, they encouraged an agricultural export-led development strategy as the surest path out of underdevelopment. They also fostered a labor and cash-cropping policy environment that was favorable to peasant farmers, especially when compared to other African countries.[19] In addition, the Ivorian policymakers took advantage of the context of the Cold War to further the chances of catch-up modernization of their country. In this regard, not only did they opt for liberalism as the economic principle of the state—a choice that secured them a steady flow of investment capital from the capitalist West—but they also played the former colonial power against the United States to get a better deal on developmental assistance.[20]

To maximize the chances of success for these strategies, the mobilization of the power of the mass media proved apposite. Domestically, the state-run newspaper, for instance, was used to extol the "facts" and benefits of the modernization of the country. In article after article, the policy choices of the Ivorian leadership were portrayed not only as the best but also as likely to lead Ivory Coast toward a Western-type modernity. In line with the ambient discourse of the miracle, the economic realizations of the country were reported in celebratory terms and its infrastructural development magnified.[21] Advertisements that targeted the Ivorian people, especially in the cities, participated in a similar effort, and in the process attempted to make the miracle real for the Ivorians. Pierre Thizier Seya has highlighted this point, showing in the early 1980s that during the years of the economic boom, "the imagery of the Ivory Coast, as apparent from the [advertising] messages [was] virtually that of a paradise on earth. The country itself [was] painted as the materialization of economic success, and the inhabitants appear as extremely happy to live in such a wonderful setting."[22]

On the international scene, the public relations endeavors to sell the Ivorian miracle were no less proactive. For instance, in the early 1960s, Ivory Coast was one of the first newly independent African countries to hire lobbying firms to polish their images in the United States.[23] If anything, this suggests that the mobilization of the "new methods of political communication" that Spicka has identified as a particular strategy in realizing the *Wirtschaftswunder* was not limited to West Germany.[24] To be sure, unlike in Germany, the primary aim of the Ivorian PR campaigns was to attract American investment. However, even the quickest skim of the artifacts that the lobbying campaigns produced (e.g., ad displays, country profiles) convinces one that they had the added value of constructing Ivory Coast as indeed an economic miracle.[25] Other industrialized countries were the targets of similar campaigns, including Japan, where, in the late 1970s, the Ivorian embassy began publishing in the columns of the *Japan Times* yearly one-page profiles around the time of the anniversary of Ivorian independence. Like the ad displays that appeared in the American media, these pages not only highlighted the achievements of Ivory Coast but, by calling such achievements "miracles," they made them as such.[26]

Ironically, these public relations efforts were heightened at the very time when the relatively rapid growth of the Ivorian economy was losing steam. By the early 1980s, prices for Ivory Coast's main export commodities had dropped precipitously; the foreign debt had reached exponential proportions; peasant farmers were increasingly resorting to contraband to sell their products for better remuneration; and the Western-educated urbanites were defiantly asking for more Ivorianization of the economy; that is, more control of the economy by Ivorian nationals and/or the government. The emergence of these issues revealed the fragility of the country's model of development. Their conceptualization as historical social facts provide new insights into the limits of a hegemonic construction of the Ivorian economic miracle.

. . . . .

The problems Ivory Coast faced in the late 1970s did not grow from thin air. Nor was knowledge about them new. In fact, even as pundits marveled at Ivory Coast's achievements and called its economic growth an African miracle, keen observers had been sounding the alarm about the possible dead ends of the Ivorian model of development. Not only were their criticisms dismissed promptly, but steps were also taken to attempt to muzzle the critics themselves. The discomfitures of René Dumont and Samir Amin with the Ivorian authorities in the 1960s provided an early insight into this type of politics and gatekeeping regarding the dissemination of critical knowledge on the Ivorian miracle.

A French agricultural economist, Dumont had researched extensively on colonial agriculture. In the 1960s, he began publishing some of his findings on Africa, which culminated in his *L'Afrique est mal partie*—a landmark work that raised questions about the future of the agricultural economies of the African continent.[27] In the lead-up to the book's publication, the French expert had voiced concerns about the agricultural policy choices of various francophone African countries, including Ivory Coast, whose reliance on cash-crop agriculture was criticized for creating the illusion of wealth. More significantly, Dumont pointed out the issue of commodity price instability, which could have dire consequences for the Ivorian economy. He also warned about the rising inequality that cash cropping was introducing among the Ivorians.[28] In many respects, these criticisms challenged the image of success that the Ivorian officials strived to cultivate, and they responded promptly in an attempt to limit their propagation. In the wake of a conference in which Dumont had expanded on his ideas, the Ivorian authorities, through their ambassador in Bern, complained to the French authorities and asked them to rein in their compatriot.[29]

The media scuffle with Samir Amin revealed a similar logic in the Ivorian effort to micromanage the representation of the Ivorian miracle. On October 1, 1967, the Pan-African magazine *Jeune Afrique* had published in its columns the concluding chapter of Amin's *Le développement du capitalisme en Côte d'Ivoire*. Focused on the strengths and weaknesses of Ivory Coast's path of development, the piece offered an economist's assessment of the evolution of the Ivorian economy from 1950 to 1965. Its overall message was unequivocal: the Ivorian experience was a perfect illustration of "growth without development."[30] For a government that had been basking in the glow of media reports on the economic achievements of Ivory Coast, this was unacceptable. According to French diplomatic intelligence, Amin's media intervention was discussed during an Ivorian cabinet meeting at which the Ministry of Agriculture was tasked with providing a rebuttal, a duty the latter completed a few weeks later.[31]

Foreign critics were not the only ones to raise doubts about the claims making inherent in the discourse of the economic miracle as applied to Ivory Coast. In fact, many people within the country, including farmers, labor unionists, university professors, and students, challenged the dominant narrative—particularly beginning in the late 1960s and thereafter. Shifting the focus from macroeconomics and aggregate data, they demanded that the so-called achievements of the Ivorian miracle be assessed against the issue of social justice and the human cost of the economic choices that their leaders had made over the years. To the discourse of rapid and constant increase of the gross domestic product, they counterposed the fact of the overbearing presence of the French in the Ivorian economy. Against the backdrop of the extravagant lifestyles of the bureaucrats, they drew attention to the pittance that the farmers in the countryside received for the products of their labor. While some wrote anonymous leaflets to disseminate their criticism, others took to the streets.[32]

Fundamentally, these were counterdiscourses that revealed the underbelly of Ivory Coast's model of development. In that, they were not unlike the criticisms of Dumont or Amin. While not always explicitly, they irreverently tarnished the brand name of the Ivorian miracle. And such an affront could not be tolerated, lest it galvanize opposition to the hegemonic rule of the government's regime of truth. Consequently, their promoters faced constant persecution. While some were jailed, others were forced into exile.[33] Yet many of the critical points of the counterdiscourses were on target. By the early 1980s, it was increasingly clear that the rapid growth of the Ivorian economy had been achieved on shaky grounds. Coming to terms with such a realization, the authorities could not but accept the initiation of a series of policies to restructure the overall economic edifice of the country, a process that was underway in other African countries and that collectively came to be known as structural adjustment programs.[34]

. . . . .

In the end, did Ivory Coast ever witness an economic miracle? The answer to this question depends on how one defines "economic miracle." In the 1960s through the mid-1980s, the concept was certainly deployed in some circles to describe the Ivorian experience in postcolonial nation-building. As this think piece has underlined, however, such a characterization might have been the result of a particular regime of constructing economic truths. Indeed, as in the case of the West German *Wirtschaftswunder*, it points to the power of public relations in manufacturing reality.

Writing on the case of Botswana, another African country that has been dubbed an "economic miracle," Morten Jerven has noted that the existing literature has a tendency to focus "on the aggregate averaged growth rate." In contrast, scholars pay "relatively little attention to the source of growth as well as its timing."[35] For the economic historian, such a practice is problematic in the sense it provides a skewed picture of the economic reality of Botswana. Taking a more holistic approach, other social scientists have concluded that despite its impressive growth rate in the last forty years, Botswana's economy may be not only suffering from the "Dutch disease" but also illustrates "a clear case of growth without development."[36]

"Growth without development" is the same phrase that Samir Amin used in 1967 to raise doubt about the Ivorian economic miracle. Even as he found many aspects of the Ivorian economy to be impressive, he maintained that its overall growth had been "engendered and kept up from the outside, without the construction of socioeconomic structures that would enable automatic passage to a still further stage of a self-centered and self-maintained new dynamism."[37] This may have been a sharp criticism. However, it was not without merit, even if the authorities in Ivory Coast attempted to discredit it. Significantly, they intensified the deployment of public relations to tout the achievements of their economic policy choices. Consulting firms were hired, ad displays were designed, and Ivory Coast was made the blue-eyed boy of postcolonial development in Africa. In the end, while not quite a pipe dream, the Ivorian miracle was like a house of cards, whose edifice ultimately came crashing down in the late 1970s.

Abou B. Bamba is professor of history and Africana studies at Gettysburg College in Pennsylvania. He is author of *African Miracle, African Mirage: Transnational Politics and the Paradox of Modernization in Ivory Coast* (2016), which was a finalist for the 2018 Fage and Oliver Prize of the African Studies Association of the United Kingdom. He is currently at work on two book-length projects, including one that analyzes the historical contours of Ivorian diplomacy in the long 1960s and one that deals with the relations between the United States and francophone Africa in the wake of decolonization. Bamba presently serves as an editor of the *Journal of African History*.

Notes

1. Shub, "Ivory Coast's Golden Decade." The same article is reproduced in other international publications under different titles (Shub, "Ivory Coast Sets the Pace"; Shub, "Ivory Coast Growing Prosperous").
2. Isaak, "Making 'Economic Miracles,'" 59. On some contemporary uses of the concept of economic miracle in the prewar period, see, among others, *New York Times*, "Knudsen Warns Labor on Output"; Fisher, "Resuscitated Austria"; and Hirsch, *Das amerikanische Wirtschaftswunder*.
3. Isaak, "Making 'Economic Miracles,'" 59.
4. Chamberlin, "Japan's Miracle"; Tolischus, "Miracle in Nippon"; Alsop, "Matter of Fact"; Childs, "German Rebirth Now Complete"; Childs, "German Miracle." Some scholars have expanded on a number of these points. See, for example, Giersch, Paqué, and Schmieding, *Fading Miracle*; Nicholls, *Freedom with Responsibility*; Metzier, *Capital as Will and Imagination*; and Johnson, *MITI and the Japanese Miracle*.
5. Beckley, Horiuchi, and Miller, "America's Role," 4–6; Forsberg, *America and the Japanese Miracle*.
6. Apel, "East German Miracle," 11.
7. Spicka, "Selling the Economic Miracle: Public-Opinion Research," 51. See also Spicka, *Selling the Economic Miracle*.
8. Spicka, *Selling the Economic Miracle*, 43.
9. Apel, "East German Miracle," 10.
10. Alt and Schneider, "West Germany's 'Economic Miracle,'" 47. The historian of technology Raymond Stokes has confirmed this assessment ("Technology and the West German *Wirtschaftswunder*").
11. Spicka, *Selling the Economic Miracle*, 43.
12. Isaak, "Making 'Economic Miracles,'" 59.

13. Isaak, "Making 'Economic Miracles,'" 59.

14. *Le Monde*, "Un miracle économique"; Hecht, "Ivory Coast Economic 'Miracle'"; Tuinder, *Ivory Coast*.

15. Amin, *Le développement du capitalisme en Côte d'Ivoire*. See also Rapley, *Ivoirien Capitalism*.

16. *Bulletin du comité de l'Afrique française*, "Côte d'Ivoire"; G.J., "Un territoire en plein essor"; Blanchet, "Les cours exceptionnels du café"; Carbon, "L'importance de la Côte d'Ivoire"; Péchoux, "Ivory Coast Governor"; Rougeroc, "La Côte d'Ivoire, pays récent dans la vieille Afrique"; *Daily Boston Globe*, "Port of Abidjan on Ivory Coast"; *Christian Science Monitor*, "Africa's 'Port of the Future'"; *Pittsburgh Courier*, "Develop African Port to Attract More Trade."

17. Taton, "Pragmatique et prospère Côte d'Ivoire."

18. For a sample of the subsequent use of the term in various publications, see Lamb, "African Success Story"; *Washington Post*, "Economy of Ivory Coast Is Booming"; *Le Monde*, "M. Raphaël-Leygues évoque le 'miracle économique' ivoirien"; and Decraene, "La Côte d'Ivoire sous le signe de l'expansion."

19. Widner, "Origins of Agricultural Policy in Ivory Coast"; Kelsall, "Patrimonialism, Administrative Effectiveness, and Economic Development"; Ridler, "Comparative Advantage as a Development Model"; Diabaté, "Le modèle ivoirien du développement."

20. I have developed these points in earlier works. See, in particular, Bamba, *African Miracle, African Mirage*.

21. For a sample of these newspaper articles, see *Fraternité Matin*, "Buyo: Avec le barrage, une nouvelle ère de développement"; *Fraternité Matin*, "Le patron des patrons français"; *Fraternité Matin*, "Côte d'Ivoire, 1960–1977"; *Fraternité Matin*, "Côte d'Ivoire, 1968–69"; and *Fraternité Matin*, "Les industries alimentaires ivoiriennes."

22. Seya, "Transnational Capitalist Ideology," 387.

23. Landauer, "Swaying Uncle Sam," 18; Faltermayer, "Propaganda Push."

24. Spicka, "Selling the Economic Miracle: Public-Opinion Research," 49.

25. Bamba, "Courting American Capital."

26. For a sample of these, see Coffi, "Economic, Social Development Often Called Ivorian Miracle"; *Japan Times*, "More Effective Control Taken"; Coffi, "Assuring People of Cultural, Social, and Economic Progress"; *Japan Times*, "Ambitious Agricultural Plans."

27. Dumont, *L'Afrique noire est mal partie*. The book was later translated into English along with some paratextual materials (*False Start in Africa*).

28. Dumont, *Afrique noire, développement agricole*; Dumont, "Quelques problèmes agricoles africains et malgaches."

29. Geneva to Paris, February 18, 1963, série: Direction des Affaires Africaines & Malgaches (DAM)/sous-série: Côte d'Ivoire (CI), Carton 1888, Archives du Ministère des Affaires Etrangères, Paris, France (hereafter AMAE).

30. Amin, "Côte d'Ivoire."

31. Raphaël-Leygues to Ministre des Affaires Etrangères, February 22, 1968, DAM/CI, Carton 1888, AMAE.

32. Maalouf, "Côte d'Ivoire: Le malaise"; Bureau politique [PDCI/RDA], "Non aux tracts!"; Diallo, "Côte d'Ivoire: Les chômeurs se fâchent"; *Fraternité Matin*, "A propos des 'remous sociaux.'"

33. Bamba, *African Miracle, African Mirage*, 171–74.

34. Koumoué Koffi, *Politique économique et ajustement structurel*; *Fraternité Matin*, "'Nous devons tous accepter des sacrifices'"; *Fraternité Matin*, "Le Président de retour." For an

overview of structural adjustment programs in Africa, see Mkandawire and Soludo, *Our Continent, Our Future*.

35. Jerven, "Accounting for the African Growth Miracle," 74.
36. Pegg, "Is There a Dutch Disease in Botswana?"; Hillbom, "Diamonds or Development?"
37. Amin, *Le développement du capitalisme en Côte d'Ivoire*, 281. See also Amin, "Capitalism and Development in the Ivory Coast," 288.

References

Alt, Peter, and Max Schneider. "West Germany's 'Economic Miracle.'" *Science and Society* 26, no. 1 (1962): 46–57.

Amin, Samir. "Capitalism and Development in the Ivory Coast." In *African Politics and Society: Basic Issues and Problems of Government and Development*, edited by Irving L. Markovitz, 277–88. New York: Free Press, 1970.

Amin, Samir. "Côte d'Ivoire: Valeur et limites d'une expérience." *Jeune Afrique*, October 1, 1967.

Amin, Samir. *Le développement du capitalisme en Côte d'Ivoire*. Paris: Editions Minuit, 1967.

Apel, Hans. "East German Miracle." *Challenge* (November 1963).

Bamba, Abou B. *African Miracle, African Mirage: Transnational Politics and the Paradox of Modernization in Ivory Coast*. Athens: Ohio University Press, 2016.

Bamba, Abou B. "Courting American Capital: Public Relations and the Business of Selling Ivorian Capitalism in the U.S., 1960–1980." In *Capitalism and Diplomacy: The Political Economy of U.S. Foreign Relations in the Twentieth Century*, edited by Christopher Dietrich, 193–205. Philadelphia: University of Pennsylvania Press, 2022.

Beckley, Michael, Yusaku Horiuchi, and Jennifer M. Miller. "America's Role in the Making of Japan's Economic Miracle." *Journal of East Asian Studies* 18, no. 1 (2018): 1–21. https://doi.org/10.1017/jea.2017.24.

Blanchet, André. "Les cours exceptionnels du café et du cacao font connaître à la Côte-d'Ivoire une prospérité sans précédent." *Le Monde*, April 30, 1954.

Bulletin du Comité de l'Afrique française. "Côte d'Ivoire: Une brillante expansion économique." July-November-December 1957.

Bureau politique [PDCI/RDA]. "Non aux tracts! Tout citoyen dispose du dialogue pour s'exprimer." *Fraternité Matin*, August 16, 1978.

Carbon, Luc de. "L'importance de la Côte d'Ivoire dans l'économie de l'AOF." *Marchés Coloniaux*, April 28, 1951.

Chamberlin, William Henry. "Japan's Miracle: In Some Ways It Has Surpassed Germany's Economic Rise." *Wall Street Journal*, October 30, 1962.

Childs, Marquis. "The German Miracle: Currency Reform Proved Effective." *Washington Post*, March 10, 1954.

Childs, Marquis. "German Rebirth Now Complete." *Washington Post*, August 3, 1955.

Christian Science Monitor. "Africa's 'Port of the Future' Plans for Partial Debut in 1950." April 3, 1950.

Coffi, Pierre Nelson. "Assuring People of Cultural, Social, and Economic Progress." *Japan Times*, December 7, 1980.

Coffi, Pierre Nelson. "Economic, Social Development Often Called Ivorian Miracle." *Japan Times*, December 7, 1982.

Daily Boston Globe. "Port of Abidjan on Ivory Coast to Open Feb. 5." *Daily Boston Globe*, January 28, 1951.

Decraene, Philippe. "La Côte d'Ivoire sous le signe de l'expansion: Le miracle économique." *Le Monde*, August 19, 1964.

Diabaté, Moustapha. "Le modèle ivoirien du développement." *Annales de l'Université d'Abidjan*, sér. F, *Ethnosociologie* 5 (1973): 116–35.

Diallo, B. "Côte d'Ivoire: Les chômeurs se fâchent." *Jeune Afrique*, October 8–14, 1969.

Dumont, René. *Afrique noire, développement agricole: Reconversion de l'économie agricole des républiques de Guinée, de Côte d'Ivoire et du Mali*. Paris: Presses Universitaires de France, 1961.

Dumont, René. *False Start in Africa*. Translated by Phyllis Nauts Ott. Introduction by Thomas Balogh, with an additional chapter by John Hatch. New York: Frederick A. Praeger, 1966.

Dumont, René. *L'Afrique noire est mal partie*. Paris: Éditions du Seuil, 1962.

Dumont, René. "Quelques problèmes agricoles africains et malgaches (Madagascar, Côte d'Ivoire, Guinée)." *Présence Africaine*, nouvelle série, 31 (1960): 34–44.

Faltermayer, Edmund K. "Propaganda Push: Foreign Efforts to Win Support in U.S. Grow." *Wall Street Journal*, May 8, 1962.

Fisher, Irving. "Resuscitated Austria: Revived by the League of Nations, She Is the Economic Miracle of Europe." *Washington Post*, June 27, 1926.

Forsberg, Aaron. *America and the Japanese Miracle: The Cold War Context of Japan's Postwar Economic Revival, 1950–1960*. Chapel Hill: University of North Carolina Press, 2000.

Fraternité Matin. "A propos des 'remous sociaux': La Présidence communique." October 2, 1969.

Fraternité Matin. "Au Conseil des Ministres. Le Président: 'Nous devons tous accepter des sacrifices.'" January 15, 1980.

Fraternité Matin. "Buyo: Avec le barrage, une nouvelle ère de développement." March 8, 1978.

Fraternité Matin. "Côte d'Ivoire, 1960–1977: 17 ans de progrès grâce à notre agriculture." October 20, 1977.

Fraternité Matin. "Côte d'Ivoire, 1968–69: Un bilan économique réconfortant." October 1, 1969.

Fraternité Matin. "Le patron des patrons français aux 'Journées Ivoiriennes' de Paris: Votre voie est la meilleure." October 25, 1977.

Fraternité Matin. "Le Président de retour: Bientôt des mesures d'austérité." May 12, 1977.

Fraternité Matin. "Les industries alimentaires ivoiriennes." May 12, 1965.

Giersch, Herbert, Karl-Heinz Paqué, and Holger Schmieding. *The Fading Miracle: Four Decades of Market Economy in Germany*. Cambridge: Cambridge University Press, 1992.

G. J. "Un territoire en plein essor: La Côte d'Ivoire." *Bulletin du Comité de l'Afrique française*, July–August 1954.

Hecht, Robert M. "The Ivory Coast Economic 'Miracle': What Benefits for Peasant Farmers?" *Journal of Modern African Studies* 21, no. 1 (1983): 25–53.

Hillbom, Ellen. "Diamonds or Development? A Structural Assessment of Botswana's Forty Years of Success." *Journal of Modern African Studies* 46, no. 2 (2008): 191–214.

Hirsch, Julius. *Das amerikanische Wirtschaftswunder*. Berlin: S. Fischer, 1926.

Isaak, Robert. "Making 'Economic Miracles': Explaining Extraordinary National Economic Achievement." *American Economist* 41, no 1 (1997): 59–69.

Japan Times. "Ambitious Agricultural Plans to Finance Nation's Progress." December 7, 1978.

Japan Times. "More Effective Control Taken over Development of Country." December 7, 1981.

Jerven, Morten. "Accounting for the African Growth Miracle: The Official Evidence—Botswana 1965–1995." *Journal of Southern African Studies* 36, no. 1 (2010): 73–94.

Johnson, Chalmers. *MITI and the Japanese Miracle: The Growth of Industrial Policy, 1925–1975.* Stanford, CA: Stanford University Press, 1982.

Kelsall, Tim. "Patrimonialism, Administrative Effectiveness, and Economic Development in Côte d'Ivoire." *African Affairs* 88, no. 351 (1989): 205–28.

Koumoué Koffi, Moise. *Politique économique et ajustement structurel en Côte d'Ivoire.* Paris: L'Harmattan, 1994.

Lamb, David. "African Success Story: Ivory Coast—'Miracle' with a French Flavor." *Los Angeles Times,* August 28, 1977.

Landauer, Jerry. "Swaying Uncle Sam: Foreign Lobbying Here Grows." *Wall Street Journal,* January 21, 1963.

Le Monde. "M. Raphaël-Leygues évoque le 'miracle économique' ivoirien." December 17, 1965.

Le Monde. "Un miracle économique." September 16, 1968.

Maalouf, Amin. "Côte d'Ivoire: Le malaise." *Jeune Afrique,* September 6, 1978.

Metzier, Mark D. *Capital as Will and Imagination: Schumpeter's Guide to the Postwar Japanese Miracle.* Ithaca, NY: Cornell University Press, 2013.

Mkandawire, Thandika, and Charles Chukwuma Soludo. *Our Continent, Our Future: African Perspectives on Structural Adjustment.* Ottawa: International Development Research Centre, 1999.

New York Times. "Knudsen Warns Labor on Output." October 26, 1938.

Nicholls, Anthony J. *Freedom with Responsibility: The Social Market Economy in Germany, 1918–1963.* Oxford: Clarendon, 1994.

Péchoux, Laurent. "Ivory Coast Governor Hails Territory's Great New Port." *New York Herald Tribune,* March 29, 1951.

Pegg, Scott. "Is There a Dutch Disease in Botswana?" *Resources Policy* 35, no. 1 (2010): 14–19.

Pittsburgh Courier. "Develop African Port to Attract More Trade." March 4, 1950.

Rapley, John. *Ivoirien Capitalism: African Entrepreneurs in Côte d'Ivoire.* Boulder, CO: Lynne Rienner, 1993.

Ridler, Neil B. "Comparative Advantage as a Development Model: The Ivory Coast." *Journal of Modern African Studies* 23, no. 3 (1985): 407–17.

Rougeroc, C. "La Côte d'Ivoire, pays récent dans la vieille Afrique." *La Côte d'Ivoire,* special issue, February 1951.

Seya, Pierre Thizier. "Transnational Capitalist Ideology and Dependent Societies: A Case Study of Advertising in the Ivory Coast." PhD diss., Stanford University, 1981.

Shub, Anatole. "Ivory Coast Growing Prosperous." *Japan Times,* March 9, 1971.

Shub, Anatole. "Ivory Coast Sets the Pace for the Rest of Black Africa." *Guardian,* February 20, 1971.

Shub, Anatole. "Ivory Coast's Golden Decade: Called an 'Economic Miracle.'" *Washington Post,* February 11, 1971.

Spicka, Mark E. *Selling the Economic Miracle: Economic Reconstruction and Politics in West Germany, 1949–1957.* New York: Berghahn Books, 2007.

Spicka, Mark E. "Selling the Economic Miracle: Public-Opinion Research, Economic Reconstruction, and Politics in West Germany, 1949–1957." *German Politics and Society* 20, no. 1 (2002): 49–67.

Stokes, Raymond. "Technology and the West German *Wirtschaftswunder.*" *Technology and Culture* 32, no. 1 (1991): 1–22.

Taton, Robert. "Pragmatique et prospère Côte d'Ivoire." *Europe France Outre-mer,* June 1964.

Tolischus, Otto D. "A Miracle in Nippon." *New York Times*, May 25, 1958.

Tuinder, Bastiaan A. den. *Ivory Coast: The Challenge of Success*. Baltimore: Johns Hopkins University Press, 1978.

Washington Post. "Economy of Ivory Coast Is Booming." September 13, 1968.

Widner, Jennifer A. "The Origins of Agricultural Policy in Ivory Coast, 1960–86." *Journal of Development Studies* 29, no. 4 (1993): 25–59.

A Dubai and a Shenzhen in Gwadar?

Development Models on Pakistan's Securitized Coastline at the Turn of the Century

Hasan H. Karrar

"Gwadar Port is like a blank sheet of paper, and we can draw the most beautiful paintings on it," said Zhang Baozhang, chairperson of the China Overseas Port Holding Corporation, in 2023. Zhang, who has headed port management in Gwadar since 2016, was referring to the future developmental potential of Gwadar, located on the far end of Pakistan's western Balochistan Province.[1] Such optimistic projections for Gwadar were not new. For the last two decades, Pakistan's rulers—until 2008 a military junta, followed by successive civilian governments—had breathlessly forecast miraculous transformation of this sparsely populated and underserved stretch of Pakistan's shoreline. In this exploratory essay, I ask two questions: First, what were the pathways or development models that were referenced to forecast miraculous transformation of Gwadar? And second, at the turn of the century, what had suddenly motivated the choice of these models?

I suggest that development in Gwadar was forecast along two overlapping paths: a "Dubai model" of cascading investments in real estate, and a "Shenzhen model" of infrastructure-driven service and logistics delivery. Dubai, one of the seven emirates that constitute the United Arab Emirates (UAE), and Shenzhen, in southern China's Pearl River Delta, serve directly or indirectly as developmental archetypes for Gwadar. In Pakistan, the UAE and China are widely considered the pinnacles of developmentalist modernity. Still, it is worth underscoring that Dubai

Radical History Review
Issue 151 (January 2025)   DOI 10.1215/01636545-11506784
© 2025 by MARHO: The Radical Historians' Organization, Inc.

or Shenzhen are a poor reference because of how their reality on the ground differs from that of Gwadar. At the time of writing, in 2024, Gwadar's population of about ninety thousand suffers a lack of adequate water, electricity, schools, and medical facilities. Fishing and informal trade with Iran—besides consumer goods, petrol is routinely shuttled across the border—are common sources of livelihood.

There is also friction surrounding Balochistan's integration into the national polity. The sprawling region was never directly colonized. After Pakistan's independence, many Baloch resisted an assimilation that expected loyalty to a national Pakistani identity. Since the 1950s, the Baloch also resisted—sometimes through force—the appropriation of the province's substantial energy and mineral resources. The same Baloch will see the relationship with the center as exploitative—extractive, top-down, and non-consultative—and depriving them of benefit. At the same time, the center has routinely given free rein to security forces, turning the province into a veritable place of exception. Gwadar is dotted with checkpoints and is one of the most securitized places within Pakistan.[2] It was on this bitterly contested terrain that new development pathways were projected early in this century. Regional changes, such as the opening of the Dubai real estate market to foreign investment and China's export of foreign direct investment (FDI), help explain why.

Another pivotal event was the September 11, 2001, attacks on New York and Washington. Pakistan, which was then globally isolated and under military rule, quickly joined the Anglo-American-led military coalition. Overnight, Pakistan's fortunes revived. The country became a frontline state in the so-called War on Terror. Vast amounts of foreign currency and NATO military supplies flowed into Pakistan. Awash with cash, and with Pakistan's rulers coveted by world leaders, this moment empowered a new geopolitical imaginary among the junta and crony civilian politicians. With the swift collapse of the Taliban regime, momentarily it was possible to imagine a reconfigured, integrated Asia. Pakistan's leaders believed the country could play a new linking role between Afghanistan, Central Asia, China, the Persian Gulf, and beyond. Projecting Gwadar as the new Dubai and the new Shenzhen represented the two ways in which private capitalists and statesmen imagined Gwadar's role: as a place of multiplying personal wealth through real estate development, and as fulfilling an infrastructure-driven logistics and service delivery function. It was also believed that the development of Gwadar would bring order to the region. The Baloch were an unruly lot—at best unaware of how far the world had come, at worst tribal—to be brought into the ambit of a homogenizing state. Development would control them, using the carrot in tandem with the stick.

Recall Zhang's comment about Gwadar being a blank sheet of paper. In 1927, Mao Zedong had described the Chinese peasantry as poor and blank, which was to say they could be transformed. Mao made this assertion when no one believed in the revolutionary potential of the Chinese peasantry; in subsequent years, Mao would successfully mobilize the peasantry and lead the Communist Party to victory.

He defied the naysayers. A century later, Zhang was assuring all who cared to listen that the miraculous transformation of Gwadar was possible.[3] This essay is an attempt to excavate the thinking behind this idea and the reasons for the faith in this thinking.

This essay first introduces Gwadar's historical transnationalism. I then describe how, over the twentieth century, Dubai leveraged its location between Iran, the Persian Gulf, and South Asia to become a commercial hub. I also describe the development of the real estate sector in the new century. Further, I discuss how the Dubai model was purportedly replicated in Gwadar, where large tracts of land were acquired by real estate developers. Finally, I describe the other development pathway, the so-called Shenzhen model of infrastructure-driven service and logistics delivery. This dovetailed with Pakistan's aspiration of being a geopolitical pivot. Development, here, also was a means of bringing borderland populations into the ambit of a centralizing state.

Gwadar: Maritime Frontier to Securitized Borderlands

Gwadar is located on the westernmost extremities of Pakistan's shoreline, five hundred kilometers from Karachi, about one hundred kilometers from the border with Iran, and just over two hundred kilometers, across the Persian Gulf, from the port of Muscat in the Sultanate of Oman. For nearly two hundred years, from the late eighteenth until the mid-twentieth century, the Sultanate of Oman exercised sovereignty over Gwadar. The Sultanate of Oman was never colonized. Throughout modern history it was a seaward-facing mercantilist state boasting an economy that was "highly sophisticated, developed and organized."[4]

Prior to its inclusion in the Sultanate of Oman, Gwadar had been part of the Khanate of Kalat. In 1784, the Khan of Kalat, Mir Nasir Khan (1749–95) had offered Gwadar as his jagir (endowment) to Sultan bin Ahmad (d. 1804) of the Sultanate of Oman. (In 1794, Bandar Abbas, today in Iran, was likewise awarded to the Sultanate of Oman.) Gwadar became a node in the western Indian Ocean maritime network dominated by the Omanis. African slaves, Baloch mercenaries, dates, and spices passed through Gwadar, which connected the western Indian Ocean circuit primarily to India but also northward to Central Asia. The Omanis remained a formidable regional power—and the coastal Baloch a maritime community—until the second half of the nineteenth century, at which point circulation in the western Indian Ocean declined as European imperial power began to enclose this space through the construction of the Indo-European telegraph line, steam navigation, and patrolling by warships.[5]

Amid the European enclosure of the Indian Ocean, the nineteenth century saw the appearance of a new transnational community in Gwadar, the Khojas, an Ismaili Shi'a community, originally from Gujrat. The Ismailis were followers of the Aga Khan, who communicated with the Ismaili community by way of *farmans*, or decrees.[6] In the nineteenth century, Hasan Ali Shah, or Aga Khan I (1817–81), who had migrated from Iran to India, decreed that the Khojas seek better economic opportunities outside India; this led to a migration of the Khojas to the littoral region of the western Indian Ocean, primarily to Muscat and Zanzibar, but also to Gwadar.[7] Given that they were a transnational community, the Khojas were a literate people. In the early twentieth century the Khojas ran the only dispensary and school in Gwadar and owned sailing vessels. Unlike the Baloch, the Khojas remained subjects of the British.[8]

In August 1947, Pakistan gained independence. Gwadar remained under the suzerainty of the Sultanate of Oman, becoming a part of Pakistan only on September 8, 1958, when, against the sum of three million pounds, Gwadar came under Pakistan's fold.[9] A substantial portion of the money paid to the Sultanate of Oman came from Karim al-Husayni, the present Aga Khan IV, which speaks to the then importance of Gwadar for the transnational Ismaili ecumene.

In the meantime, since 1948, in Balochistan Province—of which Gwadar would become a part—a terse new relationship with the postcolonial state was being forged. During colonial rule, Balochistan had not been a single unit but comprised smaller, adjacent polities over which the British exercised varying degrees of influence. The largest of these autonomous units was the Khanate of Kalat, which, along with the other surrounding polities, acceded to Pakistan in March 1948. Since the beginning, the postcolonial state was wary of the Baloch desire for autonomy, and after the accession it sought to make national subjects of the Baloch.[10] Pakistan's leaders, whether civilian or military, have viewed Balochistan as an unruly borderland that needs to be brought into the ambit of the nation-state.[11] Ideally, this would happen through development, or otherwise, through force.

In 1964, the Pakistani government first identified Gwadar for seaport development. There was some interest in developing Gwadar in the 1970s, and then again in the 1990s. Development of the port would not take off until the new century, when a combination of global and regional developments thrust this desolate stretch of Pakistan's Indian Ocean shoreline into the commercial and geopolitical limelight.

Dubai: Real Estate Frontier

In the 1960s, when plans for Gwadar port development were first proposed, nearby Dubai and the surrounding sheikdoms were under an imperial protectorate system that allowed the local rulers a high degree of autonomy, albeit with British oversight; Dubai and the surrounding sheikhdoms, together known as the Trucial States, would remain a protectorate until 1971.

Contrary to popular perception, Dubai was not a backwater. Since the early twentieth century, Iranian merchants settled in Dubai to evade Iranian state control over trade. By the middle of the century, Arab, Iranian, and South Asian merchants were shuttling goods through Dubai, not just across the western Indian Ocean but as far as Brazil. The register of goods was extensive and ranged from rice, wheat, coffee, and tinned fruit to pickup trucks, cars, and gold.[12] Thus contemporary Dubai has been at least half a century in the making, with pivotal roles played by its leaders, foreign technical experts, and diaspora labor. Todd Reisz describes developmentalist imaginaries of Dubai's sudden transformation as "conveyer belt fairytales," in which magnificent infrastructure purportedly arises from the desert in what is nothing short of an economic miracle.[13] The miracle economy story erases long swathes of history and fuels a hubris that if it can happen in Dubai, it can happen elsewhere, too.

A landmark development occurred in the new century when the Dubai real estate market opened to foreign investors. This followed a peak in oil production in 1991, after which Dubai's oil output was in steady decline. As oil played a less prominent role in Dubai's economy, the emirate began to rebrand itself as a transit hub at the crossroads of energy-abundant Gulf states. Simultaneously, foreign entities could enjoy ownership rights, beginning with the Jebel Ali industrial zone, followed by other enclaves such as the Dubai Internet City and Dubai Media City. Soon thousands of companies, many of them high-profile multinationals, had offices in Dubai; many had their regional headquarters there. This was followed by liberalization of the real estate sector, allowing renewable ninety-nine-year leases as well as residency visas for foreigners.

After 9/11, increasing scrutiny made banks less attractive to store wealth; globally, the real estate sector became a more attractive sector to discreetly stash personal wealth. Demand for real estate in Dubai soared as A-list global celebrities fueled a worldwide now-is-the-time-to-invest frenzy. In Dubai, prospective buyers would frequently line up to enter a lottery to buy coveted developments. Dubai's real estate growth was fueled by hype, glamour, and global flows of private wealth.[14] The result is that today Dubai is the world's largest offshore property market, where approximately $146 billion is invested.[15]

Wealth from Pakistan played an important role in the growth of the Dubai real estate market, as it enjoyed a new liquidity through an unlikely turn of events. Just previously, in May 1998, Pakistan's then civilian government had conducted nuclear tests in reaction to India's nuclear tests, leading to international condemnation and sanctions; the country's foreign exchange reserves dried up. Pakistan's precarity was amplified when, the following year, the head of the military General Pervez Musharraf overthrew the civilian government. For over a year, Pakistan was in a state of defiant isolation, when the attacks on New York and Washington on September 11, 2001, offered Musharraf a lifeline. Pakistan hastily joined the Anglo-American-led military campaign to oust the Taliban. By the end of the year, Pakistan had successfully rescheduled outstanding debts of $400 million to the United States and what it owed to the IMF and the Paris Club. Between 2001 and 2008, Pakistan

received over \$5 billion in aid, as well as an estimated \$4.75 billion in coalition support. After Afghanistan, Pakistan was the largest beneficiary of the US military operation. Pakistan was awash in dollars, documented and undocumented.[16]

Gwadar, Redux: Reimagining Pakistan's Indian Ocean Shoreline

By this time, Dubai had become the reference point for Pakistan's wealthy. It had
one advantage for Pakistanis that London or New York could never match: proxim-
ity. In Pakistan, the wealthy boasted that it took the same amount of time to fly to
Dubai that it did to fly within Pakistan. The opulent city became a place of leisure
and a place to discreetly park private wealth; recent reports have revealed that at
least seventeen thousand Pakistanis own twenty-three thousand properties in
Dubai worth \$12.5 billion (Pakistanis are the third largest investors in Dubai after
people from the UK and India).[17] Additionally, at least some of the cash that was
flowing in for reconstruction of Afghanistan was channeled by contractors into the
Dubai property market.[18]

   The years 2001 to 2008, when the Dubai property market attracted increasing investment, corresponded with real estate development in Gwadar, too, as thousands of acres of "empty" land was appropriated by real estate developers. One of
the early developers was Sadruddin Hashwani, a self-made billionaire, who as a
small-scale transporter in the 1960s had traveled the length and breadth of Balochistan. By the late 1990s, his fortunes had multiplied. Now one of the richest men in
Pakistan, his Hashoo Group owned five-star hotels and held investments in energy
and mining as well as property development and construction across the country.
Because Hashwani was a high-profile Khoja, and Gwadar continued to host a
small Ismaili community, this resulted in the Karachi Ismaili community being
early investors in the burgeoning real estate sector in Gwadar.

   Hashwani was also one of the earliest supporters of General Musharraf. "It is
a turning point, a chance to make a good country of Pakistan," Hashwani was
reported as saying shortly after Musharraf overthrew the civilian government in
1999.[19] Consequently, as Gwadar was projected as a site of geopolitical interest—a
topic I take up in the next section—Hashwani was one of the earliest property developers, constructing the only five-star hotel in town and developing a one-thousand-
acre real estate project, the Golden Palms, the plan for which was drawn up by the
Singapore consultancy Meinhardt.

   Hitherto there had been no outside investment in Gwadar. Land settlement
began in 1992; prior to this point, there were no official land records along this
stretch of the shoreline. Once land settlement began, vast tracts of land were
acquired by developers from outside Gwadar.[20] In Karachi, anecdotes abound of
how property developers snapped up land at as little as 500 rupees (today less than
\$2) per yard. Housing schemes proliferated. Gwadar was the new Dubai, property
developers announced, and this was the time to get in the market. Many of the real

estate developments were scams where buyers living in other parts of Pakistan bought property that did not exist. Few buyers traveled to Gwadar to personally see what they were buying, and for those that did, there was an endless stretch of desert and shoreline that property developers could randomly point to. It was easy to buy into this myth because the buyers were speculating. No one buying property in Gwadar had any intention of living there; they were only holding on to it until it turned a profit. Thus the Dubai model was far removed from Dubai's coterminous experience as a real estate frontier. At best, property development in Gwadar was speculative, at worst, fraudulent.

But the Gwadar property market soon started losing its sheen. By 2007 the influx of dollars coming into Pakistan had dried up. Pakistan's economy now teetered on the brink of collapse. The anthropologist Hafeez Jamali, who did fieldwork in Gwadar shortly afterward, describes how, early in the second decade, many of the real estate offices in Gwadar were abandoned or had become corner stores, bakeries, and tea stalls.[21] Across the Persian Gulf, the Dubai real estate market was also hit hard by the 2008 global financial crisis, requiring intervention from the central bank in the next year.[22]

This model also failed to take hold because of the Pakistani state's inability to address demands for autonomy by the Baloch, who wanted a greater say in provincial decision-making. On August 26, 2006, Nawab Bugti, a popular, intransigent Baloch nationalist leader, was assassinated. Bugti's killing, which was widely believed to be the work of state security agencies, triggered the latest provincial insurgency, prompting the Pakistani state to deploy what are essentially dirty war tactics, such as enforced disappearances and extrajudicial killings.

As Balochistan became mired in violence, a new development model was unfolding alongside the Dubai model. This development pathway was based on geopolitical reconfiguration through an Asia connected via infrastructure. This model would also supposedly bring development to the recalcitrant Baloch.

The Shenzhen Model: Controlling the Unruly Frontier

This next model was the so-called Shenzhen model. While, in Pakistan, Shenzhen does not have the name recognition that Dubai does, this development pathway, too, assumed miraculous transformation.

In 1978, Deng Xiaoping, who emerged as the leader of China following the death of Mao Zedong in 1976, initiated a policy of reform and opening to the outside world. Shenzhen, across the border from Hong Kong, which was under British control at the time, was China's first special economic zone (SEZ). Shenzhen's transformation is depicted within and outside China as a story of miraculous transformation; a *China Daily* article, for example, describes it as a transformation from a "fishing village" to "an economic juggernaut" or "China's Silicon Valley."[23] This transformation, too, was assumed to be replicable; Pakistani's leaders have invoked Shenzhen as a pathway for coastal development. Here, too, the way the highly centralized Chinese state, which carefully manages macroeconomic planning, was able to mobilize and direct financial and human resources has been overlooked by Pakistani leadership.

Chinese interest in Gwadar dates to 2002, when on March 23 General Musharraf, dressed in military khakis, accompanied by Wu Bangguo, then Chinese vice premier, laid the foundation stone for the construction of the Gwadar port. China offered 80 percent of the projected $250 million costs. For Pakistan, this was an opportunity for economic revival.[24] Simultaneously, it was a chance to leverage a geopolitical imaginary—one that had become popular after the Cold War—which envisioned Pakistan becoming a connectivity hub. At the groundbreaking of the port, Musharraf described Afghanistan, Central Asia, and western China as "the top of the funnel" and Gwadar, "the inlet and the outlet into it." Musharraf also described plans to develop industrial zones, export processing zones, and technical training centers.[25]

Five years later, on May 20, 2007, Musharraf returned to Gwadar to inaugurate the port. Now he was accompanied by Li Shenglin, China's minister for communication. In his speech, Musharraf described how five years earlier, there had been "nothing" in Gwadar except "sand and dust, no road or buildings." Musharraf described new infrastructure that was coming up—roads, buildings, power supply, and "a hotel equivalent to other hotels in Islamabad, Karachi or Lahore"—a reference to the Pearl Continental built by his compatriot Sadruddin Hashwani. Musharraf again spoke about connecting the port to Central Asia. With connectivity infrastructure, everything would snap into place. An economic miracle was forecast. The plan was illogically simple, and it was peddled by Musharraf and the ruling clique not just for Gwadar but across the country, including in north Pakistan.

But unlike 2002, in 2007 Musharraf emphasized not connectivity but how development would heel this unruly frontier. The bulk of the speech was directed at the local people, whom he variously addressed as "brothers and sisters," "natives of this land," and "fishermen." Dressed in civilian clothes, with the sleeves of his *kameez* (flowing shirt) scrunched up, and wearing sunglasses, Musharraf played the strongman. "I want to show you a proper direction," he announced. He dismissed fears of land grabbing. He warned his audience that the nations that develop are those that are "not afraid of outsiders," whereas "those who resist investors remain backward and poor." He schooled the Baloch, saying that "when you go abroad your identity is Pakistani." He promised a "Fishery Training Centre"—because "you are using old-fashioned fishing techniques"—as well as gas, potable water, and electricity. He listed soon-to-be completed infrastructure linkages, roads, railways, dams ("it is for you"), an airport, and of course, the seaport. Still, while the state was giving developmental projects it was up to the Baloch, who had to "go forward and work hard." At the end of this rambling speech Musharraf called out unnamed adversaries who were "disrupting developmental projects . . . who are creating hindrances . . . and want to see [the people of Gwadar] underdeveloped," before obliquely stating that the adversaries would be "wiped out of this area."[26] This was a thinly veiled reference to attacks on Chinese engineers in Gwadar—three of them had been killed in 2004—and the escalation in Baloch armed resistance following the assassination of Nawab Bugti.

Conclusion

This essay has focused on the first decade of the new century, when the projection of economic miracles onto Gwadar came about through a combination of factors: junta rule, the emergence of the Dubai real estate market, an ascendant China, and finally 9/11, which offered a fleeting opportunity for Pakistan to end its global isolation and reimagine its regional role, which a strongman general grabbed with both hands.

During this decade, Dubai and Shenzhen were development archetypes, one through anticipating cascading investments in real estate, the other through infrastructure-driven service and logistics delivery. This was a vision for Gwadar imagined from outside the region. "My brothers and sisters," Musharraf had asked at the inauguration, after he had rattled off all the infrastructure projects his government was purportedly pursuing, "what else do you want?"[27] Musharraf's solution to Baloch grievances against top-down integration and extraction, which dates to the beginning of Pakistan, was more top-down development and extraction.

While today it is less common to hear Gwadar being referred to as the new Dubai, Pakistan has cast its lot with China as an enthusiastic proponent of the Belt and Road Initiative (BRI). Indeed, Pakistani leaders' favorite adjective to describe BRI in Pakistan is "game changer"—in other words, a miracle. Gwadar is a centerpiece of this story, in Pakistan often described as the "crown jewel" of the BRI in Pakistan. Even after military rule ended in 2008, successive civilian governments continue to deploy a playbook that rests on the development of heavy infrastructure, securitization, and extraction. With more than 90 percent of the revenue from Gwadar port reportedly going to China for the next forty years,[28] and Balochistan remaining a site of extraction—most notably by the Canadian mining giant Barrick Gold—Balochistan remains mired in a peripheralized past despite the miraculous futures that have been imagined for it. While the Pakistani leadership has oversold the idea of miraculous transformation, at a basic level, these economic pathways have served their purpose. Real estate developers walked away with handsome projects. Development funds were channeled to political constituencies. Rent was extracted. Spectacular infrastructure was meant to cement political legitimacy, and when that failed, as it often did, securitization was the default option.

Hasan H. Karrar is associate professor in the Department of Humanities and Social Sciences at the Lahore University of Management Sciences, Pakistan. A specialist on China and Central Asia, he researches transnational connections and contemporary geopolitical alignments. More broadly, he is interested in development, governance, and securitization and in the deployment and representation of Chinese economic and strategic power, including how Chinese authority responds to—and is contoured by—realities in countries where China is pursuing partnership.

Notes

1. Chu, "Gwadar Being Transformed."
2. Akhtar, "Checkpost State," 1372; Asma Faiz, pers. comm., May 31, 2024. For insights into ethnic politics in Pakistan, see Faiz, *In Search of Lost Glory.*
3. Gwadar Development Authority, "Gwadar to Become Logistics Hub." A year earlier, Zhang had emphasized the transformation that had already occurred. He recalled that when he first arrived in Gwadar in 2016, he thought he was on Mars. "The whole city was without any environment for doing business." Now, he said, the Gwadar port and free trade zone are "as good as any other . . . in the world." Looking to the future, Zhang predicted that "Gwadar will become one of the attractive cities in the world—a dreamland for human beings!"
4. Nicolini, "Maritime Indian Ocean Routes," 71.
5. Jamali, "Shorelines of Memory," 173.
6. Nicolini, "Maritime Indian Ocean Routes," 71–72.
7. Tejpar, "Migration of Indians," 34–37, 41.
8. Hirji, "Socio-Legal Formation of the Nizari Ismailis," 132–33. The British colonial archive offers insights into the Khojas community. See, for example, India Office Records, File 22/16 II, A66 (Gwadur), May 11, 1929–June 13, 1932, Ref: IOR/R/15/1/379.
9. Nicolini, "Maritime Indian Ocean Routes," 71.
10. Sheikh, *Genesis of Baloch Nationalism*, 78–90.
11. Jamali, "Shorelines of Memory," 165.
12. Reisz, *Showpiece City*, 31–41.
13. Reisz, *Showpiece City*, 8.
14. Davidson, "Dubai," 9–10.
15. Iqbal, "Pakistani Businesses."
16. Hashmi, "War on Terrorism," 6–9.
17. Rehman, "Dubai Unlocked."
18. *Dawn*, "Amid US Rebuilding of Afghanistan."
19. Weiner and Levine, "Pakistan General Forms New Panel."
20. On real estate development in Gwadar, see Jamali, "A Harbor in the Tempest," esp. chap. 3. For an investigative report, see Ahmed, "Unreal Estate."
21. Jamali, "Harbor in the Tempest," 90.
22. Mathiason, "UAE Central Bank."
23. Zhou, "Fishing Village."
24. Boni, "Civil Military Relations in Pakistan," 503–4.
25. Musharraf, "President at Ground Breaking Ceremony."
26. Musharraf, "President Musharraf's Address."
27. Musharraf, "President Musharraf's Address."
28. Khan, "China to Get 91pc Gwadar Income."

References

Ahmed, Maqbool. "Unreal Estate: The Boom in Gwadar's Property Market." *Herald*, June 22, 2017. https://herald.dawn.com/news/1153788.

Akhtar, Aasim Sajjad. "The Checkpost State in Pakistan's War of Terror: Centres, Peripheries, and the Politics of the Universal." *Antipode* 54, no. 5 (2022): 1365–85.

Boni, Filippo. "Civil-Military Relations in Pakistan: A Case Study of Sino-Pakistani Relations and the Port of Gwadar." *Commonwealth and Comparative Politics* 54, no 4 (2016): 498–517.

Chu Daye. "Gwadar Being Transformed into Modern Hub via BRI." *Global Times*, July 31, 2023. https://www.globaltimes.cn/page/202307/1295398.shtml.

Davidson, Christopher M. "Dubai: Foreclosure of a Dream." *Middle East Report*, no. 251 (2009): 8–13.

Dawn. "Amid US Rebuilding of Afghanistan, Contractors Snap Up UAE Properties." May 16, 2024. https://www.dawn.com/news/1833778.

Faiz, Asma. *In Search of Lost Glory: Sindhi Nationalism in Pakistan*. London: Hurst, 2021.

Gwadar Development Authority. "Gwadar to Become Logistics Hub in Region within Five Years: Zhang Baozhang." January 4, 2022. https://gda.gov.pk/gwadar-to-become-logistic-hub-in-region-within-five-years-zhang-baozhong/.

Hashmi, Rehana Saeed. "War on Terrorism: Impact on Pakistan's Economy." *Journal of Political Studies* 11 (2007): 1–15.

Hirji, Zulfikar. "The Socio-Legal Formation of the Nizari Ismailis of East Africa, 1800–1950." In *A Modern History of the Ismailis: Continuity and Change in a Muslim Community*, edited by Farhad Daftary, 129–60. Ismaili Heritage. London: I. B. Tauris, 2011.

Iqbal, Shahid. "Pakistani Businesses Opt for Dubai amid Uncertainty." *Dawn*, February 11, 2024. https://www.dawn.com/news/1813198.

Jamali, Hafeez. "A Harbor in the Tempest: Megaprojects, Identity, and the Politics of Place in Gwadar, Pakistan." PhD diss., University of Texas at Austin, 2014.

Jamali, Hafeez. "Shorelines of Memory and Ports of Desire: Geography, Identity, and the Memory of Oceanic Trade in Mekran Coast (Balochistan)." In *Reimagining Indian Ocean Worlds*, edited by Smriti Srinivas, Bettina Ng'weno, and Neelima Jeychandran, 165–79. New York: Routledge, 2020.

Khan, Iftikhar. "China to Get 91pc Gwadar Income, Minister Tells Senate." *Dawn*, November 25, 2017. https://www.dawn.com/news/1372695.

Mathiason, Nick. "UAE Central Bank Vows to Honour Dubai's Debts." *Guardian*, November 29, 2009. https://www.theguardian.com/business/2009/nov/29/banking-global-economy.

Musharraf, Pervez. "President at Ground Breaking Ceremony of Gwadar Deep-Sea Port." March 22, 2002. https://presidentmusharraf.wordpress.com/2005/01/24/musharraf-ground-breaking-gwadar/.

Musharraf, Pervez. "President Musharraf's Address at the Inauguration of the Gwadar Deep Seaport." March 20, 2007. https://presidentmusharraf.wordpress.com/2008/01/07/gwadar-deep-seaport/.

Nicolini, Beatrice. "Maritime Indian Ocean Routes: The Port of Gwadar/Gwātar." *Quaderni Asiatici* (June 2013): 69–80.

Rehman, Atika. "Dubai Unlocked: Pakistan's Multi-billion Dollar Property Pie." *Dawn*, May 14, 2024. https://www.dawn.com/news/1833476.

Reisz, Todd. *Showpiece City: How Architecture Made Dubai*. Stanford, CA: Stanford University Press, 2021.

Sheikh, Salman Rafi. *The Genesis of Baloch Nationalism: Politics and Ethnicity in Pakistan, 1947–1977*. New York: Routledge, 2018.

Tejpar, Azizeddin. "The Migration of Indians to Eastern Africa: A Case Study of the Ismaili Community, 1866–1966." Master's thesis, University of Central Florida, 2019.

Weiner, Tim, and Steve Levine. "Pakistan General Forms New Panel to Govern Nation." *New York Times*, October 18, 1999. https://www.nytimes.com/1999/10/18/world/pakistani -general-forms-new-panel-to-govern-nation.html.

Zhou Mo. "A Fishing Village Becomes China's Economic Juggernaut." *China Daily*, October 22, 2018. https://www.chinadaily.com.cn/a/201810/22/WS5bce720ba310eff303283e8d.html.

Teaching about the Brazilian Military Dictatorship (1964–85)

James N. Green

During the twenty years that I have taught Brazilian history at Brown University, by far my favorite seminar course has been "Politics and Culture during the Brazilian Military Dictatorship," which I have offered almost every year. The seminar, which is listed as an upper-division course, also usually includes several graduate students. Drawing from my own research agenda, which in part has focused on this period in Brazilian history, the course features an intensive consideration of the historiographic debates about the nature of the regime, the internal dynamics within the armed forces, and the processes that led to the slow-motion decade-long return to democratic rule, among other questions. Because the economy had a direct impact on the day-to-day lives of its citizens and became a source of legitimacy for the regime, the course pays close attention to the dictatorship's economic policies, especially the efforts to control inflation in the mid-to-late 1960s, the effects on society of the dramatic increase in the gross domestic product between 1968 and 1973, known as the "Brazilian economic miracle," and the results of the crises that ensued after the oil price shock of 1973–74.

Most students learn nothing, or nearly nothing, about Brazil in middle or high school. Therefore, they bring little knowledge about the country (including the military regime) to the seminar or have only vague, general notions about the dictatorship, which are usually based on analogies with periods of authoritarianism in other countries. An additional challenge in teaching this seminar is aiding

Radical History Review
Issue 151 (January 2025)   DOI 10.1215/01636545-11506840

students in analyzing the contradictions and complexities of a regime that carried out repressive policies against the opposition while simultaneously retaining certain political rituals associated with a democracy, such as keeping the Congress open most of the time, allowing for an opposition political party, and carrying out periodic elections. Students are almost universally surprised to discover, for example, that the regime's violent repression of the radical opposition coexisted with the fact that large swaths of the population supported the regime.

Moreover, because Brazil went through profound changes during the two decades of military rule, an important theme in this course is understanding historical contingencies and the ways in which the regime's policies had many unintended consequences, despite the generals' attempts to carefully control politics, the economy, society, and culture. For example, the elimination of Brazil's traditional parties and the creation of a pro-government party (National Renovating Alliance, ARENA) and an opposition political party (Brazilian Democratic Movement, MDB) in 1965 was an attempt to sever the population's historic links with popular political organizations. The maneuver worked for a time as the military channeled government resources to ARENA politicians to help their electoral victories. However, as opposition to the military grew in the mid-1970s, the two-party political system ended up creating a situation in which, by 1974, voting became a plebiscite in which the public could express opposition to the dictatorship. Although the generals in power decided to impose a law eliminating the two existing parties in 1980 and allow for politicians to organize new political parties, this divide-and-conquer strategy, designed to split up the opposition, eventually backfired. Whereas the reformulated Party of the Brazilian Democratic Movement (PMDB) swept gubernatorial elections in 1982, the party reorganization law also led to the formation of the Workers' Party, which eventually coalesced into the main political opposition party. Over the same period, the PMDB transformed into a party associated with politicians' personal self-interest in enriching themselves while in office. The seminar examines this and other examples of unintended consequences of the dictatorship's policies throughout the semester.

The seminar syllabus outlines the extensive required weekly readings of primary documents and secondary sources, as well as the viewing of feature-length films and documentaries. The seminar also includes guiding students on how to use over sixty thousand US government documents about Brazil available through the Opening the Archives Project at Brown University.[1] Finally, biweekly Brazilian biography assignments allow students to create a character whose life history coincides with the events taking place in Brazil during the dictatorship.

Since Brown students have significant leeway in choosing which courses they can take, there are usually thirty or more students visiting the introductory meeting of the seminar to decide whether they want to enroll. To pare down its size and weed out less-dedicated students, the first hour consists of a detailed discussion of the course content, emphasizing the heavy reading load, which is designed to scare students away from the course. The excessively detailed syllabus serves a similar purpose. In earlier versions, I also limited the seminar to those students who had taken at least one other course about Brazil, visited or lived in the country, or were from a Brazilian background. Here, the criteria were meant to ensure that participants had at least some previous knowledge of Brazilian history and culture. In recent years, I have dropped this requirement since I have found that most students, including the first-year enrollees whom I allowed to slip into the course, were as serious and engaged as graduating seniors and able to quickly immerse themselves in the course's content as easily as those with more extensive familiarity with Brazil. Most of the international students from Brazil who take the seminar later conclude that the experience of learning about their country's history while abroad, together with those who initially knew little about their homeland, enriched their own understanding of this period.

The course uses Thomas E. Skidmore's classic work *The Politics of Military Rule in Brazil, 1964–85* as the underlying chronological narrative. While the volume is somewhat dated so lacks any discussion of recent debates among historians about how to interpret the twenty-one years of military rule, the clear chronological narrative and analysis of the country's political economy throughout the book seem to reassure students without deep background knowledge of late twentieth-century Brazil. Over the years, I have found it useful to assign a student to lead discussions about Brazil's political economy every week to focus on how the military dictatorship's economic policies had a direct impact on the overall direction of the regime. The ongoing issues of inflation, wage adjustments, labor unrest, trade agreements, and the foreign debt, along with a detailed study of the years of the Brazilian "economic miracle" (1968–73), link macroeconomics to macropolitics and help students make sense of the ways in which the generals enjoyed support during years of significant growth and lost backing of large sectors of the society as the economy started to decline in 1974.

A counterpoint to the well-documented involvement of Washington in the overthrow of the João Goulart government (1961–64) and the bipartisan US support of the new military regime is an examination of the decentralized and loosely coordinated campaign of clergy, exiles, academics, and "friends of Brazil" in the United States, who engaged in multiple activities to denounce the dictatorship, especially its use of torture and repression to sustain itself in power. My book *We Cannot Remain Silent: Opposition to the Brazilian Military Dictatorship in the United States* documents these efforts; it is supplemented by *A Mother's Cry*, a personal account of the arrest and torture of Marcos Arruda, a trained geologist and revolutionary opponent of the regime, told from the different perspectives of his mother, his family, and his own experiences while under custody in 1970 and 1971 and subsequently in exile in the United States.[2]

The radicalized student movement and the decision by several thousand youths to take up arms against the regime are two interwoven themes that attract significant interest. Victoria Langland's comprehensive history of student activism, focusing on the protest movement in 1968 and its legacy, and my biography of Herbert Daniel, medical student turned guerrilla fighter, capture the ethos of members of a generation who imagined that they had the power to bring down the military regime through revolutionary politics and the armed struggle.[3]

In previous iterations of this course, students observed that too much attention was given to the radical opposition to the dictatorship, given the fact that those who engaged in revolutionary contestation were a small percentage of Brazilian youth. Bryan Pitts's recent work, *Until the Storm Passes*, partially addresses that problem with the course content design. Pitts looks at the legal opposition to the generals in power that was largely aggregated in the Brazilian Democratic Movement.[4] The study examines how congressional politicians responded to the wave of authoritarian measures and political maneuvers that the armed forces employed to stay in power for more than two decades. Although Skidmore tells this story in general terms, Pitts offers details that deepen students' comprehension of the role those traditional politicians played in challenging (and collaborating) with the regime.

Culture and film are two additional important components of the course. Although it is a demanding requirement, students view and write brief essays about seven films seen outside the classroom. The first, *Vidas Secas* (*Barren Lives*; dir. Nelson Pereira dos Santos, 1963), a classic of the Cinema Novo movement, represents the ways in which the poverty-stricken Northeast was employed by the Left to demonstrate why structural reforms (*reformas de base*) prior to the 1964 coup were urgent, and by the Right (as well as by US journalists and policymakers) as a location where communist subversion might prevail. *O dia que durou 21 anos* (*The Day That Lasted 21 Years*; dir. Camilo Tavares, 2013) documents US support for the 1964 coup. Three feature films, *O que é isso, companheiro* (*Four Days in September*; dir. Bruno Barreto, 1997), *Marighella* (dir. Wagner Moura, 2019), and *O ano em que meus pais saíram de férias* (*The Year My Parents Went on Vacation*; dir. Cao Hamburger, 2006), portray different aspects of the armed struggle, in the first two cases, and everyday life under the dictatorship, in the third. Two additional documentaries capture the ambivalences of the experience of exile and return.[5] *Tropicália*, a new musical genre that burst onto the music scene in 1967 during a São Paulo song festival, is the subject of a book and a documentary, and students are also provided with a twenty-five-item song list linked to publicly available YouTube recordings (with an English translation of most of the lyrics), so that they can listen to the music that Brazilian youth consumed in the 1960s and 1970s.[6] Finally, a documentary film study of the gender-bending theater group Dzi Croquettes (*Dzi Croquettes*, dir. Tatiana Issa and Raphael Alvarez, 2009) captures the ambiguities of the liberalization process, when content thought morally "subversive" managed to circumvent state censors' control.

Many students taking courses on Brazil do not have enough fluency in Portuguese to conduct research in that language. Thus the Opening the Archives Project offers a wealth of government documents from the US National Archives, presidential libraries, and other institutions about the relations between Brazil and the United States in the 1960s, 1970s, and 1980s.[7] Detailed indexing and a searchable database provide access to over sixty thousand documents that students can use to explore hundreds of topics for final research papers. One suggested approach to this material is to analyze the ways in which US government legislators, bureaucrats, and policymakers understood the nature of the Brazilian dictatorship and how to respond to it.

A particularly original aspect of the course is the Brazilian biographies assignment. At the beginning of the semester students create a character and move that personality through the years of military rule, beginning on the eve of the coup and ending as the country returns to democratic governance. They make website entries every other week describing how their character interacts with the political, social, and cultural events taking place, and usually students enthusiastically engage in this creative exercise. In fact, I have to remind students that Brazilian biographies is supposed to be a short assignment, as many embark on wildly imaginative (and sometimes lengthy) story-telling adventures. By creating and placing their characters amid mundane or momentous events, students seem to engage more deeply with the content of the weekly readings and with an overall goal of the course—to understand life under authoritarian rule and the diverse ways it affected different people.

Finally, the seminar is designed to be student led. The syllabus presents some of the historiographical debates related to each week's themes through basic questions to guide the reading. But the success of the seminar resides with the student leaders, who prepare their own questions and orient the discussion of the readings and films. The professor reserves the right to intervene in the debates to add points, ask follow-up questions, or answer students' queries. The array of approaches that the student leaders bring to the weekly seminar sessions further enhances the quality of the classroom discussion. In anonymous evaluations, the seminar is almost universally ranked as among the best courses that students have taken while at Brown University.

Syllabus: Politics and Culture during the Brazilian Military Dictatorship, 1964–89

This seminar focuses on the political, social, economic, and cultural changes that took place in Brazil during the military dictatorship that ruled the country from 1964 to 1985. We will examine the context in which the generals took power; the role of the US government in backing the new regime; the political, social, economic, and cultural transformations that occurred during this period; and the process that led to redemocratization.[8]

This is going to be a fun and extremely challenging seminar. Join us if you want to delve into the reality of Brazil during the dictatorship, use your creative

Figure 1. 1964 military coup d'état, Rio de Janeiro. Fundo Correio da Manhã, Arquivo Nacional.

Figure 2. Student protests, Rio de Janeiro. Fundo Correio da Manhã, Arquivo Nacional.

Figure 3. LGBT movement, São Paulo, May 1, 1980. Photo by Fernando Ochoa. Author's archive.

Figure 4. Signs from demonstration in front of the Brazilian embassy, Washington, DC. Photo by Harry Strharsky. Author's archive.

energies, expand your intellectual horizons, read intensely and critically, view films analytically, carry out interesting research, and write elegant prose. Otherwise, I would suggest you not take this course. You must do all the readings prior to the seminar (an average of 220 pages per week), participate in all seminar sessions, lead seminar discussions, view seven films outside the classroom, write short reflections on the films, and write a final research paper based on Opening the Archives documents. You cannot get an A in this class unless you excel in all aspects of the seminar.

Learning Goal

This seminar is designed to afford students the opportunity to read, think, discuss, and write critically about various interpretations of the history of the Brazilian military dictatorship (1964–85) and understand the political, social, economic, and cultural context in which it took place. This will include learning or strengthening the following skills:

- How to read historical narratives (secondary sources) carefully and critically to understand different scholars' arguments and their interpretations of history;
- How to articulate a wide-ranging understanding of the complex interplay of diverse economic, social, political, and cultural phenomena in a specific historical moment;
- How to view and think analytically about the ways that films are used as a means of communicating specific narratives about a given culture and its historical context;
- How to understand and interpret documents and other material (primary sources) produced contemporaneously to a period under investigation as a means of understanding political, economic, social, and cultural events;
- How to construct an argument about the meaning of primary sources through persuasive essays about their significance that can shed light on our comprehension of this period in Brazilian history.

Race, Gender, and Inequality

This course is structured around understanding the history of the Brazilian military dictatorship through the analytical lenses of race, gender, class, and socioeconomic inequality and how systems of power are structured and reproduced. This will be apparent in the documents we will analyze, as well as in the readings, lectures, and films. We will pay particular attention to the ways in which the US government intervened in the politics of Brazil, as well as how US citizens, Brazilian exiles, and others opposed these imperial policies. The final research paper, using US government documents found on the Opening the Archives website, will allow students to analyze internal State Department debates about US policies toward Brazil before and during the two decades of authoritarian rule to understand unequal power relationship between the United States and Brazil.

Academic Integrity

Each student in this course is expected to abide by the University Academic Code. Any work submitted by a student in this course for academic credit must be the student's own work. All outside sources, whether quoted word for word or paraphrased, must be duly cited and footnoted.

Course Workload and Expectations

The total of in-class hours and out-of-class work for all full-credit courses is approximately 180 hours over the length of a semester. In this class, students seeking to maximize their learning can expect to spend: 42 hours in class (3 hours per week for 14 weeks; 91 hours reading for class (approx. 7 hours per week for 13 weeks); 20 total hours viewing 6 assigned films outside the classroom and writing response papers; 6 hours writing your Brazilian biography postings; and 21 hours researching and writing the final paper. Actual times will vary for each student; final grades are not determined by the amount of time a student spends on the course.

Required Readings

These books make be purchased at the campus bookstore. They are also on 24-hour reserve in the library.

- Dunn, Christopher. *Brutality Garden: Tropicália and the Emergence of a Brazilian Counterculture*. Chapel Hill: University of North Carolina Press, 2001.
- Green, James N. *Exile within Exiles: Herbert Daniel, Gay Brazilian Revolutionary*. Durham, NC: Duke University Press, 2018.
- Green, James N. *We Cannot Remain Silent: Opposition to the Brazilian Military Dictatorship in the United States*. Durham, NC: Duke University Press, 2009.
- Langland, Victoria. *Speaking of Flowers: Student Movements and the Making and Remembering of 1968 in Military Brazil*. Durham, NC: Duke University Press, 2013.
- Pitts, Bryan. *Until the Storm Passes: Politicians, Democracy, and the Demise of Brazil's Military Dictatorship*. Berkeley: University of California Press, 2023.
- Sattamini, Lina Penna. *A Mother's Cry: A Memoir of Politics, Prison, and Torture under the Brazilian Military Dictatorship*. Introduction by James N. Green; translated by Rex P. Nielson and James N. Green; epilogue by Marcos P. S. Arruda. Durham, NC: Duke University Press, 2010.
- Skidmore, Thomas E. *The Politics of Military Rule in Brazil, 1964–85*. New York: Oxford University Press, 1988.
- Green, James N., Victoria Langland, and Lilia Moritz Schwarcz, eds. *The Brazil Reader: History, Culture, and Politics*. 2nd edition. Durham, NC: Duke University Press, 2019.
- Assigned articles, documents, and films are on the website.

Recommended Readings

These books are on reserve in the library on 24-hour reserve. They are noted elsewhere in the syllabus as excellent additional secondary sources for the material we will study and are recommended for the enthusiast.

- Alves, Maria Helena Moreira. *State and Opposition in Military Brazil*. Austin: University of Texas Press, 1985.
- Dunn, Christopher. *Contracultura*: *Alternative Arts and Social Transformation in Authoritarian Brazil*. Chapel Hill: University of North Carolina Press, 2016.
- McGowan, Chris, and Ricardo Pessanha. *The Brazilian Sound: Samba, Bossa Nova and the Popular Music of Brazil*. Philadelphia: Temple University Press, 1998.
- Serbin, Kenneth P. *From Revolution to Power in Brazil: How Radical Leftists Embraced Capitalism and Struggled with Leadership*. Notre Dame, IN: University of Notre Dame Press, 2019.
- Serbin, Kenneth P. *Secret Dialogues: Church-State Relations, Torture, and Social Justice in Authoritarian Brazil*. Pittsburgh: University of Pittsburgh Press, 2000.
- Skidmore, Thomas, E. *Politics in Brazil, 1930–1964: An Experiment in Democracy*. 2nd ed. New York: Oxford University Press, 2007. Especially pages 205–330.
- Veloso, Caetano. *Tropical Truth: A Story of Music and Revolution in Brazil*. Translated by Isabel de Sena. New York: Alfred A. Knopf, 2002.

Course Assessment

1. 30% Active participation in seminar discussions, including leading sessions.
2. 10% *Brazilian biographies* entries (six short postings on the website) (6 pages).
3. 30% Reflections on seven assigned films seen outside the classroom (total of 12 pages).
4. 30% Final paper based on documents in the Opening the Archives Project website or on an original research topic (12–15 pages).

Note: Graduate students taking this course should meet with me to discuss additional expectations.

This course requires a heavy reading load (an average of 200 pages a week), significant writing, and other out-of-classroom assignments. If you think that you cannot keep up with the reading for all seminar sessions, the writing, and the other assignments, you should not take the class. (It also should not be your fifth class; there is simply too much work for this seminar.)

1. **Seminar attendance and participation (30% of the final grade)**

This is an advanced seminar. Active participation in the discussions about the readings is essential for success. Along with another person, you will be required to lead the discussion of the assigned readings (chapters, articles, and documents) of seminar sessions. Some students will also lead the Economic Forum Discussions. If you are hesitant or shy about contributing to or leading the seminar discussion, you must talk to me so that we can find ways to encourage your active participation and leadership in the weekly meetings.

2. **BB Brazilian Biography (10% of the final grade)**

Between the first and second class, you will create a character, give her/him a name, identity, profession, political perspectives and then follow that person throughout the twenty-one years of the dictatorship. We will then divide the class into two groups: Group I (Last name A–L); Group II (Last name M–Z). Every other week you will post a brief account on the *Canvas website in the Discussion Section* about how that character interacted with the changing social, economic, political, and cultural changes that took place in the period about which we will have prepared for classroom discussion. You may be as creative as you wish, as long as your character's actions, life story, changes, etc. have some logic to them, and are plausible within the context of Brazilian culture and society. You will have a total of six entries during the semester related to your character. The questions listed in the syllabus about each time period are merely guidelines for thinking about how your character might have responded to the society around her or him during that moment in Brazilian history. Feel free to use your imagination and go beyond those suggestions. You should also consider interacting with other characters in the class. You may bring other people into your narrative, including other characters created by other members of the seminar. Brazilian Biographies is designed to be a fun exercise that will allow you, through your character, to imagine yourself in Brazil during the time covered in this seminar. The entries do not have to be too long, as we want people in the class to follow them. You should not spend too much time on this assignment. When it is your week to post an entry, you will also give a one-minute oral summary of the posting to the other members of the seminar.

3. **Out-of-class film viewings (30% of the final grade)**

During the semester, you will view seven different films about Brazil in the 1960s, 1970s, and 1980s and write a two-page reflection about each one. They will be available on the website. Your reflections should not be summaries of the films, but rather your thoughts about how they relate to the themes of the seminar. You should send them to me. They should be in Word.

The films are:

-   *Vidas Secas* (*Barren Lives*), dir. Nelson Pereira dos Santos, 1963.
-   *O dia que durou 21 anos* (*The Day That Lasted 21 Years*), dir. Camilo Tavares, 2013.
-   Two of three: Option A: *O que é isso, companheiro* (*Four Days in September*), dir. Bruno Barreto, 1997; Option B: *O ano em que meus pais saíram de férias* (*The Year My Parents Went on Vacation*), dir. Cao Hamburger, 2006. Option C: *Marighella,* 2019, dir. Wagner Moura.

- *Uma noite em 1967* (*A Night in 1967*), dir. Renato Terra and Ricardo Calil, 2010.
- *Dzi croquettes*, dir. Tatiana Issa and Raphael Alvarez, 2009.
- One of two: Option A: *Diário de uma busca* (*Diary of a Search*), dir. Flávia Castro, 2010; Option B: *Fico te devendo uma carta sobre o Brasil* (*I Owe You a Letter about Brazil*), dir. Carol Benjamin, 2019.

4. **Opening the Archives project or research paper with an original theme (30% of the final grade)**

Option A: Over the last decade, teams of Brown University students have been involved in a multi-year project to digitize, index, and make available to the public US government documents on Brazil from the 1960s, 1970s, and 1980s. These include US State and Defense Department documents held at the National Archives II in College Park, Maryland, and materials in the Kennedy, Johnson, Carter, and Ford Presidential Libraries. To date we have made available 60,000 documents on the Opening the Archives website: http://library.brown.edu/openingthearchives/. We have a long-term goal of digitizing, indexing, and making available to the public 100,000 US documents about Brazil.

For your final seminar project, you will choose a topic related to the Brazilian military dictatorship and then seek out documents in the Opening the Archives Project database that deal with that issue. While the focus of your research should be the primary sources in the State Department, Defense Department, or Presidential Libraries archives, you will need to do some additional research with secondary sources to augment the analysis of the documents that you choose. Your topic may vary from looking at how the US embassy understood a particular moment in Brazilian history to seeing how the mechanisms of diplomacy functioned.

We will have a brief in-house training session about how to use the Opening the Archives database. You will need to present a very brief statement of your research topic along with excerpts from at least one of the documents to me. The final papers should be *12 to 15 pages long, double-spaced, 12 pt. font, with an original title, page numbering, and Chicago Manual of Style footnoting for a historical paper.* The best papers will be published on the website. Two examples will be posted on the website during the semester.

Option B: You may choose a research topic related to the period of the Brazilian military dictatorship or regarding its legacy in the aftermath of authoritarian rule, which draws on primary and secondary sources, has a clear argument, and offers a new or original study of a specific theme. You should send me a short research proposal, with the topic, a summary of the idea, and primary and secondary sources you are considering. The final papers should be *12 to 15 pages long, double-spaced, 12 pt. font, with an original title, page numbering, and Chicago Manual of Style footnoting for a historical paper.* The best papers will be published on the website. Two examples will be posted on the Canvas website during the semester.

Seminar Schedule

Week #1 An Introduction to the Course

- Brief introduction of students and professor: your background, concentration, interests, and the answer to the question: Why are you taking this seminar?
- Outline of course expectations; review of the syllabus; explanation of Brazilian Biographies, film viewings and reflections expectations, Opening the Archives Project research paper.
- What do we know about the topic of the seminar? How can we systematize our knowledge? How are we going to learn together? How do we read a chapter, an academic article, or a primary document? View a film?
- *Mini-lecture: Brazil's "Experiment in Democracy": 1946–64*
- *Historiographic Debate:* What kind of democracy did Brazil have in the post–World War II period? What were the legacies of Vargas and their relationship to the 1964 coup d'état?
- Assignment of seminar discussion leader teams

Out of classroom film viewing of *Vidas Secas*. Two-page reflection paper. (Double-spaced, original title, student's name).

      Please send in Word with your last name and the short film title as the file name: e.g., Green—21 Years).

      Recommended Film Article No. 1: Randall Johnson and Robert Stam, "The Cinema of Hunger: Nelson Perreira dos Santos's *Vidas Secas*." In *Brazilian Cinema*, Randall Johnson and Robert Stam, eds. (New York: Columbia University Press, 1995), 120–27.

Week #2 Jânio, Jango, and Radical Politics (1961–64)

Seminar Discussion

Historiographic Debate: Was the coup inevitable? If so, why? If not, why not?

Discussion of *Vidas Secas*. To what extent did the discussion about the hunger and poverty in the Brazilian Northeast politicize Brazilian youth in the early 1960s and create a "discourse" about the nation's problems and their solutions?

Economic Forum No. 1: What economic problems did Goulart's government face?

Economic Forum Discussion

Secondary Source Readings (92 pages):

- Skidmore, *The Politics of Military Rule*, chapter 1, 3–17.
- Green, *We Cannot Remain Silent*, introduction and prologue, 1–18.
- Langland, *Speaking of Flowers*, 1–60.

Primary Documents (approx. 24 pages):

- Document No. 1: Jânio Quadros, "Brazil's New Foreign Policy," *Foreign Affairs* 40, no. 1 (1961): 19–27.

- Document No. 2: Tad Szulc, "Northeast Brazil Poverty Breeds Threat of a Revolt," *New York Times*, October 31, 1960.
- Document No. 3: Editorial, "The 'Fidelists' of Brazil," *New York Times*, November 1, 1960.
- Document No. 4: Tad Szulc, "Marxists Are Organizing Peasants in Brazil: Leftist League Aims at a Political Army 40 Million Strong," *New York Times*, November 1, 1960.
- Document No. 5: Leonard Gross, "How Red Is Brazil," *Look Magazine*, May 21, 1963.

Recommended Reading (for the enthusiast):

o   Skidmore, *Politics in Brazil, 1930–1964*, 205–330.

Out of classroom viewing of *The Day That Lasted 21 Years* (2013), director Camilo Tavares.

Two-page film reflection sent to me.

See Document No. 6 for US State Department documents cited in documentary.

(Double-spaced, original title, student's name.) Please send in Word with your last name and the short film title as the file name: e.g., Green—21 Years.

BB *Brazilian Biographies #1* (Group I and II): Name, social class, race, gender, origin, profession, political ideology, family history, etc. What is your character's attitude to the Goulart regime?

Week #3 The 1964 Coup d'état
Seminar Discussion
(Readings and *The Day That Lasted 21 Years*)

Historiographic Debate: Was the role of the US government in supporting the coup essential for its success? What do we call the new regime? Is it a military dictatorship, a civilian-military dictatorship, a fascist regime, an authoritarian regime?

Discussion of *The Day That Lasted 21 Years*. To what extent does the focus of attention on US participation in the 1964 military coup obscure the role of Brazilians?

Economic Forum No. 2: What were the economic problems facing the new regime government? (Skidmore, *Politics of Military Rule*, 29–38).

Economic Forum Discussion

Secondary Source Readings (94 pages):

- Green, *We Cannot Remain Silent*, chap. 1, 19–48.
- Skidmore, *Politics of Military Rule*, chap. 2, 18–45.
- Article No. 1: W. Michael Weis, "Government News Management, Bias and Distortion in American Press Coverage of the Brazilian Coup of 1964," *Social Science Journal* 34, no. 1 (1997): 35–55.

- Article No. 2: Jan Knippers Black, "Lincoln Gordon and Brazil's Military Counterrevolution," in *Ambassadors in Foreign Policy: The Influence of Individuals on U.S.-Latin American Policy*, ed. C. Neale Ronning and Albert P. Vannucci (New York: Prager, 1987): 95–113.

Primary Source Documents (approx. 45 pages):

- Document No. 6: "Brazil Marks Fortieth Anniversary of Military Coup," National Security Archive Documents 1–7. Retrieve from http://www.gwu.edu/~nsarchiv/NSAEBB/NSAEBB118/index.htm
- Document No. 7: Clarence W. Hall, "The Country That Saved Itself," *Readers Digest*, November 1964, 35–59.

Recommended Reading (for the enthusiast):

- Alves, *State and Opposition in Military Brazil*, 3–28.

BB *Brazilian Biographies* #2 (Group I and II): What is your character's attitude to the new government? What changes have taken place in her/his life?

Week #4 Castelo Branco and Institutionalizing the Dictatorship (1965–66)
Seminar Discussion

Historiographic Debate: Was Castelo Branco really a "moderate"? Does the "moderate/hard-line" binary work in analyzing the military regime?

Economic Forum No. 3: What is Skidmore's assessment of the economic situation during the Castelo Branco government?

Economic Forum Discussion

Secondary Source Readings (176 pages):

- Skidmore, *Politics of Military Rule*, 46–65.
- Green, *We Cannot Remain Silent*, 49–75.
- Langland, *Speaking of Flowers*, 61–106.
- Green, *Exile within Exiles*, 1–54.
- Pitts, *Until the Storm Passes*, 1–32.

Primary Source Documents (approx. 24 pages):

- Document No. 8: "Institutional Act"
- Document No. 9: "The Inaugural Speech of Castelo Branco."
- Document No. 10: "Ambassador Juracy Magalhães Comments on the Revolution of 1964."
- Document No. 11: Senator Wayne Morse's speeches in the *Congressional Record*.

Recommended Reading (for the enthusiast):

○ Alves, *State and Opposition in Military Brazil*, 29–79.

For next week, please write on TWO films (total of three pages):

Film No. 3: Option A: *O que é isso, companheiro* (*Four Days in September*), dir. Bruno Barreto, 1997.

Recommended Reading: *Film Article No. 2:* Valerie Elbrick Hanlon, "They've Got Your Father," *Washingtonian*, April 1998, 70. See also James N. Green, "Kidnappings of Diplomats and Revolutionary Politics in Authoritarian Brazil: The Tale of Two Films," in *Latin American History at the Movies: The Sequel*, ed. Donald Stevens (Lanham, MD: Rowman and Littlefield, 2022).

Option B: *The Year My Parents Went on Vacation*, dir. Cao Hamburger, 2006.

Recommended Reading: *Film Article No. 3:* Karen Backstein, review of *The Year My Parents Went on Vacation*, *Cinéaste* 33, no. 2 (Spring 2008), 54–55.

Option C: *Marighella* (2019), dir. Wagner Moura.

Recommended Reading: *Film Article No. 4:* James N. Green, "Kidnappings of Diplomats and Revolutionary Politics in Authoritarian Brazil: The Tale of Two Films," in *Latin American History at the Movies: The Sequel*, ed. Donald Stevens (Lanham, MD: Rowman and Littlefield, 2022).

BB *Brazilian Biographies #3A* (Group I, Last name A–K): What is your character's attitude to the 1965 elections? What changes have taken place in her/his life?

Week #5 Costa e Silva: Hard-liner or More of the Same? (1967–69)
Seminar Discussion

Historiographic Debate: Was Costa e Silva "hard-line" in relationship to Castelo Branco or is this a false dichotomy (hard-line/moderate)? How has the dictatorship changed?

Discussion of *Four Days in September/The Year My Parents Went on Vacation/Marighella*. How is the revolutionary left that chose the armed struggle portrayed in these three different films?

Economic Forum No. 4: What is Costa e Silva's new economic policy?

Economic Forum Discussion

Secondary Source Readings (203 pages):

• Skidmore, *Politics of Military Rule*, 66–104.
• Green, *We Cannot Remain Silent*, 77–136.
• Langland, *Speaking of Flowers*, 107–66.

- Green, *Exile in Exiles*, 55–83.
- Pitts, *Until the Storm Passes*, 33–52.

Primary Documents (approx. 6 pages):

- Document No. 12: "Institutional Act No. 5."
- Document No. 13: ALN, MR-8 "Text of Manifesto from Kidnappers of U.S. Ambassador," *New York Times*, September 6, 1969.
- Document No. 14: Editorial, "Terror in Brazil," *New York Times*, September 6, 1969.
- Document No. 15: Joseph Novitski, "Brazil to Free Fifteen to Win Release of U.S. Envoy," *New York Times*, September 6, 1969.

Recommended Reading (for the enthusiast):

- ○ Alves, *State and Opposition in Military Brazil*, 80–100.

For next week: *Film No. 4: Uma noite em 1967 (A Night in 1967)*, dir. Renato Terra and Ricardo Calil, 2010.

BB *Brazilian Biographies #3B* (Group II, Last name L–W): What is your character's attitude toward the student movements of 1968, Institutional Act No. 5, the forced retirement of professors from the university? What has changed in her/his life?

Film reflection on *Uma noite em 1967 (A Night in 1967)*, dir. Renato Terra and Ricardo Calil, 2010.

Week #6 Tropicália and the Brazilian Counterculture (1967–71)
Seminar Discussion
(Discussion of the readings and *Uma noite em 1967*)

Historiographic Debate: Does it make sense to understand Brazilian music of the 1960s as polarized between politically engaged music and "alienated" or nonpolitical music? If so, why? If not, why not?

Secondary Source Reading (228 pages):
- Dunn, *Brutality Gardens* (entire book)

Primary Documents:

- CD No. 1: A selection of music from the 1960s and 1970s (24 songs). A sheet with the words and translations of most of the titles along with links to performances is on the website. Enjoy!

Recommended readings (for the enthusiast):

- ○ Veloso, Caetano. *Tropical Truth: A Story of Music and Revolution in Brazil.* Translated by Isabel de Sena. New York: Alfred A. Knopf, 2002.

○   McGowan, Chris, and Ricardo Pessanha. *The Brazilian Sound: Samba, Bossa Nova and the Popular Music of Brazil*. Philadelphia: Temple University Press, 1998.

BB *Brazilian Biographies #4A* (Group I): What is your character's relationship to Brazilian popular music, *tropicália*, the Beatles, hippies, the contracultural, and US music?

Week #7 Médici: "Years of Lead" and the "Economic Miracle" (1969–73)
Seminar Discussion

Historiographic Debate: How can we characterize the Médici government? What was life like for "ordinary people" during these years?

Economic Forum No. 5: What were the economic bases for the "miracle"? Was the "economic miracle" essential for the legitimacy of the Médici government?

Economic Forum Discussion

Secondary Source Readings (230 pages):

• Skidmore, *Politics of Military Rule*, 105–59.
• Langland, *Speaking of Flowers*, 167–214.
• Green, *Exile within Exiles*, 84–153.
• Pitts, *Until the Storm Passes*, 53–80.
• Article No. 3: Kenneth P. Serbin, "The Anatomy of a Death: Repression, Human Rights, and the Case of Alexandre Vannucchi Leme in Authoritarian Brazil," *Journal of Latin American Studies* 30, no. 1 (1998): 1–33.

Recommended Reading (for the enthusiast)

○   Alves, *State and Opposition in Military Brazil*, 101–38.
○   Serbin, Kenneth P. *Secret Dialogues: Church-State Relations, Torture, and Social Justice in Authoritarian Brazil*. Pittsburgh: University of Pittsburgh Press, 2000.

BB *Brazilian biography #4B* (Group II): How does your character relate to the armed struggle/terrorist movements, the economic situation, the Médici government?

Recommended viewing of *Brazil: A Report on Torture* (dir. Saul Landau, 1971).

Warning: This film was shot in Chile in 1971 with former political prisoners released in exchange for the freedom of the kidnapped Swiss ambassador. (You will encounter some of the characters—Dedora, Marcos, Jean Marc—in seminar readings.) They describe and demonstrate the methods of torture they endured in Brazil. Many students find these enactments upsetting, so you should view the film with these considerations in mind. *It is not required viewing*, but recommended if you can tolerate the graphic descriptions of torture.

Week #8 The International Campaign against the Dictatorship, Part I:
Torture, (1969–73)
Seminar Discussion

Historiographic Debate: To what extent did the international campaign against the dictatorship have an effect (or not) on the regime's human rights policies? For those of you who watched *Brazil: A Report on Torture*, how effective do you think it is as a means of raising interest in the situation in Brazil?

Brief in-seminar training on how to use the Opening the Archives database and discussion of other possible research paper topics

Secondary Source Readings (194 pages):

- Green, *We Cannot Remain Silent*, 137–232.
- Sattamini, *A Mother's Cry* (introduction, 1–99).

Primary Documents (12 pages):

- Document No. 16. Ralph Della Cava, "Torture in Brazil," *Commonweal*, April 24, 1970, and exchange with Lincoln Gordon.
- Document No. 17. Lincoln Gordon, "Letter to the Editor," *Commonweal*, August 7, 1970, and Ralph Della Cava, "Reply."

View for next class: *Film No. 5: Dzi croquettes*, dir. Tatiana Issa and Raphael Alvarez, 2009.

Recommended Reading: *Film Article No. 5:* David William Foster, review of *Dzi Croquettes*, *Chasqui* 39, no. 2 (2010): 243–44.

BB *Brazilian Biographies* #5A (Group I): What is your character's relationship to news of torture and repression in Brazil?

Week #9 Spring Break: No class

Week #10 Geisel: The Slow-Motion Return to Democratic Rule (1974–79)
Seminar Discussion

(Discussion of readings and the film *Dzi Croquettes*)

Historiographic Debate: How do we understand the return to democratic rule? Was it a top-down process initiated by the military or a bottom-up process reflected in the electoral defeat of ARENA in 1974 and the emergence of new social movements? Or was it a combination of both? If so, what was that dynamic? How did the MDB manage to channel much of the legal opposition to the regime?

Dzi Croquettes: What does this film tell us about changes in notions of gender and the process of liberalization in Brazil under Geisel?

Economic Forum No. 6: What are the factors that lead to Geisel's economic woes? How does he address them?

Economic Forum Discussion

Secondary Source Readings (215 pages):

- Skidmore, *Politics of Military Rule*, 160–209.
- Green, *We Cannot Remain Silent*, 233–92.
- Green, *Exile within Exiles*, 154–205.
- Pitts, *Until the Storm Passes*, 81–124.

Primary Documents (approx. 10 pages):

- Document No. 18: Editors, *Nós Mulheres*, "Second-Wave Brazilian Feminism," in *The Brazil Reader*, 479-80.
- Document No. 19: Aguinaldo Silva, "LGBT Rights and Democracy," in *The Brazil Reader*, 481–83.
- Document No. 20: Various authors, "The Movement for Political Amnesty," in *The Brazil Reader*, 484–85.

Recommended Reading (for the enthusiast):

- Alves, *State and Opposition in Military Brazil*, 139–251.

BB *Brazilian Biography #5B* (Group II): What are your character's attitudes toward the *abertura* process? How did she/he vote in the 1974 elections?

Week #11 The International Campaign against the Dictatorship, Part II: Beyond Torture (1971–79)
Seminar Discussion

Historiographic Debate: To what extend did the shift in US policy toward Brazil actually have an effect on the internal politics in Brazil? What other issues were raised?

Secondary Source Readings (163 pages):

- Green, *We Cannot Remain Silent*, 233–320.
- Sattamini, *A Mother's Cry*, 100–176.

Primary Documents (approximately 20 pages):

- Document No. 21 (A-D): Selections, *Brazilian Information Bulletin*, 1971–75.
- Document No. 22: Richard M. Morse, Thomas E. Skidmore, Alfred Stepan, Stanley Stein, and Charles Wagley, Letters to the Editor: "Brazil: The Sealed Coffin," *New York Review of Books*, November 27, 1975.

- Document No. 23: *Brazilian Labor Information and Resource Bulletin*, 1980.

Film No. 6: Option A: *Diário de uma busca*, dir. Flavia Castro, 2010; Option B: *Fico te devendo uma carta sobre o Brasil*, dir. Carol Benjamin, 2019.

Week #12 Figueiredo: Liberalization, Strikes, and a Return to Democracy (1979–85)
Seminar Discussion

Historiographic Debate: Was political *conciliação* (conciliation), including the 1979 Amnesty Law, the only way to achieve an exit from military rule? What was the role of the strike wave on the return to democracy? What is the nature of the transition to democracy?

Diário de uma busca, dir. Flavia Castro, 2010; *Fico te devendo uma carta sobre o Brasil*, dir. Carol Benjamin, 2019. What is the relationship of these films to the process of democratization, reconciliation, and memory?

Economic Forum No. 7: What is the relationship between Brazil's economic situation and the process of *abertura*?

Economic Forum Discussion

Secondary Source Readings (128 pages):

- Skidmore, *Politics of Military Rule*, 210–55.
- Langland, *Speaking of Flowers*, 215–48.
- Green, *Exile within Exiles*, 206–66.

Week #13 The Citizens' Constitution and the Legacies of the Military Regime
Seminar Discussion

Historiographic Debate: Why is the Constitution of 1988 called the Citizens' Constitution? What are the progressive provisions in the constitution? What changed, and what stayed the same? How are the legacies of the dictatorship still manifested in Brazil? In what ways were the Constituent Assembly and the Constitution democratic?

Secondary Source Readings (130 pages):

- Pitts, *Until the Storm Passes*, 125–80.
- Article No. 4: Daniel McDonald, "Making the 'Citizen Constitution': Popular Participation in the Brazilian Transition to Democracy, 1985–1988," *The Americas* 79, no. 4 (2022): 619–52.
- Article No. 5: Jorge Zaverucha, "The 1988 Brazilian Constitution and Its Authoritarian Legacy: Formalizing Democracy While Gutting Its Essence," *Journal of Third World Studies* 15, no. 1 (1998): 105–24.

- Article No. 6: André Pagliarini, "'De onde? Para onde?': The Continuity Question and the Debate over Brazil's 'Civil'-Military Dictatorship," *Latin American Research Review* 52, no. 5 (2017): 760–74.

James N. Green is the Carlos Manuel de Céspedes Professor Emeritus of Latin American History and Professor Emeritus of Brazilian History and Culture at Brown University, where he directed the Center for Latin American and Caribbean Studies (2005–2009) and the Brazil Initiative (2012–2022). He is the author of four monographs and coeditor of eight collections on Brazilian history. The former president and executive director of the Brazilian Studies Association (BRASA), Green currently serves as the president of the board of directors of the Washington Brazil Office (WBO), a nonpartisan advocacy group and think tank that works with Brazilian social movements and non-government organizations in developing international articulations of their sociopolitical agendas.

Notes

1. The collection is available online through the Brown Digital Repository, https://library .brown.edu/create/openingthearchives/en/.
2. Green, *We Cannot Remain Silent*; Sattamini, *A Mother's Cry*.
3. Langland, *Speaking of Flowers*; Green, *Exile within Exiles*.
4. Pitts, *Until the Storm Passes*.
5. *Diário de uma busca* (*Diary of a Search*; dir. Flávia Castro, 2010); *Fico te devendo uma carta sobre o Brasil* (*I Owe You a Letter about Brazil*; dir. Carol Benjamin, 2019).
6. Dunn, *Brutality Garden*; *Uma noite em 1967* (*A Night in 1967*; dir. Renato Terra and Ricardo Calil, 2010).
7. Opening the Archives: Documenting US-Brazil Relations 1960s–80s, https://library .brown.edu/create/openingthearchives/en/.
8. Please acknowledge the source of ideas from this course syllabus are used in preparing and teaching a seminar about the Brazilian dictatorship.

References

Dunn, Christopher. *Brutality Garden: Tropicália and the Emergence of a Brazilian Counterculture*. Chapel Hill: University of North Carolina Press, 2001.

Green, James N. *Exile within Exiles: Herbert Daniel, Gay Brazilian Revolutionary*. Durham, NC: Duke University Press, 2018.

Green, James N. *We Cannot Remain Silent: Opposition to the Brazilian Military Dictatorship in the United States*. Durham, NC: Duke University Press, 2009.

Langland, Victoria. *Speaking of Flowers: Student Movements and the Making and Remembering of 1968 in Military Brazil*. Durham, NC: Duke University Press, 2013.

Pitts, Bryan. *Until the Storm Passes: Politicians, Democracy, and the Demise of Brazil's Military Dictatorship*. Berkeley: University of California Press, 2023.

Sattamini, Lina Penna. *A Mother's Cry: A Memoir of Politics, Prison, and Torture under the Brazilian Military Dictatorship*. Introduction by James N. Green; translated by Rex P. Nielson and James N. Green; epilogue by Marcos P. S. Arruda. Durham, NC: Duke University Press, 2010.

Skidmore, Thomas E. *The Politics of Military Rule in Brazil, 1964–85*. New York: Oxford University Press, 1988.

Teaching the History of Development

Jacob Blanc

Until two years ago, I was only nominally a scholar of development. My first book was about the world's largest hydroelectric dam, but I was far more interested in the political movements and livelihoods of those displaced by the dam than I was by the construction, energy, or geopolitical implications of the dam itself. And although each of my subsequent books also had development-adjacent themes (nationalism, political change, dictatorship, transitional justice), the vagueness of the term *development* meant that I could invoke it when it suited but never had to confront its deeper meanings or histories.

In June 2023, I left the University of Edinburgh after six years and accepted a new position at McGill University in Montreal. My position was part of a spousal hire, which was facilitated by an agreement for me to hold a joint appointment between the Department of History and Classical Studies (HCS) and the Institute for the Study of International Development (ISID). On the heels of several years of uncertainty trying to solve our "two body problem," I would have accepted any faculty appointment if it allowed my family to be in the same city and institution. Needless to say, I was thrilled. But I was also a bit uneasy, in no small measure because I had to design a new course on the history of development. I was the first full-time historian in ISID, making a history of development an obvious course for me to offer.

I did what every historian does at the start of a new project: I went to the archives, which in this case meant Google searching for sample syllabi and checking out library books related to histories of development. There was no shortage of

Radical History Review
Issue 151 (January 2025)   DOI 10.1215/01636545-11506875
© 2025 by MARHO: The Radical Historians' Organization, Inc.

material to take inspiration from, and as I compiled my corpus of texts, I sought to design a course that would both be interesting for me to teach (thereby making the newness of everything seem less daunting) and appeal to students in the development studies program. Given that most of the students would not be history majors, I saw this as an opportunity to show students different histories, vocabularies, and case studies of development, while at the same time exposing them to the intricacies of the discipline of history. How do historians ask questions? What kinds of evidence can we compile to answer those questions? And what does it means to write analytically about the past in a way that honors the challenges of the present?

In a certain way, I reverse-engineered the course. Normally I design a syllabus first by mapping out the weekly readings and thematic sections, and only once that structure is in place do I construct the graded assignments. But here, I knew early on that I wanted the final project to be what I called a "history and practice report." This capstone project requires students to adopt the role of a consultant hired by an international aid organization and to present at least two historical case studies in order to make a set of policy recommendations around a chosen theme: for example, gender, poverty, agriculture, health, or the environment. My goal was for students to engage seriously with how to conduct historical research and then present their analysis with an eye toward contemporary issues.

I incorporated the final assignment into the progression of the course through several features. First, by also assigning three primary source assignments, in which students had to write a short (400–500 words) reflection on a document from a list that I provided for every lecture. By helping students contextualize a source, analyze its content, and situate it in the themes of a given week, the course scaffolded the skills that students would need to write an effective final project.

The curation of the primary source lists was the hardest and most time-consuming aspect of building this course. I aimed to give between three and seven sources for each lecture (twice a week) and to have the sources represent a broad range of regions, authors, positionings, and historical perspectives. This was a challenge in a new course. For my normal rotation of Latin American history classes, I already have a series of primary source lists that I have compiled over the years. For a new and entirely global course, I was starting from scratch.

Here, the written assignments again served as a catalyst for fleshing out the structure and content of the course. It was at this point, while preparing the list of primary sources, that I started mapping out the weekly assigned readings and, by extension, the framework of what I would lecture on. I did not provide primary sources for the first two weeks—that is the add/drop period at McGill, during which time no assignments can be given, and I also wanted those initial weeks to introduce students to the course and the major themes, narratives, and periodizations of the course. (Though for weeks one and two, I did assign "hybrid" readings that were both primary and secondary sources: chapters from Walter Rodney's 1972 *How Europe Underdeveloped Africa* and Edward Said's 1979 *Orientalism*). But from week three onward, I needed to prepare two weekly sets of primary sources. So I worked backward, locating primary sources that were digitally available (or could be scanned by our librarians), and then choosing readings that would complement the sources. I figured that there was essentially a limitless number of fascinating secondary sources from a range of academic disciplines that I could assign, and that it would thus be more engaging (for students) and productive (for their exercise in working as historians) to give priority to the primary sources.

In week three, for example, which was the start of the primary source options, a digital database shared with me by McGill's excellent resource librarian, Dr. Kristen Howard, gave several options for newspapers in the late nineteenth century from colonial India. These sources showed news articles, editorials, and a variety of advertisements showing sporting events, products for sale, and classifieds. These were great sources, but they of course also showed a thoroughly top-down view. I paired these colonial sources with a selection of Mahatma Gandhi's 1909 text *Hind Swaraj; or, Indian Home Rule*, allowing for alternative perspectives on life in that period and also counternarratives about how to enact "change" and "improvement." And it was only then, once I had a set of three primary sources, that I chose the assigned reading for that day, David Arnold's article on agriculture and improvement in early colonial India, which I found to be an excellent example of what the author explicitly treats as a "pre-history" of development.

I took a similar source-first approach to most weeks. A rich selection of documents relating to labor in Africa from the 1890s and early 1900s (touching on themes of technology, geography, and local social/kindship structures), then pointed me toward a chapter from Helen Tilley's book *Africa as a Living Laboratory*. Building the course in this manner remained useful even after the opening section on colonialism. For week eight's theme of "Development from and for the Global South," I knew that I wanted to focus on the Bandung Conference of 1955, and I was able to find several reports from participants of that global summit as well as those of subsequent meetings of anti-imperialist and pro-"third worldist" attempts to reorient the global financial and political sectors. These included reports from what became the Group of 77, the United Nations Commission on Trade and Development, and also South-South solidarity movements such as the Black Panthers' support for independence in Algeria. The idea here, as throughout the course, is to help students rethink their assumptions about what development is, who the "implementors/interveners" are, as well as the "recipients," and what languages are available for articulating different visions of how to improve society. In that vein, many of the weeks have a primary source from W. E. B. Du Bois, taken from a recently published anthology of his writings on the theme of "international thought." The inclusion of Du Bois was meant to show students that questions of development are not the sole purview of the Global South but have also operated within the Global North, including as a tool and logic for economic and social liberation for historically marginalized groups.

Admittedly, not all of the assigned readings emerged from a source-first approach. There were several secondary texts that I always planned on using, such as Priya Lal's work on gender and *ujamaa* in postcolonial Tanzania, as well as Nick Cullather's research on the green revolution. In those cases, I then collected primary sources around the respective themes of postcolonial development/self-help and agricultural technology and modernization. And in two instances, I also assigned secondary readings from scholars whom I know personally and could ask to share primary sources from their own research which I could then give to students. These were publications by Emily Brownell (on the built environment in Dar es Salaam) and Nicole Bourbonnais (on the early history of global family planning). These pairings were among the most productive (and fun) for students, as we were able to see behind the curtain and directly analyze the types of documents that scholars used as the basis of the academic texts we were reading.

Among the many challenges of this course was how to balance a chronological and thematic progression. Especially because we would essentially be covering all of the world, there was inevitably going to be a lot of bouncing around from week to week. There is a rough chronology that starts in the 1880s (the Berlin Conference of 1884, which sparked the so-called Scramble for Africa) and ends in the present day, but in the span of a week or two, we also go backward in time, sometimes retracing the same periods covered in earlier weeks. To ease what might otherwise be a disorienting progression, whenever possible I tried to ground those "step-back" examples in case studies that we had already covered. So even if the chronology was sometimes a roller coaster, the regional coverage provided some familiarity. And with a consistent focus on the narratives of development and how certain vocabularies have, or have not, changed over time, each week also had a specific theme. Examples of these weekly themes are "Colonialism, Science, and the Civilizing Mission"; "Postwar Planning and Development"; "Global Finance and Multilateralism"; "The Countryside"; "Cities"; "Economists with Guns"; and "Money without Borders." Gradually, across each week, we made our way through the twentieth century.

Regarding the central theme of this issue of *Radical History Review*— economic miracles and their afterlives—my course grappled with a key tension not just for historians of development (for whom economic booms and busts are a central story) but above all for students interested in the development sector. When reflecting on the nature of an economic "miracle"—for example, by asking who benefits from a miracle, for how long, and who even has the power to label a miracle as such—one sees strong parallels with how historians can approach the study of development. This line of thinking can naturally lead to the question of whether a critical understanding of development means discarding the idea of development in its entirety. In the course, we study the work of scholars who have explicitly called for this approach, the so-called post-development scholars, who argue that development is nothing more than a dressed-up version of (neo)colonial exploitation. This includes readings and lecture discussions about the work of scholars such as Arturo Escobar, Chandra Mohanty, Gayatri Spivak, and James Scott, among others. Providing that perspective is an important pillar in the conceptual framework of the course. But I also know that students want to go out into the world feeling capable of changing it, and in those instances, we need to consider the history of development through from the perspective of an emerging generation of future scholars and practitioners.

Influenced by the pedagogical approach of my wife, Isabel Pike—herself a sociologist of development—I tell my students that our goal can be to remain *critical* but not *pessimistic*. I also tell them that my job is not to give them a template for how to do development well—or even how to do it poorly. To be sure, the course leans toward more critical examples of development (pointing out the contradictions and hierarchical dimensions of everything from colonialism to the United Nations and neoliberal trade policy). Yet I found that students also connected strongly to examples where efforts at improving society were made, if not perfectly, then at least with a broader consideration of all potential stakeholders—doing the least amount of harm while trying to do good. A low bar, perhaps, but one which nonetheless stands out. Yes, students are eager to show their criticisms of neoliberalism, colonialism, and their legacies, but they are also eager for examples from which to draw motivation. I might even say they thirst for such examples.

The history of development, like all histories, offers countless lessons for how to change (or conversely, how not to change) society. Sometimes the point of a class is to study history just for its own sake, without having to show its "relevance" to the contemporary world. Sometimes teaching history is so obviously pressing for the current world that students and professors alike opt in to a constant mode of presentism. And sometimes a course can swing between the two. A class in the history of development seems like a great example of the latter: it explores a broad range of case studies from across the globe in a way that does justice to those histories on their own terms but also builds a steady trajectory of how development—as a practice, an ideology, a vocabulary—grew into one of the defining features of the contemporary world.

History of Development
McGill University
Winter semester 2024
Course Outline
This course looks at the origins, context, and practices of development from a historical perspective. It locates the beginning of international development in colonial times and examines how ideas of economic progress and social welfare evolved from imperial settings to the UN system, and how it continued to spread to areas such as foreign aid, trade, and philanthropy. The course will examine relevant episodes in

the conceptualization of international development such as interwar planning and social engineering, as well as Cold War modernizing missions and green revolutions. It will explore cases of development policies created by actors in the Global North aimed at the Global South, but it will give equal importance to the ideologies, practices, and networks developed within and between countries in the South. Themes will include, among others, colonialism, gender, race, economic growth, poverty, geopolitics, multilateralism, foreign aid, South-South relations, philanthropy, and the environment.

Paying close attention to the shifting institutional landscapes of development and to continuity and change in the configuration of its actors and subjects, the course seeks to bring depth and nuance to our understanding of contemporary development practices. We will ask: How and why did development emerge and become a goal of policy and a tool of intervention? How have development ideas, policies, and practices been shaped by changing ideological or geopolitical imperatives? The goal of this course is to make students familiar with a wide range of cases spanning roughly the past one hundred years, and to gain a familiarity with the historical trajectory of modern development practices.

Course Requirements
History and practice report (due April 10): 32%
Midterm exam: 20%
Final exam: 30%
Attendance: 6%
Primary-source analysis: three x 4%, 12% total

Primary Source Analysis, three x 4%, 12% total
In addition to the assigned weekly articles and chapter readings, students will also be provided with a list of primary sources. Each student will be required to write three short responses (min. 300 words, max. 500, double-spaced, 12-point font), which critically analyze the particular source.

More than just a summary of the information presented in the primary source, the response must analyze its connection to the themes and events covered in class that week:

- Who produced the document? Why? Who was the intended audience?
- In addition to analyzing the meanings of the document itself, students must place it in dialogue with the themes for that week, including the assigned academic reading.
- How does the primary source deepen our understanding of the themes for the week? And, if relevant, how does the source deepen our understanding of the course as a whole?

Technical requirements of this assignment:

- The word count must be included at the top of the page.
- Minimum of 300 words and maximum of 500. No exceptions.
- All referenced content (direct quotations and also indirect paraphrasing) must be properly cited.
- The assignment must be submitted prior to the relevant lecture.

Submissions will receive only one of three potential grades: 95, 75, or 55. This corresponds to an assessment of *exceeds expectations*, *meets expectations*, or *does not meet expectations*.

History and Practice Report

How can history help inform current development practices? To answer this question, you must write a report as if you were a historical consultant hired by a contemporary development organization.

First, you must choose one of the following four organizations as your "client":

1. United Nations Development Program
2. The World Bank
3. The Gates Foundation
4. Canadian International Development Platform

Second, you must choose one of the following themes as the main focus of your report:

1. Gender
2. Poverty
3. Trade
4. Political sovereignty
5. Agriculture
6. Urban planning
7. Reproductive rights
8. Health
9. Energy
10. The environment

In a report of between 1,500 and 2,000 words, you must explain to the development organization how a historical perspective can help address contemporary challenges related to your chosen theme.

This requires that you:

- Show an awareness of the goals and structures of the development organization itself, e.g., you must also research the organization, so that your report is tailored to a particular audience.

- Draw on at least two historical examples; this can be from the course readings and lectures, or from your own outside research.
- Discuss the examples with an eye toward analyzing the policies that had been implemented, the rationale at the time for why those interventions were pursued, the challenges faced, and the results/consequences.
- The report must end with an outline of at least three policy recommendations, informed by your analysis of the historical case studies.

Academic Integrity

"McGill University values academic integrity. Therefore, all students must understand the meaning and consequences of cheating, plagiarism and other academic offences under the Code of Student Conduct and Disciplinary Procedures (see www.mcgill.ca/students/srr/honest/ for more information). (approved by Senate on 29 January 2003) / "L'université McGill attache une haute importance à l'honnêteté académique. Il incombe par conséquent à tous les étudiants de comprendre ce que l'on entend par tricherie, plagiat et autres infractions académiques, ainsi que les conséquences que peuvent avoir de telles actions, selon le Code de conduite de l'étudiant et des procédures disciplinaires (pour de plus amples renseignements, veuillez consulter le site www.mcgill.ca/students/srr/honest/)."

Language

"In accord with McGill University's Charter of Students' Rights, students in this course have the right to submit in English or in French any written work that is to be graded." (approved by Senate on 21 January 2009—see also the section in this document on Assignments and evaluation.) / "Conformément à la Charte des droits de l'étudiant de l'Université McGill, chaque étudiant a le droit de soumettre en français ou en anglais tout travail écrit devant être noté (sauf dans le cas des cours dont l'un des objets est la maîtrise d'une langue)."

Il me ferait plaisir de vous adresser en français par courriel ou en personne.

Course Outline
Week 1: Introduction
History, Practice, and Concepts of Development
Cullather, Nick. "Development? It's History." *Diplomatic History* 24, no. 4 (2000): 641–53.

Week 2: History of Development, Development as History
Inventing Development, Conceptualizing Inequality
Cooper, Frederick. "Writing the History of Development." *Journal of Modern European History* 8, no. 1 (2010): 5–23.

Post-development? Postcolonial, Postmodern, and Feminist Critiques

- Rodney, Walter. "Colonialism as a System for Underdeveloping Africa." In *How Europe Underdeveloped Africa*, chap. 6, part I. Washington, DC: Howard University Press, 1972.
- Said, Edward W. 1979. *Orientalism*. 1st Vintage Books ed. New York: Vintage Books. "Knowing the Oriental," 31–48.

Week 3: Colonialism, Science, and the Civilizing Mission
The Roots of Colonialism
Arnold, David. "Agriculture and 'Improvement' in Early Colonial India: A Prehistory of Development." *Journal of Agrarian Change* 5, no. 4 (2005): 505–25.

Primary sources:

Hind Swaraj; or, Indian Home Rule, M. K. Gandhi, 1909, "What Is Swaraj?"
Newspapers from colonial India:

  o *Baluchistan Gazette*, March 14, 1891.
  o *The Pioneer*, March 10, 1891.

Colonialism, Knowledge, and Power
Tilley, Helen. *Africa as a Living Laboratory: Empire, Development, and the Problem of Scientific Knowledge, 1870–1950*. Chicago: University of Chicago Press, 2011. Chap. 1, 31–68.

Primary sources:

- *The Native Labour Question in South Africa*, 1900.
- Carl Peters, *Lecture on the Future of Africa*, 1897.
- *Emigration to Liberia*, American Colonization Society, 1883.
- Général Gallieni, *Madagascar: Chemins de fer, routes et sentiers*, 1900.
- Marcus Garvey, *Explanation of the Objectives of the Universal Negro Improvement Association*, 1921.

Week 4: Colonialism and the Social Order
Gender, Family, and Health
Burton, Antoinette. *Burdens of History: British Feminists, Indian Women, and Imperial Culture, 1865–1915*. Chapel Hill: University of North Carolina Press, 1994. Chap. 3, "Female Emancipation and the Other Woman."

Primary sources:

- "Behind the Purdah, the Lives and Legends of our Hindu Sisters," Milly Cattell, 1916.
- "Hindoo Female Education," Priscilla Chapman, 1909.

- *The Diary of a Civilian's Wife in India, 1877–1882*, by Mrs. Robert Moss King.
- "To the Girls at Home, from One of the Girls," Eva M. Swift, 1888.

Religion and Morality

Daughton, J. P. *An Empire Divided: Religion, Republicanism, and the Making of French Colonialism, 1880–1914*. Oxford: Oxford University Press, 2006. Chap. 4, "Silent Sisters in the South Seas."

Primary sources:

- *Missionary Landscapes in the Dark Continent*, James Johnston, 1892.
- *Life of Mrs. Ann H. Judson, Late Missionary to Burmah; with an Account of the American Baptist Mission to That Empire*, 1830.
- *Remarks on the "Tour around Hawaii," by the Missionaries, Messers. Ellis, Thurston, Bishop, and Goodrich, in 1823*.
- "Evangelistic Efforts for the Women of India," Mrs. M. E. Bissell, 1893.

Week 5: Postwar Planning and Development

Postwar Middle East

Norris, Jacob. "Development and Disappointment: Arab Approaches to Economic Development in Mandate Palestine." In *The Routledge Handbook of the History of the Middle East Mandates*, edited by Cyrus Schayegh and Andrew Arsan, 275–90. New York: Routledge, 2015.

Primary sources:

- W. E. B. Du Bois, *The African Roots of War*, 1915.
- Palestine Railways, poster, 1922.
- Palestine crafts and industries exhibition, poster, 1922.
- With Allenby in Palestine, poster, 1923.
- Carmel Oriental advertisement, 1925.

Postwar Latin America

Marino, Katherine M. "A New Force in the History of the World." In *Feminism for the Americas: The Making of an International Human Rights Movement*. Chapel Hill: University of North Carolina Press, 2019. Chap. 1, 13–39.

Primary sources:

- Abella de Ramírez, "Basic Plan for a Vindication of the Rights of Women," 1906.
- Ernestina A. López, "What Feminists Stand For," 1910.
- Paulina Luisi, "A Call for Solidarity of the Sexes and Social Classes," 1936.
- W. E. B. Du Bois, *To the World (Manifesto of the Second Pan-African Congress)*, 1921.

Week 6: The Post-WWII Global Order

Reconstruction, Underdevelopment, and the United Nations

Reinisch, Jessica. "'Auntie UNRRA' at the Crossroads." *Past and Present* 218, suppl. 8 (2013): 70–97.

Primary sources:

- Charter of the United Nations and Statute of the International Court of Justice, 1945.
- United Nations Universal Declaration of Human Rights, 1948.
- National Film Board, *Mexico Today*, 1947.
- CEPAL documents:
  o *The Social Development of Latin America in the Post-war Period*, 1963.
  o *Economic Development in Latin America, Sociological Considerations*, Echavarría, 1963.
  o *The Textile Industry in Latin America*, 1964.

Foreign Aid

Campbell-Miller, Jill. "Encounter and Apprenticeship: The Colombo Plan and Canadian Aid in India, 1950–1960." In *A Samaritan State Revisited: Historical Perspectives on Canadian Foreign Aid*, edited by Greg Donaghy and David Webster, 27–52. Calgary: University of Calgary Press, 2020.

Primary sources:

- Canadian House of Commons, May 15, 1952, relating to Plan Colombo.
- "US Is Favorable to Colombo Plan." *Montreal Gazette*, February 21, 1951, p. 10.
- "Three Plants Share India Aid Scheme." *Windsor Daily Star*, September 25, 1952, pp. 3, 12.

Week 7: Global Finance and Multilateralism

Bretton Woods and the International System

Helleiner, Eric. "Silences of Bretton Woods: Gender Inequality, Racial Discrimination, and Environmental Degradation." *Review of International Political Economy* 30, no. 5 (2023): 1701–22.

Primary sources:

- Bretton Woods attendees list.
- Questions and Answers on the Bank for Reconstruction and Development, June 10, 1944.
- Minutes of Executive Plenary Session, July 20, 1944.
- First Meeting, Commission I, Purposes, Policies, and Quotas of the Fund, July 4, 1944.

Development Banks and Financial Organizations
Guest lecture by Bart Edes (ISID Professor of Practice).
Goldman, Michael. *Imperial Nature: The World Bank and Struggles for Social Justice in the Age of Globalization*. New Haven, CT: Yale University Press, 2005. Chap. 2, "The Rise of the Bank," 46–99.

Primary sources:

Examples of World Bank loan documents:

- World Bank, report on Bokaro-Konar Project loan application, 1950.
- World Bank, loan application report, Guayas Highway Project, 1954.
- World Bank loan report, Burma Railway Project, 1956.
- World Bank, loan agreement with Iran, 1957.

Week 8: Development from and for the Global South
South-South Visions
Prakash, Gyan, and Jeremy Adelman. "Introduction, Imagining the Third World: Genealogies of Alternative Global Histories." In *Inventing the Third World: In Search of Freedom for the Postwar Global South*, edited by Gyan Prakash and Jeremy Adelman, 7–27. New York: Bloomsbury, 2002.

Primary sources:

- W. E. B. Du Bois, *Black Africa Tomorrow*, 1938.
- "Report from the Chinese Foreign Ministry, 'The Asian-African Conference,'" April 1, 1955, Bandung Conference.
- Joint Declaration of the Developing Countries made at the eighteenth session of the General Assembly, November 11, 1963.
- *Towards a New Trade Policy for Development*, aka the Prebisch report, 1964.
- The UN Development Decade, proposals for action, 1962.
- Charter of Algiers, 1967.
- *Black Panther News* 3, no. 18, August 9, 1969. Issue on Algeria.
- Lima Declaration and Plan of Action on Industrial Development and Co-operation, 1975.

Decolonization and Independence
Lal, Priya. "Militants, Mothers, and the National Family: *Ujamaa*, Gender, and Rural Development in Postcolonial Tanzania." *Journal of African History* 51, no. 1 (2010): 1–20.

Primary sources:

- W. E. B. Du Bois, "The Realities in Africa: European Profit or Negro Development?,"
- by the president of the All-African Convention, 1950.

- FRELIMO, Mozambique Liberation Front Constitution, 1962.
- American Committee on Africa, 1962 report.
- *Ten Years toward African Freedom*, 1964 bulletin.
- *New Perspectives on Sub-Saharan Africa*, 1962 pamphlet.
- CIA book review of Kwame Nkrumah, *Neo-colonialism, the Last Stage of Imperialism*, 1965.
- The Arusha Declaration, TANU, 1967.

Week 9: The Countryside
Rural Development
Cullather, Nick. "Miracles of Modernization: The Green Revolution and the Apotheosis of Technology." *Diplomatic History* 28, no. 2 (2004): 227–54.

Primary sources:

- 1968 speech by William S. Gaud coining the term "Green Revolution."
- Paarlberg, Don. *Norman Borlaug, Hunger Fighter*. Washington, DC: Foreign Economic Development Service, U.S. Dept. of Agriculture, 1970.
- Rockefeller Archive Center, "Photo Essay: Mexico and the Launch of the Green Revolution," https://resource.rockarch.org/story/photo-essay-mexico-and-the-launch -of-the-green-revolution/.
- Digitized album documenting "Visit of Dr. N. Borlaug to Indian Institute of Horticultural Research," Bangalore, India, August 1982, https://umedia.lib.umn.edu/item /p16022coll345:82751/p16022coll345:82506?child_index=0&facets%5Bsuper_col lection_name_ss%5D%5B%5D=The%20Green%20Revolution&query=&sidebar _page=1.
- "CIMMYT at 50: Keeping Our Commitments," 2016.
- International Bank for Reconstruction and Development, "An Appraisal of the Development Program of Mexico, Vol III, Annex II, Agriculture," 1964.

Week 10: Cities
Planned Cities and Utopian Visions
Scott, James C. 2008. *Seeing Like a State: How Certain Schemes to Improve the Human Condition Have Failed*. New Haven, CT: Yale University Press. Chap. 4, "The High-Modernist City," 103–46.

Primary sources:

- Ebenezer Howard's Garden City design, 1898.
- Lucio Costa's 1957 master plan for Brasília.
- Photos and designs for Habitat '67.
- PG Patankar, plan for underground railway, Mumbai, 1963.

Construction and the Built Environment

Brownell, Emily. 2020. *Gone to Ground: A History of Environment and Infrastructure in Dar Es Salaam*. Pittsburgh: University of Pittsburgh Press. Chap. 3, 62–90.

Primary sources:

- World Bank, "Project for the Preparation of an Integrated Urban Program for Istanbul, Turkey, 1972."
- Colonial Dar es Salaam District Book, 1948, observations on housing.
- Colonial Dar es Salaam District Book, 1948, "What is a house?"

Week 11: Economists with Guns? The Militarization of Aid

Foreign Aid and Counterinsurgency in Southeast Asia

Trisko Darden, Jessica. 2020. *Aiding and Abetting: U.S. Foreign Assistance and State Violence*. Stanford, CA: Stanford University Press. Chap. 3, "Indonesia," 45–62.

Primary sources:

- Telegram from the US Department of State to the Embassy in Indonesia, October 22, 1965.
- Memo on National Security Council meeting about Indonesia, August 9, 1967.

Week 12: Population and the Global Body

Demographic Interventions

Bourbonnais, Nicole. "The Intimate Labor of Internationalism: Maternalist Humanitarians and the Mid-twentieth-century Family Planning Movement." *Journal of Global History* 17, no. 3 (November 2022): 515–38.

Primary sources:

- Collection of bulletins, *News of Population and Birth Control*, published by the International Planned Parenthood between 1952 and 1962.
- UN Resolution establishing the UN Population Fund, July 11, 1967.
- *Birthing Reproductive Justice: 150 Years of Images and Ideas*, online exhibit, https://apps.lib.umich.edu/online-exhibits/exhibits/show/reproductive-justice.
- National Film Board documentary, 1995, *Who's Counting? Marilyn Waring on Sex, Lies, and Global Economics*, https://www.nfb.ca/film/whos_counting/.

Health on the Front Lines

Jézéquel, Jean-Hervé. "Staging a 'Medical Coup'? Médecins Sans Frontières and the 2005 Food Crisis in Niger." In *Medical Humanitarianism: Ethnographies of Practice*, edited by Sharon Alane Abramowitz and Catherine Panter-Brick, 119–36. Philadelphia: University of Pennsylvania Press, 2015.

Primary sources:

- UN Resolution establishing the World Food Programme on an experimental basis, December 19, 1961.
- Posters from Live Aid concert, 1985.
- UNAID summary booklet of best practices, 2000.
- MSF news release on Peru earthquake, 2001.
- MSF news release, supplies to Afghanistan, October 2001.
- Examples of "Straight Talk," NGO newsletters, Uganda, 2006–9 (English and Luganda).

Week 13: Money without Borders
Free Trade

Trentmann, Frank. "Before 'Fair Trade': Empire, Free Trade, and the Moral Economies of Food in the Modern World." *Environment and Planning D: Society and Space* 25, no. 6 (2007): 1079–102.

Primary sources:

- W. E. B. Du Bois, "A Cup of Cocoa and Chocolate Drops," 1946.
- EZLN Demands at the Dialogue Table, 1994.
- Assorted documents related to WTO protests, Seattle, 1999.
- Assembly of First Nations, "First Nations Trade Relations Overview," December 3, 2018.
- Tina Ngata, "Lessons from Aotearoa: The Indigenous 'Exception' Clause in Free Trade Agreements," February 2019.
- "Fyffes Farms Exposed: The Fight for Justice in the Honduran Melon Fields," 2020.

Philanthropy

Singer, Peter. "Famine, Affluence, and Morality." *Philosophy and Public Affairs* 1, no. 3 (1972): 229–43.

Primary sources:

- Peter Singer, "The Drowning Child and the Expanding Circle," *New Internationalist*, April 1997.
- William MacAskill, "Introducing CEA's Guiding Principles," Centre for Effective Altruism, online forum, March 2017.
- "Global Philanthropy Report: Perspectives on the Global Foundation Sector," 2018.
- Bill and Melinda Gates Foundation, overview brochure, 2010.

Week 14: Climate Crises and an Uncertain Future

Developing a Green Future?

Riofrancos, Thea. 2023. "The Security-Sustainability Nexus: Lithium Onshoring in the Global North." *Global Environmental Politics* 23, no. 1 (2023): 20–41.

Primary sources:

- Joseph Fourier, "General Remarks on the Temperatures of the Globe and the Planetary Spaces," 1824.
- Roger Revelle, Testimony before the House Committee on Appropriations, February 8, 1956.
- US Central Intelligence Agency, "A Study of Climatological Research as It Pertains to Intelligence Problems," 1974.
- "Acid Rain: An Increasing Threat," *New York Times*, November 6, 1979.
- Proposed compensation offer, Union Carbide, March 1985.
- Intergovernmental Panel on Climate Change, First Assessment Report, 1990.
- Pope Francis, *Laudato Si'—On Care for Our Common Home*, 2016.